Sakura, Saku

STORY & ART BY **IO SAKISAKA**

1

CONTENTS

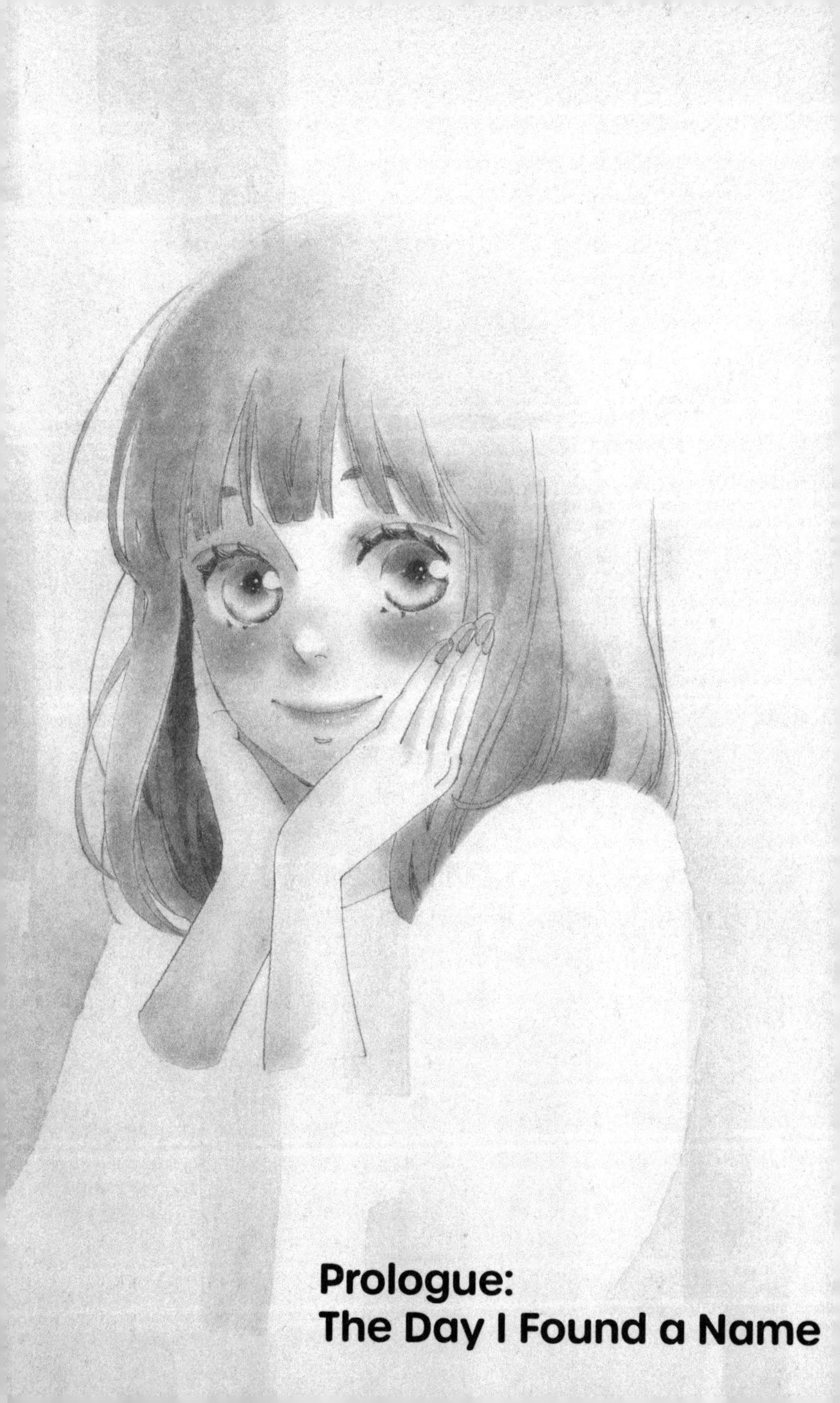

Prologue:
The Day I Found a Name

GREETINGS

Hello. I'm Io Sakisaka.
Whether you're a new reader or already familiar with my work, thank you very much for picking up the first volume of *Sakura, Saku*!!!

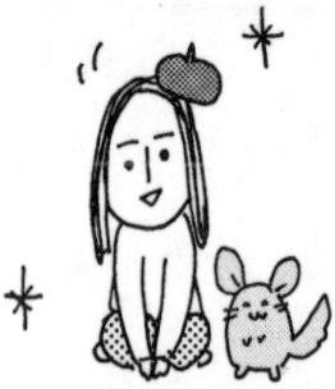

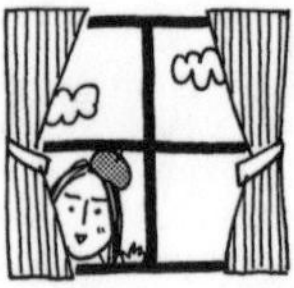

As you might expect, it's always nerve-racking to start a new series. But this nervous feeling is a special experience I can't have at any other time, so I plan to cherish it along with the rest of the fun of creating this story. I hope you all enjoy the journey with me.

Io Sakisaka

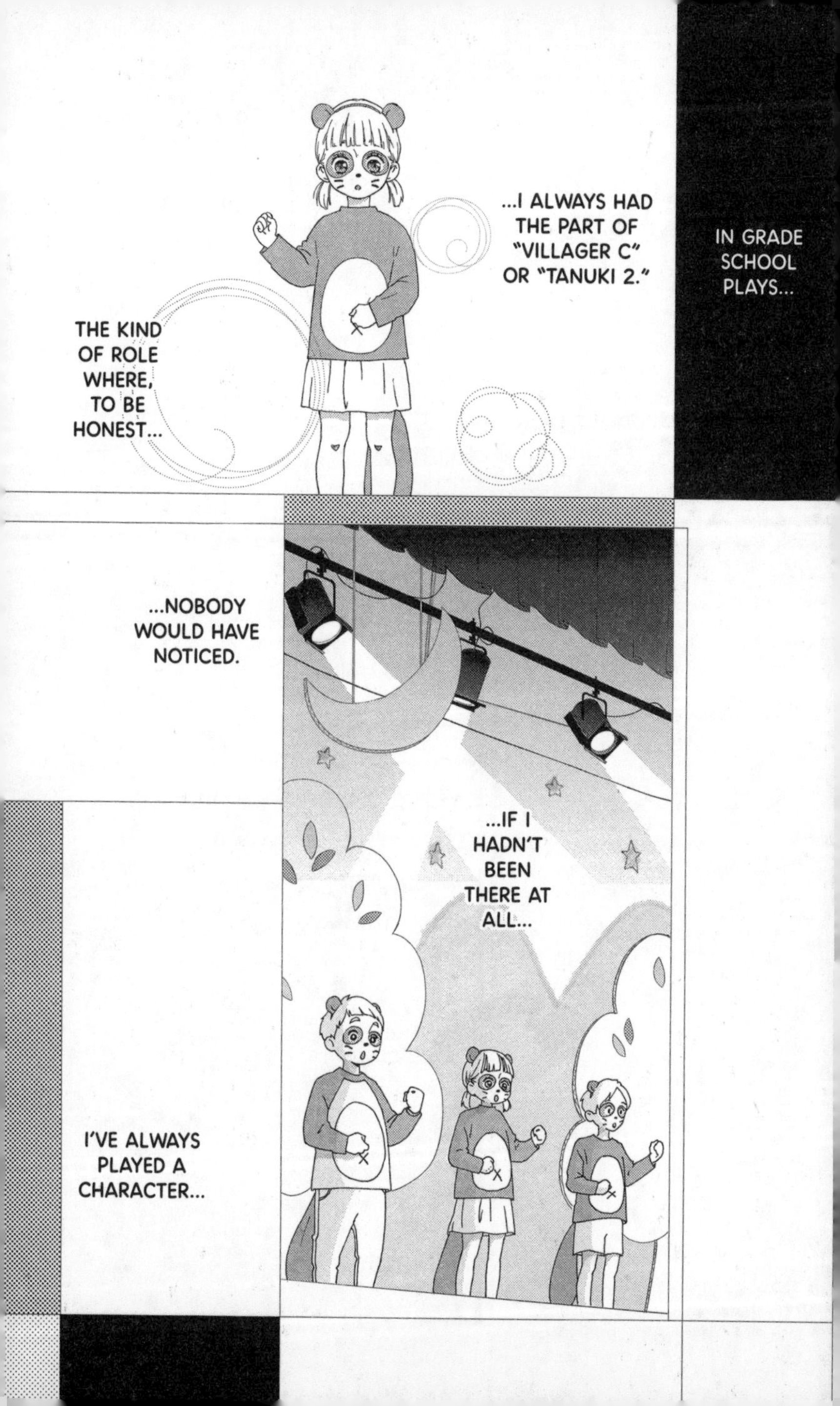
IN GRADE SCHOOL PLAYS...
...I ALWAYS HAD THE PART OF "VILLAGER C" OR "TANUKI 2."
THE KIND OF ROLE WHERE, TO BE HONEST...
...IF I HADN'T BEEN THERE AT ALL...
...NOBODY WOULD HAVE NOTICED.
I'VE ALWAYS PLAYED A CHARACTER...

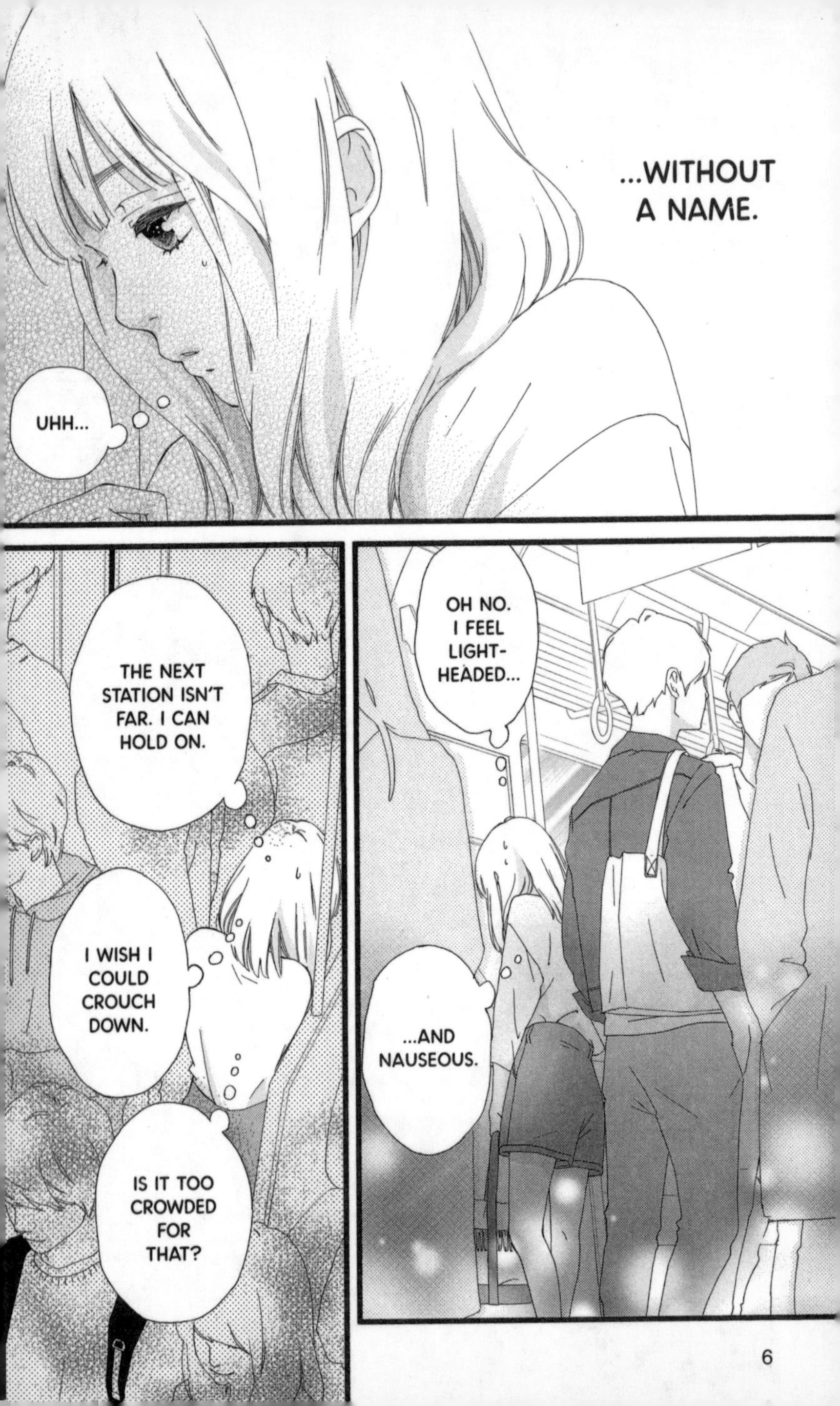
...WITHOUT A NAME.
UHH...
OH NO. I FEEL LIGHT-HEADED...
...AND NAUSEOUS.
THE NEXT STATION ISN'T FAR. I CAN HOLD ON.
I WISH I COULD CROUCH DOWN.
IS IT TOO CROWDED FOR THAT?

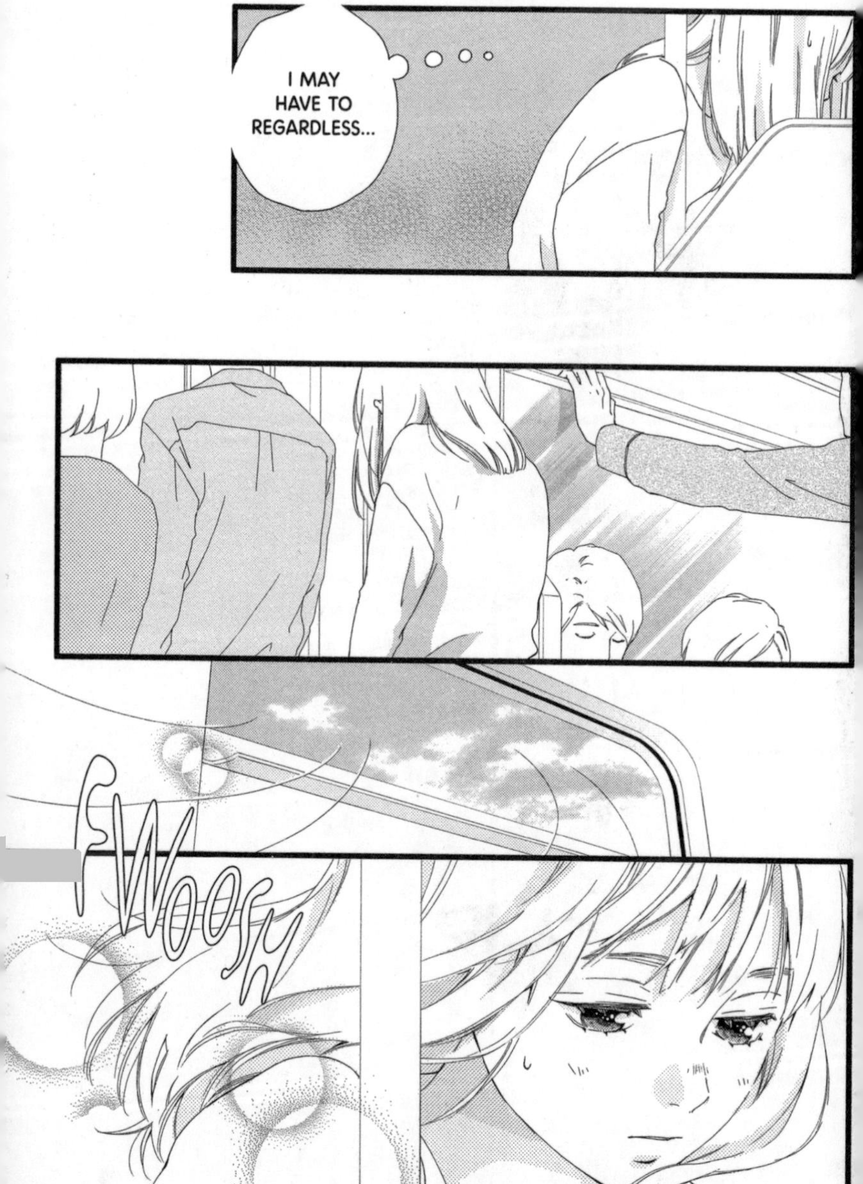
I MAY HAVE TO REGARDLESS...
FWOOSH

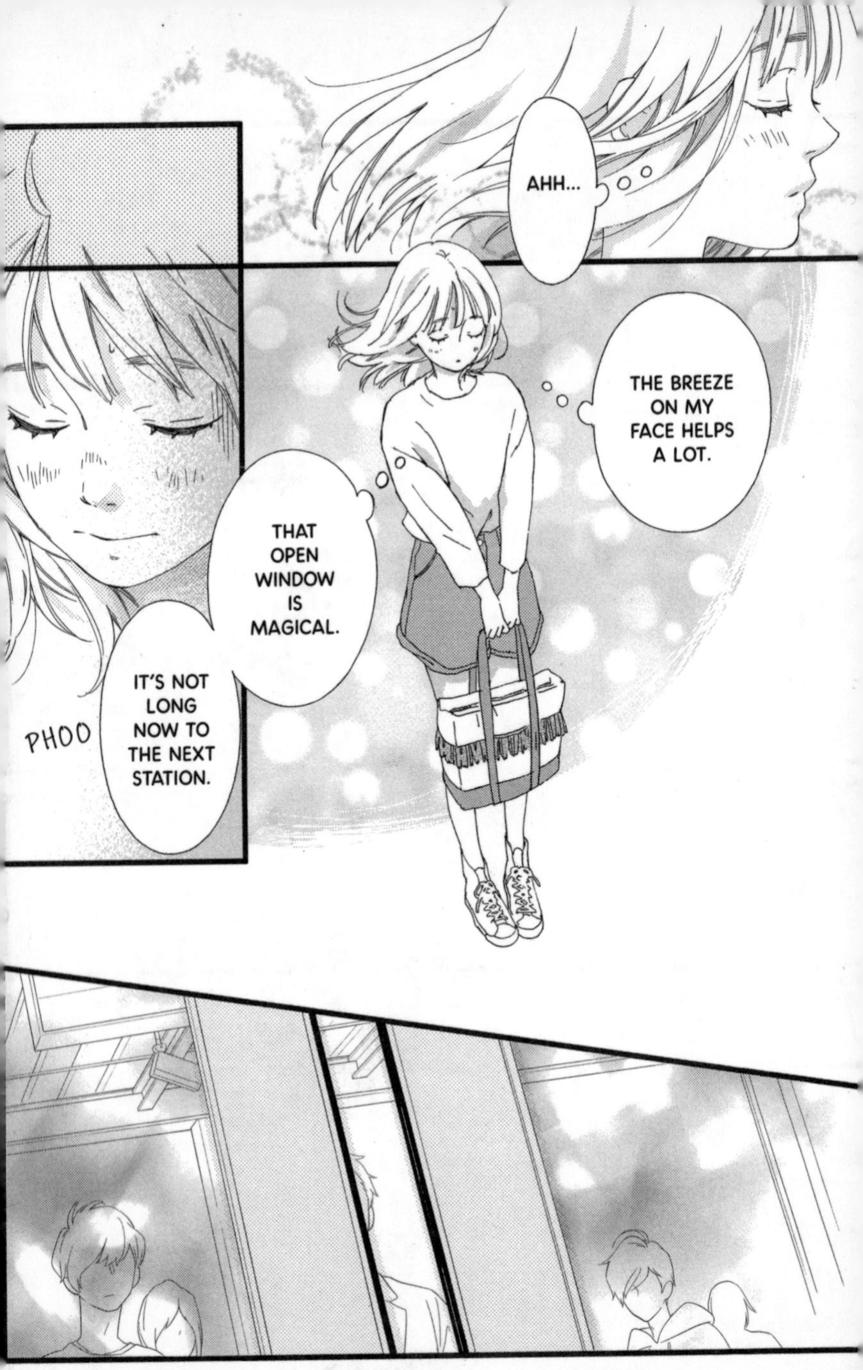
AHH...
THE BREEZE ON MY FACE HELPS A LOT.
THAT OPEN WINDOW IS MAGICAL.
IT'S NOT LONG NOW TO THE NEXT STATION.
PHOO

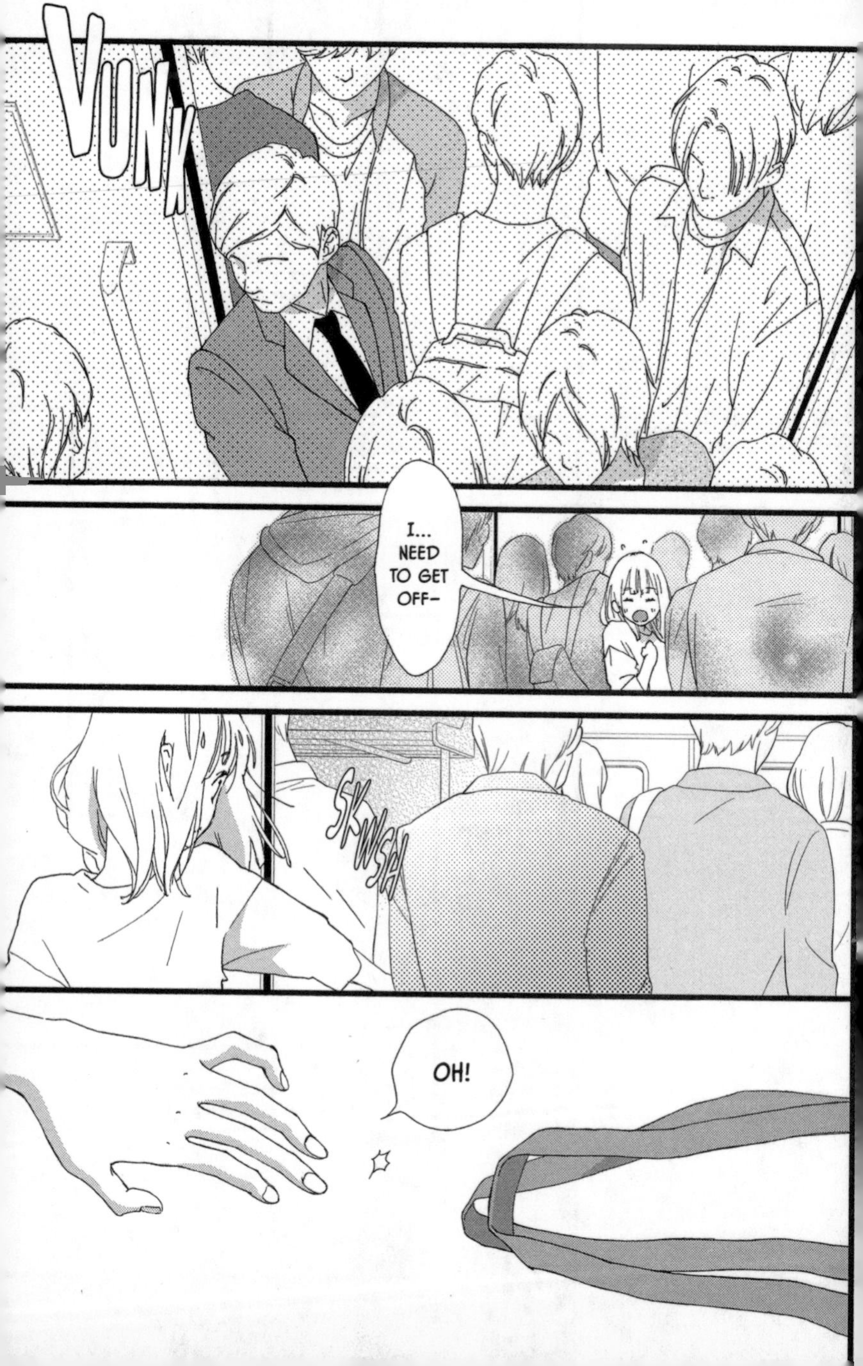
VUNK
I... NEED TO GET OFF–
SKWSH
OH!

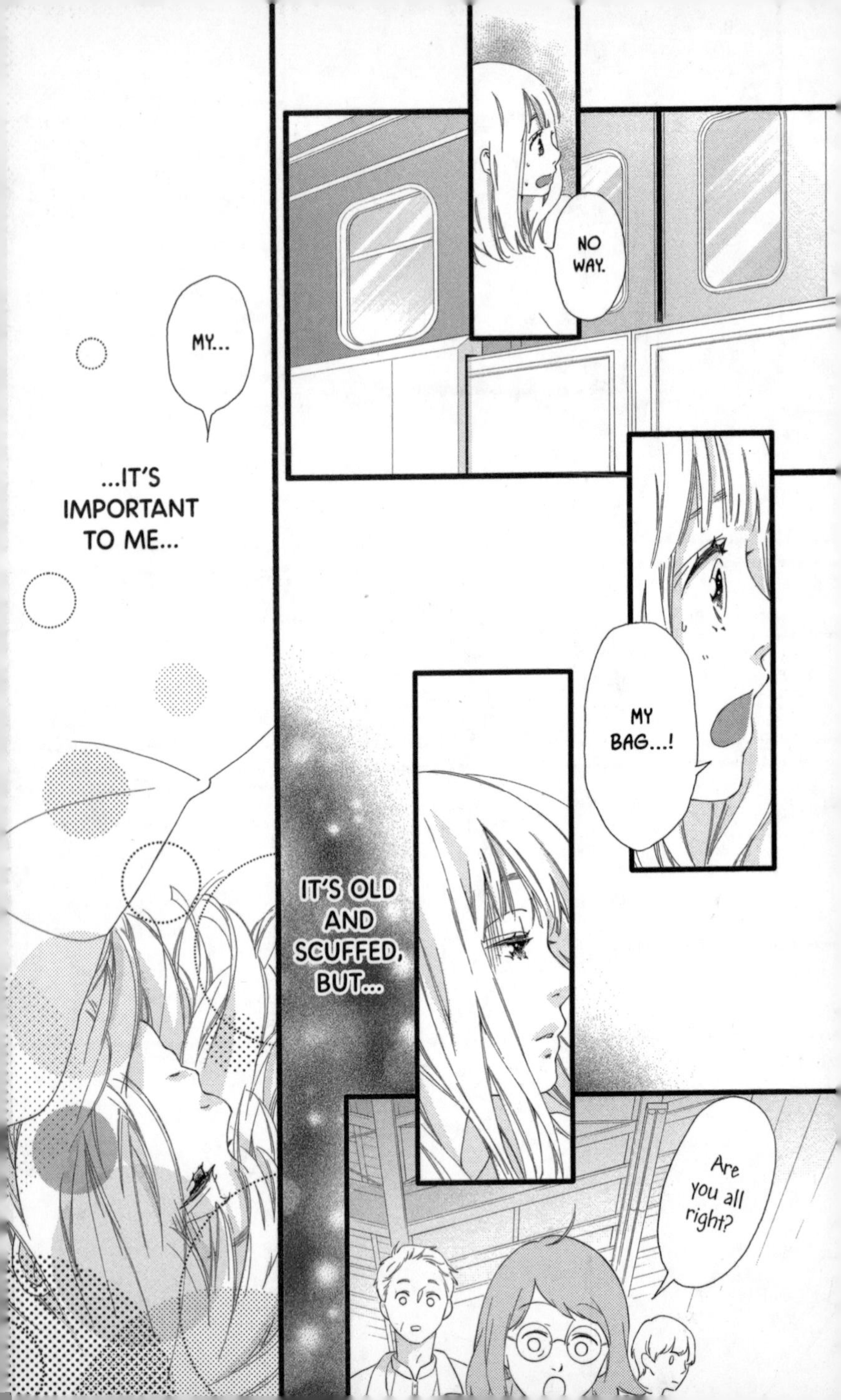
NO WAY.
MY BAG...!
IT'S OLD AND SCUFFED, BUT...
Are you all right?
MY...
...IT'S IMPORTANT TO ME...

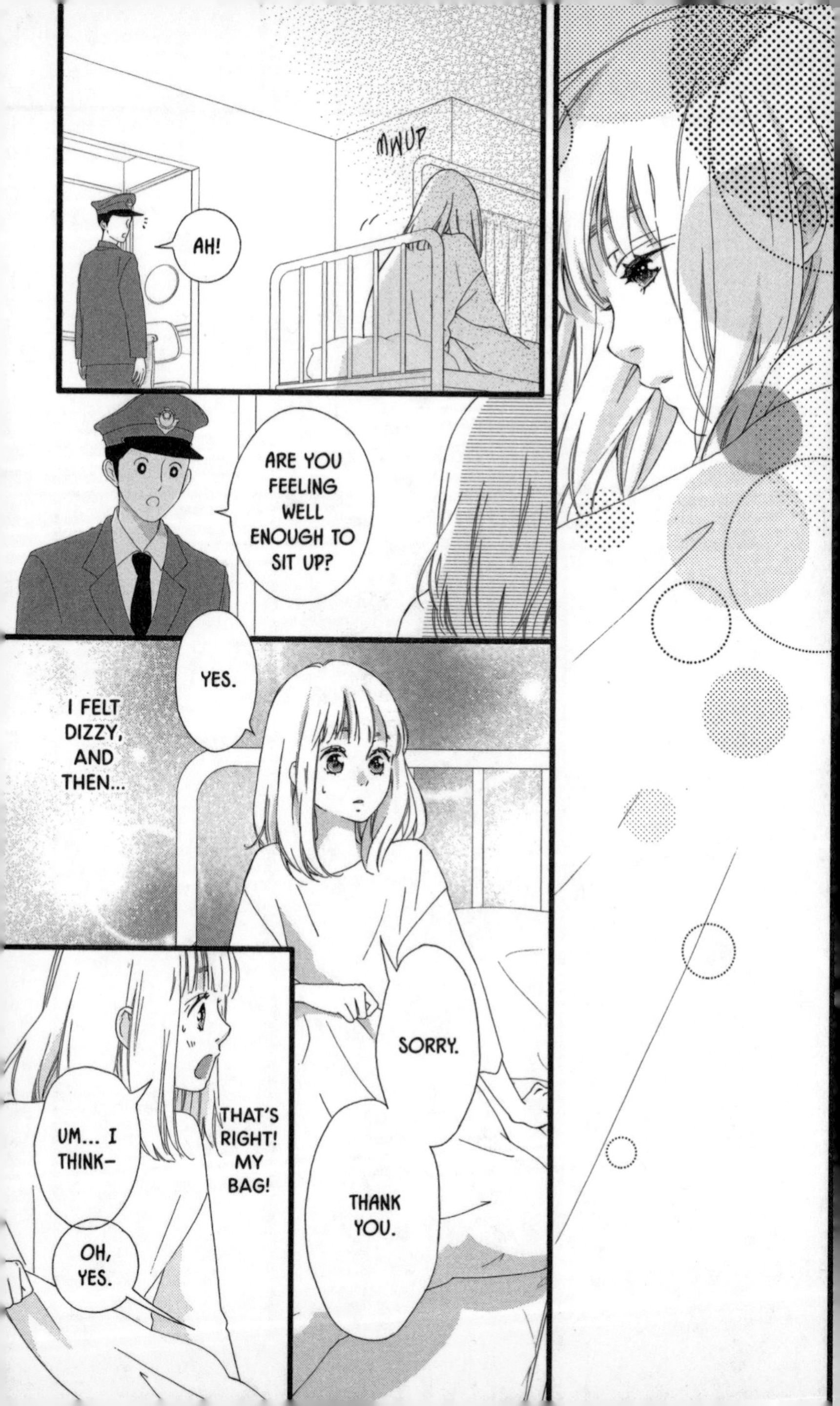
MWUP
AH!
ARE YOU FEELING WELL ENOUGH TO SIT UP?
YES.
I FELT DIZZY, AND THEN...
SORRY.
THANK YOU.
THAT'S RIGHT! MY BAG!
UM... I THINK—
OH, YES.

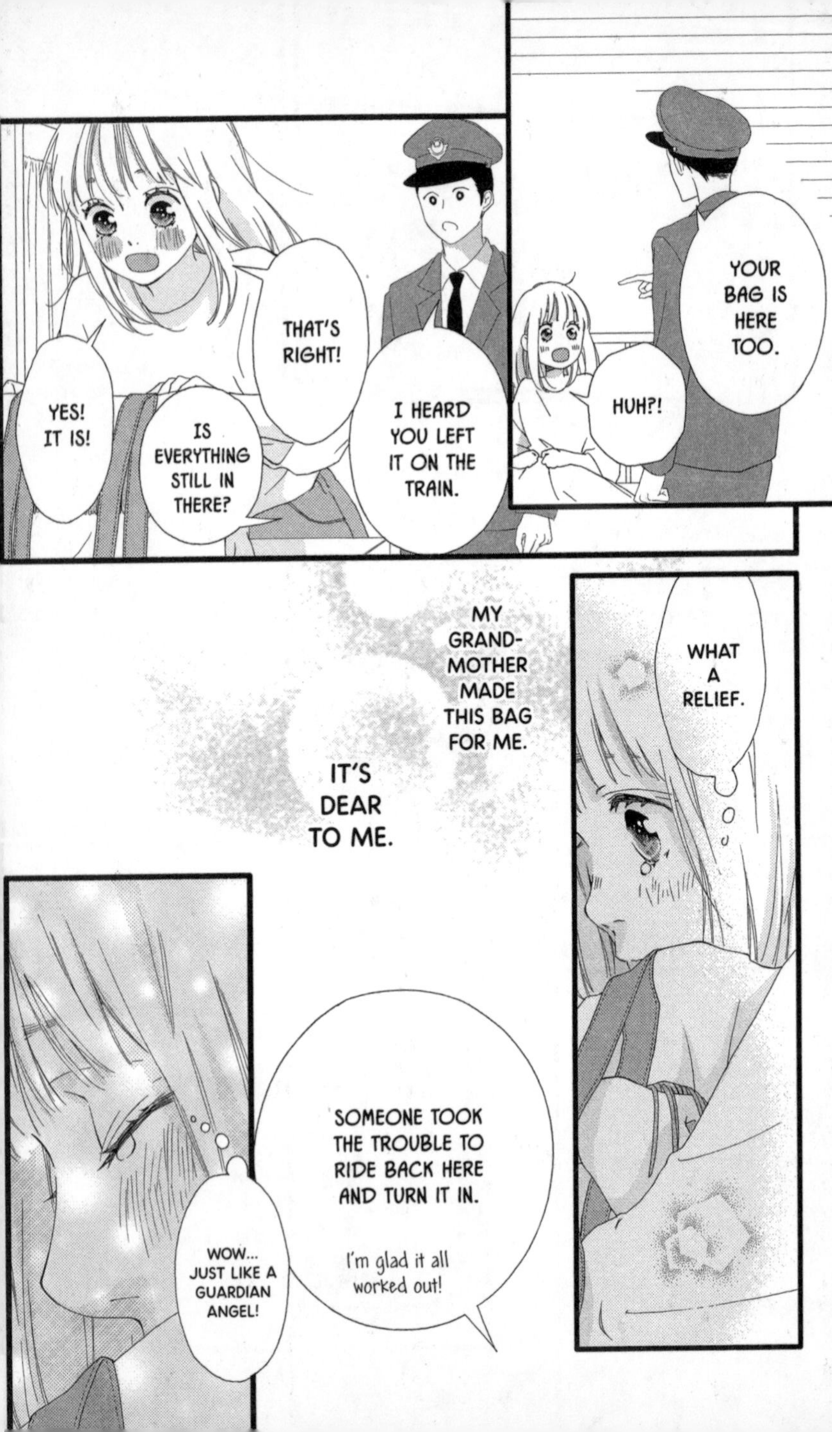
YOUR BAG IS HERE TOO.
HUH?!
I HEARD YOU LEFT IT ON THE TRAIN.
THAT'S RIGHT!
IS EVERYTHING STILL IN THERE?
YES! IT IS!
WHAT A RELIEF.
MY GRAND-MOTHER MADE THIS BAG FOR ME.
IT'S DEAR TO ME.
SOMEONE TOOK THE TROUBLE TO RIDE BACK HERE AND TURN IT IN.
I'm glad it all worked out!
WOW... JUST LIKE A GUARDIAN ANGEL!

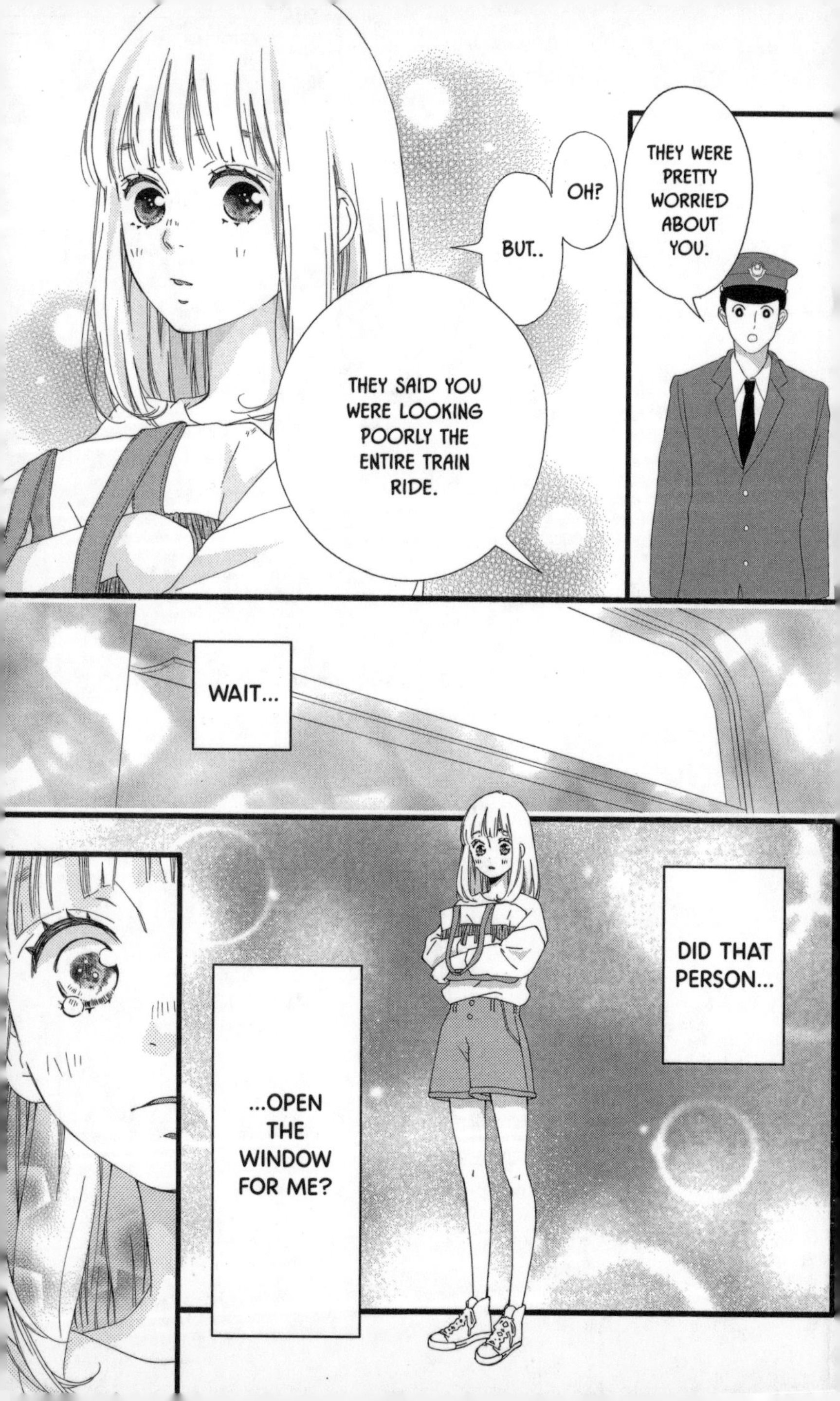
THEY WERE PRETTY WORRIED ABOUT YOU.
OH?
BUT..
THEY SAID YOU WERE LOOKING POORLY THE ENTIRE TRAIN RIDE.
WAIT...
DID THAT PERSON...
...OPEN THE WINDOW FOR ME?

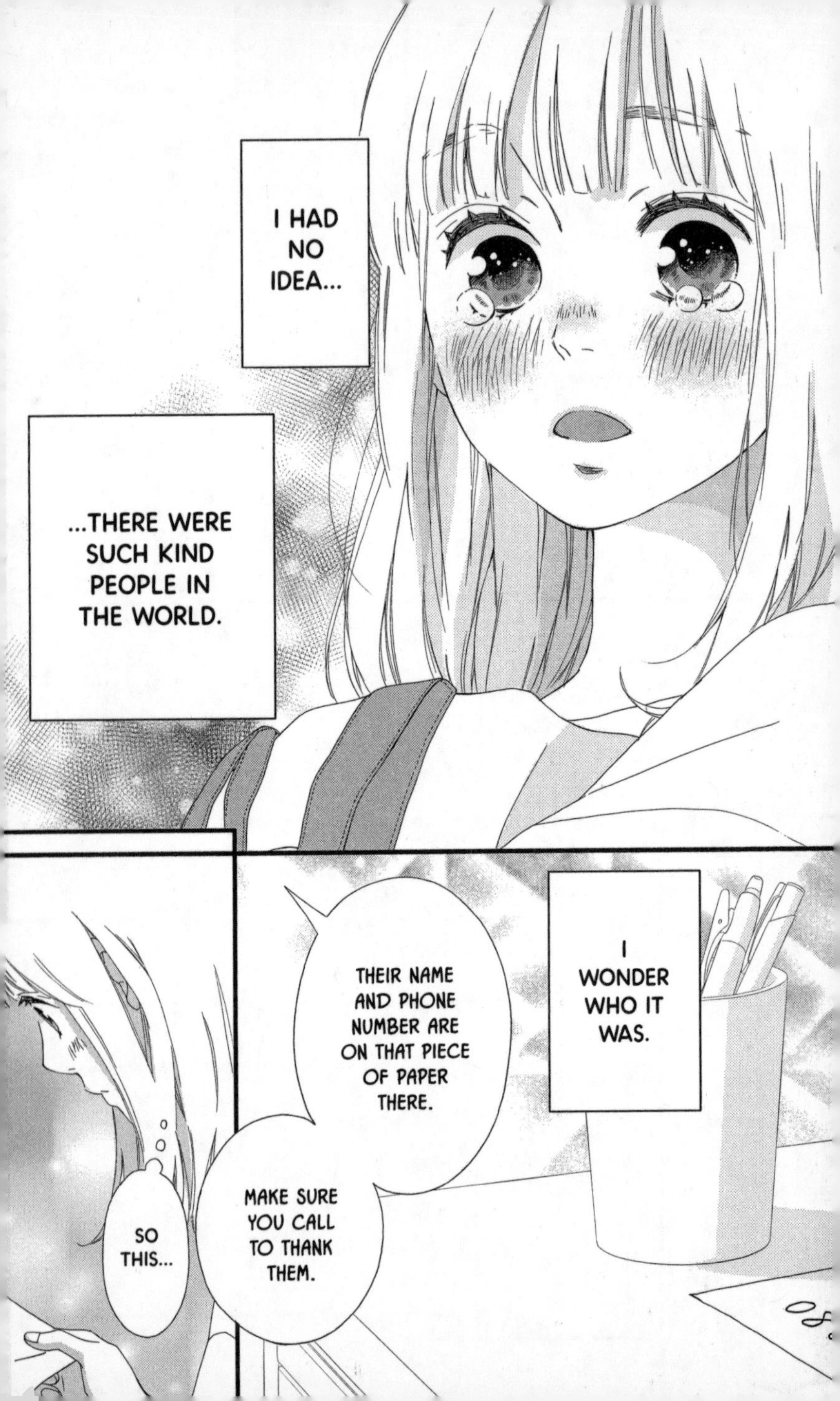
I HAD NO IDEA...
...THERE WERE SUCH KIND PEOPLE IN THE WORLD.
I WONDER WHO IT WAS.
THEIR NAME AND PHONE NUMBER ARE ON THAT PIECE OF PAPER THERE.
MAKE SURE YOU CALL TO THANK THEM.
SO THIS...

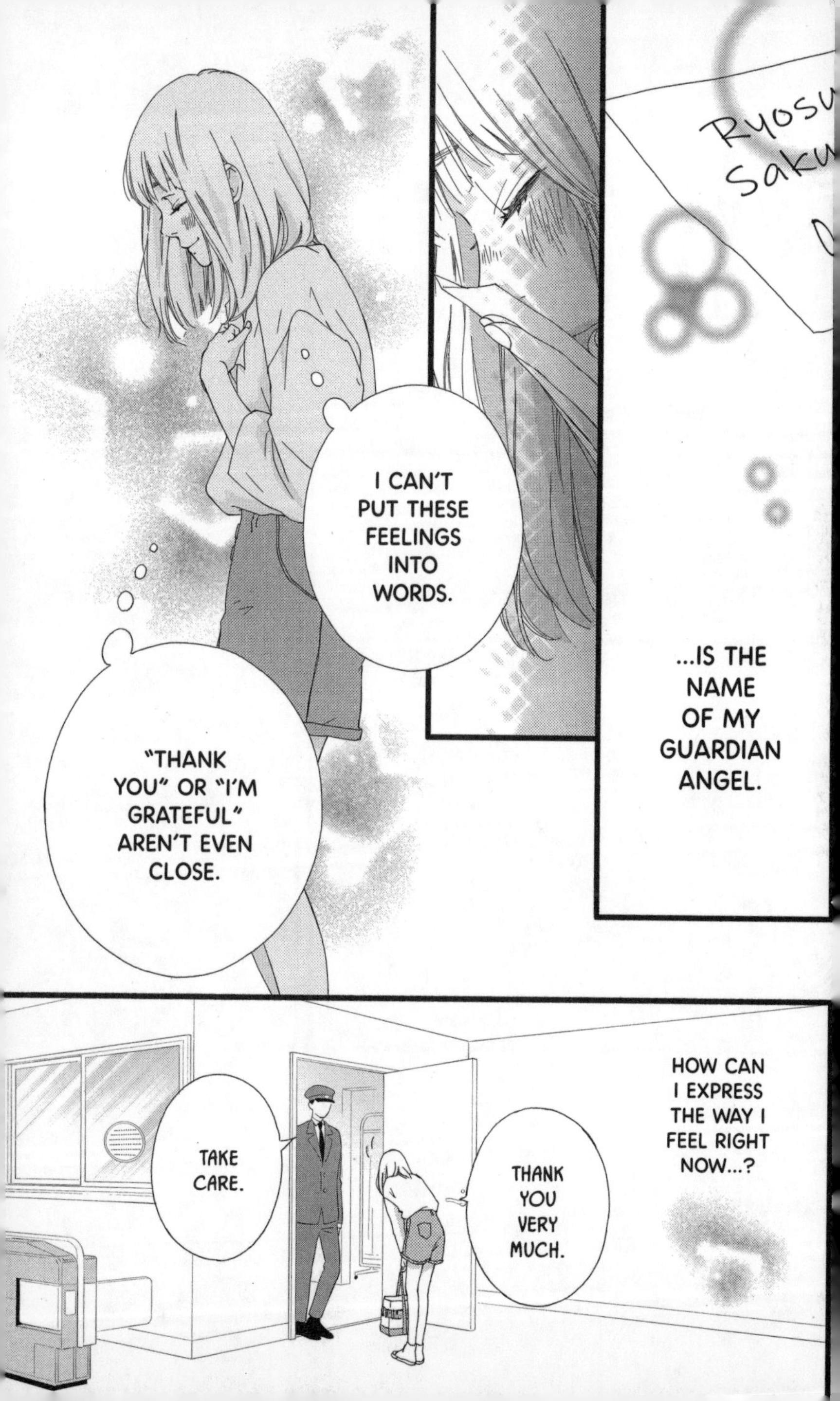
Ryosu
Saku
...IS THE NAME OF MY GUARDIAN ANGEL.
I CAN'T PUT THESE FEELINGS INTO WORDS.
"THANK YOU" OR "I'M GRATEFUL" AREN'T EVEN CLOSE.
HOW CAN I EXPRESS THE WAY I FEEL RIGHT NOW...?
THANK YOU VERY MUCH.
TAKE CARE.

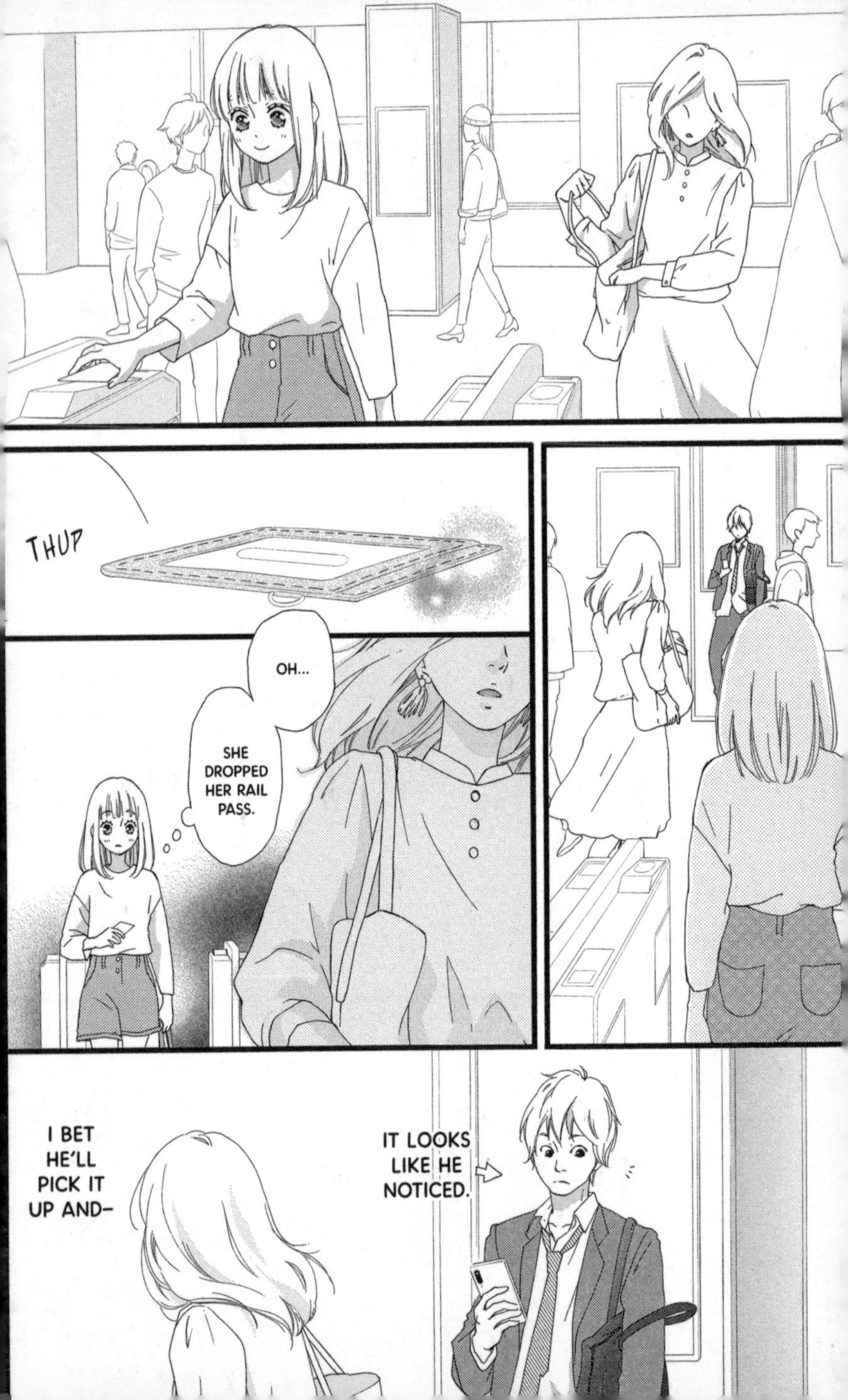

THUP
OH...
SHE DROPPED HER RAIL PASS.
IT LOOKS LIKE HE NOTICED.
I BET HE'LL PICK IT UP AND–

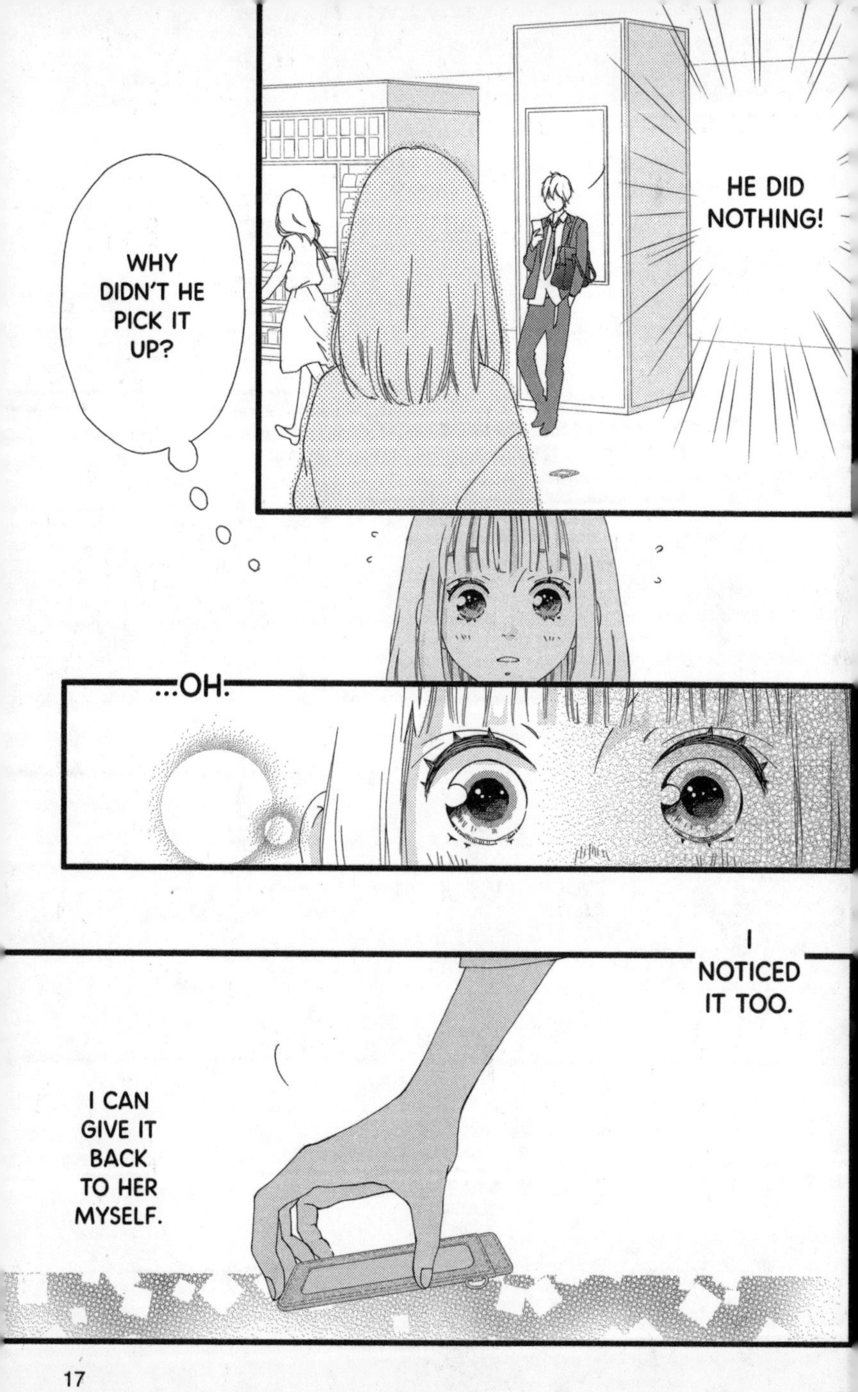
HE DID NOTHING!
WHY DIDN'T HE PICK IT UP?
...OH.
I NOTICED IT TOO.
I CAN GIVE IT BACK TO HER MYSELF.

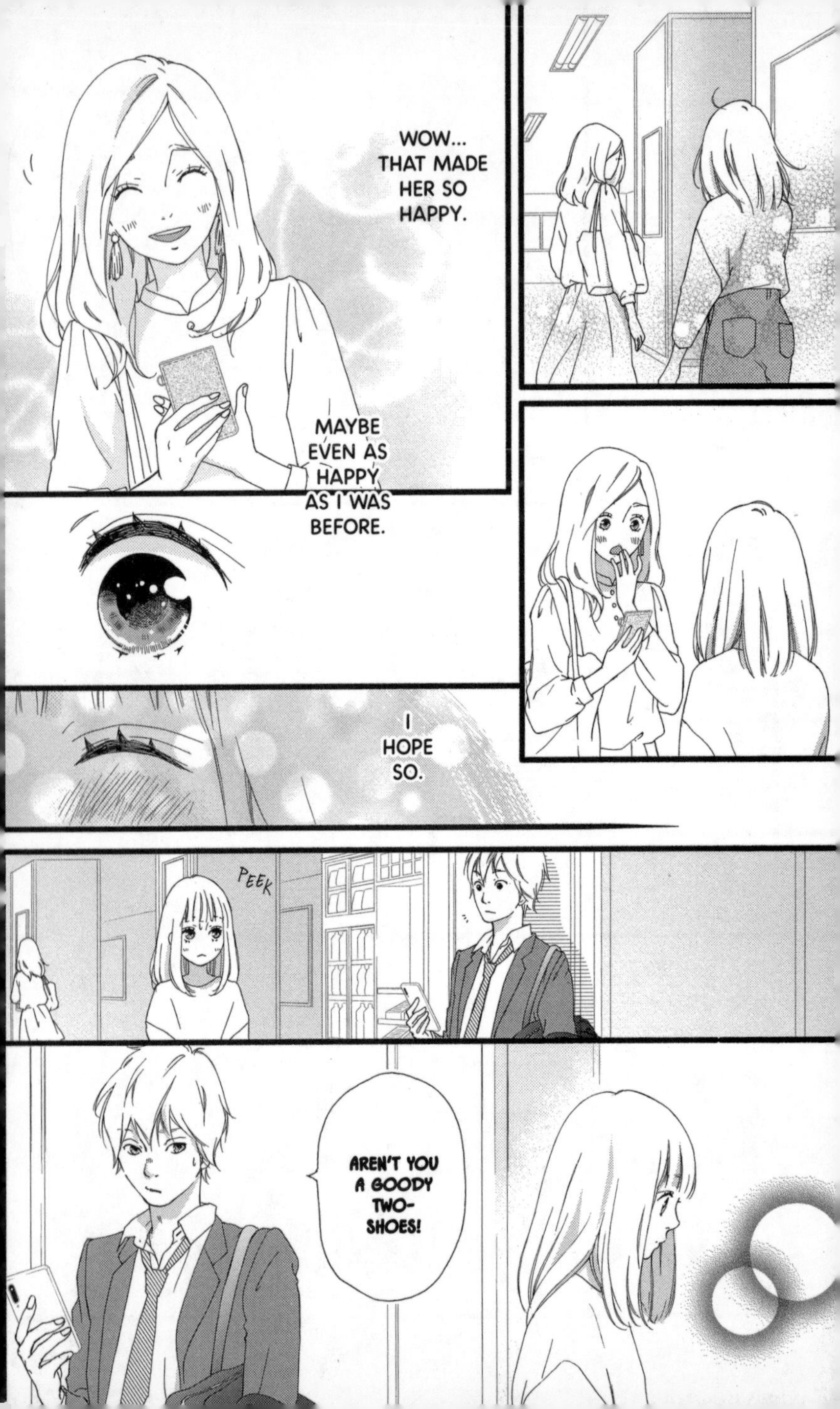
WOW... THAT MADE HER SO HAPPY.
MAYBE EVEN AS HAPPY AS I WAS BEFORE.
I HOPE SO.
PEEK
AREN'T YOU A GOODY TWO-SHOES!

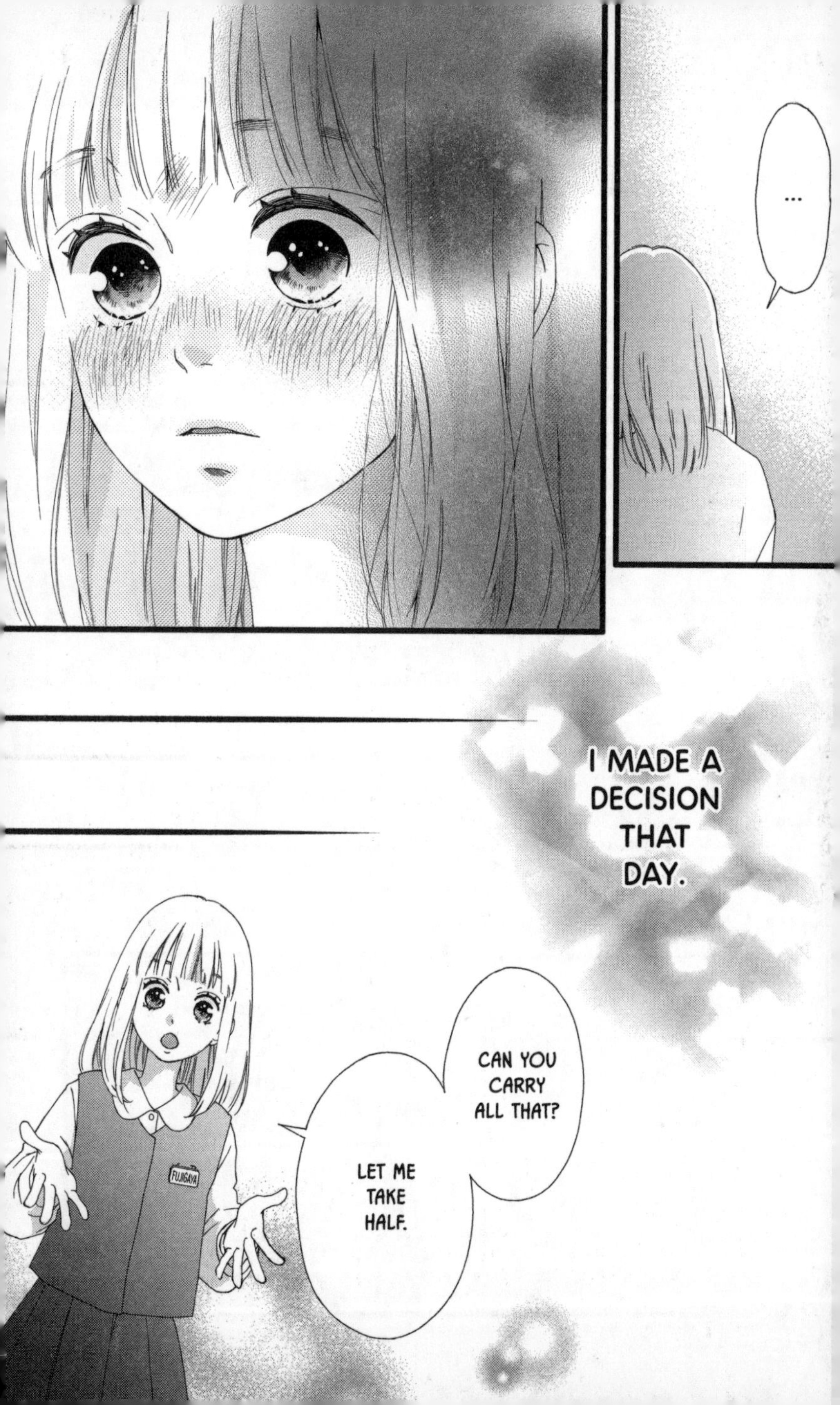
...
I MADE A DECISION THAT DAY.
CAN YOU CARRY ALL THAT?
LET ME TAKE HALF.
FUJIGAYA

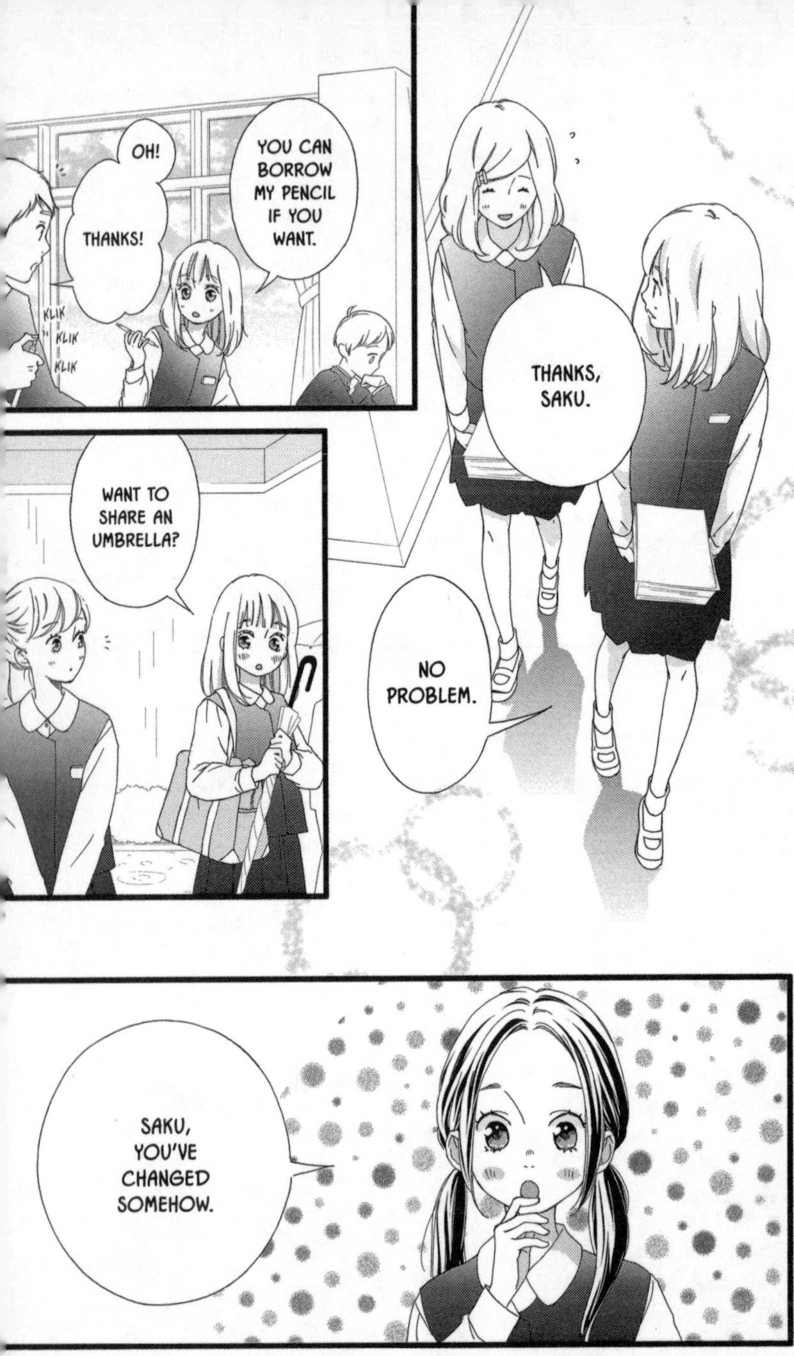
THANKS, SAKU.
NO PROBLEM.
YOU CAN BORROW MY PENCIL IF YOU WANT.
OH!
THANKS!
KLIK
KLIK
KLIK
WANT TO SHARE AN UMBRELLA?
SAKU, YOU'VE CHANGED SOMEHOW.

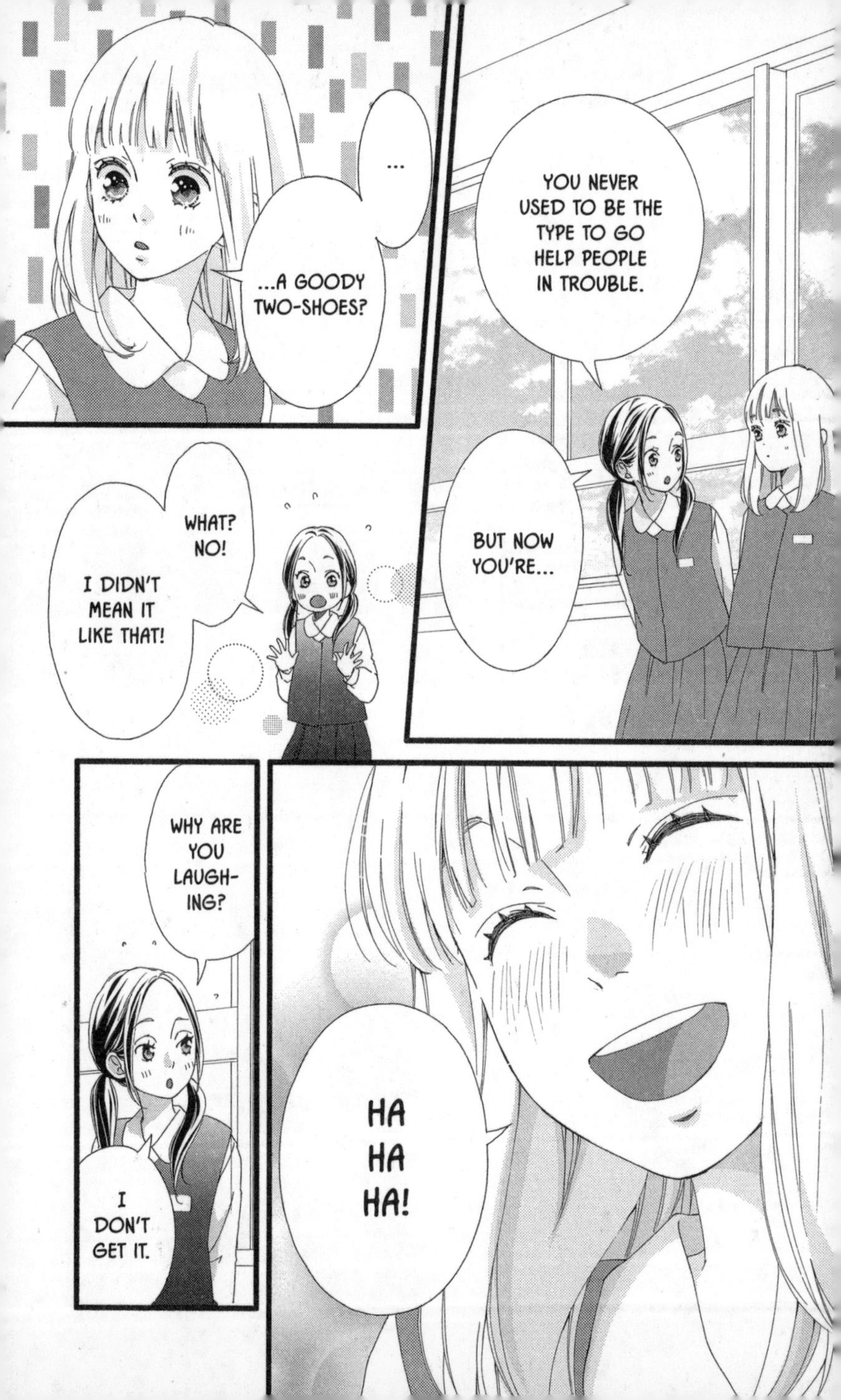
YOU NEVER USED TO BE THE TYPE TO GO HELP PEOPLE IN TROUBLE.
BUT NOW YOU'RE...
...
...A GOODY TWO-SHOES?
WHAT? NO!
I DIDN'T MEAN IT LIKE THAT!
HA HA HA!
WHY ARE YOU LAUGH-ING?
I DON'T GET IT.

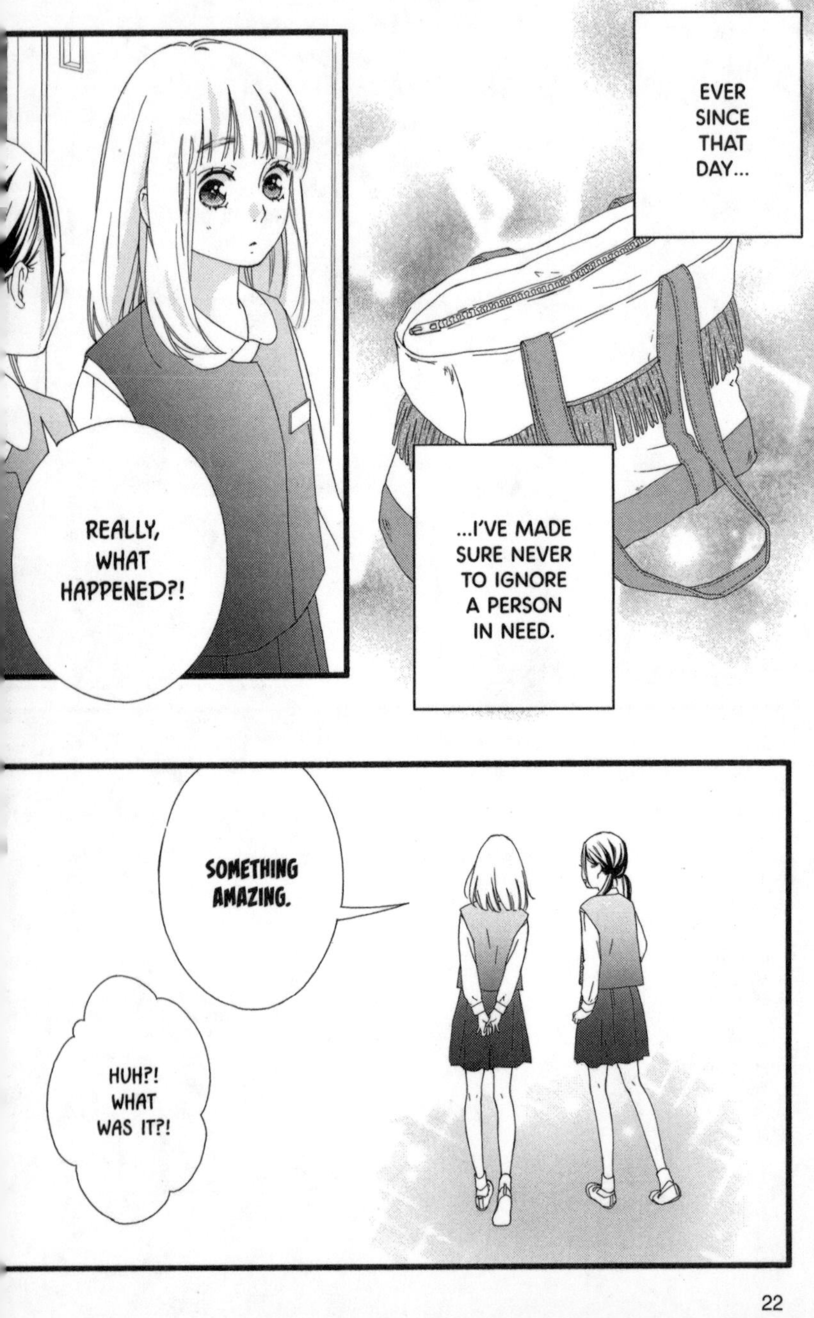
EVER SINCE THAT DAY...
...I'VE MADE SURE NEVER TO IGNORE A PERSON IN NEED.
REALLY, WHAT HAPPENED?!
SOMETHING AMAZING.
HUH?! WHAT WAS IT?!

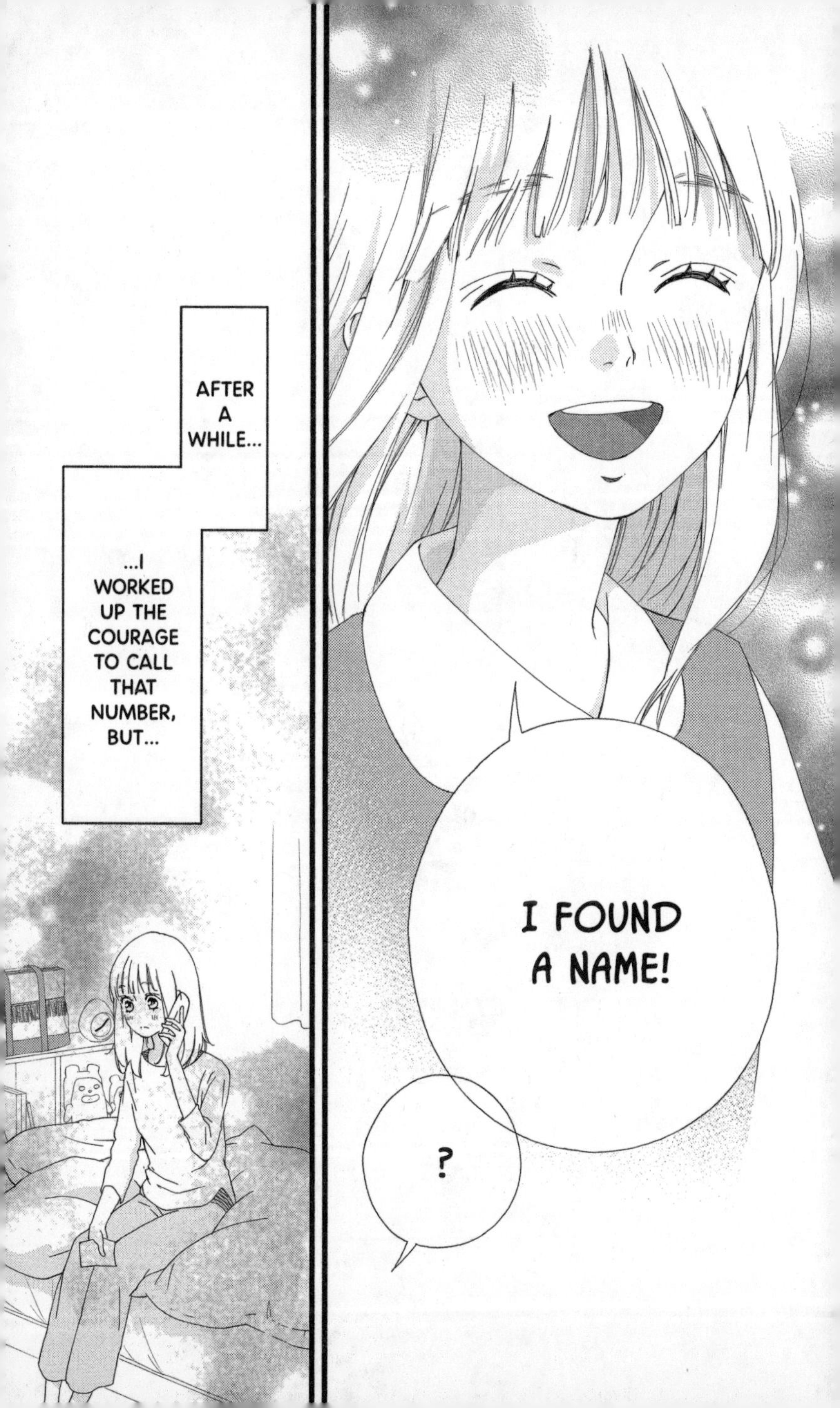
I FOUND A NAME!
?
AFTER A WHILE...
...I WORKED UP THE COURAGE TO CALL THAT NUMBER, BUT...

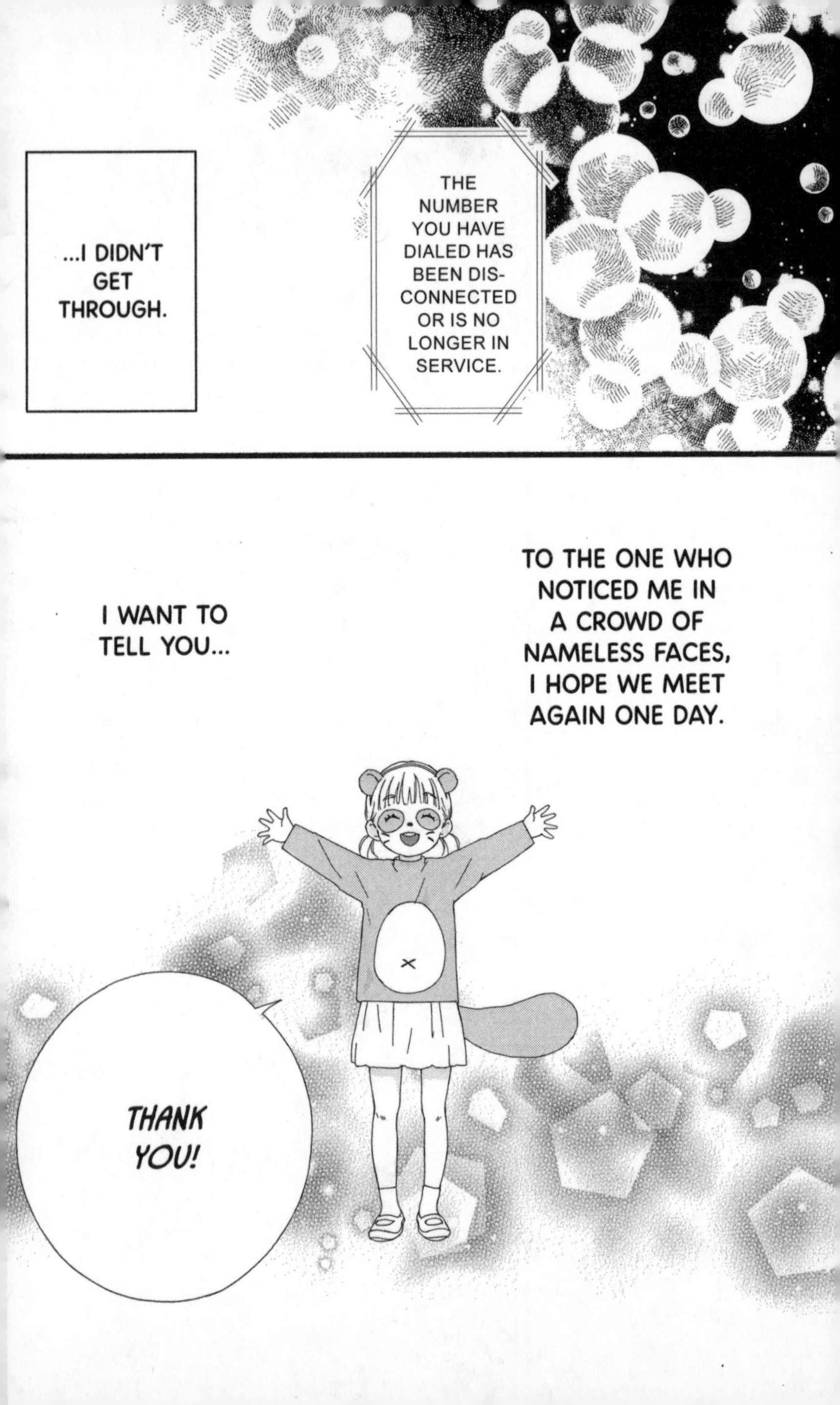
THE NUMBER YOU HAVE DIALED HAS BEEN DIS-CONNECTED OR IS NO LONGER IN SERVICE.
...I DIDN'T GET THROUGH.
TO THE ONE WHO NOTICED ME IN A CROWD OF NAMELESS FACES, I HOPE WE MEET AGAIN ONE DAY.
I WANT TO TELL YOU...
THANK YOU!

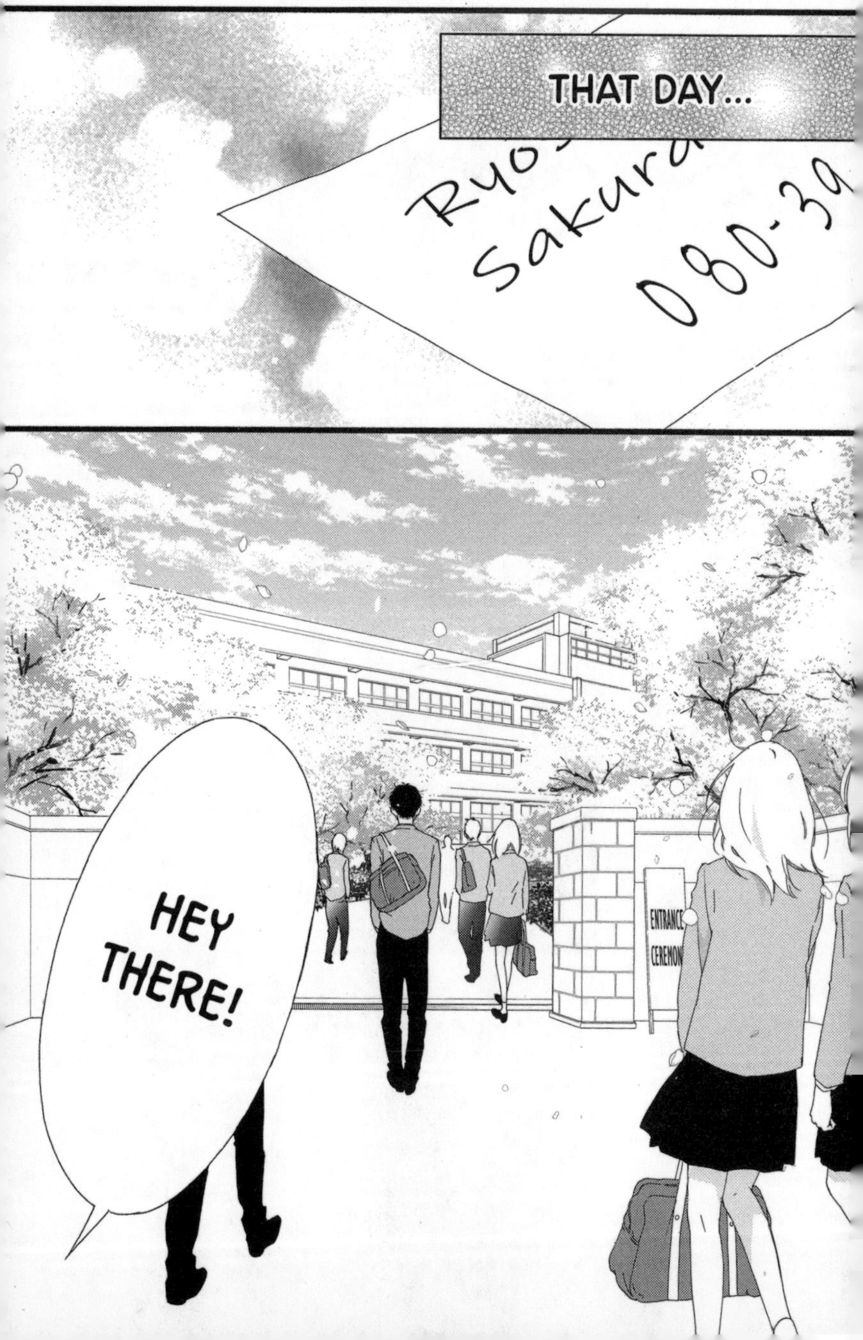
THAT DAY...
HEY THERE!
ENTRANCE

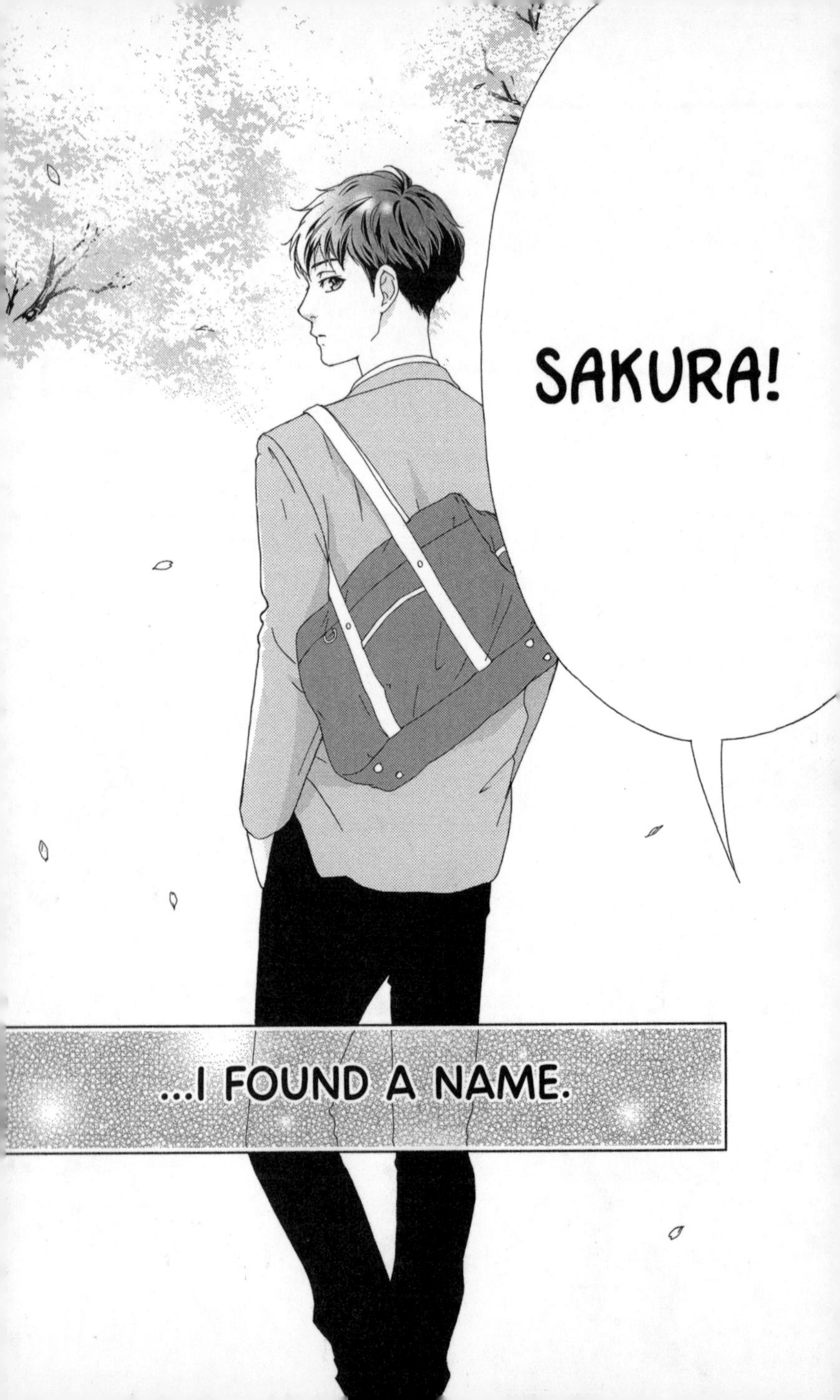
SAKURA!
...I FOUND A NAME.

Sakura, Saku

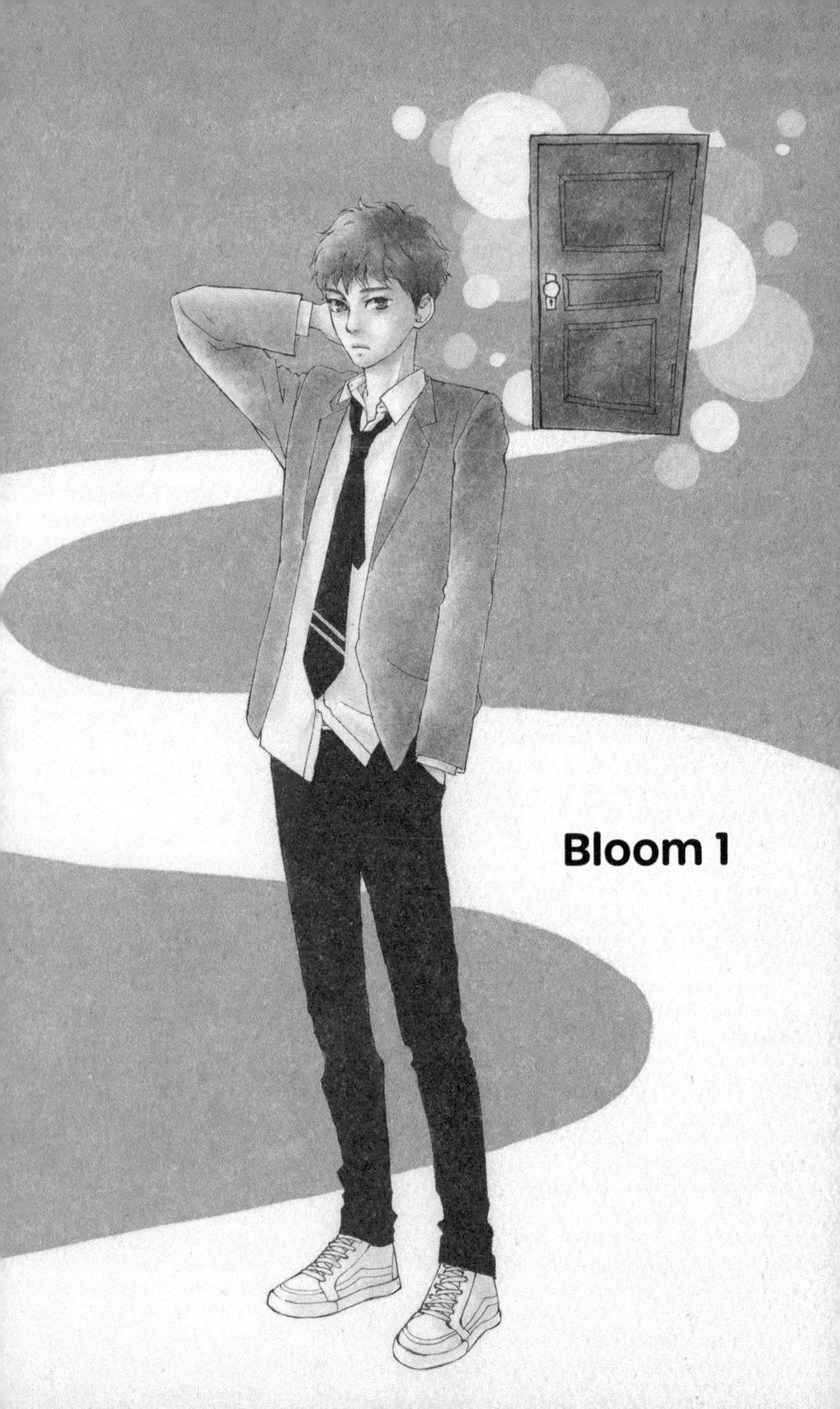
Bloom 1

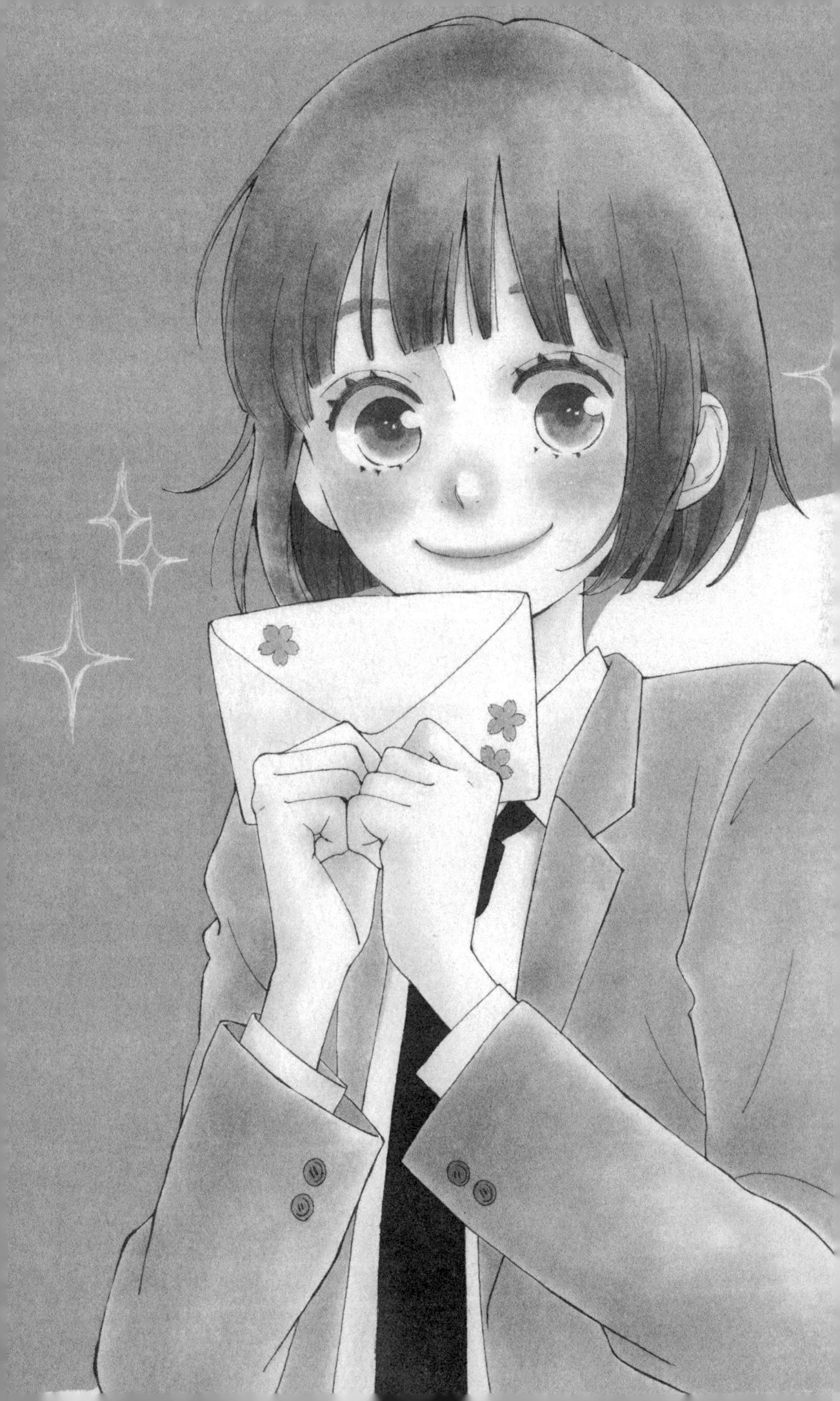

Sakura, Saku

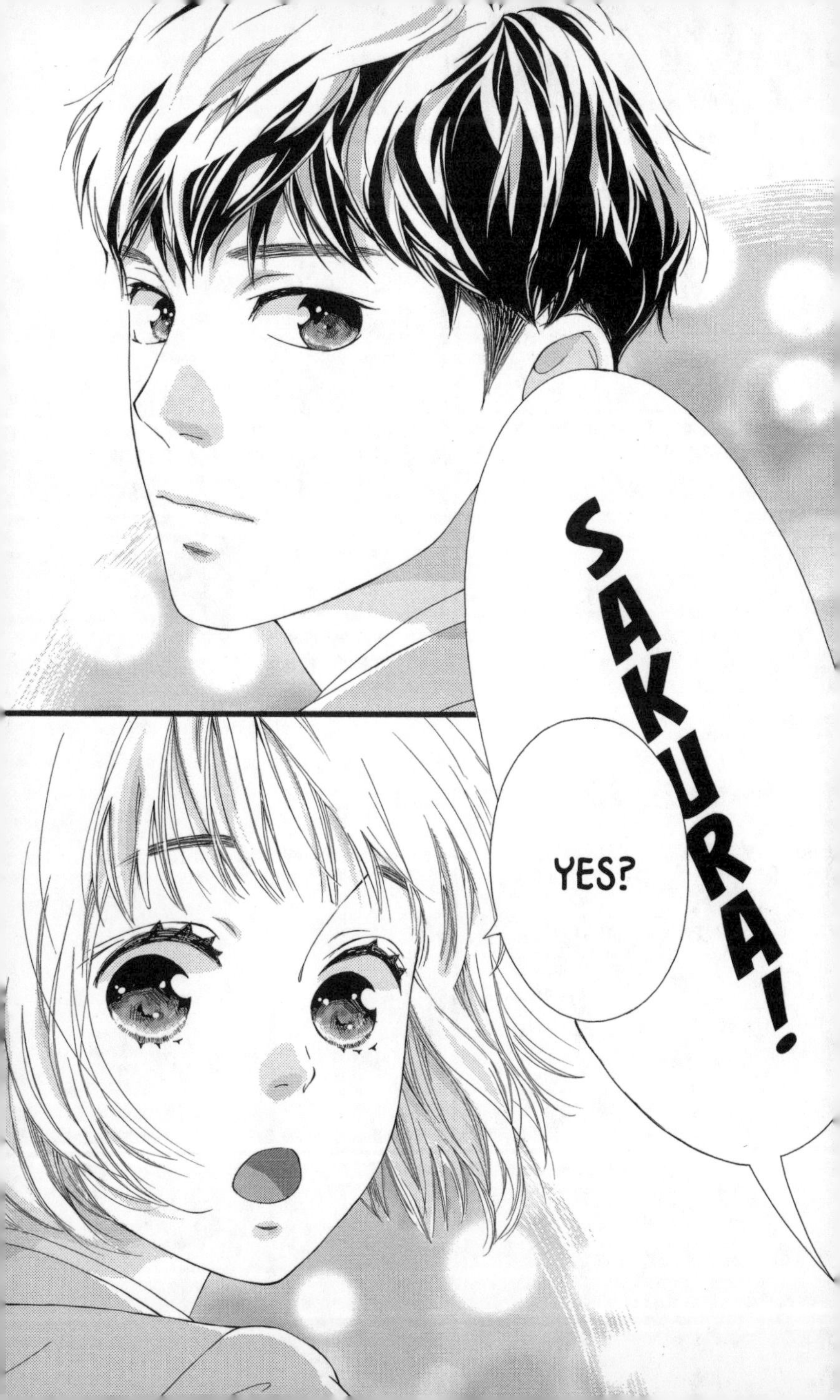
SAKURA!
YES?

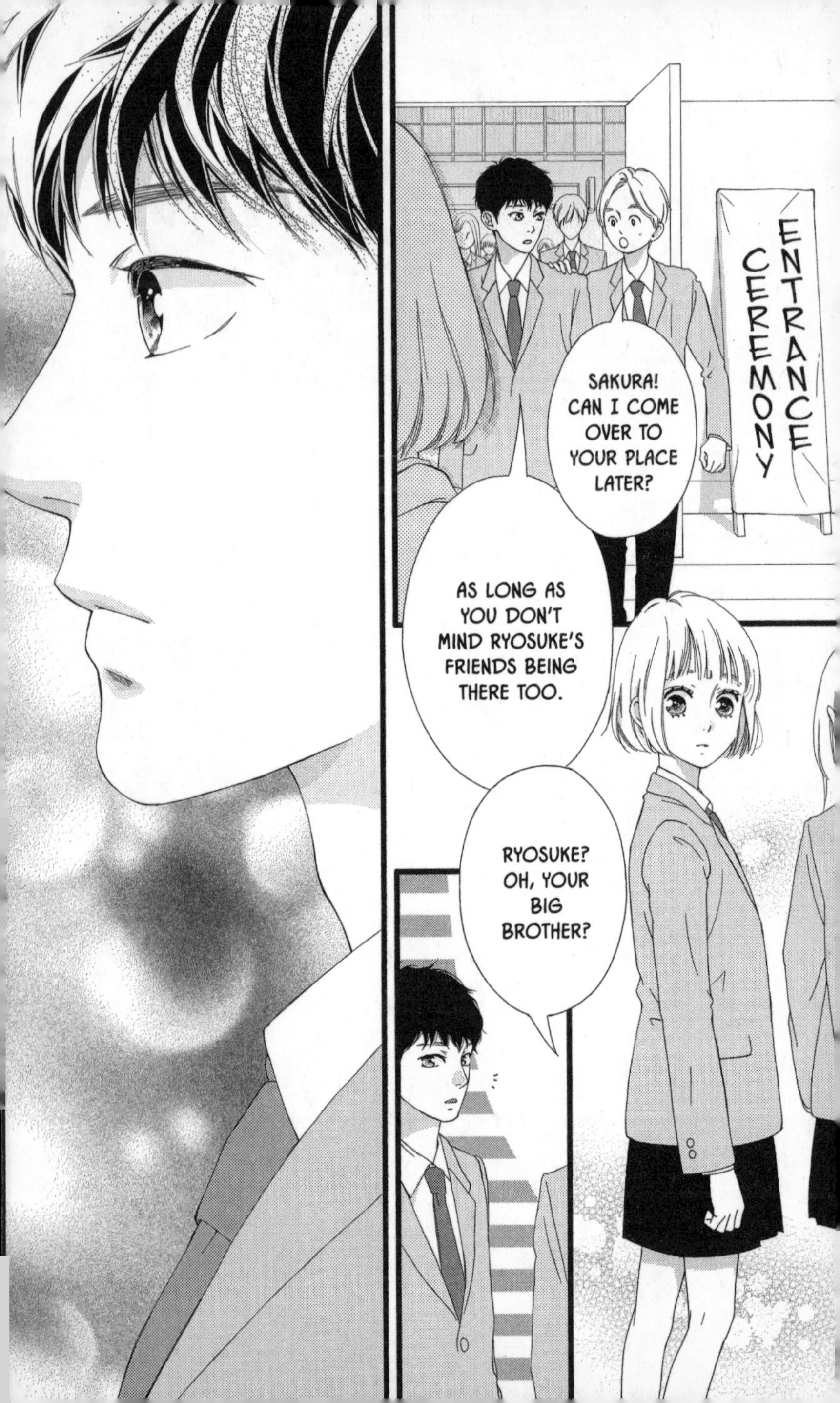
ENTRANCE CEREMONY
SAKURA! CAN I COME OVER TO YOUR PLACE LATER?
AS LONG AS YOU DON'T MIND RYOSUKE'S FRIENDS BEING THERE TOO.
RYOSUKE? OH, YOUR BIG BROTHER?

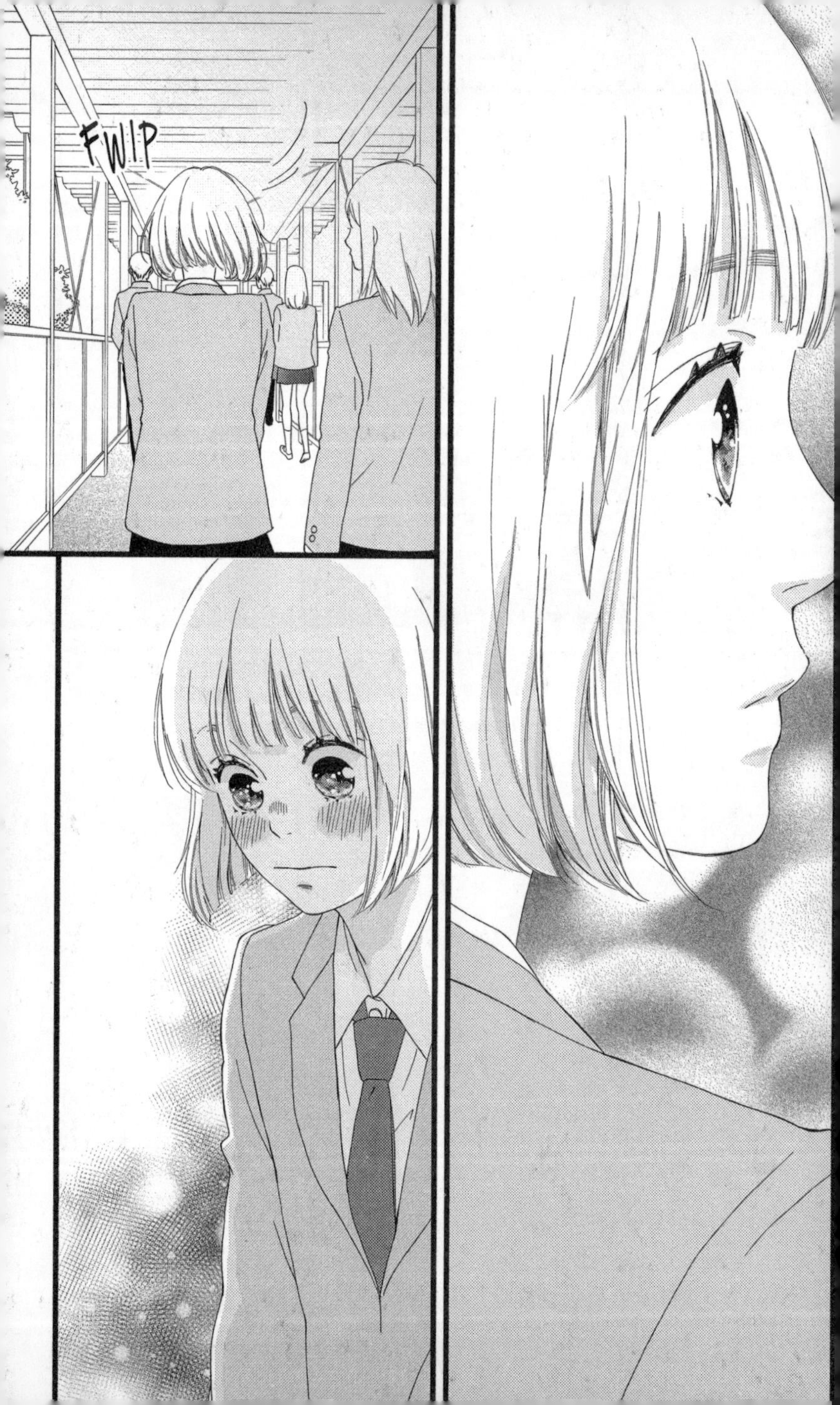
FWIP

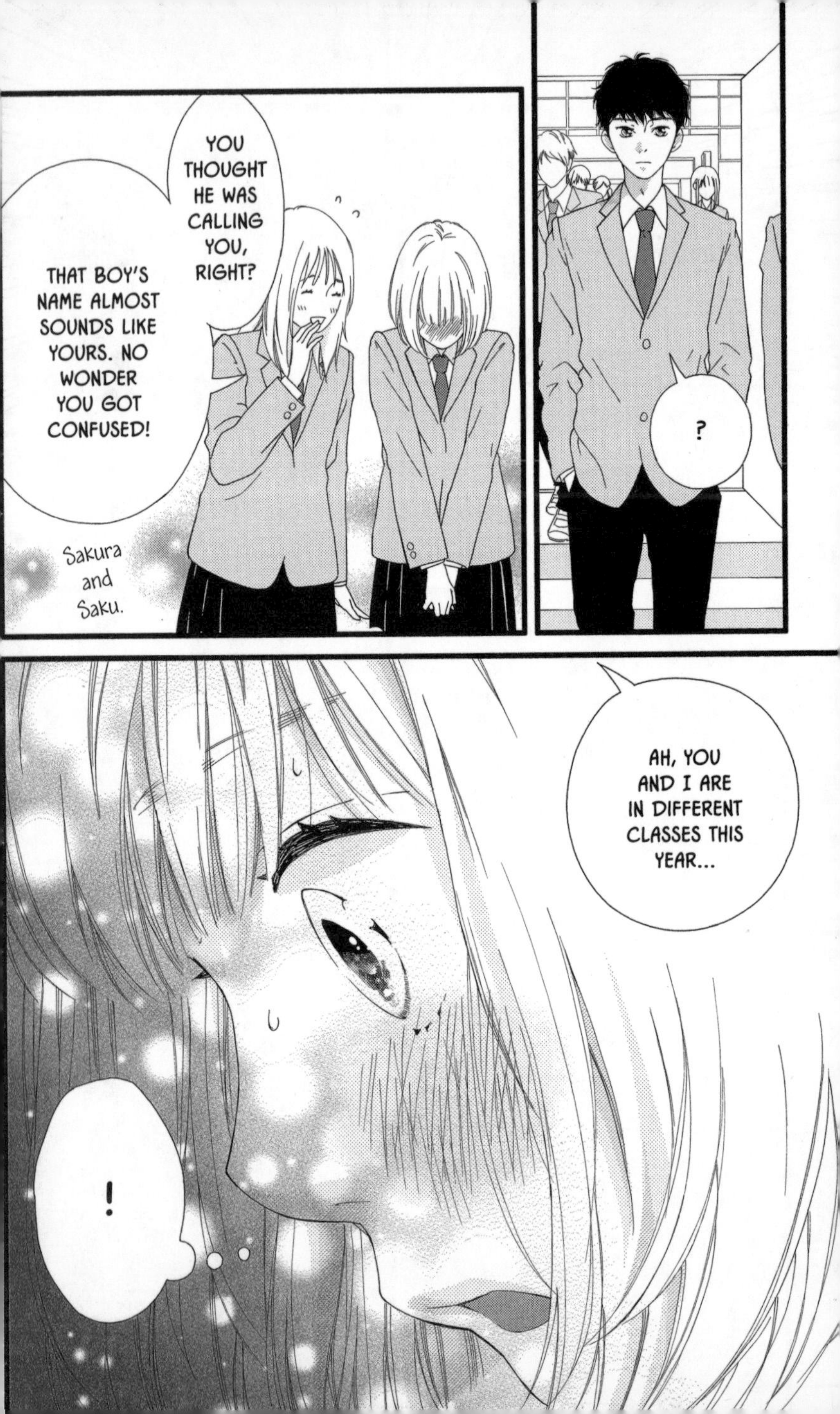
?
YOU THOUGHT HE WAS CALLING YOU, RIGHT?
THAT BOY'S NAME ALMOST SOUNDS LIKE YOURS. NO WONDER YOU GOT CONFUSED!
Sakura and Saku.
AH, YOU AND I ARE IN DIFFERENT CLASSES THIS YEAR...
!

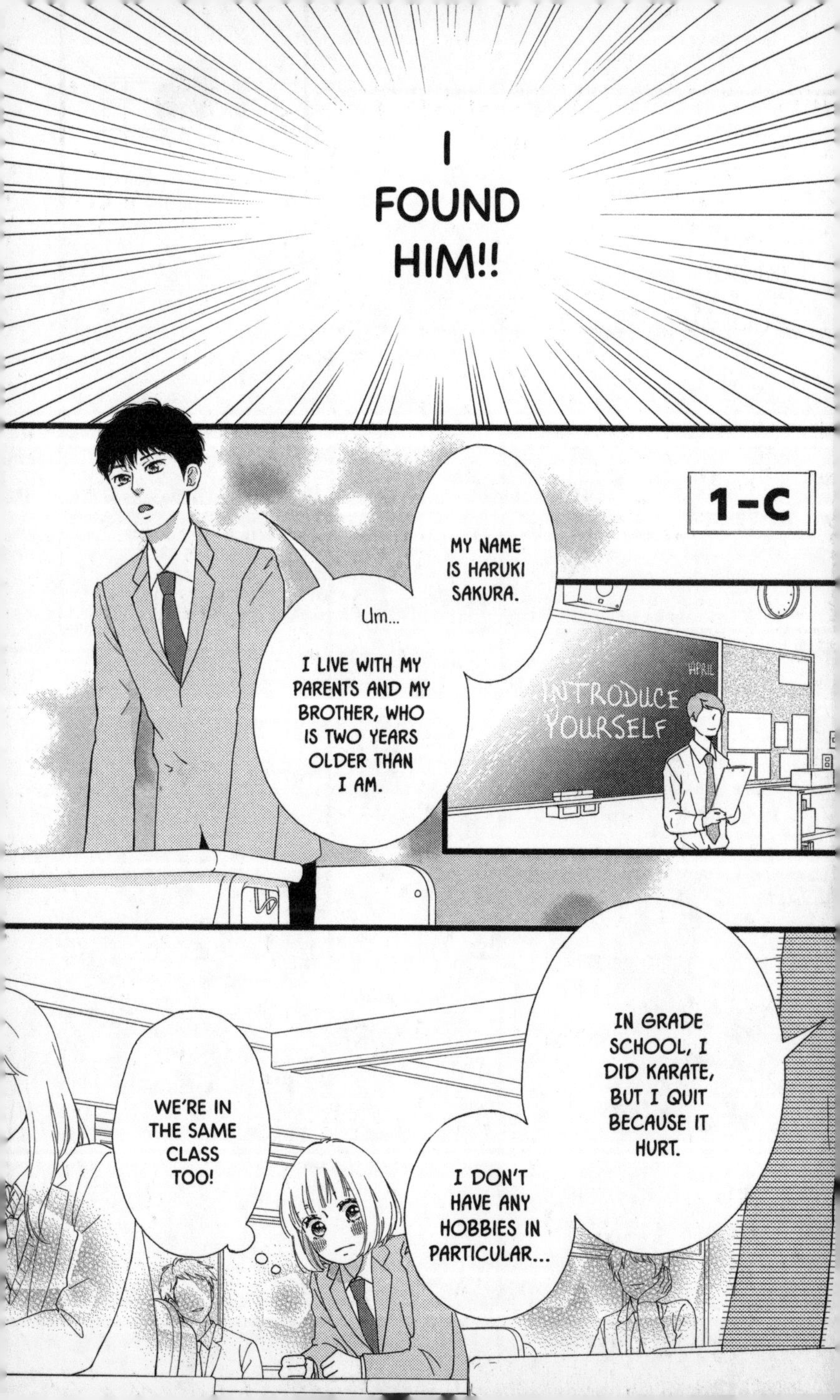
I FOUND HIM!!
1-C
APRIL
INTRODUCE YOURSELF
MY NAME IS HARUKI SAKURA.
Um...
I LIVE WITH MY PARENTS AND MY BROTHER, WHO IS TWO YEARS OLDER THAN I AM.
IN GRADE SCHOOL, I DID KARATE, BUT I QUIT BECAUSE IT HURT.
I DON'T HAVE ANY HOBBIES IN PARTICULAR...
WE'RE IN THE SAME CLASS TOO!

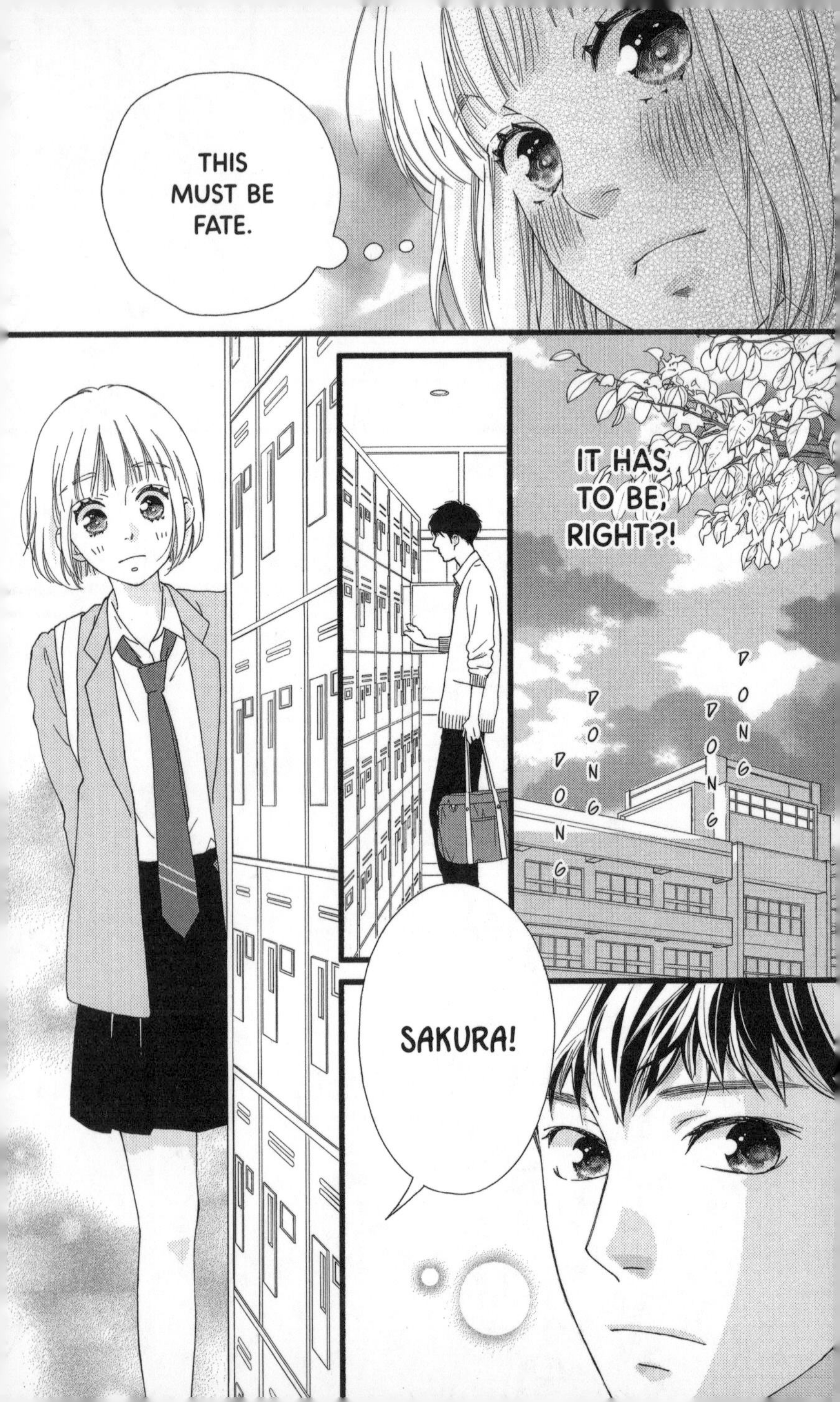
THIS MUST BE FATE.
IT HAS TO BE, RIGHT?!
DONG DONG
DONG DONG
SAKURA!
SAKURA!

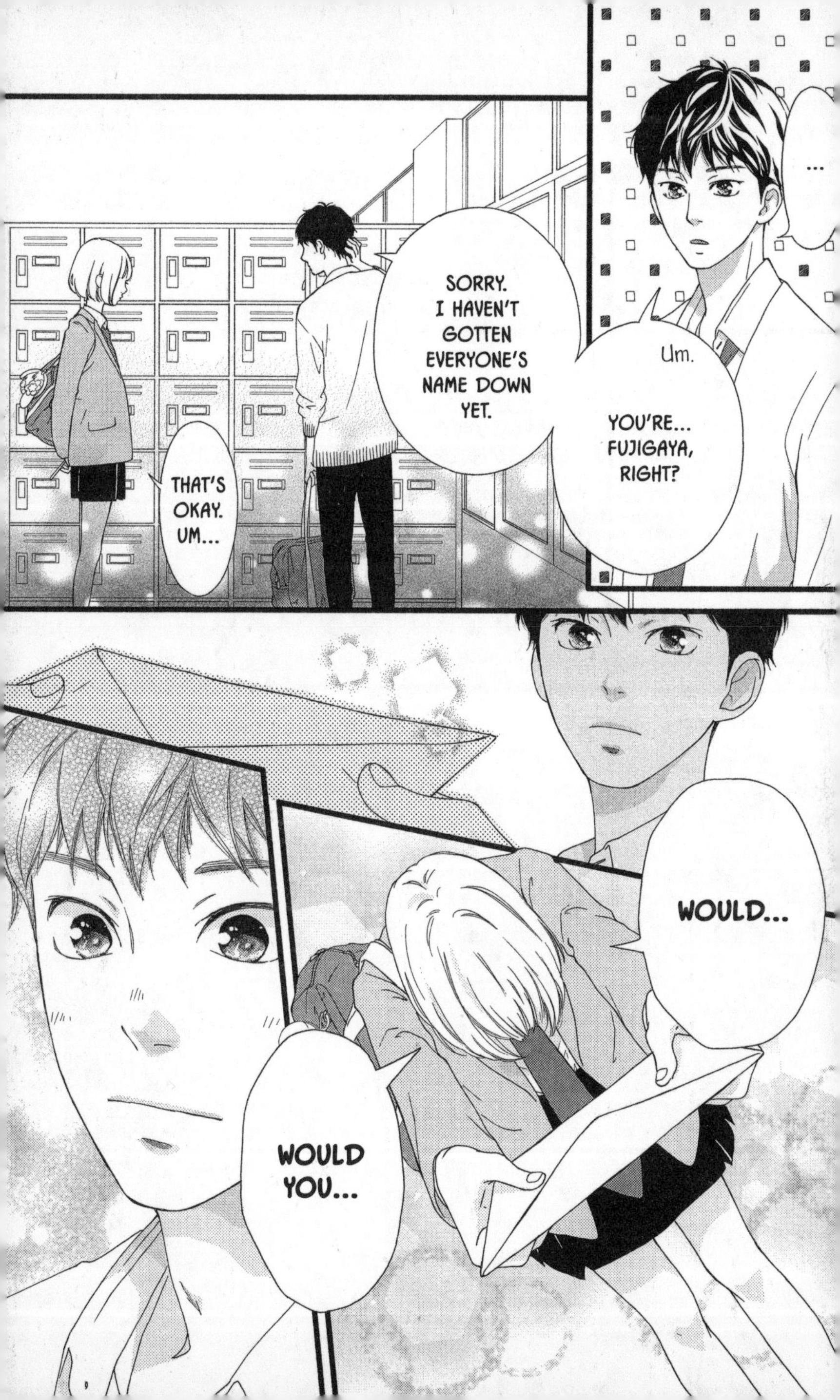
...
Um.
YOU'RE... FUJIGAYA, RIGHT?
SORRY. I HAVEN'T GOTTEN EVERYONE'S NAME DOWN YET.
THAT'S OKAY. UM...
WOULD...
WOULD YOU...

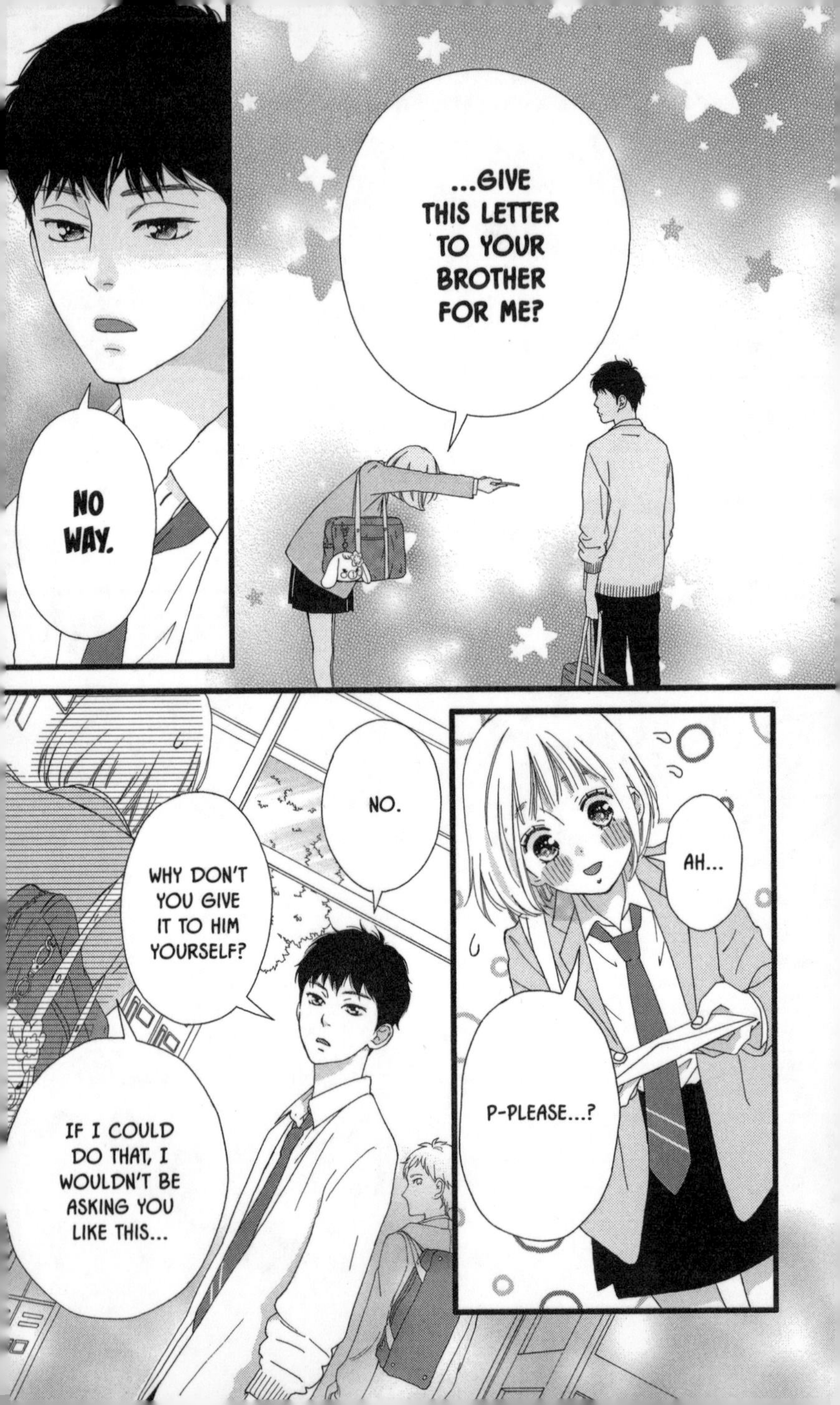
...GIVE THIS LETTER TO YOUR BROTHER FOR ME?
NO WAY.
AH...
P-PLEASE...?
NO.
WHY DON'T YOU GIVE IT TO HIM YOURSELF?
IF I COULD DO THAT, I WOULDN'T BE ASKING YOU LIKE THIS...

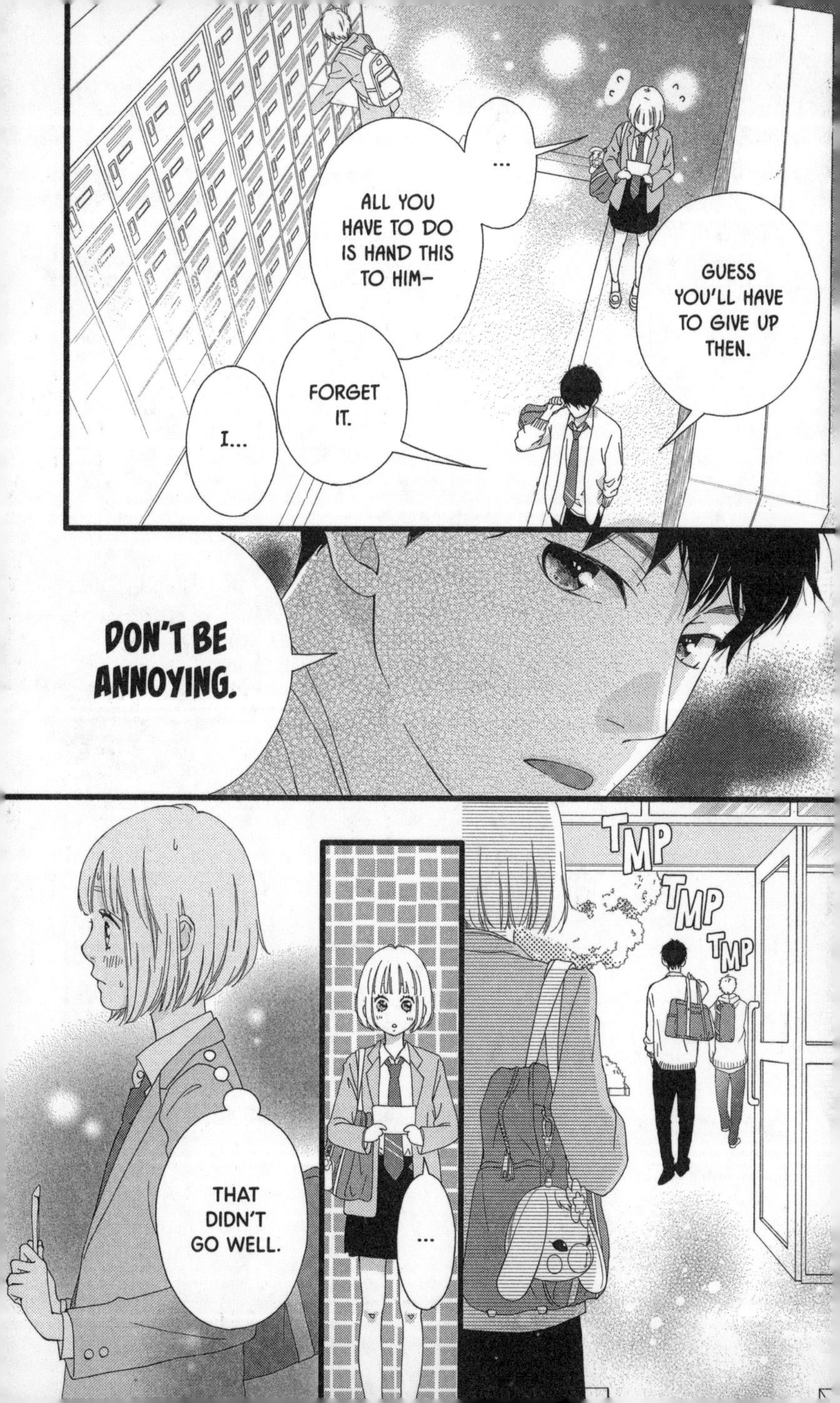

...
GUESS YOU'LL HAVE TO GIVE UP THEN.
ALL YOU HAVE TO DO IS HAND THIS TO HIM—
FORGET IT.
I...
DON'T BE ANNOYING.
TMP TMP TMP
...
THAT DIDN'T GO WELL.

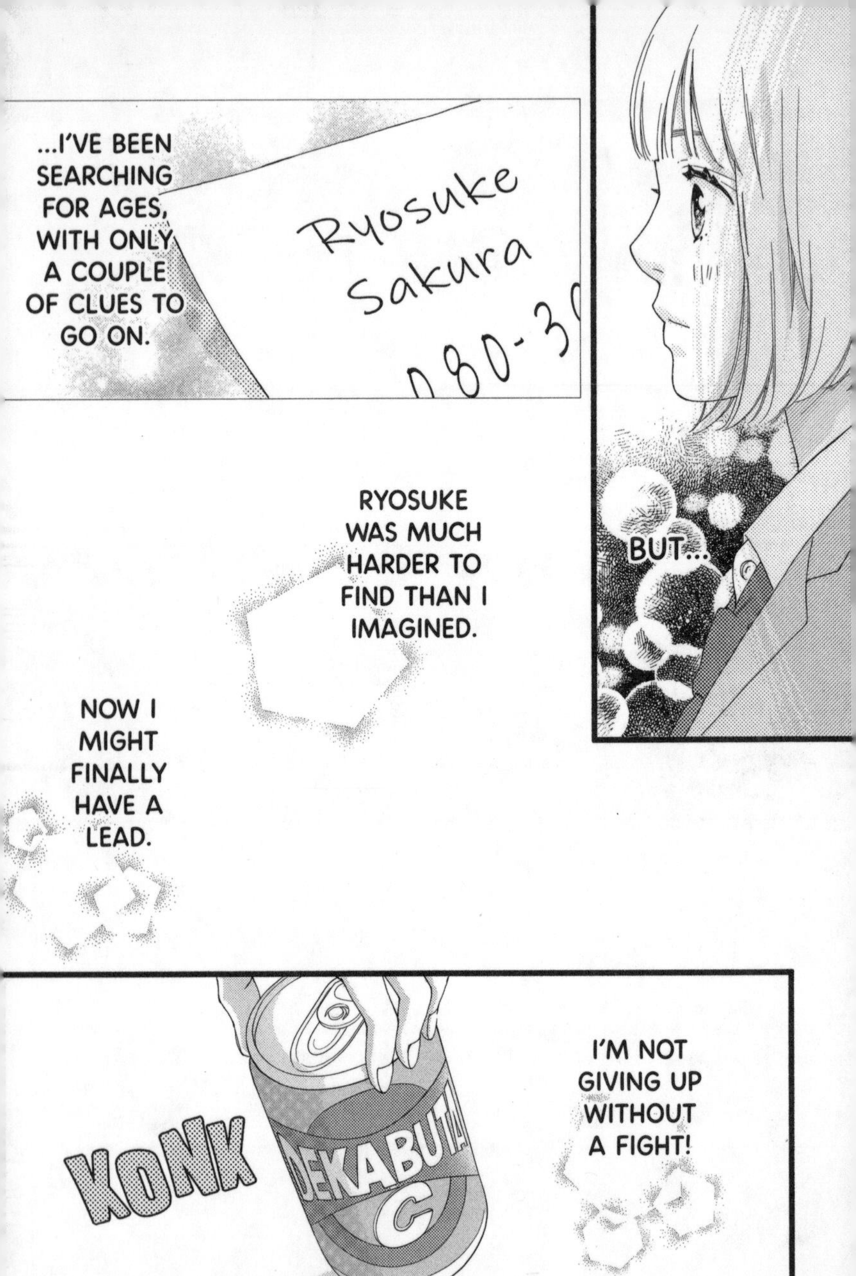

BUT...
...I'VE BEEN SEARCHING FOR AGES, WITH ONLY A COUPLE OF CLUES TO GO ON.
Ryosuke Sakura
080-3
RYOSUKE WAS MUCH HARDER TO FIND THAN I IMAGINED.
NOW I MIGHT FINALLY HAVE A LEAD.
I'M NOT GIVING UP WITHOUT A FIGHT!
KONK
DEKABUTA
C

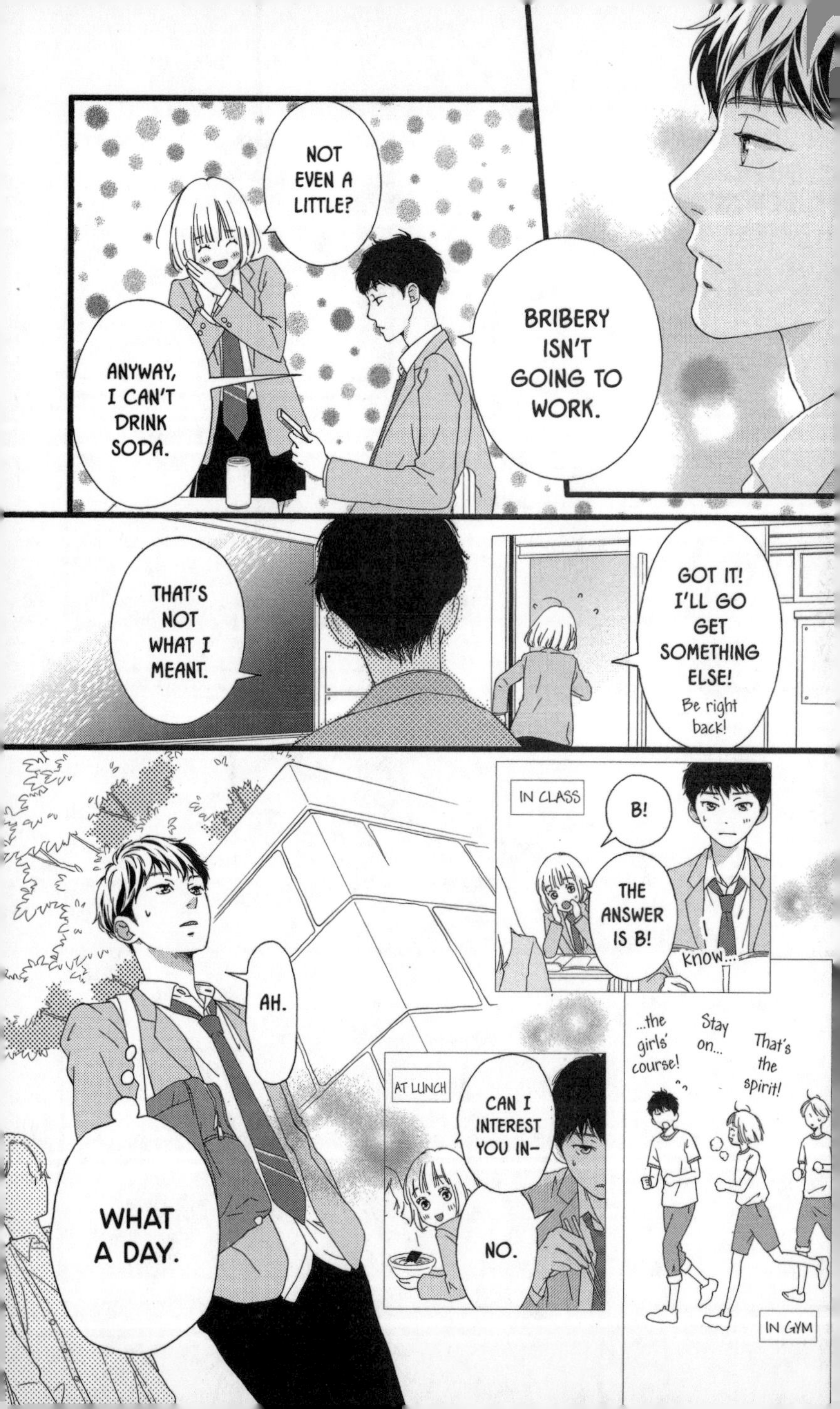
NOT EVEN A LITTLE?
BRIBERY ISN'T GOING TO WORK.
ANYWAY, I CAN'T DRINK SODA.
GOT IT! I'LL GO GET SOMETHING ELSE!
Be right back!
THAT'S NOT WHAT I MEANT.
IN CLASS
B!
THE ANSWER IS B!
I know...
That's the spirit!
Stay on...
...the girls' course!
IN GYM
AT LUNCH
CAN I INTEREST YOU IN–
NO.
AH.
WHAT A DAY.

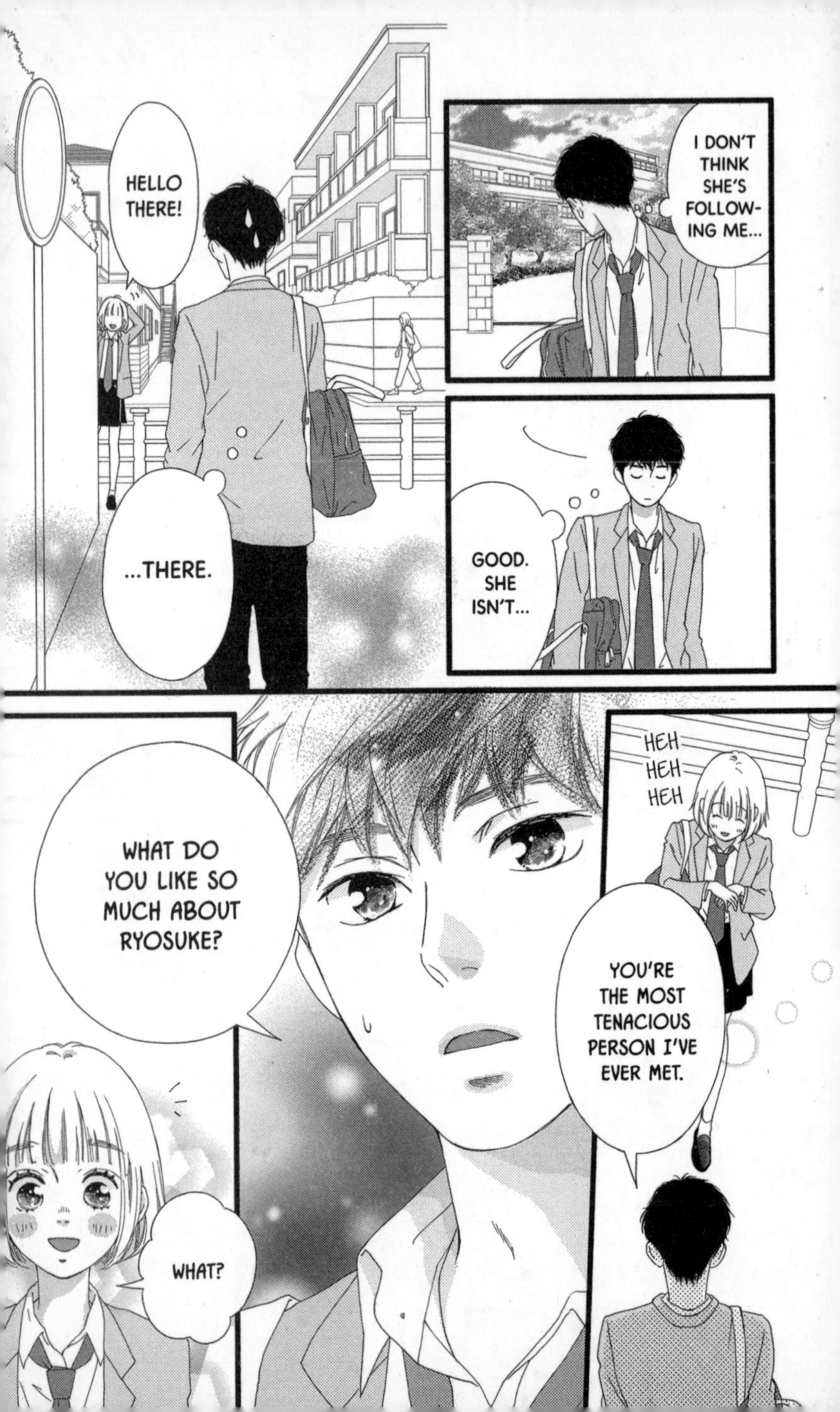
I DON'T THINK SHE'S FOLLOW-ING ME...
GOOD. SHE ISN'T...
HELLO THERE!
...THERE.
HEH HEH HEH
YOU'RE THE MOST TENACIOUS PERSON I'VE EVER MET.
WHAT DO YOU LIKE SO MUCH ABOUT RYOSUKE?
WHAT?

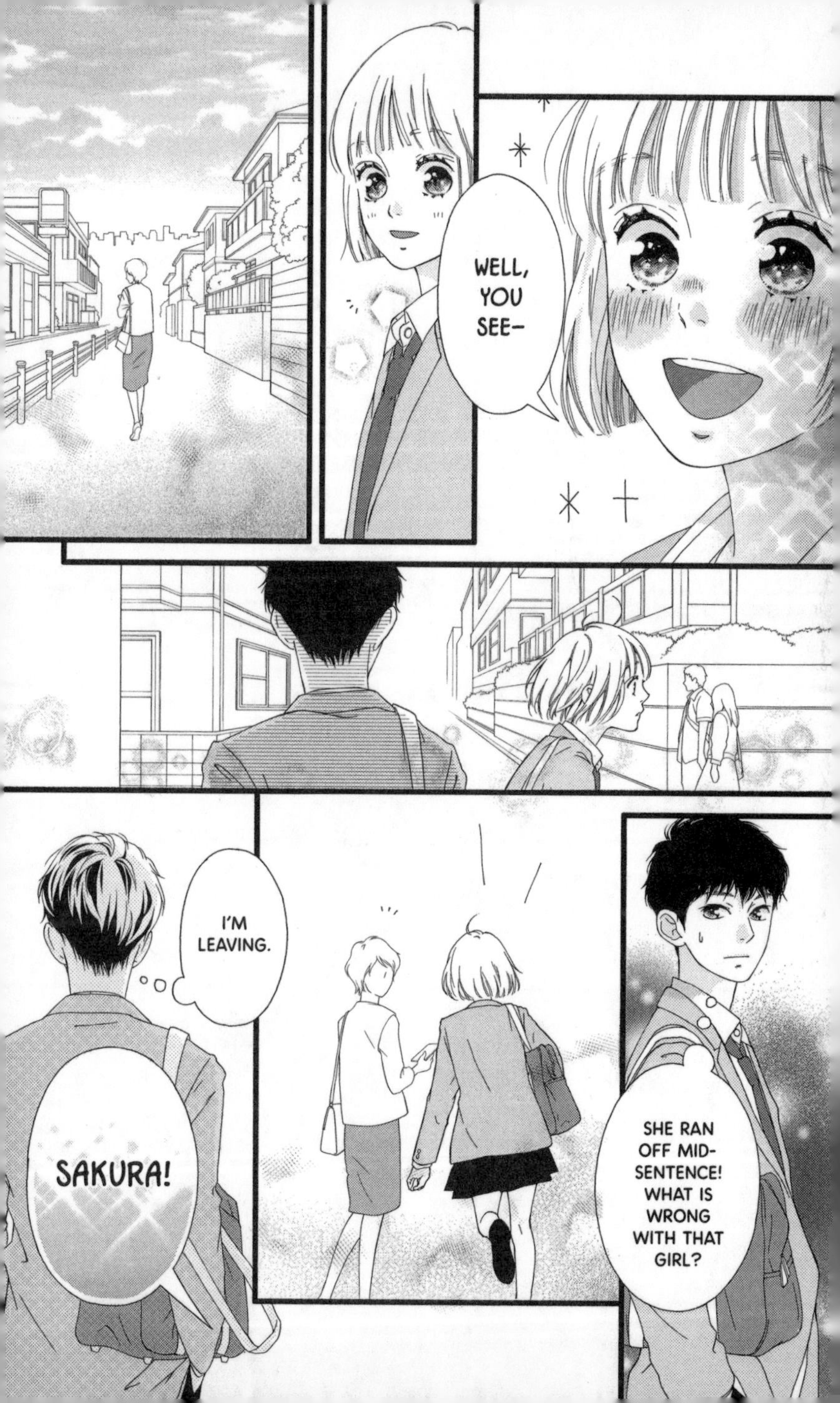
WELL, YOU SEE—
SHE RAN OFF MID-SENTENCE! WHAT IS WRONG WITH THAT GIRL?
I'M LEAVING.
SAKURA!

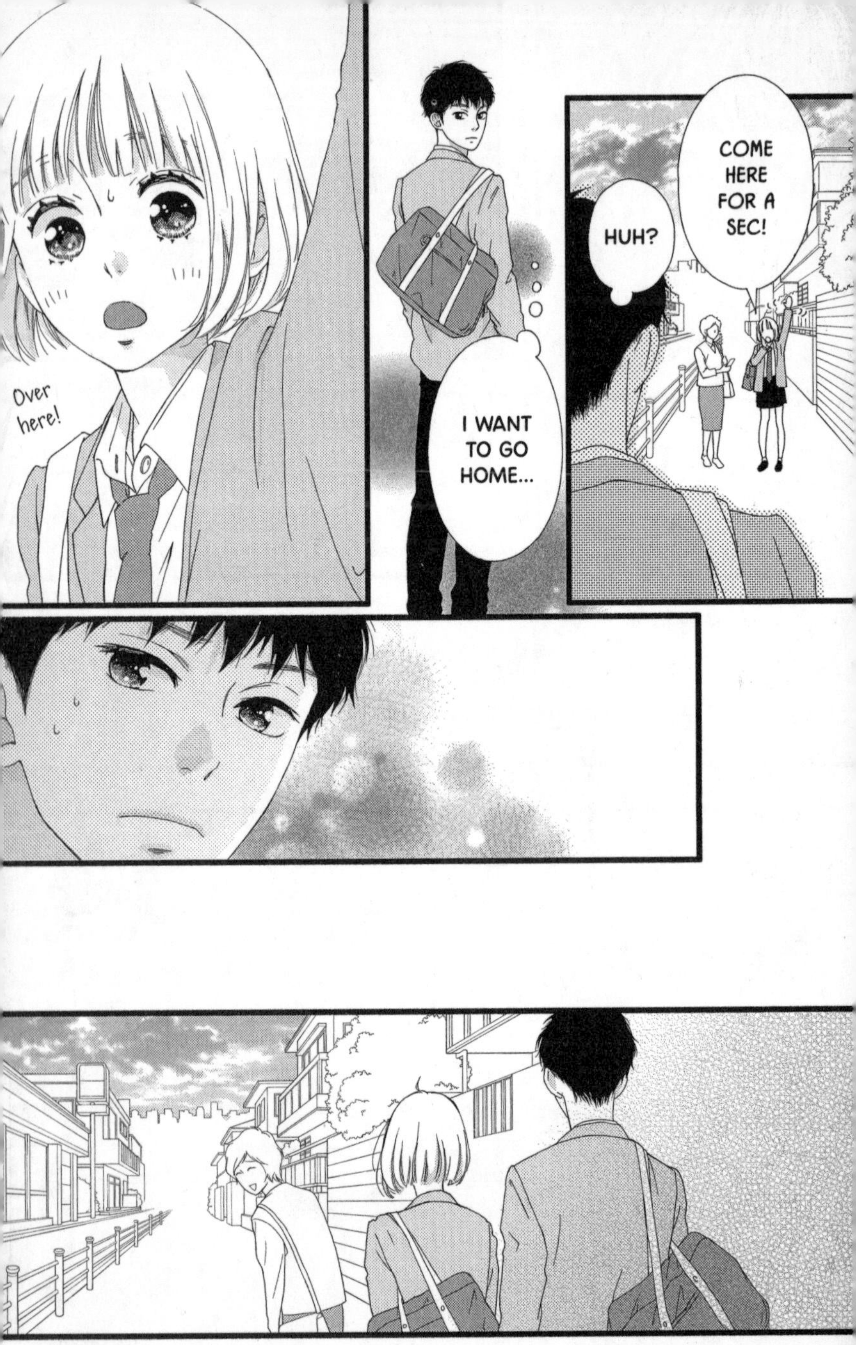
COME HERE FOR A SEC!
HUH?
I WANT TO GO HOME...
Over here!

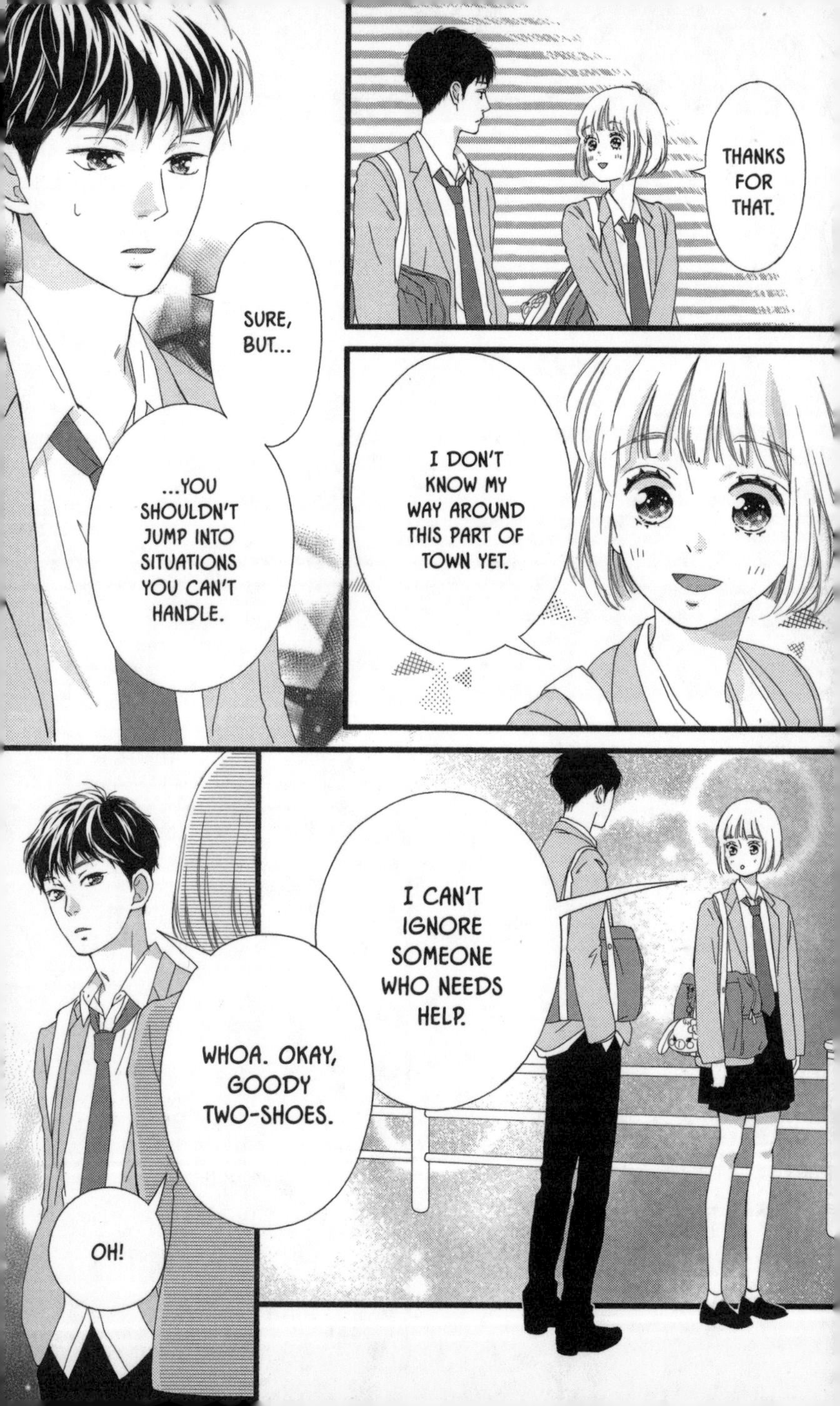
THANKS FOR THAT.
I DON'T KNOW MY WAY AROUND THIS PART OF TOWN YET.
SURE, BUT...
...YOU SHOULDN'T JUMP INTO SITUATIONS YOU CAN'T HANDLE.
I CAN'T IGNORE SOMEONE WHO NEEDS HELP.
WHOA. OKAY, GOODY TWO-SHOES.
OH!

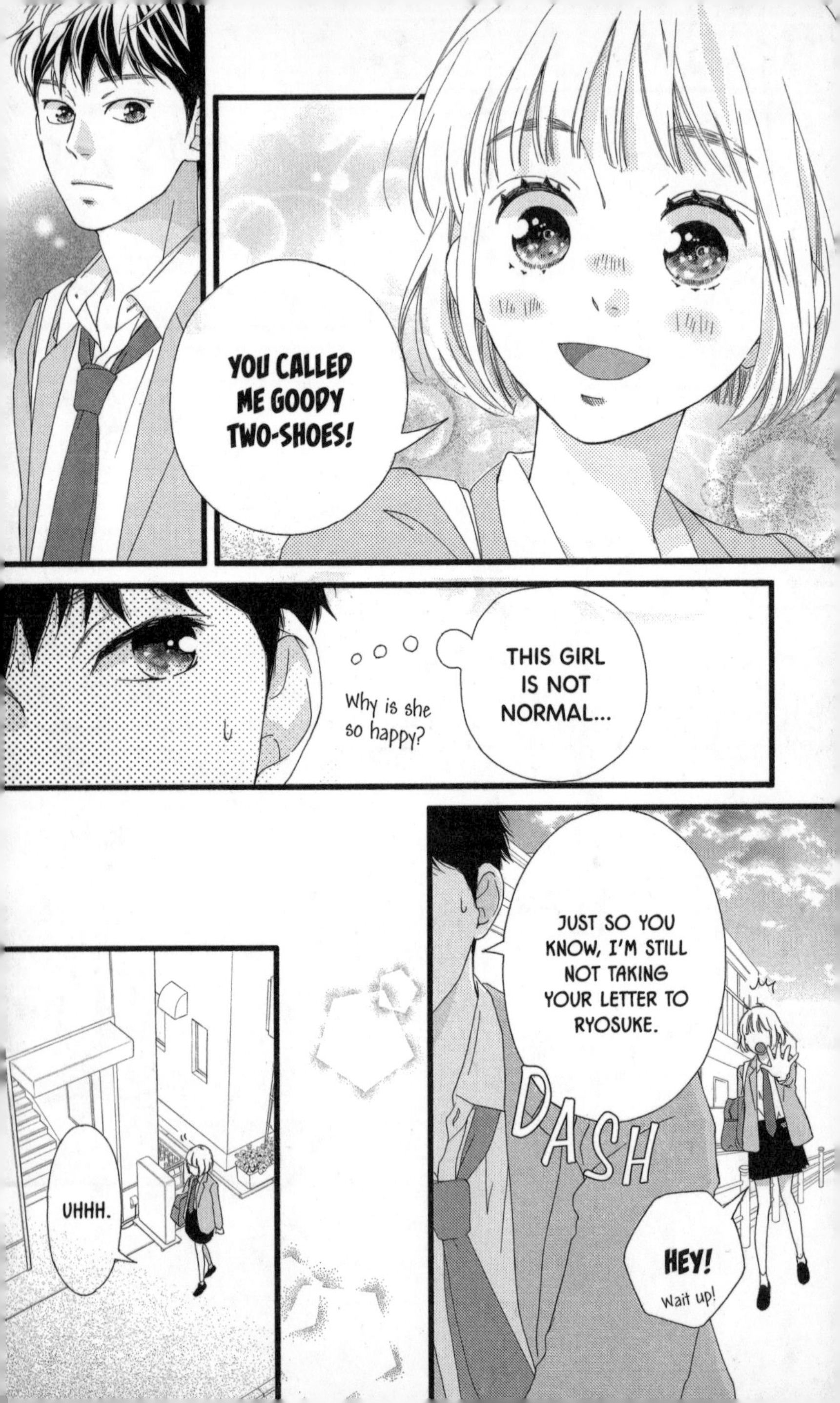
YOU CALLED ME GOODY TWO-SHOES!
THIS GIRL IS NOT NORMAL...
Why is she so happy?
JUST SO YOU KNOW, I'M STILL NOT TAKING YOUR LETTER TO RYOSUKE.
DASH
HEY!
Wait up!
UHHH.

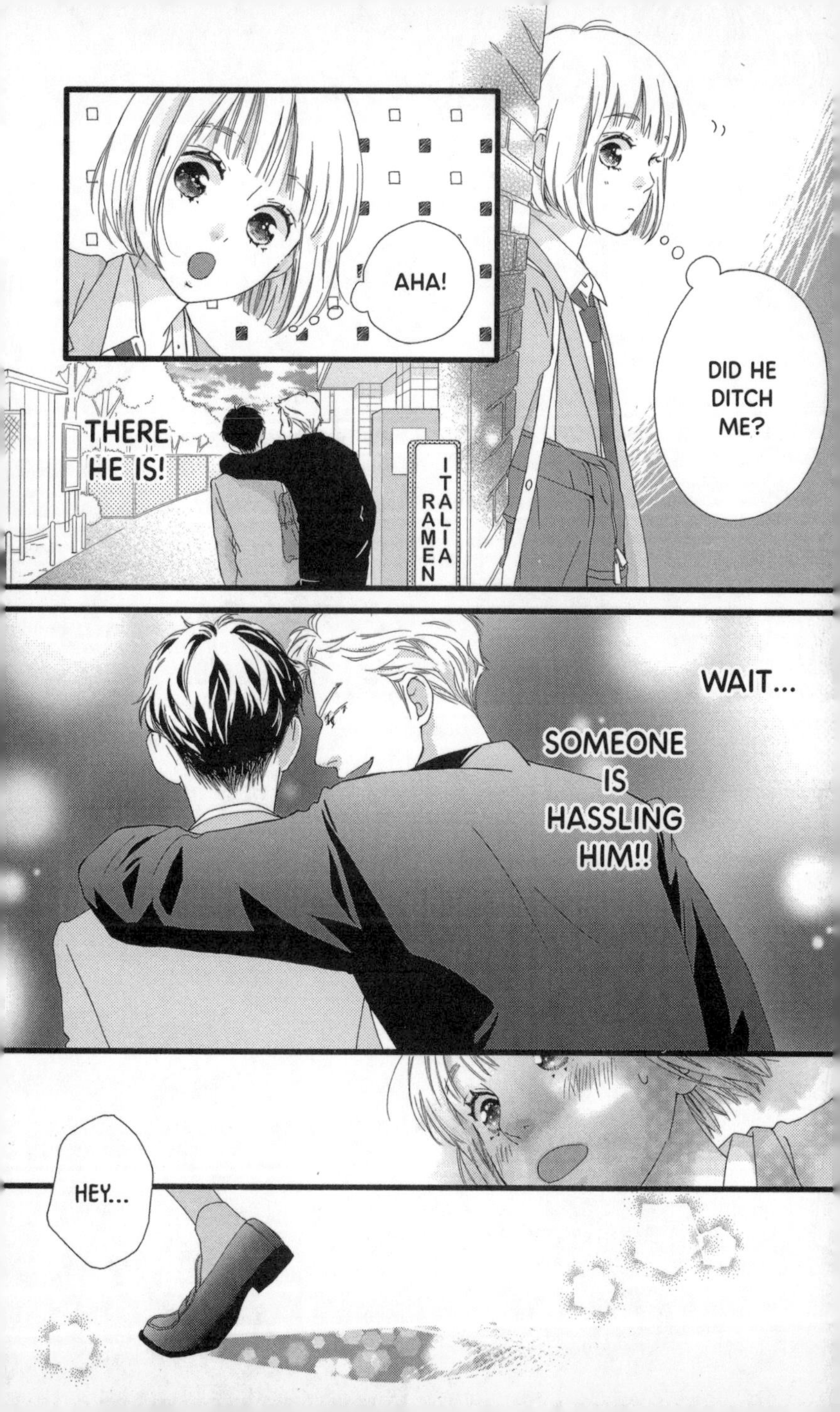
DID HE DITCH ME?
AHA!
THERE HE IS!
ITALIA
RAMEN
WAIT...
SOMEONE IS HASSLING HIM!!
HEY...

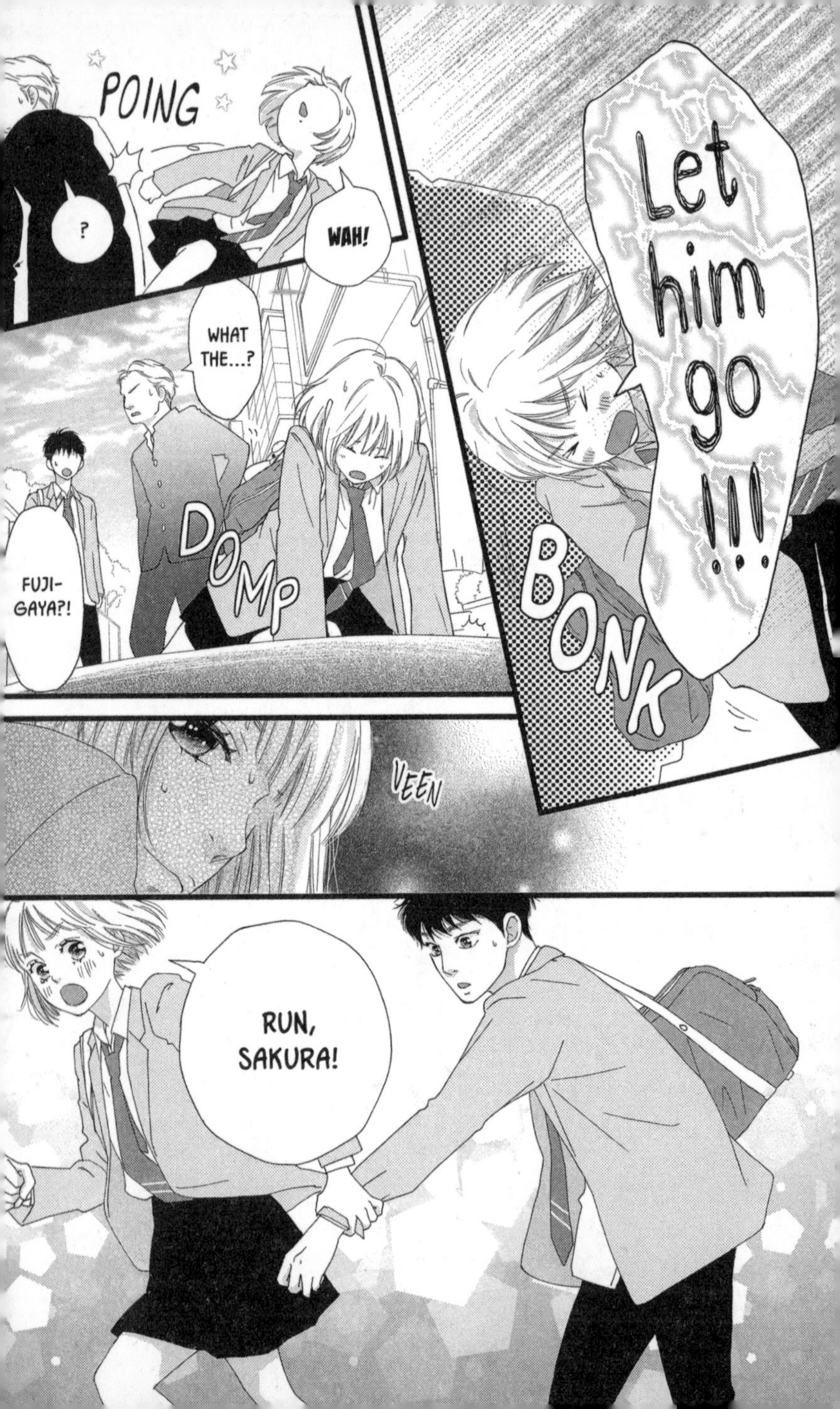
Let him go!!!
BONK
POING
WAH!
?
WHAT THE...?
DOMP
FUJI-GAYA?!
VEEN
RUN, SAKURA!

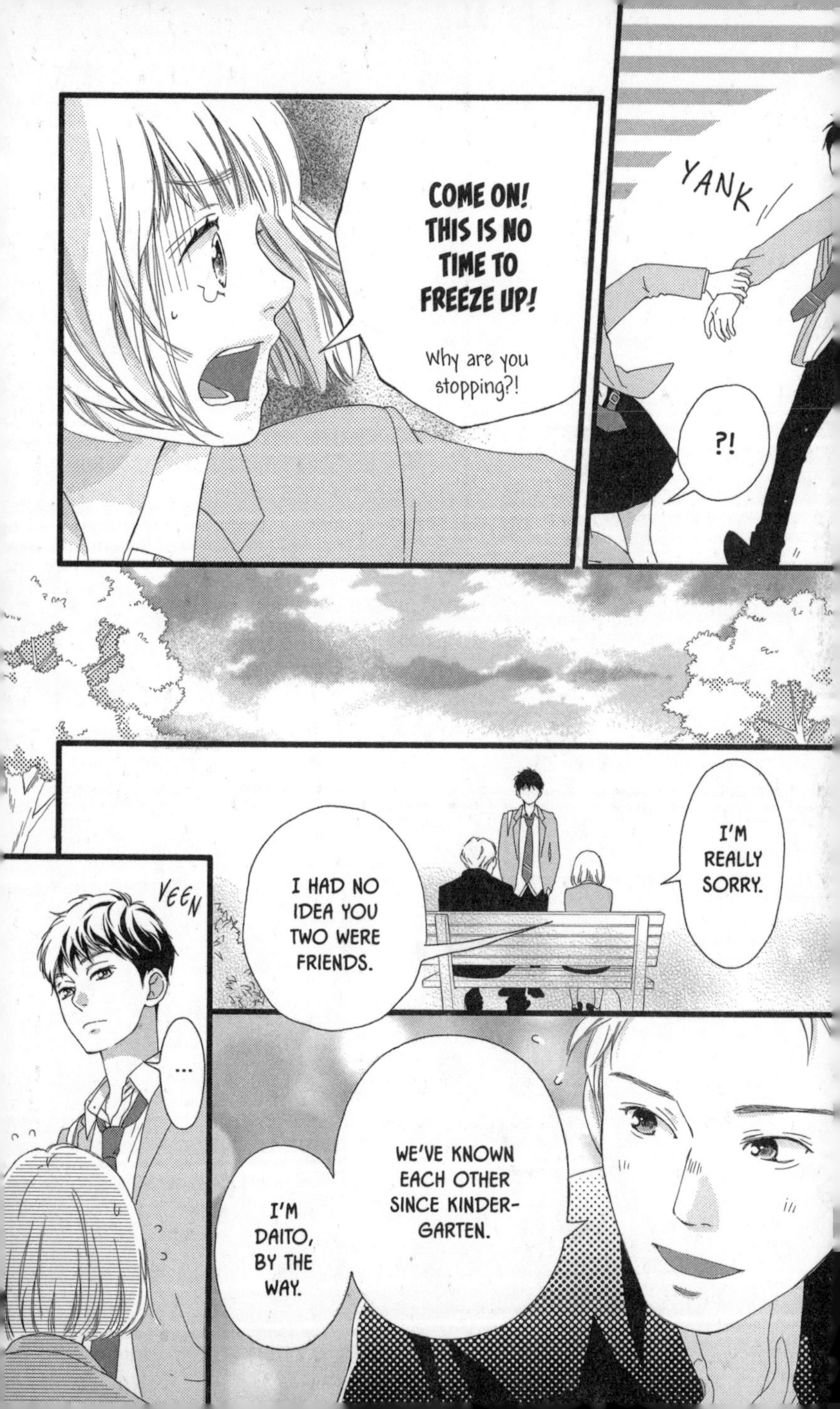
YANK
?!
COME ON! THIS IS NO TIME TO FREEZE UP!
Why are you stopping?!
I'M REALLY SORRY.
I HAD NO IDEA YOU TWO WERE FRIENDS.
WE'VE KNOWN EACH OTHER SINCE KINDER-GARTEN.
I'M DAITO, BY THE WAY.
VEEN
...

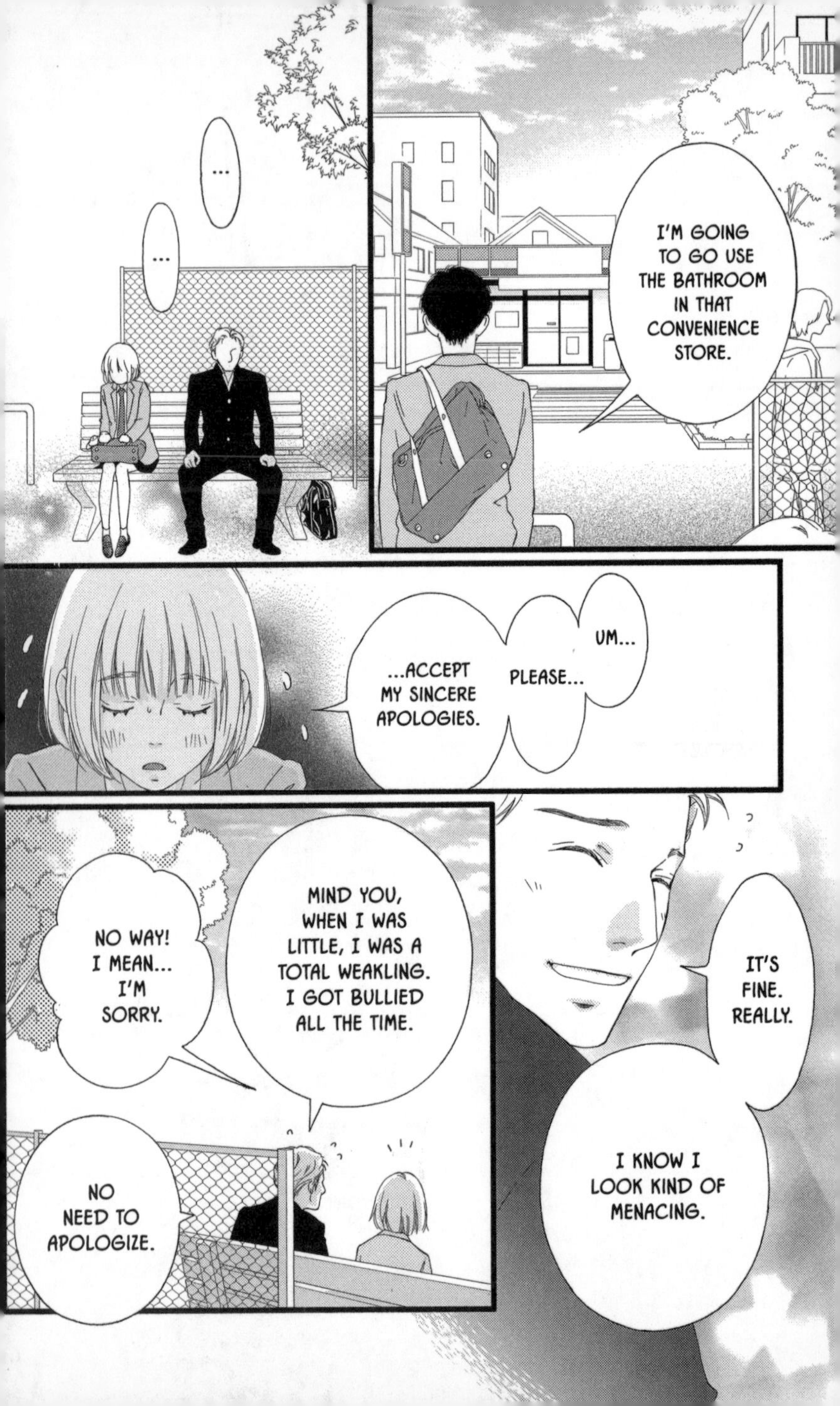

I'M GOING TO GO USE THE BATHROOM IN THAT CONVENIENCE STORE.
...
...
UM...
PLEASE...
...ACCEPT MY SINCERE APOLOGIES.
IT'S FINE. REALLY.
I KNOW I LOOK KIND OF MENACING.
MIND YOU, WHEN I WAS LITTLE, I WAS A TOTAL WEAKLING. I GOT BULLIED ALL THE TIME.
NO WAY! I MEAN... I'M SORRY.
NO NEED TO APOLOGIZE.

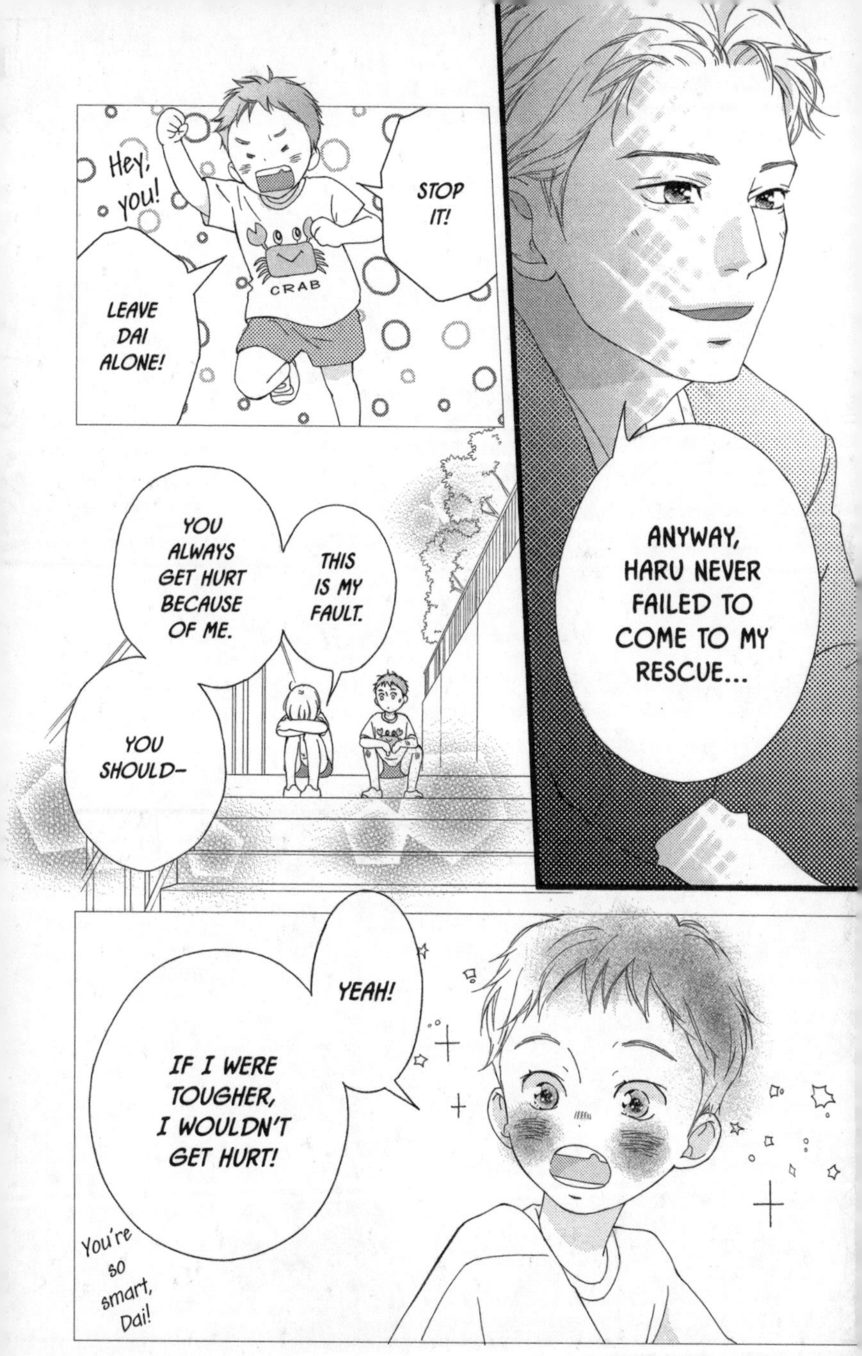
ANYWAY, HARU NEVER FAILED TO COME TO MY RESCUE...
STOP IT!
Hey, you!
LEAVE DAI ALONE!
THIS IS MY FAULT.
YOU ALWAYS GET HURT BECAUSE OF ME.
YOU SHOULD–
YEAH!
IF I WERE TOUGHER, I WOULDN'T GET HURT!
You're so smart, Dai!

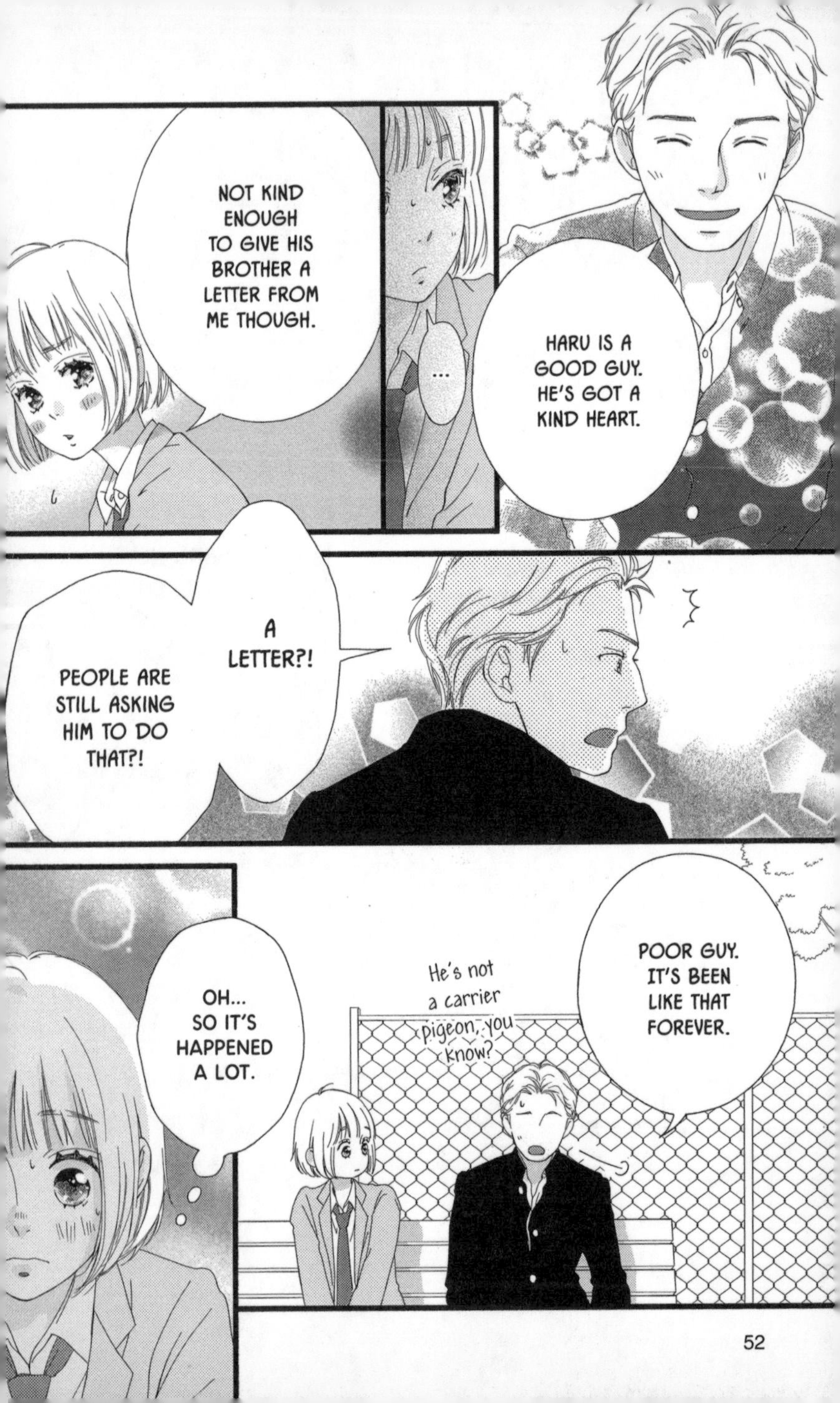
HARU IS A GOOD GUY. HE'S GOT A KIND HEART.
...
NOT KIND ENOUGH TO GIVE HIS BROTHER A LETTER FROM ME THOUGH.
A LETTER?!
PEOPLE ARE STILL ASKING HIM TO DO THAT?!
POOR GUY. IT'S BEEN LIKE THAT FOREVER.
He's not a carrier pigeon, you know?
OH... SO IT'S HAPPENED A LOT.

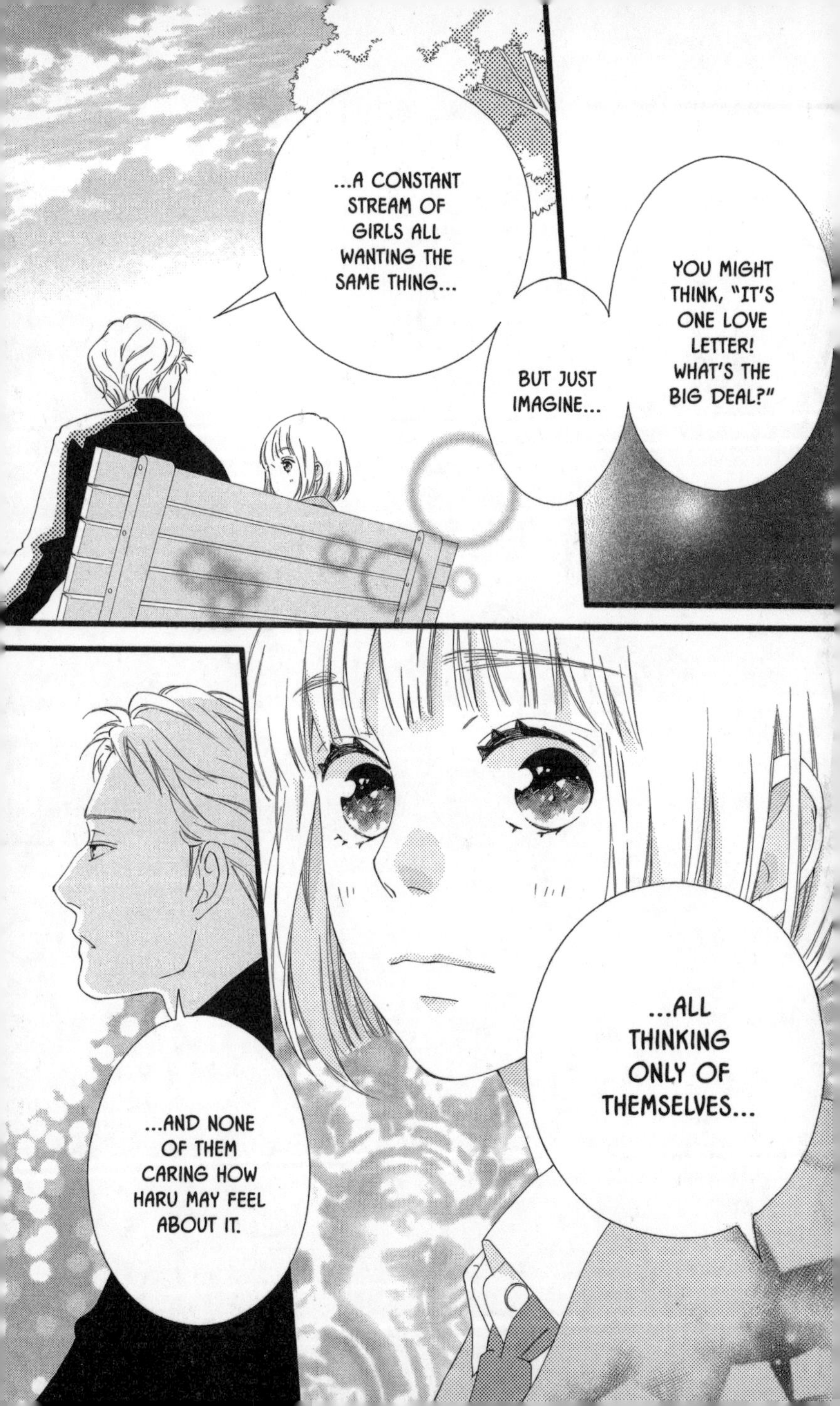
YOU MIGHT THINK, "IT'S ONE LOVE LETTER! WHAT'S THE BIG DEAL?"
BUT JUST IMAGINE...
...A CONSTANT STREAM OF GIRLS ALL WANTING THE SAME THING...
...ALL THINKING ONLY OF THEMSELVES...
...AND NONE OF THEM CARING HOW HARU MAY FEEL ABOUT IT.

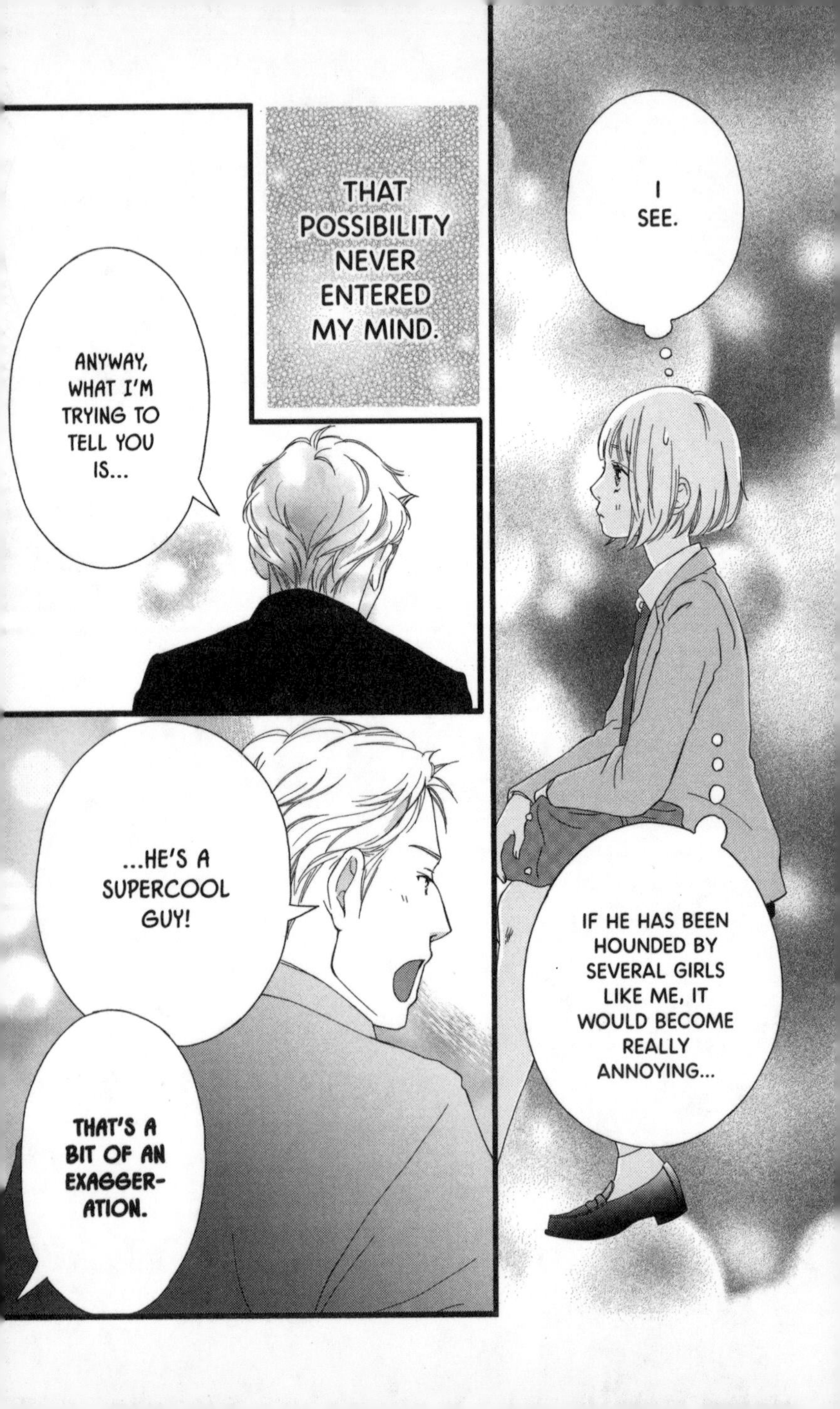
I SEE.
IF HE HAS BEEN HOUNDED BY SEVERAL GIRLS LIKE ME, IT WOULD BECOME REALLY ANNOYING...
THAT POSSIBILITY NEVER ENTERED MY MIND.
ANYWAY, WHAT I'M TRYING TO TELL YOU IS...
...HE'S A SUPERCOOL GUY!
THAT'S A BIT OF AN EXAGGER-ATION.

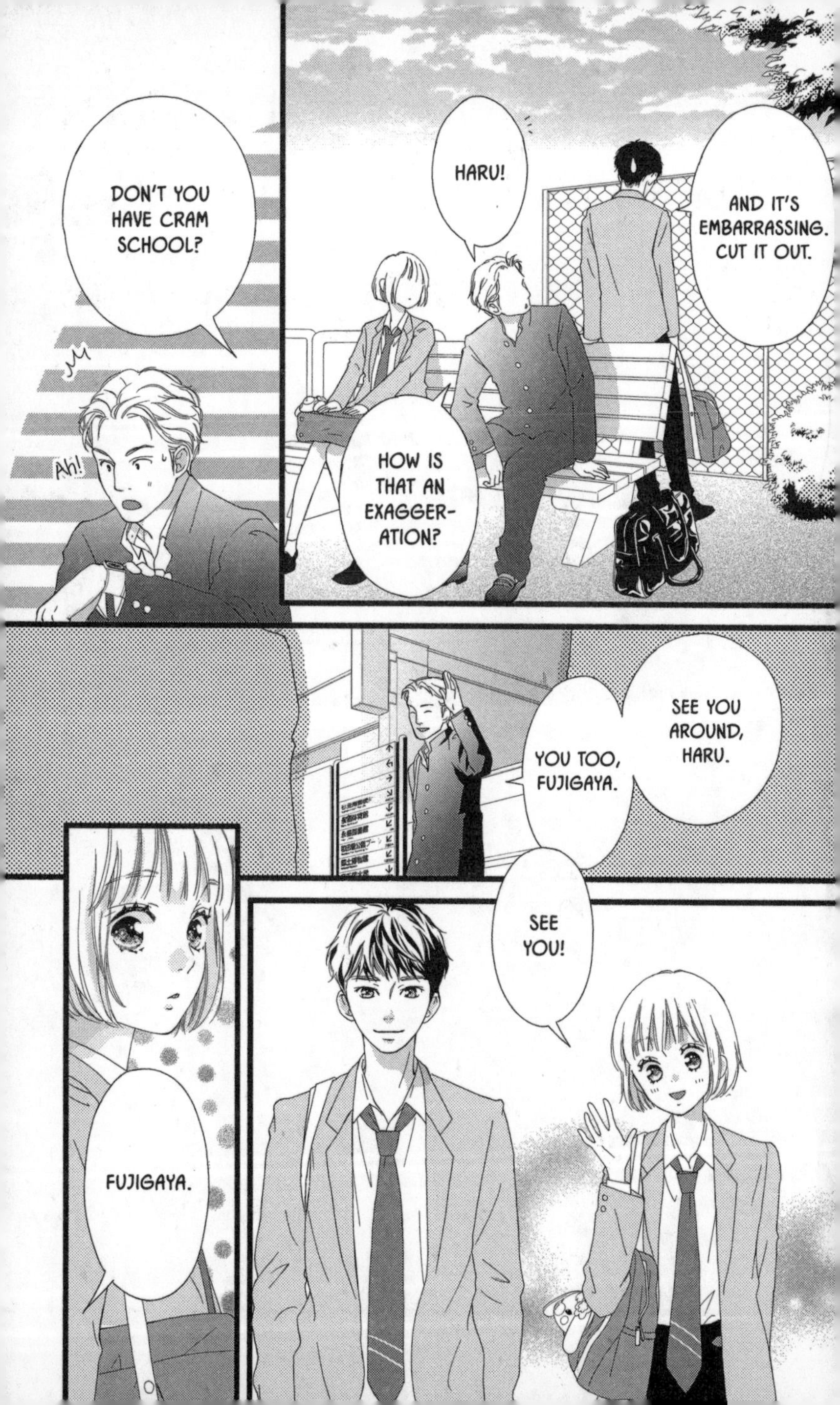

AND IT'S EMBARRASSING. CUT IT OUT.
HARU!
HOW IS THAT AN EXAGGERATION?
DON'T YOU HAVE CRAM SCHOOL?
Ah!
SEE YOU AROUND, HARU.
YOU TOO, FUJIGAYA.
SEE YOU!
FUJIGAYA.

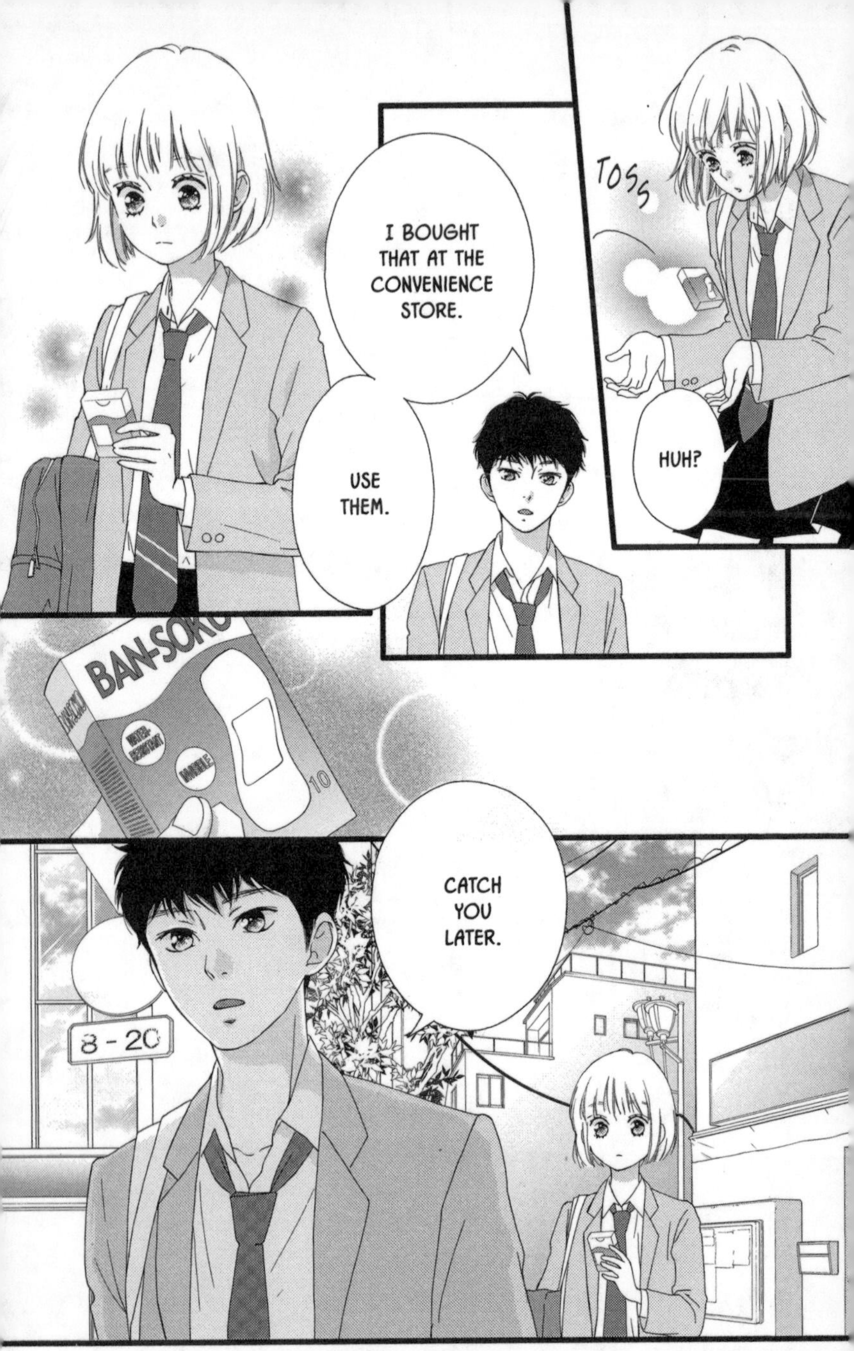
TOSS
HUH?
I BOUGHT THAT AT THE CONVENIENCE STORE.
USE THEM.
BAN-SOKO
10
CATCH YOU LATER.
8-20

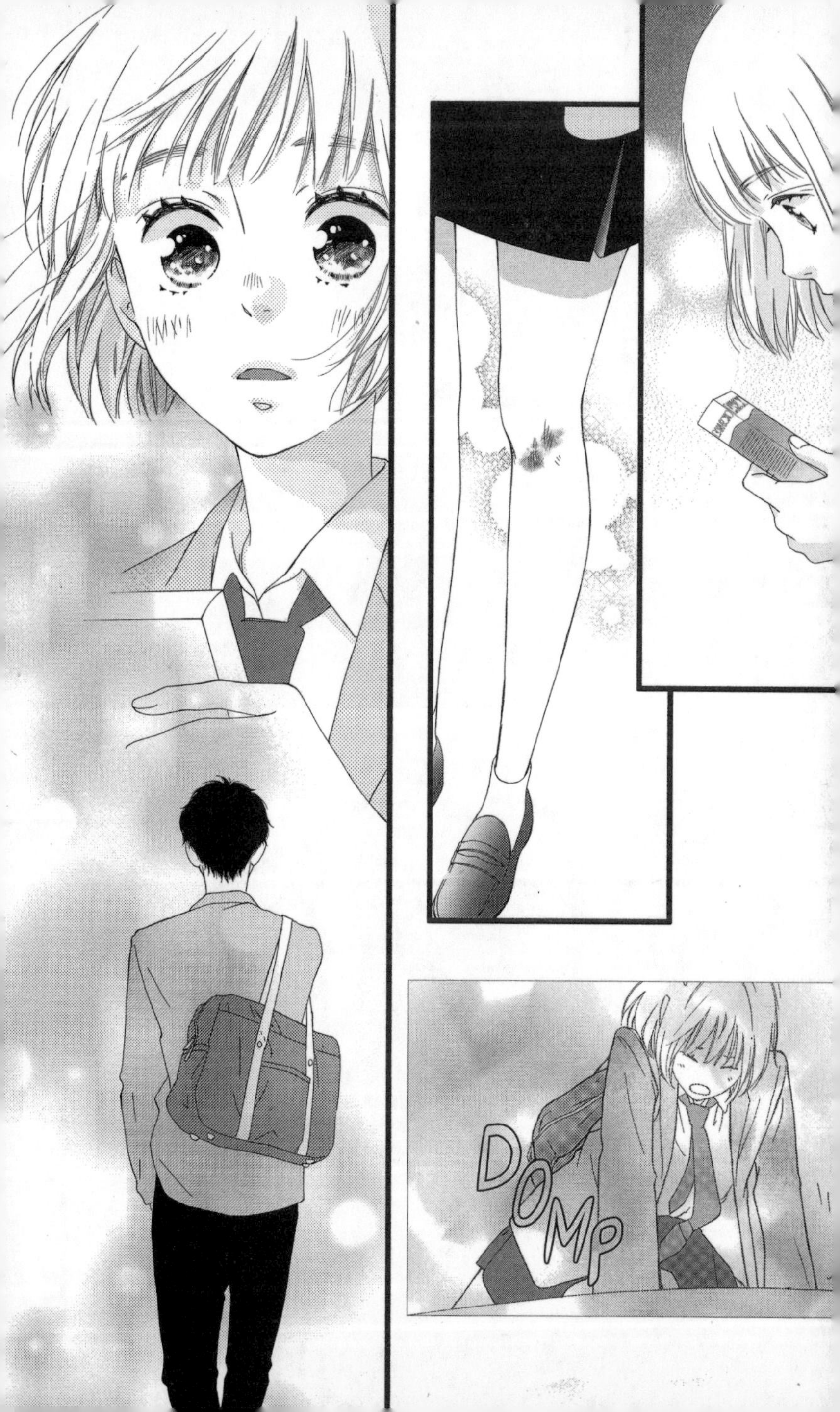
DOMP

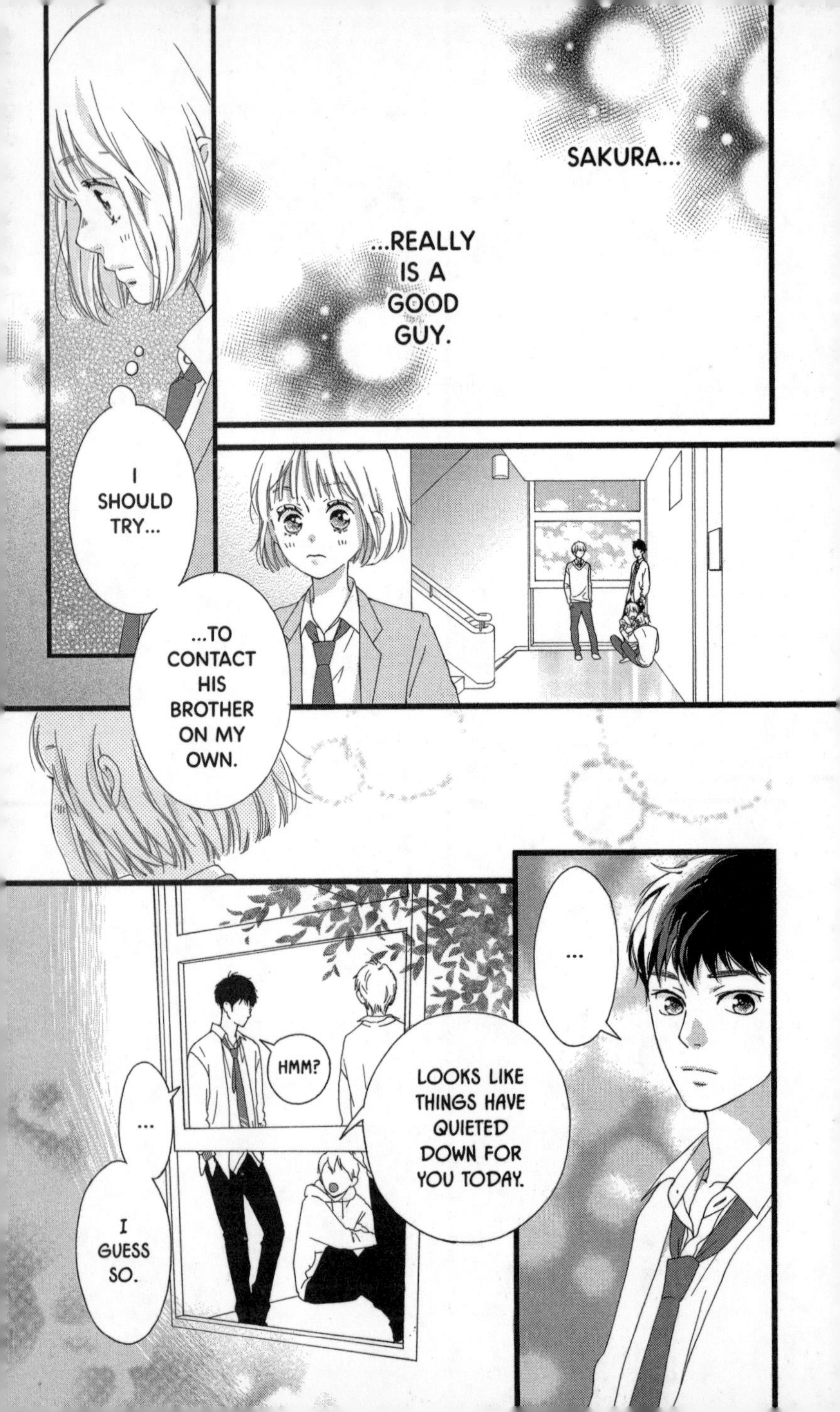
SAKURA...
...REALLY IS A GOOD GUY.
I SHOULD TRY...
...TO CONTACT HIS BROTHER ON MY OWN.
...
LOOKS LIKE THINGS HAVE QUIETED DOWN FOR YOU TODAY.
HMM?
...
I GUESS SO.

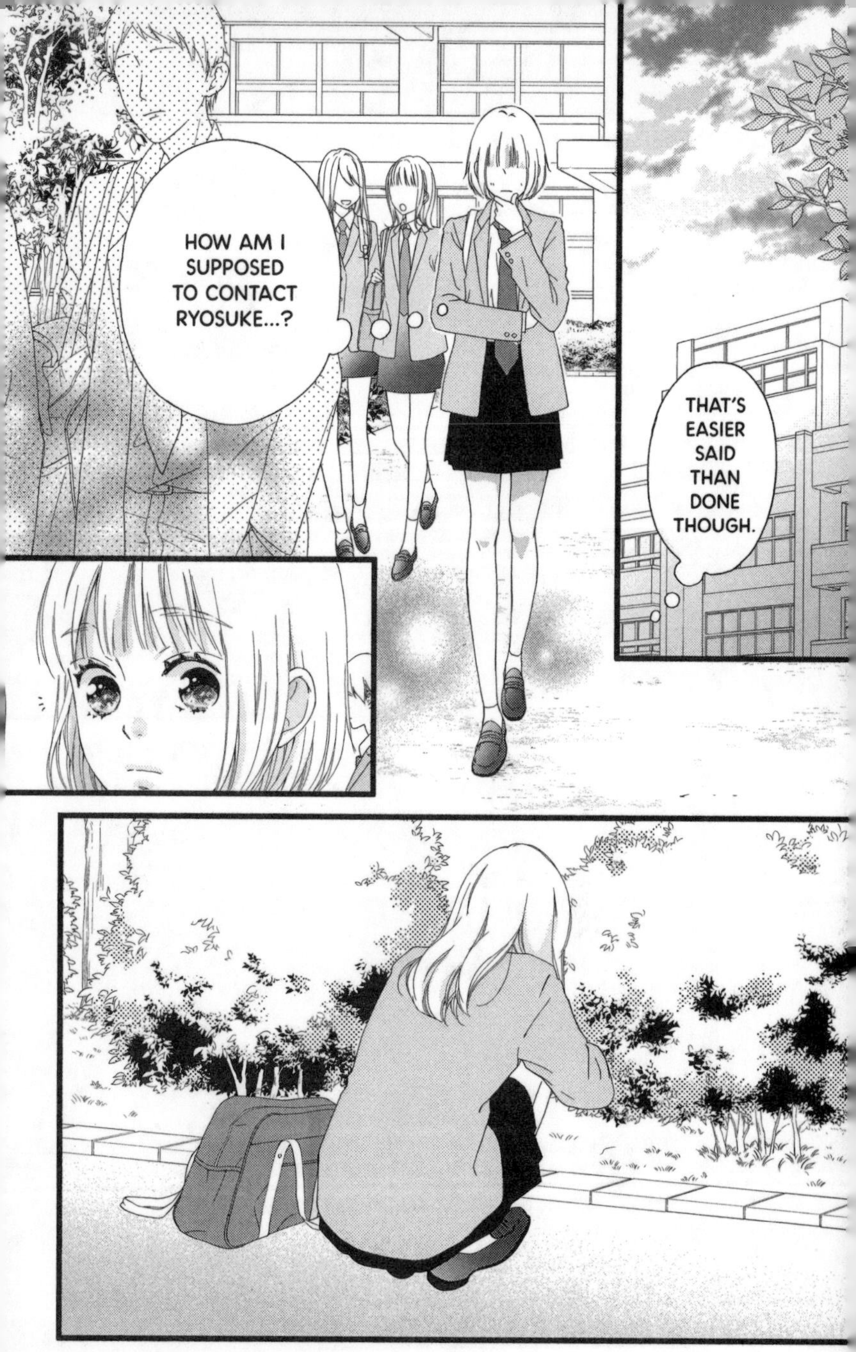
THAT'S EASIER SAID THAN DONE THOUGH.
HOW AM I SUPPOSED TO CONTACT RYOSUKE...?

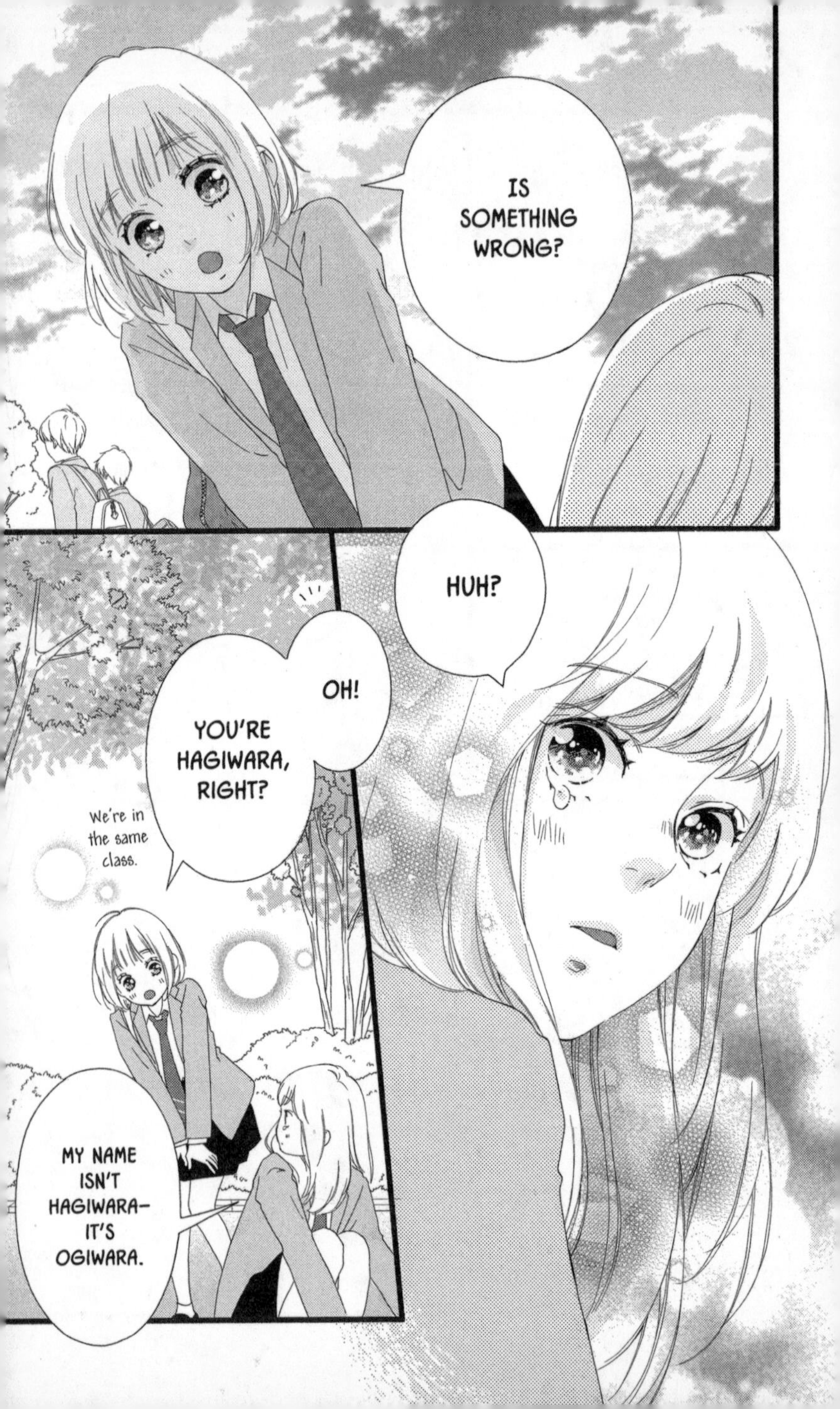
IS SOMETHING WRONG?
HUH?
OH!
YOU'RE HAGIWARA, RIGHT?
We're in the same class.
MY NAME ISN'T HAGIWARA—IT'S OGIWARA.

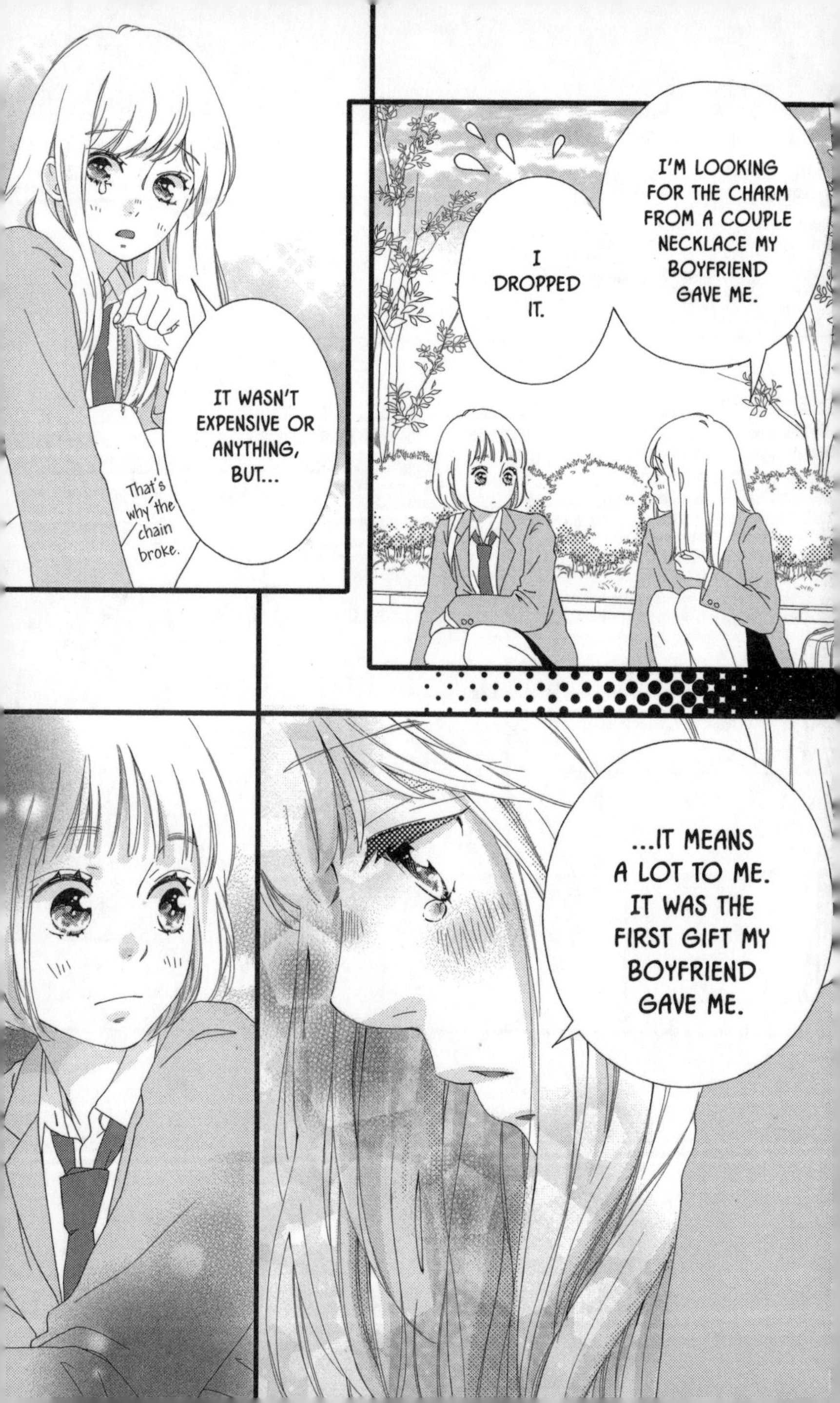
I'M LOOKING FOR THE CHARM FROM A COUPLE NECKLACE MY BOYFRIEND GAVE ME.
I DROPPED IT.
IT WASN'T EXPENSIVE OR ANYTHING, BUT...
That's why the chain broke.
...IT MEANS A LOT TO ME. IT WAS THE FIRST GIFT MY BOYFRIEND GAVE ME.

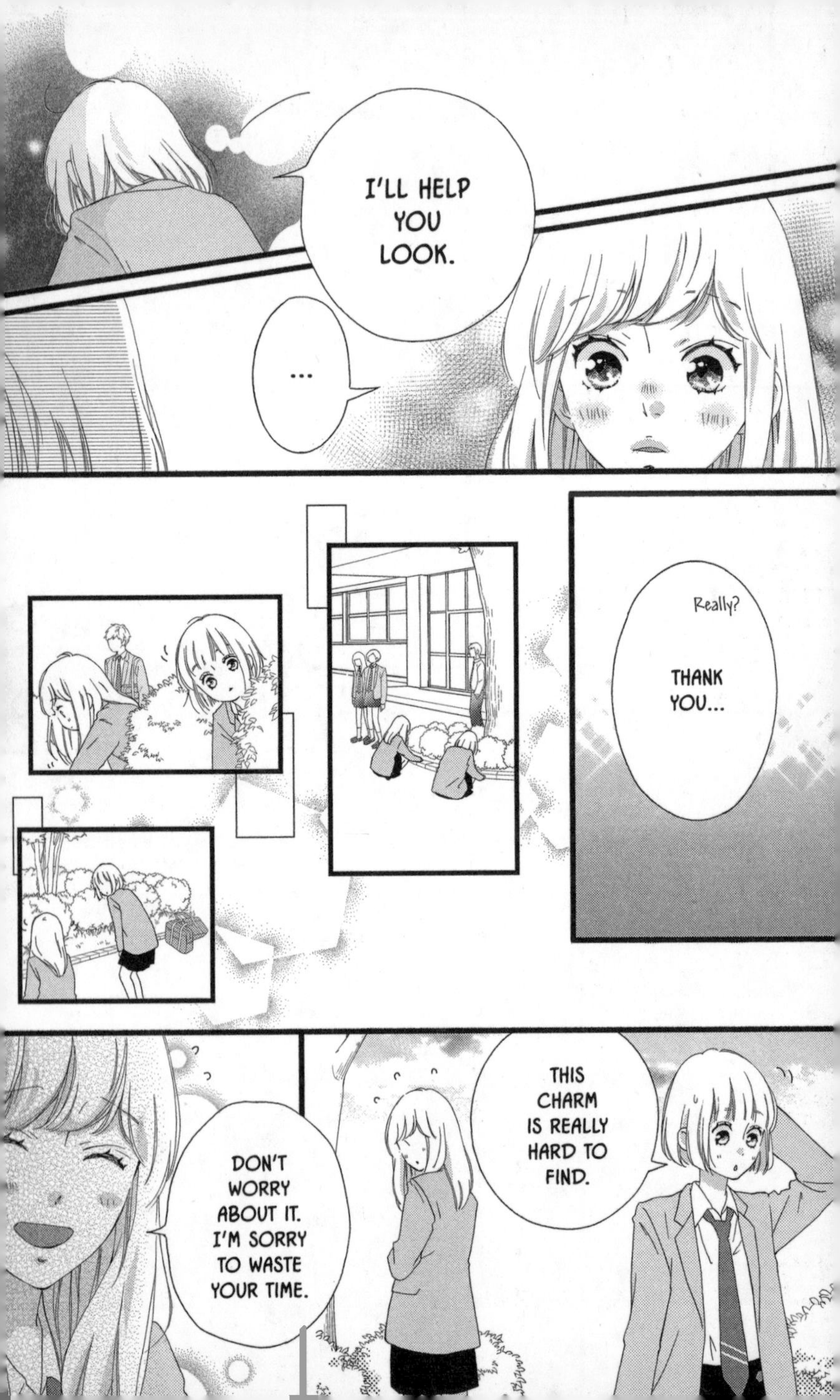
I'LL HELP YOU LOOK.
...
Really?
THANK YOU...
THIS CHARM IS REALLY HARD TO FIND.
DON'T WORRY ABOUT IT. I'M SORRY TO WASTE YOUR TIME.

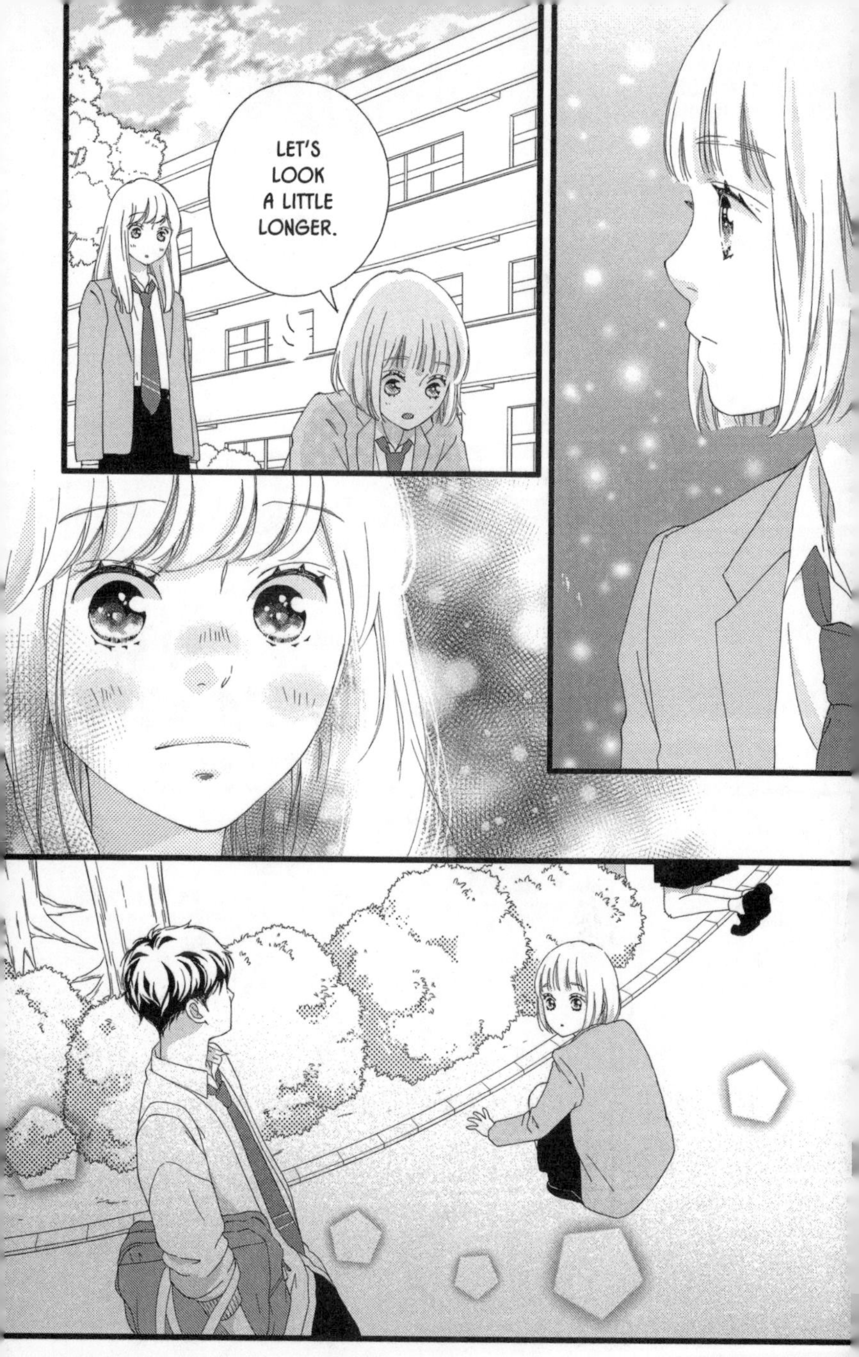
LET'S LOOK A LITTLE LONGER.

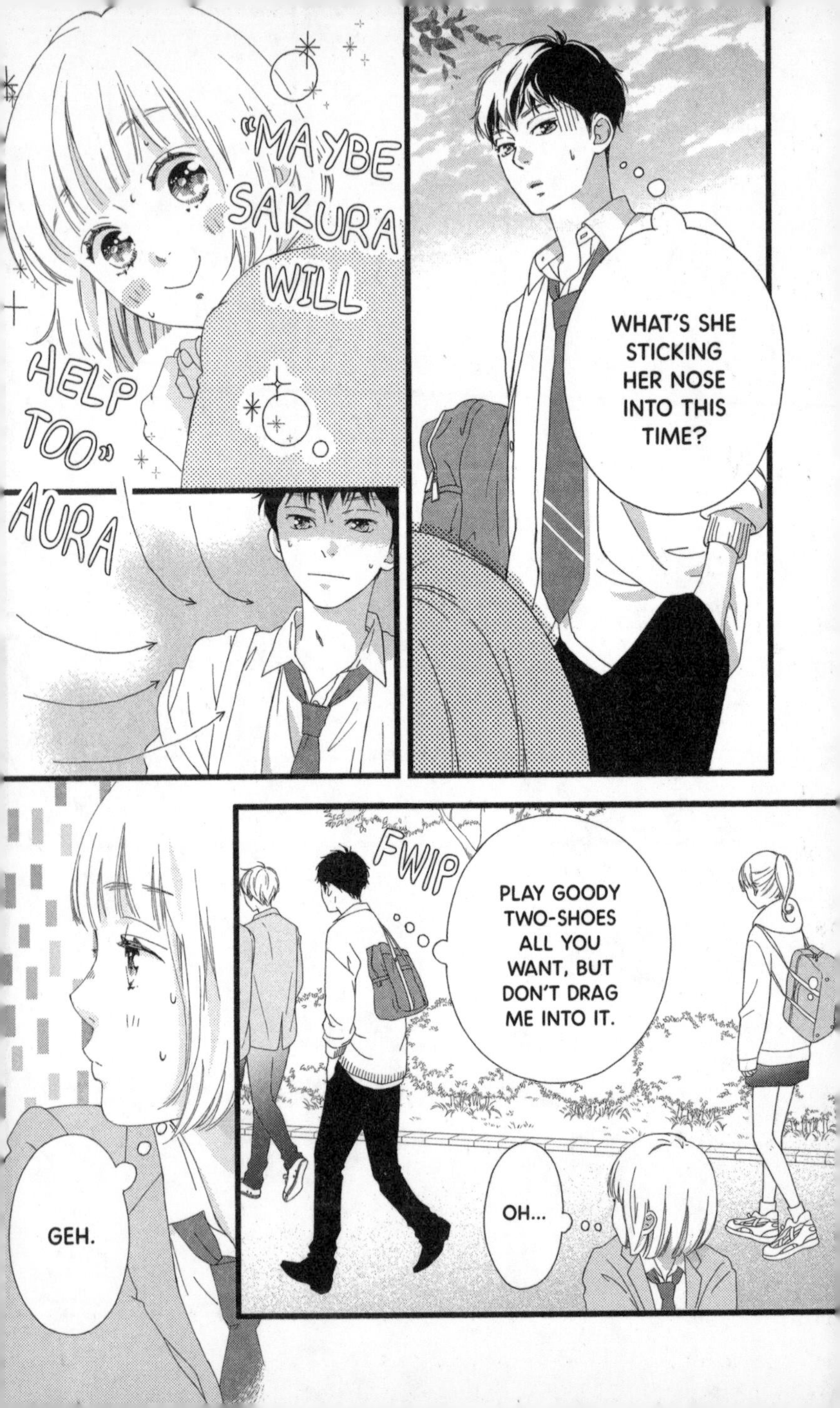

WHAT'S SHE STICKING HER NOSE INTO THIS TIME?
"MAYBE SAKURA WILL HELP TOO"
AURA
PLAY GOODY TWO-SHOES ALL YOU WANT, BUT DON'T DRAG ME INTO IT.
FWIP
OH...
GEH.

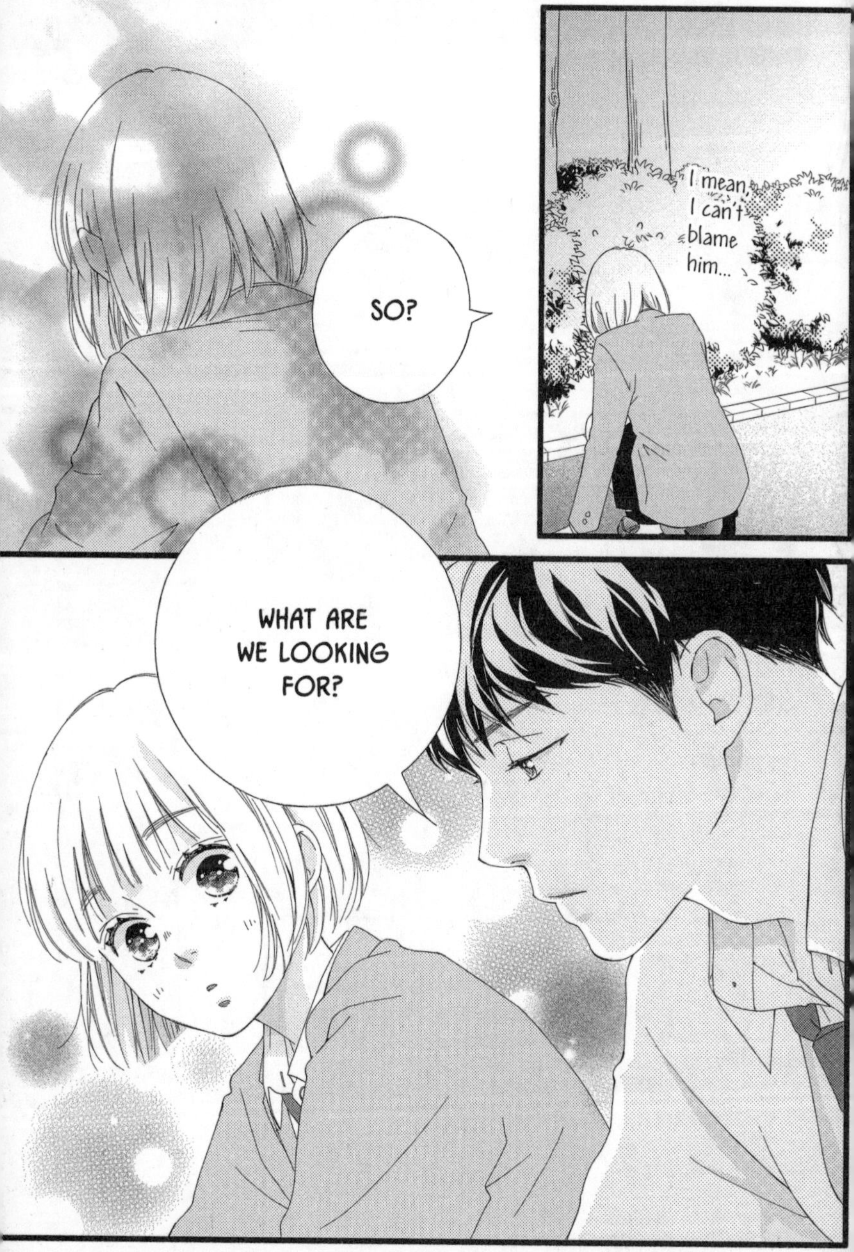
I mean, I can't blame him...
SO?
WHAT ARE WE LOOKING FOR?

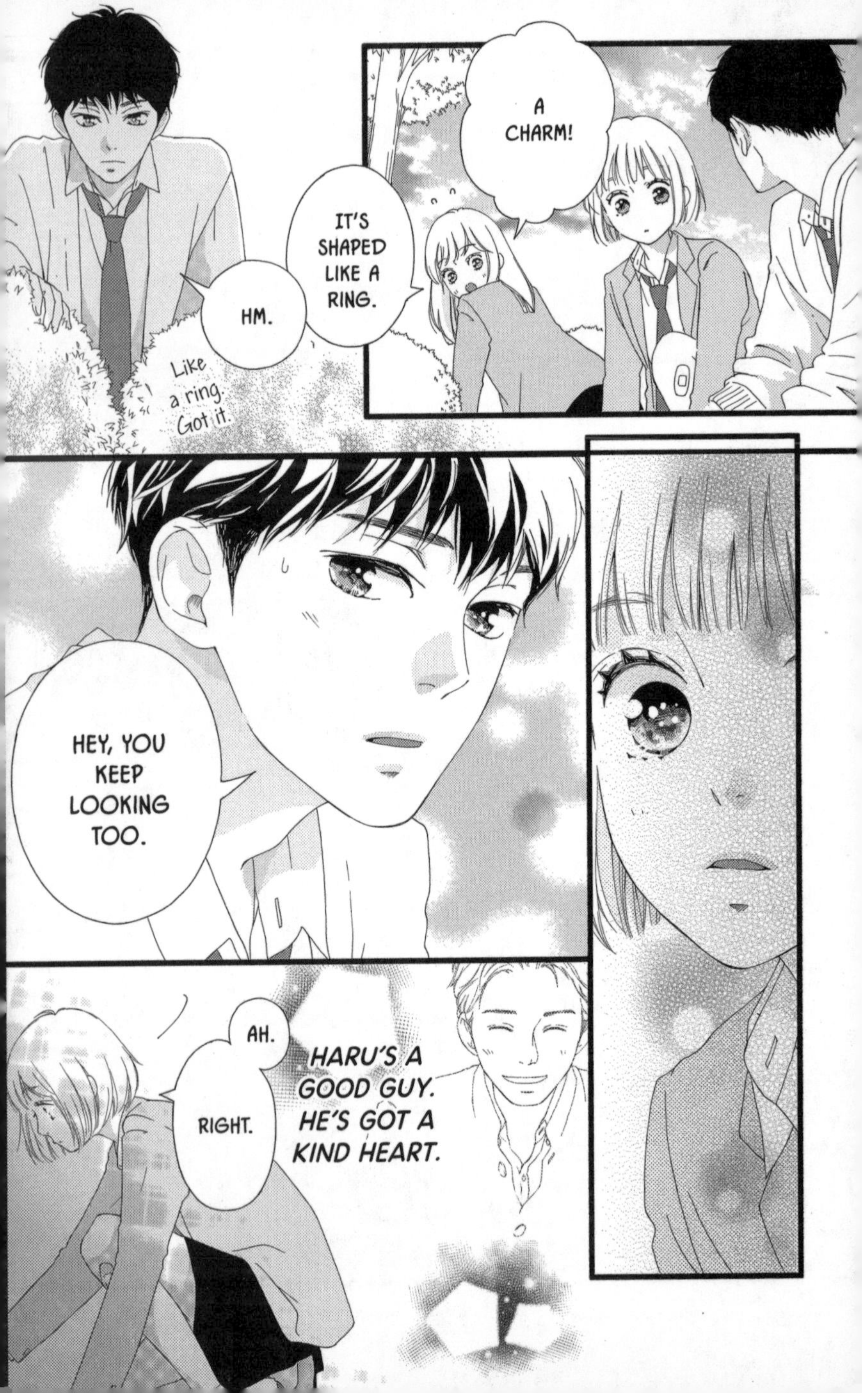

A CHARM!
IT'S SHAPED LIKE A RING.
HM.
Like a ring. Got it.
HEY, YOU KEEP LOOKING TOO.
AH.
RIGHT.
HARU'S A GOOD GUY. HE'S GOT A KIND HEART.

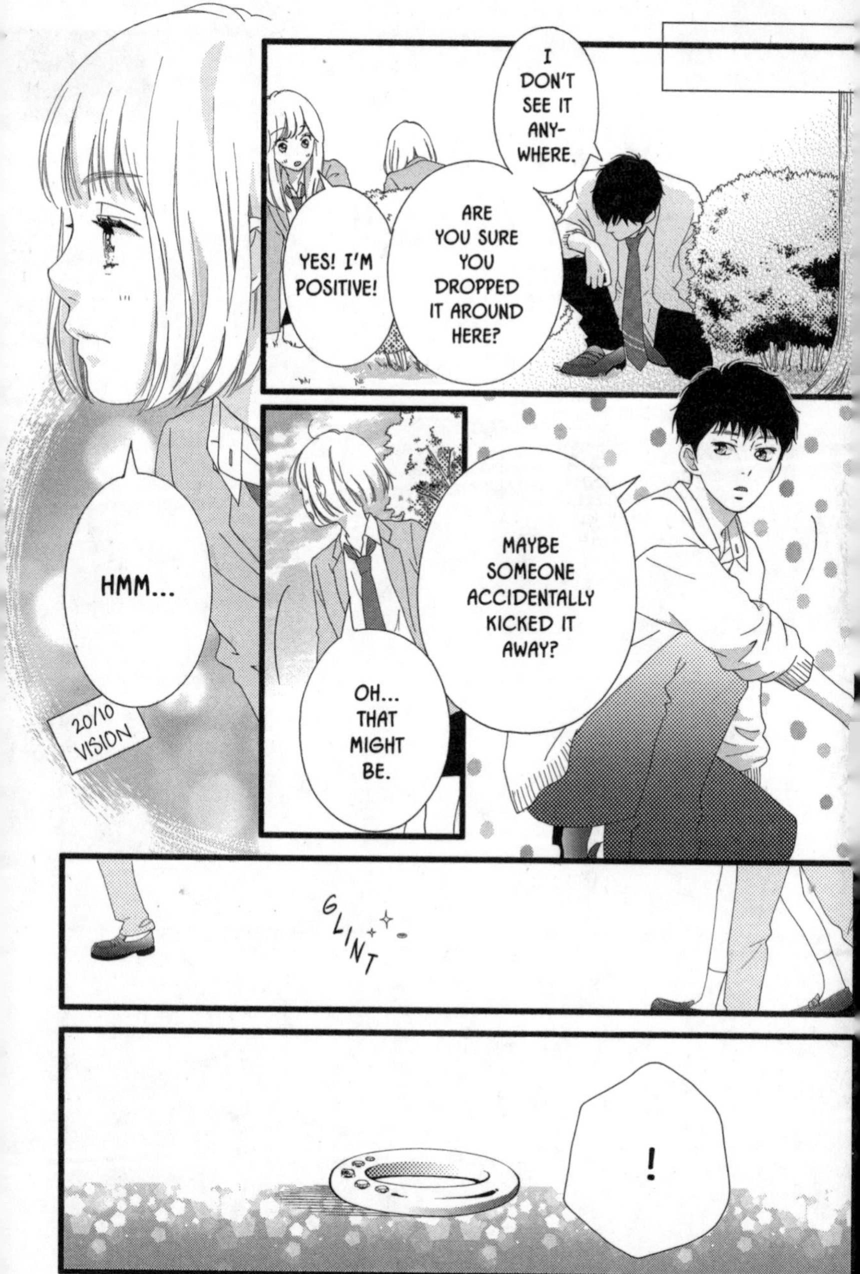

I DON'T SEE IT ANY-WHERE.
ARE YOU SURE YOU DROPPED IT AROUND HERE?
YES! I'M POSITIVE!
MAYBE SOMEONE ACCIDENTALLY KICKED IT AWAY?
OH... THAT MIGHT BE.
HMM...
20/10 VISION
GLINT
!

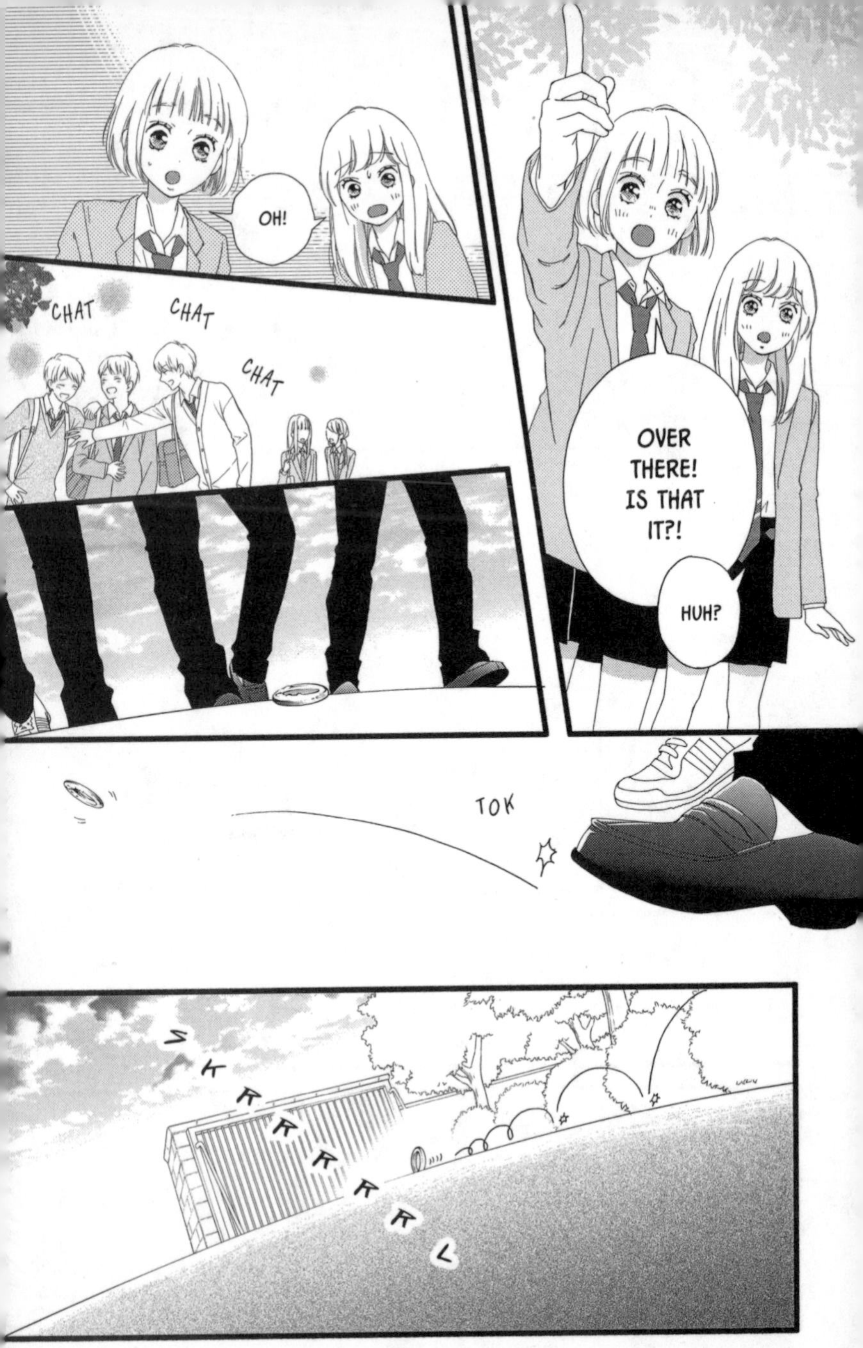
OVER THERE! IS THAT IT?!
HUH?
OH!
CHAT
CHAT
CHAT
TOK
SKRRRRRL

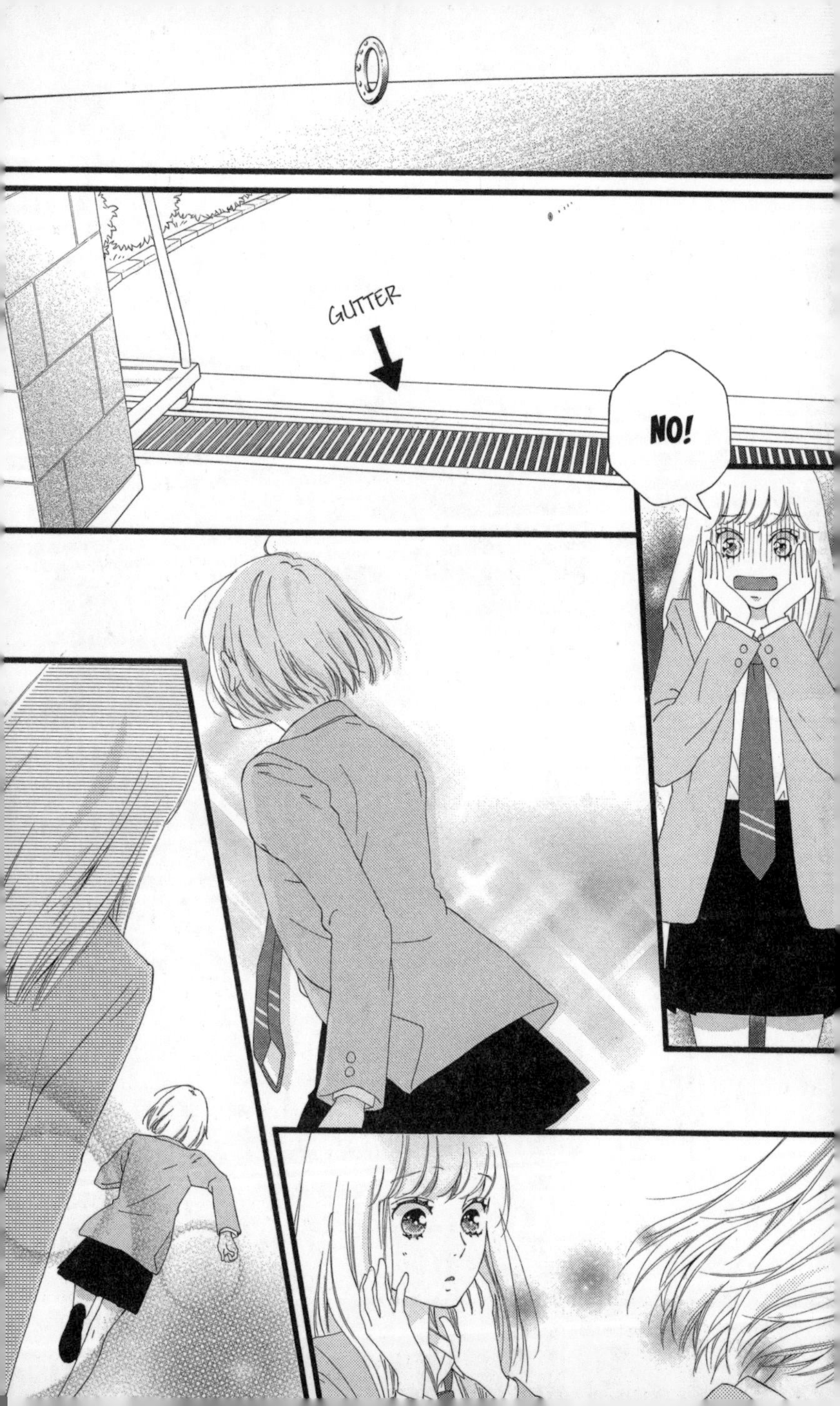
GUTTER
NO!

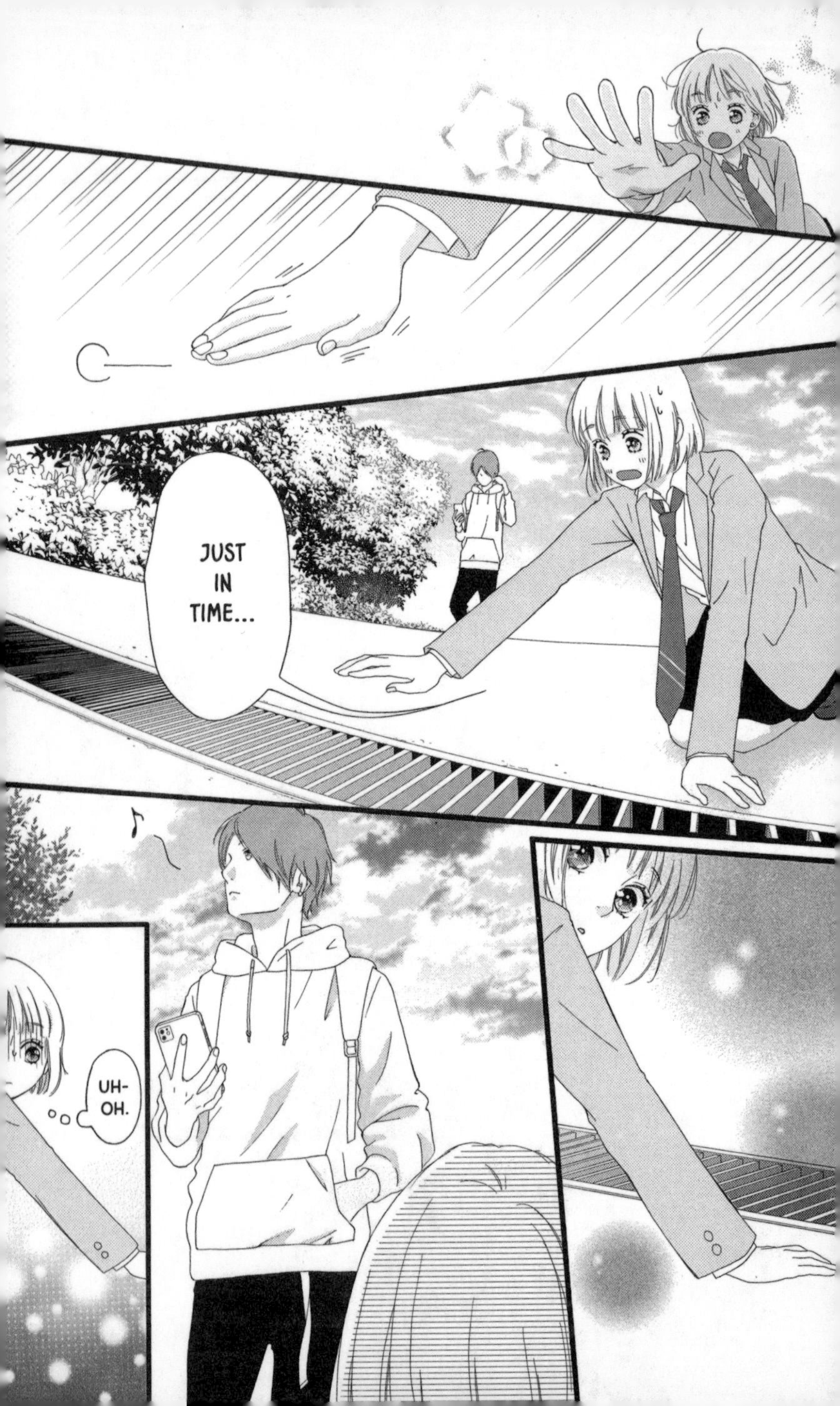

JUST IN TIME...
UH- OH.

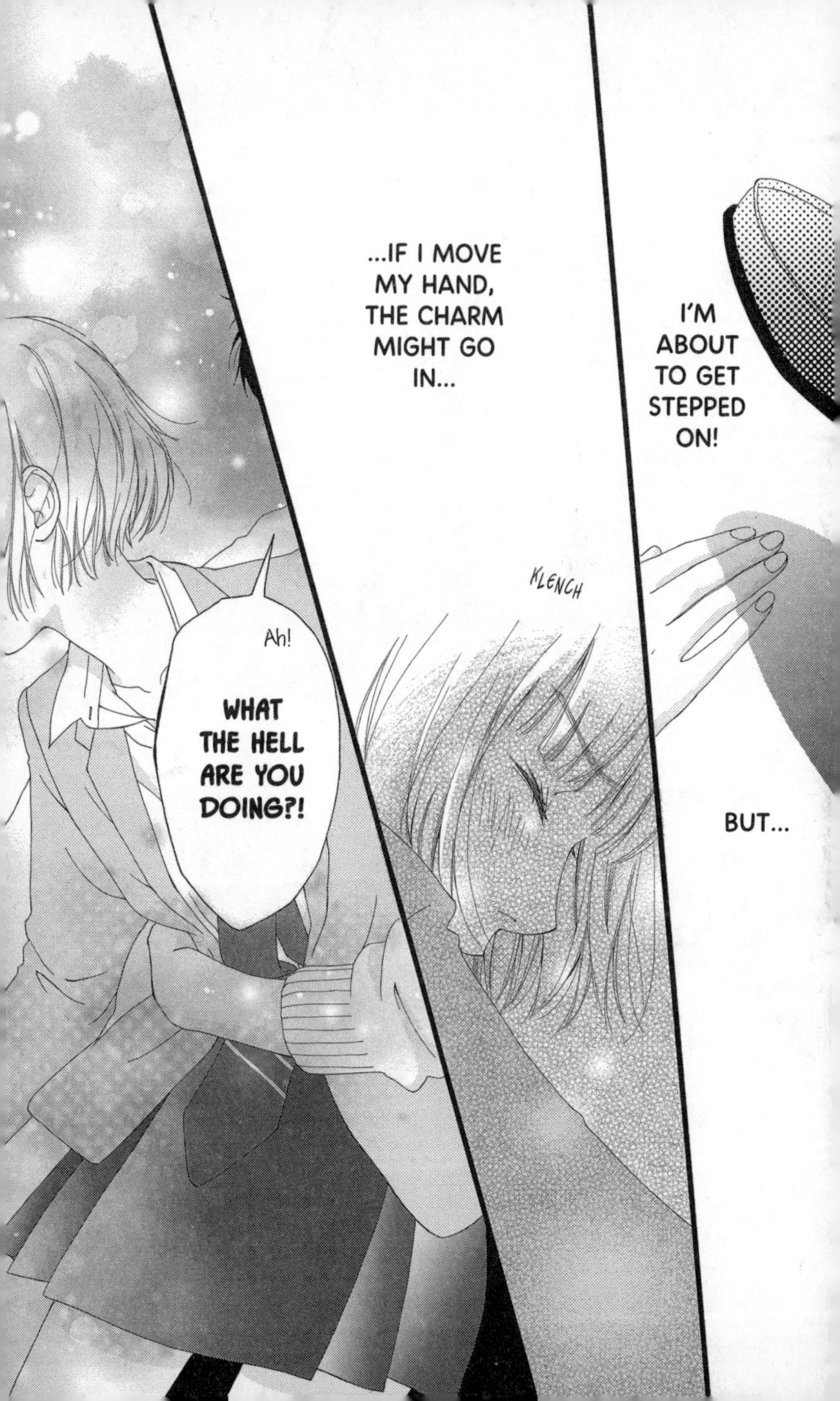
I'M ABOUT TO GET STEPPED ON!
BUT...
...IF I MOVE MY HAND, THE CHARM MIGHT GO IN...
KLENCH
Ah!
WHAT THE HELL ARE YOU DOING?!

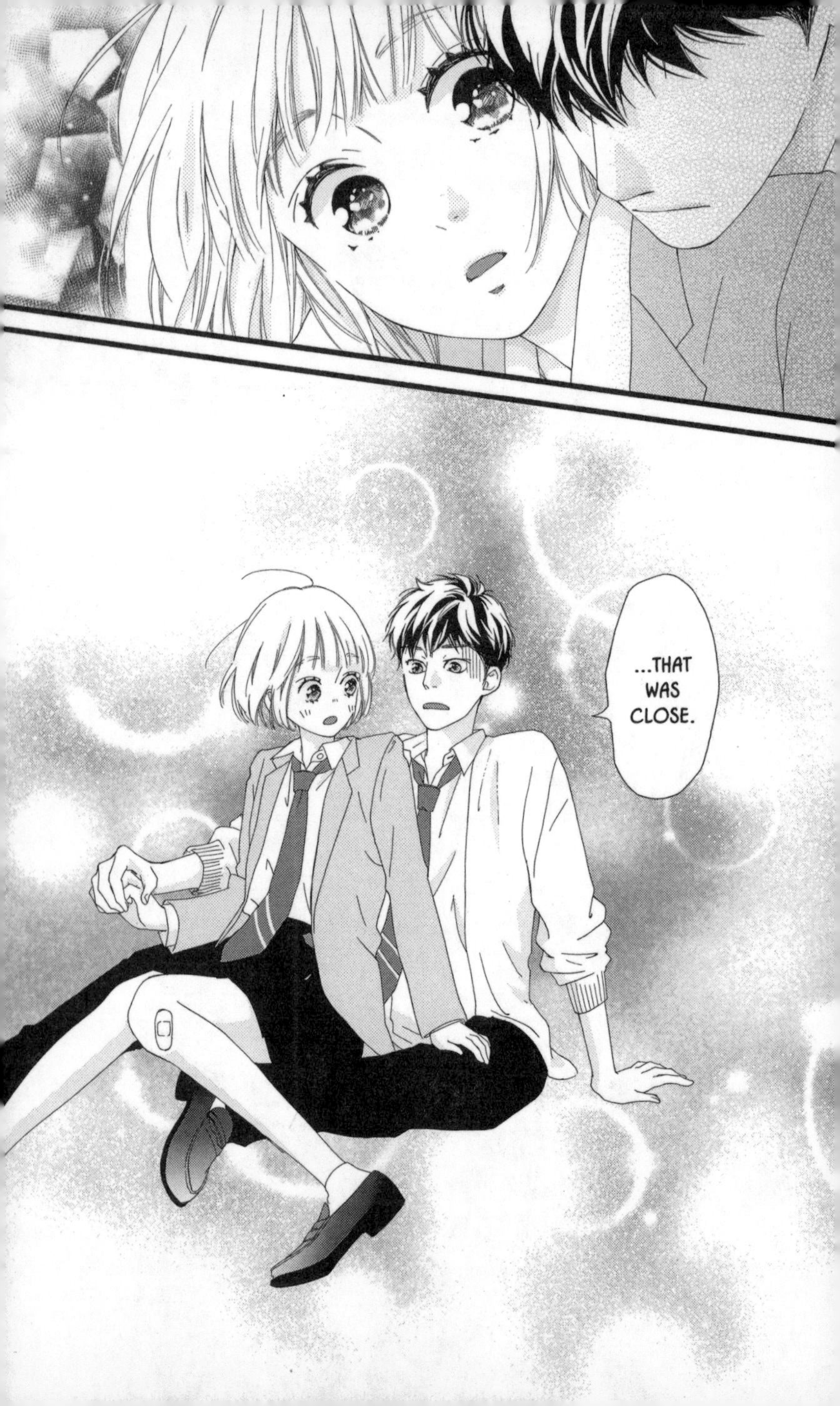
...THAT WAS CLOSE.

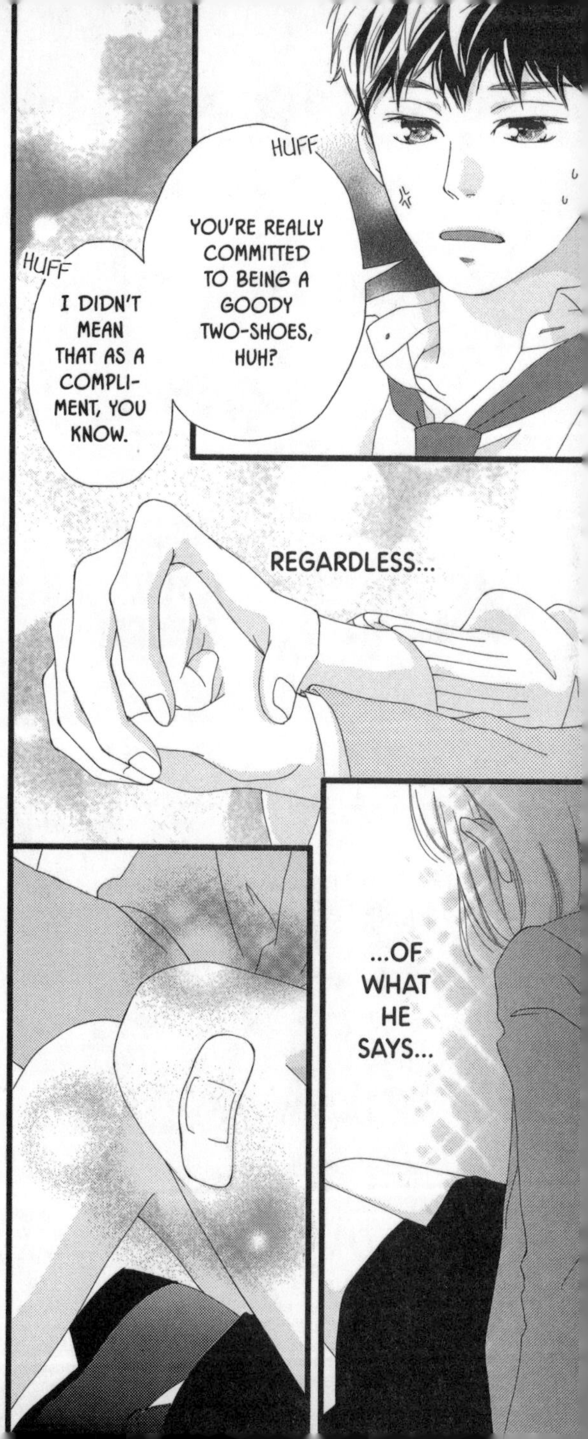
HUFF
YOU'RE REALLY COMMITTED TO BEING A GOODY TWO-SHOES, HUH?
HUFF
I DIDN'T MEAN THAT AS A COMPLI-MENT, YOU KNOW.
REGARDLESS...
...OF WHAT HE SAYS...

I had some free time after my last manga series ended, so I decided to enjoy the things I can't do when a series is ongoing. This included doing some traveling. One of the places I visited was Germany. I wanted to see the Christmas markets and also to experience a short trip across the border (Germany ⇄ Belgium). This visit to Germany was a solo trip. My flight, my hotel, my rail ticket inside Germany, and my rail ticket from Germany to Belgium—I booked them all myself. Some of the apps I used had no Japanese option, so I looked up words one by one and planned the whole trip on my own. By the way, I can't speak German or English. It's amazing what you can achieve when you try! I told myself this, feeling quite proud, but then I was late for my return flight. I couldn't help laughing at how "me" that was.

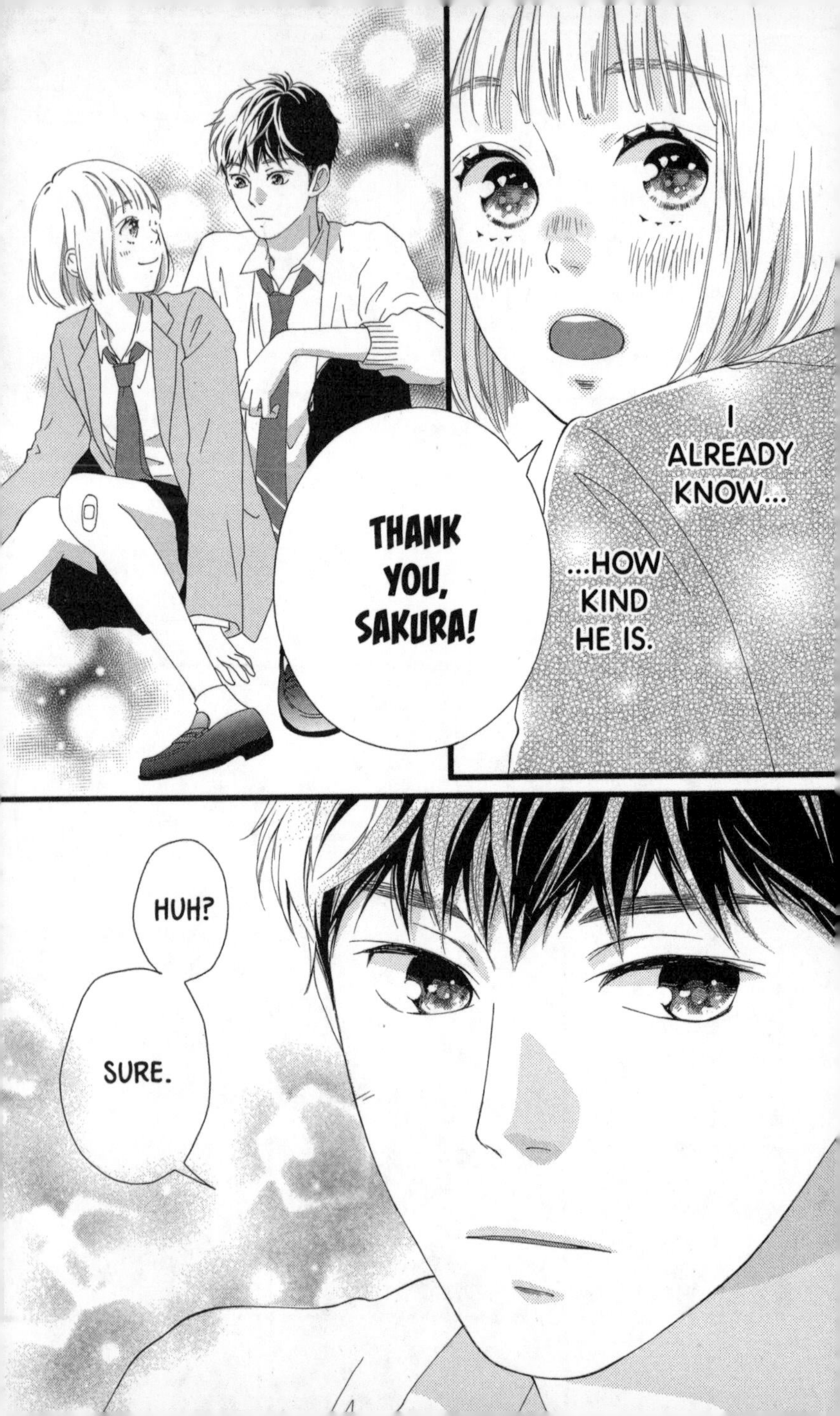
I ALREADY KNOW...
...HOW KIND HE IS.
THANK YOU, SAKURA!
HUH?
SURE.

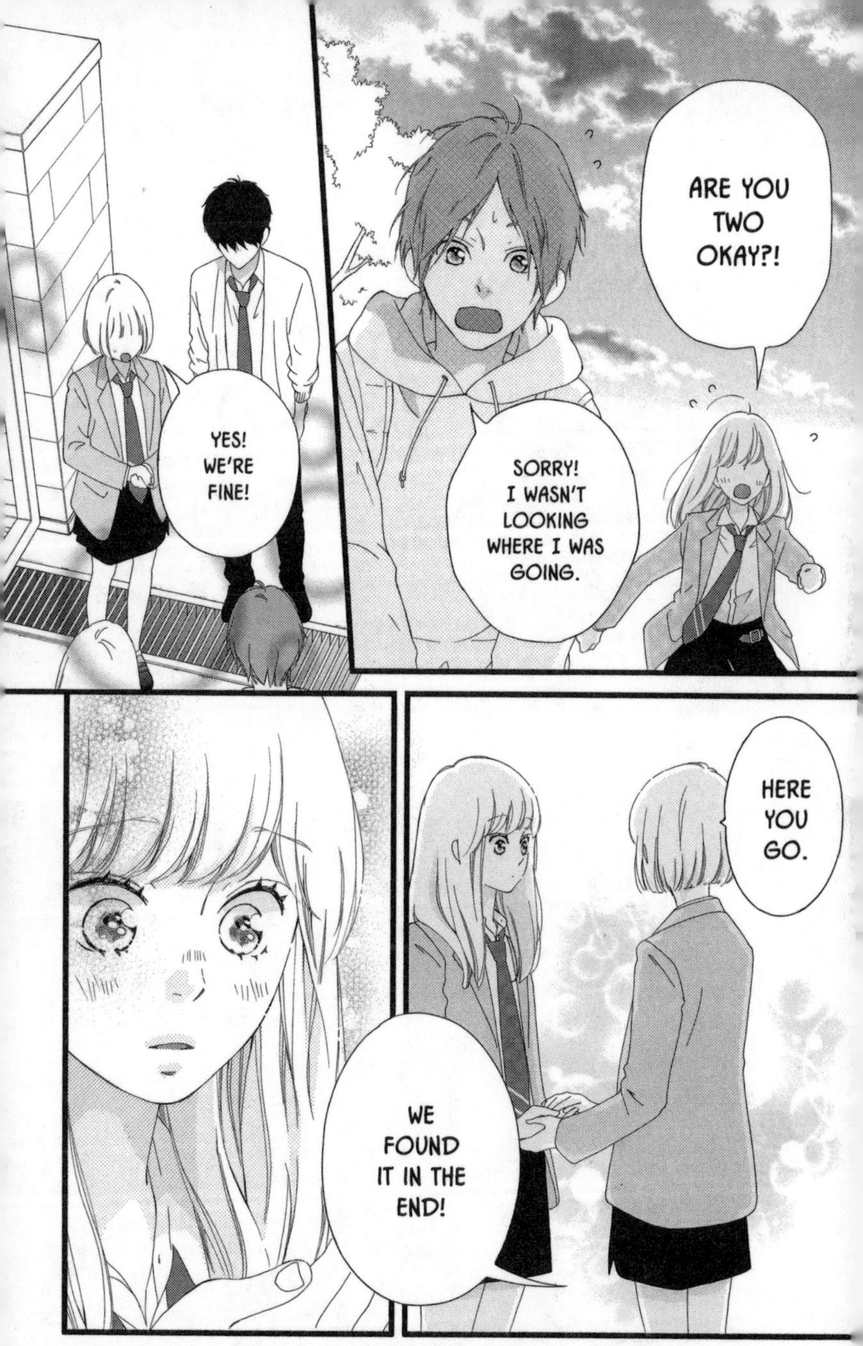
ARE YOU TWO OKAY?!
SORRY! I WASN'T LOOKING WHERE I WAS GOING.
YES! WE'RE FINE!
HERE YOU GO.
WE FOUND IT IN THE END!

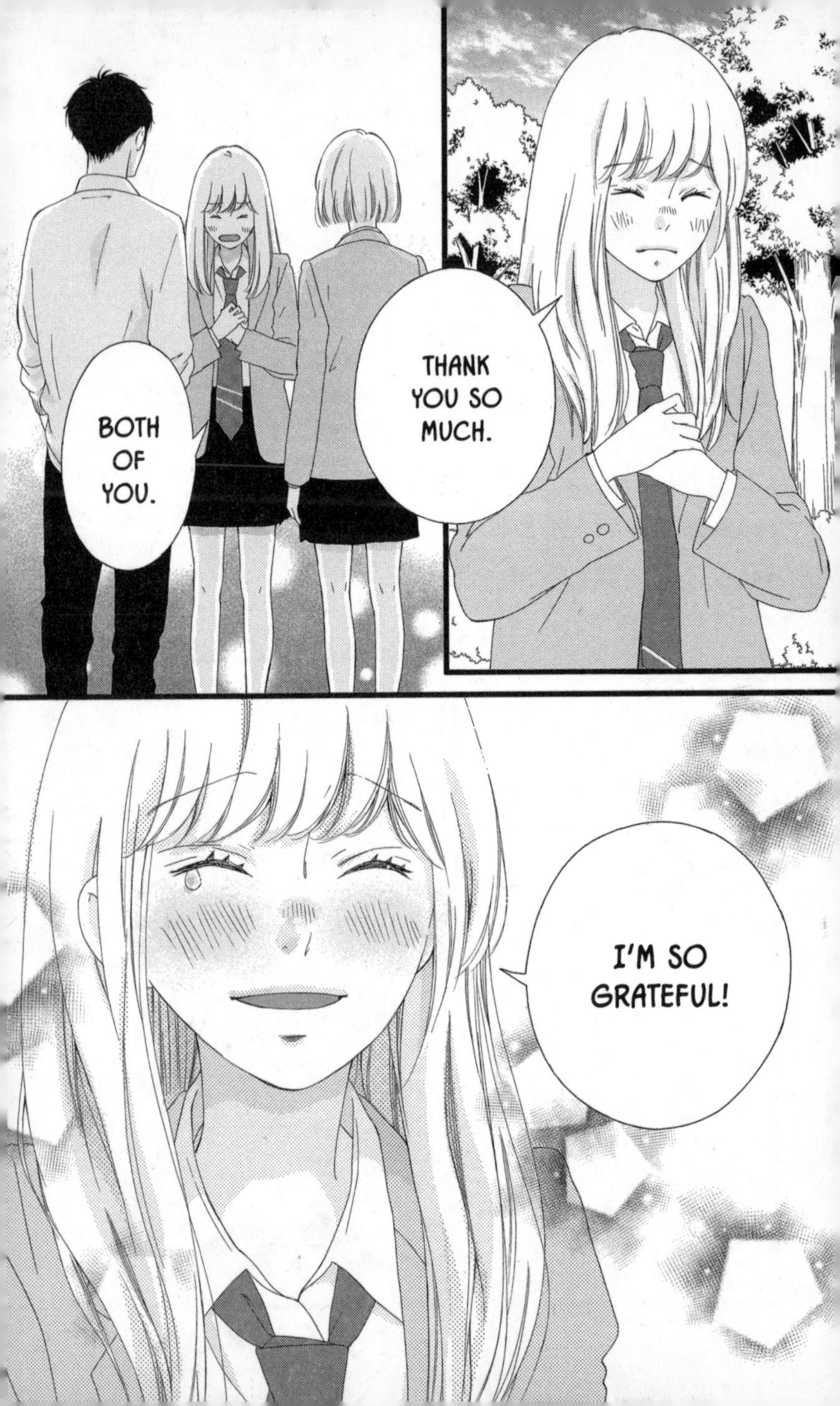
THANK YOU SO MUCH.
BOTH OF YOU.
I'M SO GRATEFUL!

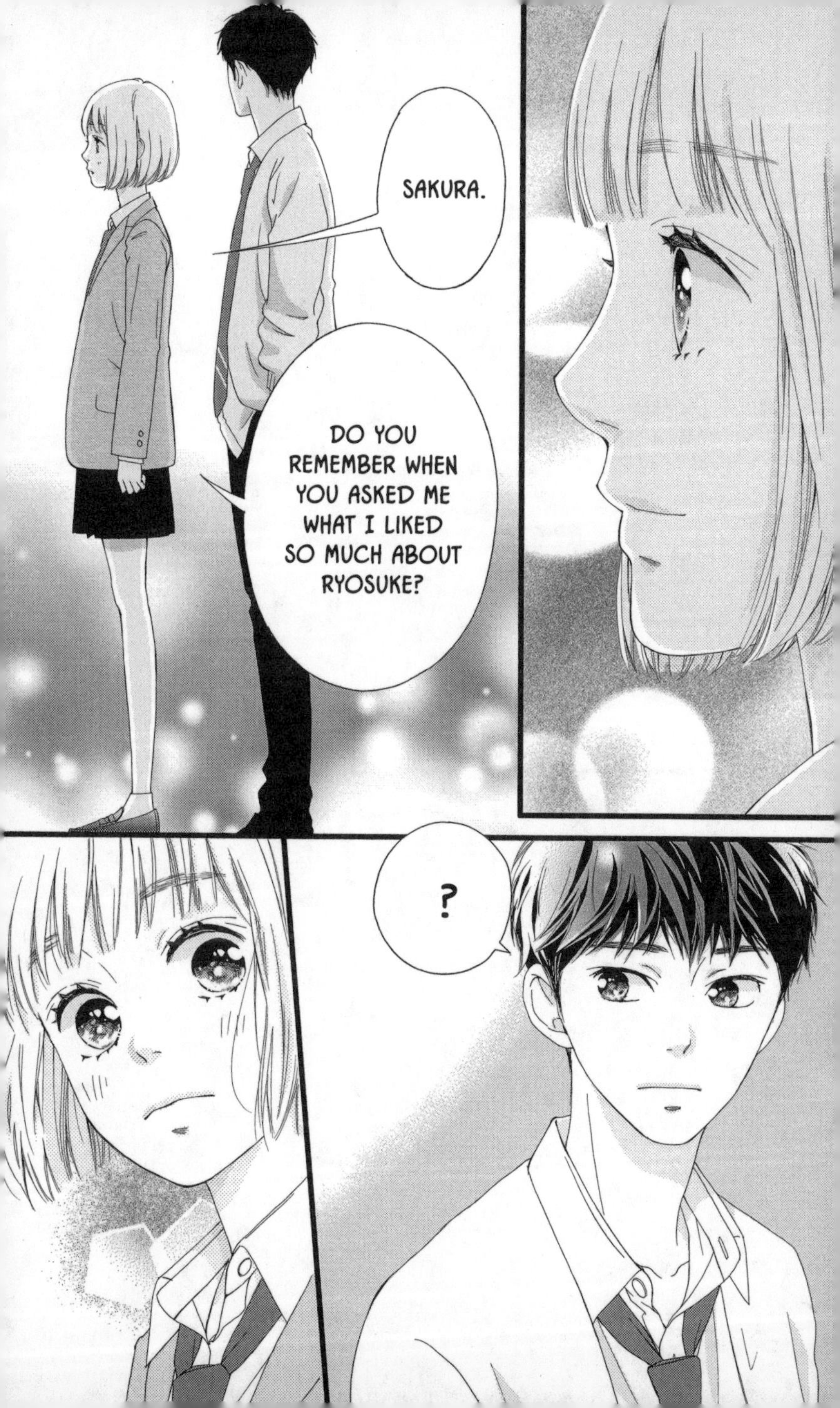
SAKURA.
DO YOU REMEMBER WHEN YOU ASKED ME WHAT I LIKED SO MUCH ABOUT RYOSUKE?
?

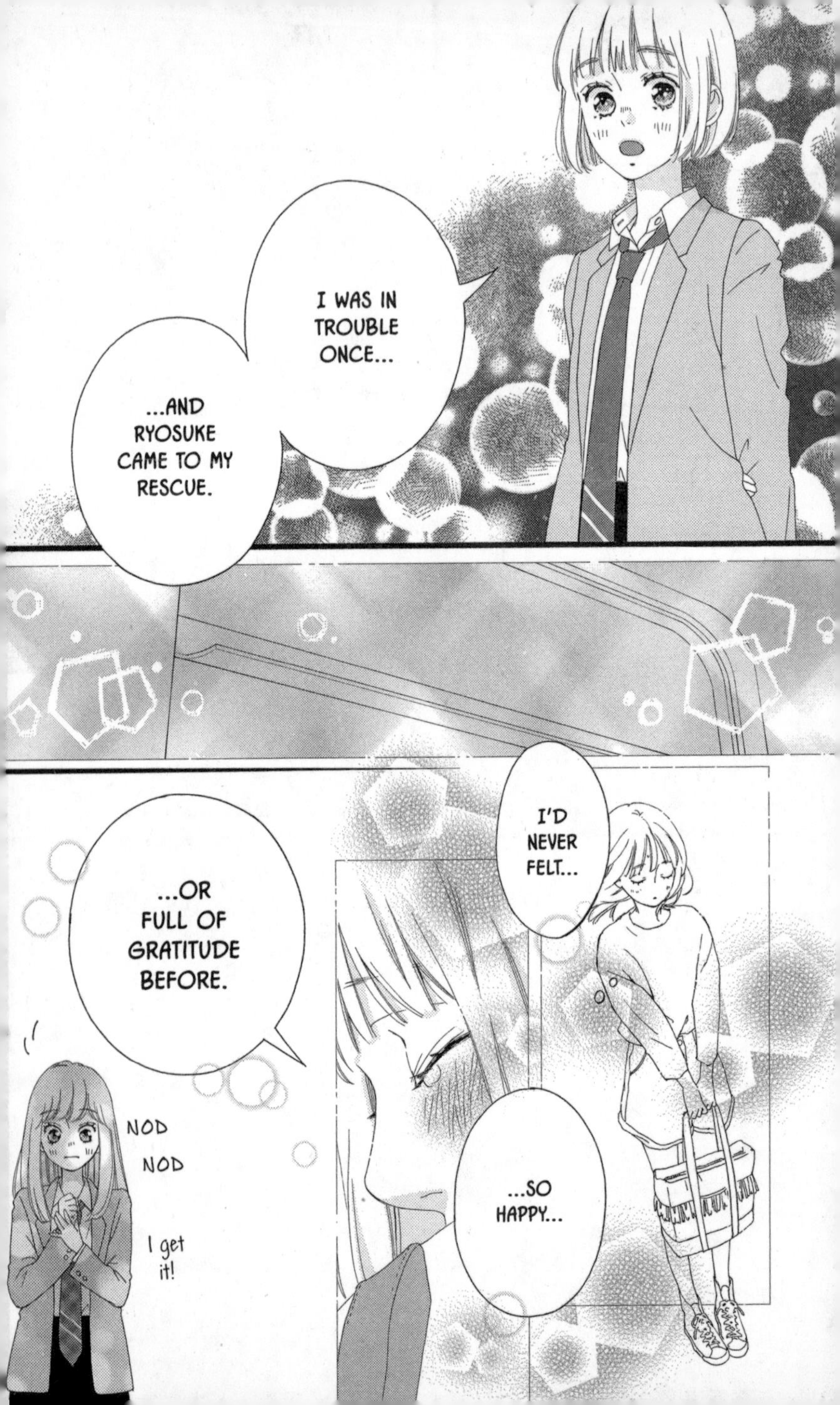
I WAS IN TROUBLE ONCE...
...AND RYOSUKE CAME TO MY RESCUE.
I'D NEVER FELT...
...SO HAPPY...
...OR FULL OF GRATITUDE BEFORE.
NOD
NOD
I get it!

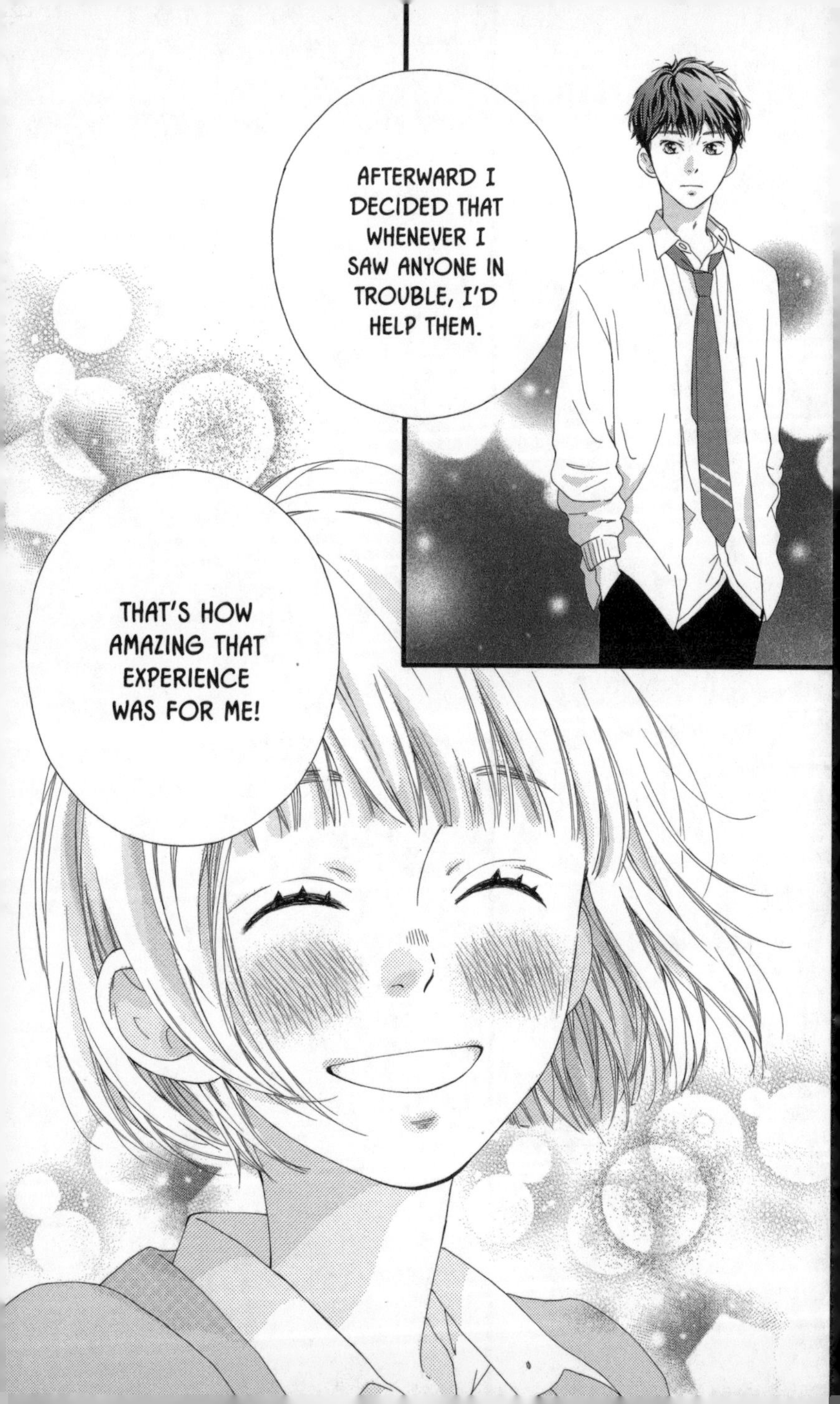
AFTERWARD I DECIDED THAT WHENEVER I SAW ANYONE IN TROUBLE, I'D HELP THEM.
THAT'S HOW AMAZING THAT EXPERIENCE WAS FOR ME!

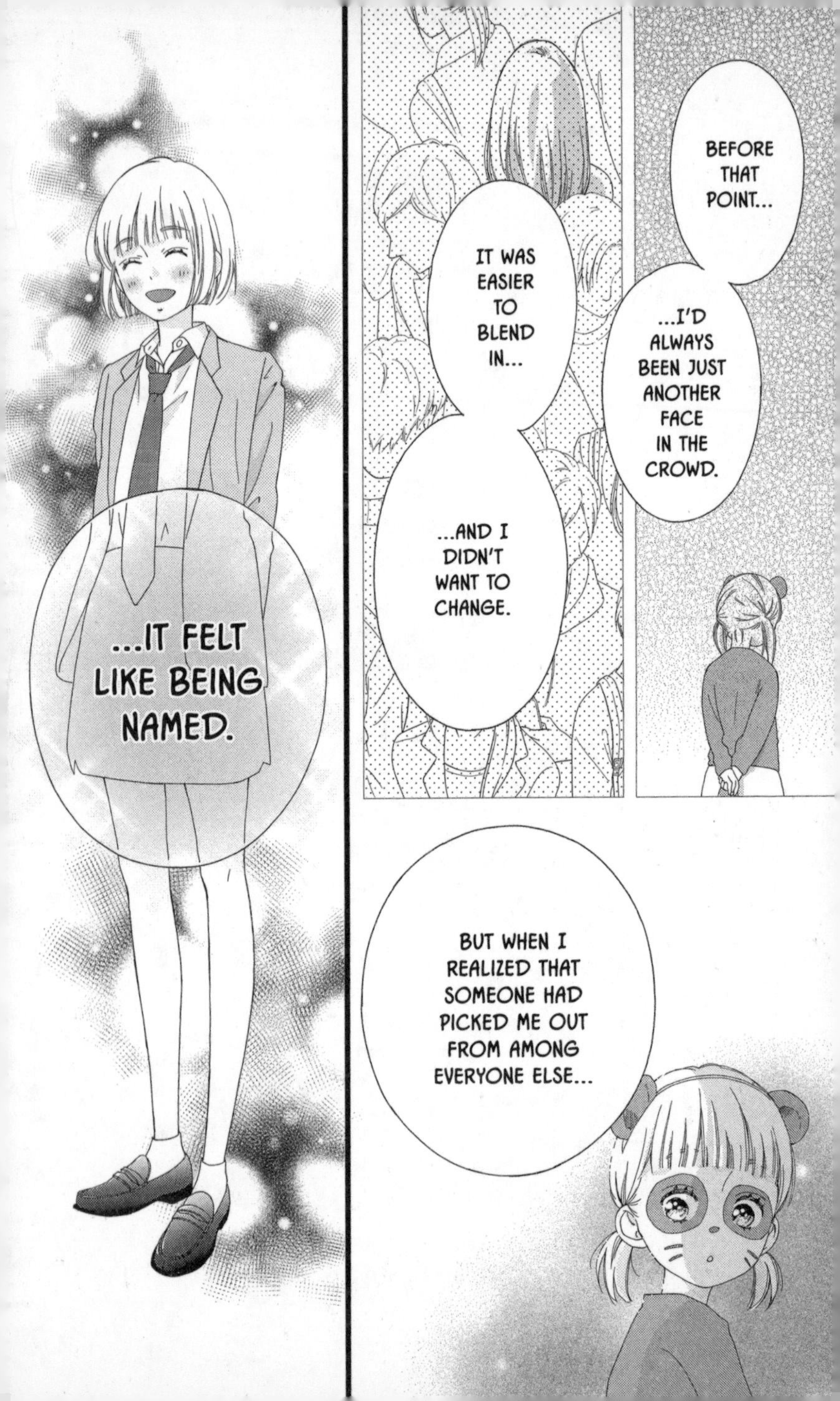
BEFORE THAT POINT...
...I'D ALWAYS BEEN JUST ANOTHER FACE IN THE CROWD.
IT WAS EASIER TO BLEND IN...
...AND I DIDN'T WANT TO CHANGE.
BUT WHEN I REALIZED THAT SOMEONE HAD PICKED ME OUT FROM AMONG EVERYONE ELSE...
...IT FELT LIKE BEING NAMED.

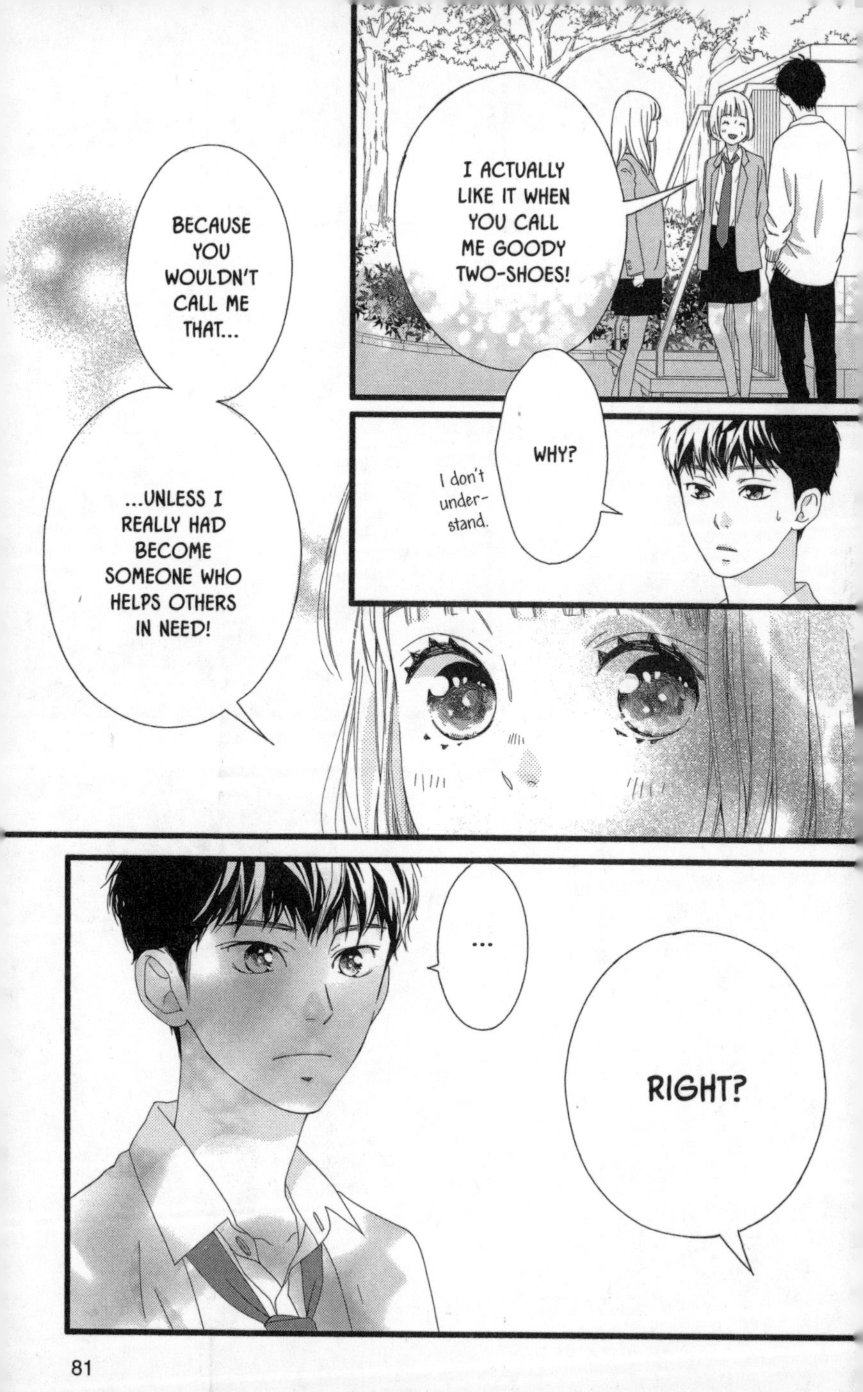
I ACTUALLY LIKE IT WHEN YOU CALL ME GOODY TWO-SHOES!
WHY?
I don't under-stand.
BECAUSE YOU WOULDN'T CALL ME THAT...
...UNLESS I REALLY HAD BECOME SOMEONE WHO HELPS OTHERS IN NEED!
RIGHT?
...

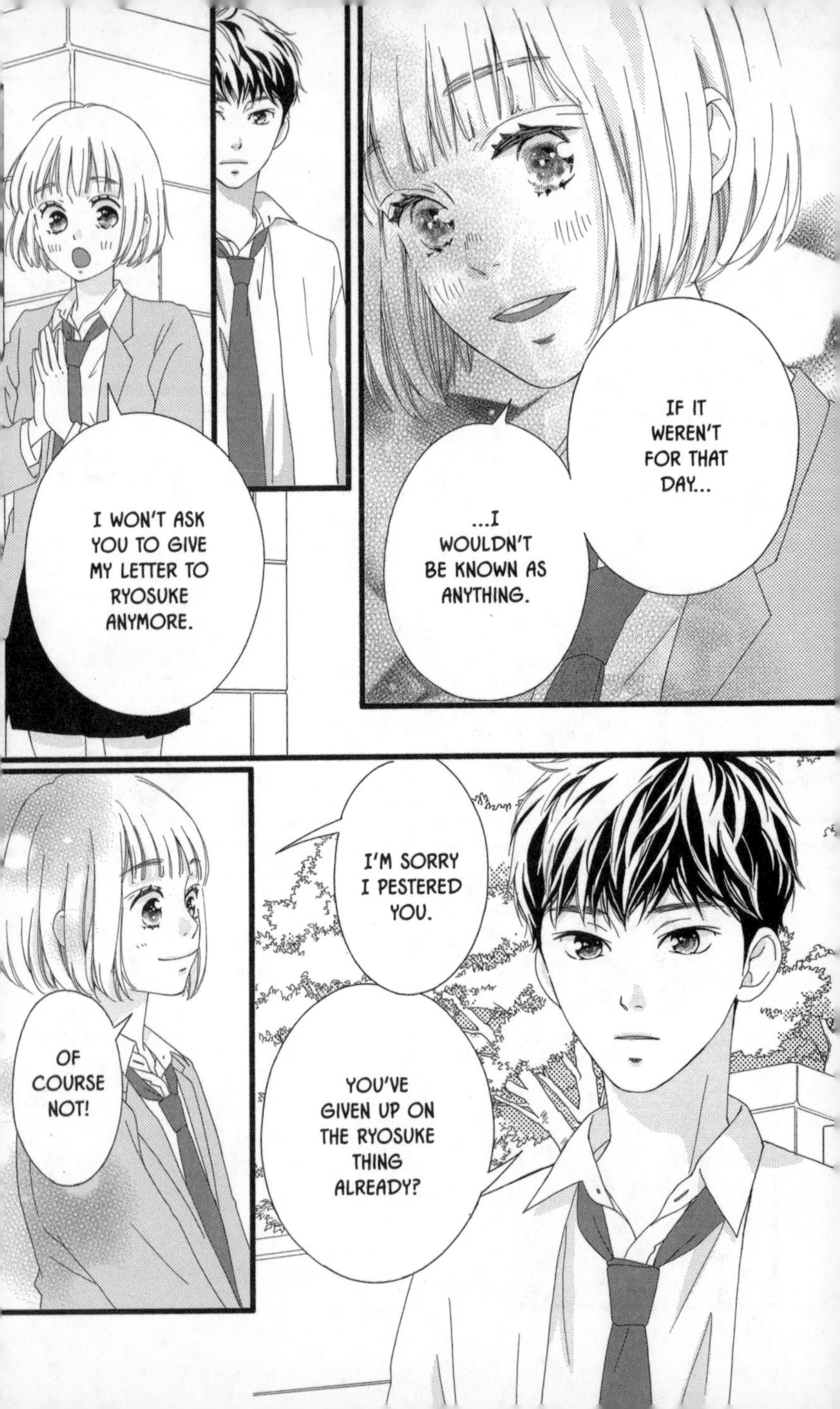
IF IT WEREN'T FOR THAT DAY...
...I WOULDN'T BE KNOWN AS ANYTHING.
I WON'T ASK YOU TO GIVE MY LETTER TO RYOSUKE ANYMORE.
I'M SORRY I PESTERED YOU.
YOU'VE GIVEN UP ON THE RYOSUKE THING ALREADY?
OF COURSE NOT!

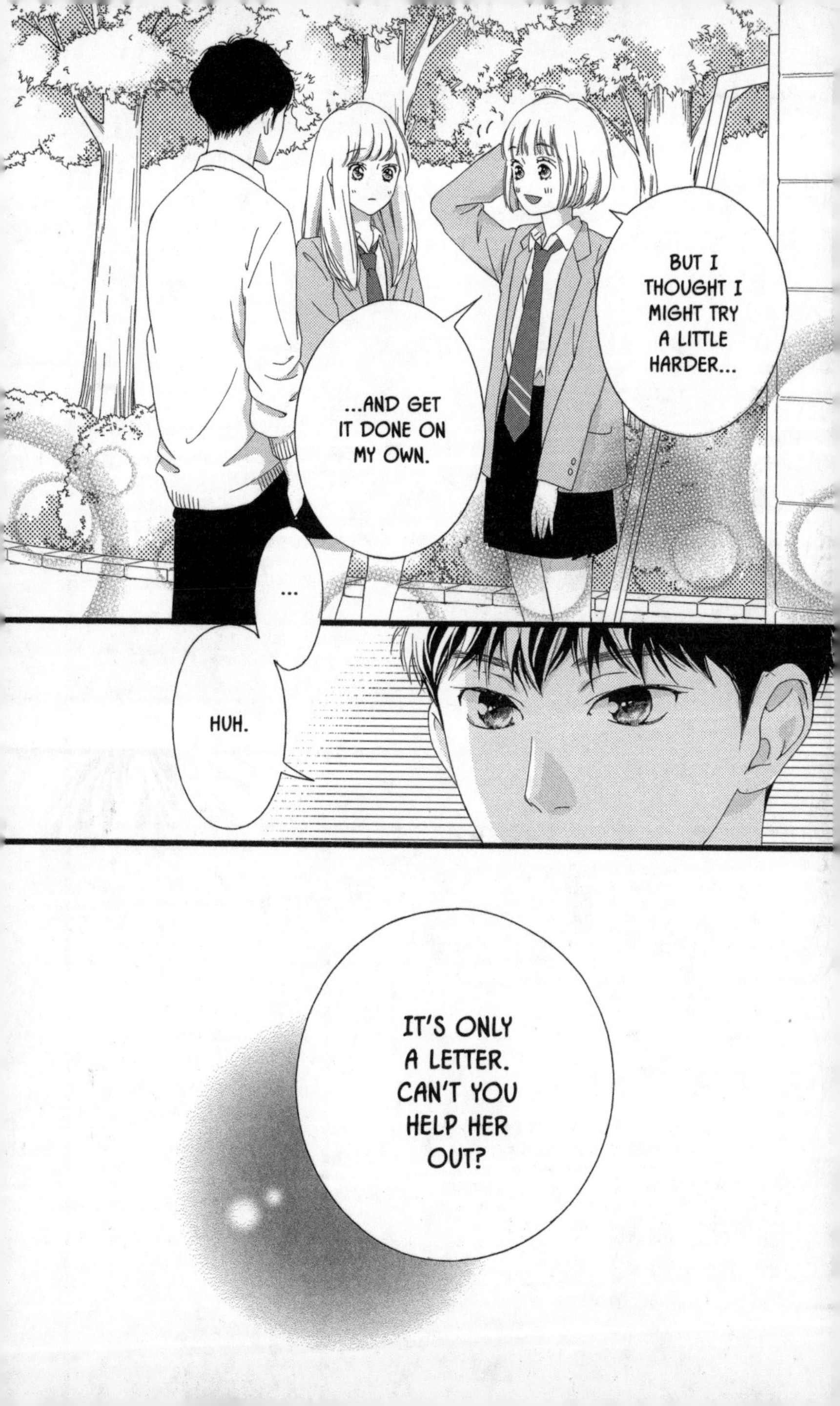
BUT I THOUGHT I MIGHT TRY A LITTLE HARDER...
...AND GET IT DONE ON MY OWN.
...
HUH.
IT'S ONLY A LETTER. CAN'T YOU HELP HER OUT?

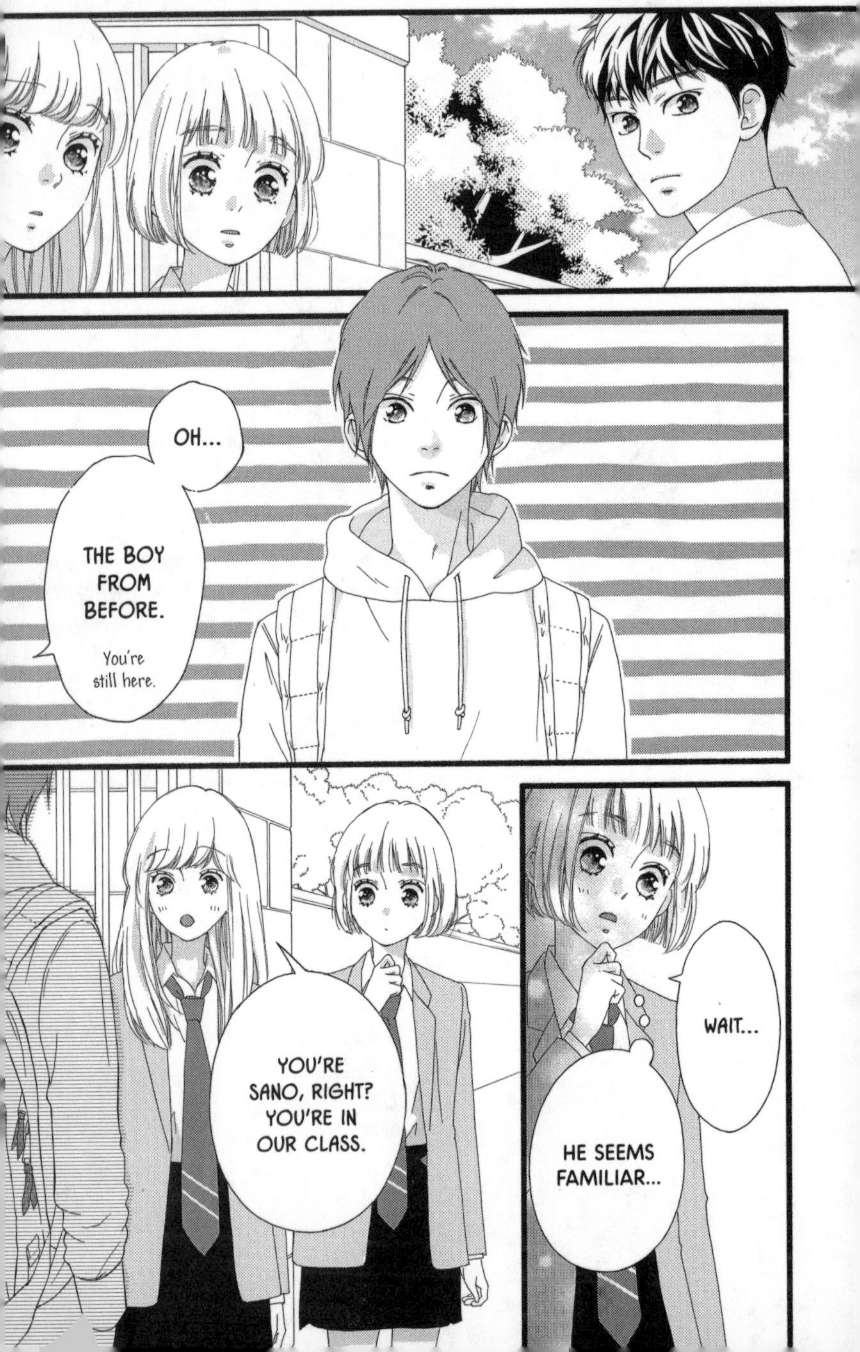
OH...
THE BOY FROM BEFORE.
You're still here.
WAIT...
HE SEEMS FAMILIAR...
YOU'RE SANO, RIGHT? YOU'RE IN OUR CLASS.

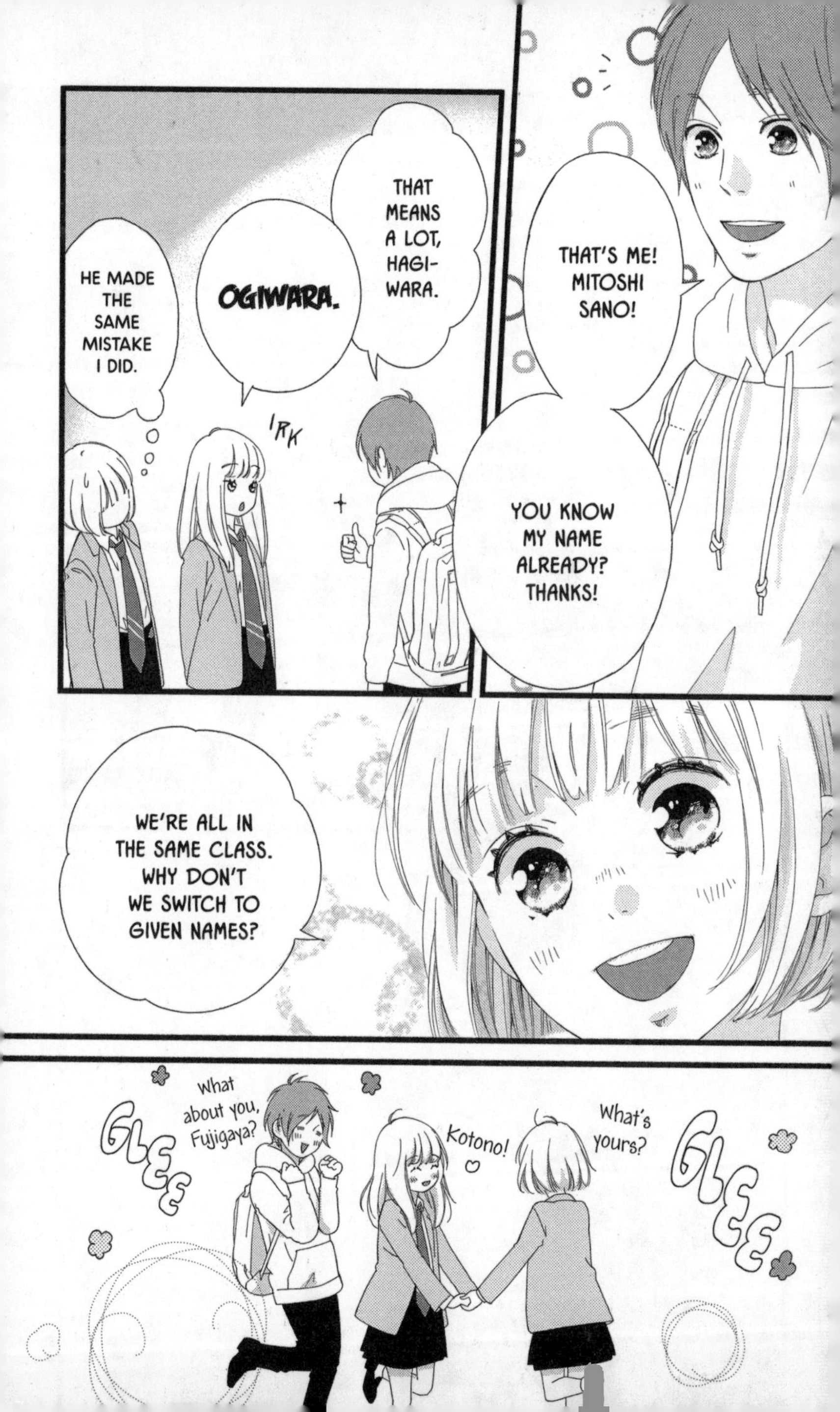
THAT'S ME! MITOSHI SANO!
YOU KNOW MY NAME ALREADY? THANKS!
THAT MEANS A LOT, HAGI-WARA.
OGIWARA.
IRK
HE MADE THE SAME MISTAKE I DID.
WE'RE ALL IN THE SAME CLASS. WHY DON'T WE SWITCH TO GIVEN NAMES?
GLEE
What's yours?
Kotono!
What about you, Fujigaya?
GLEE

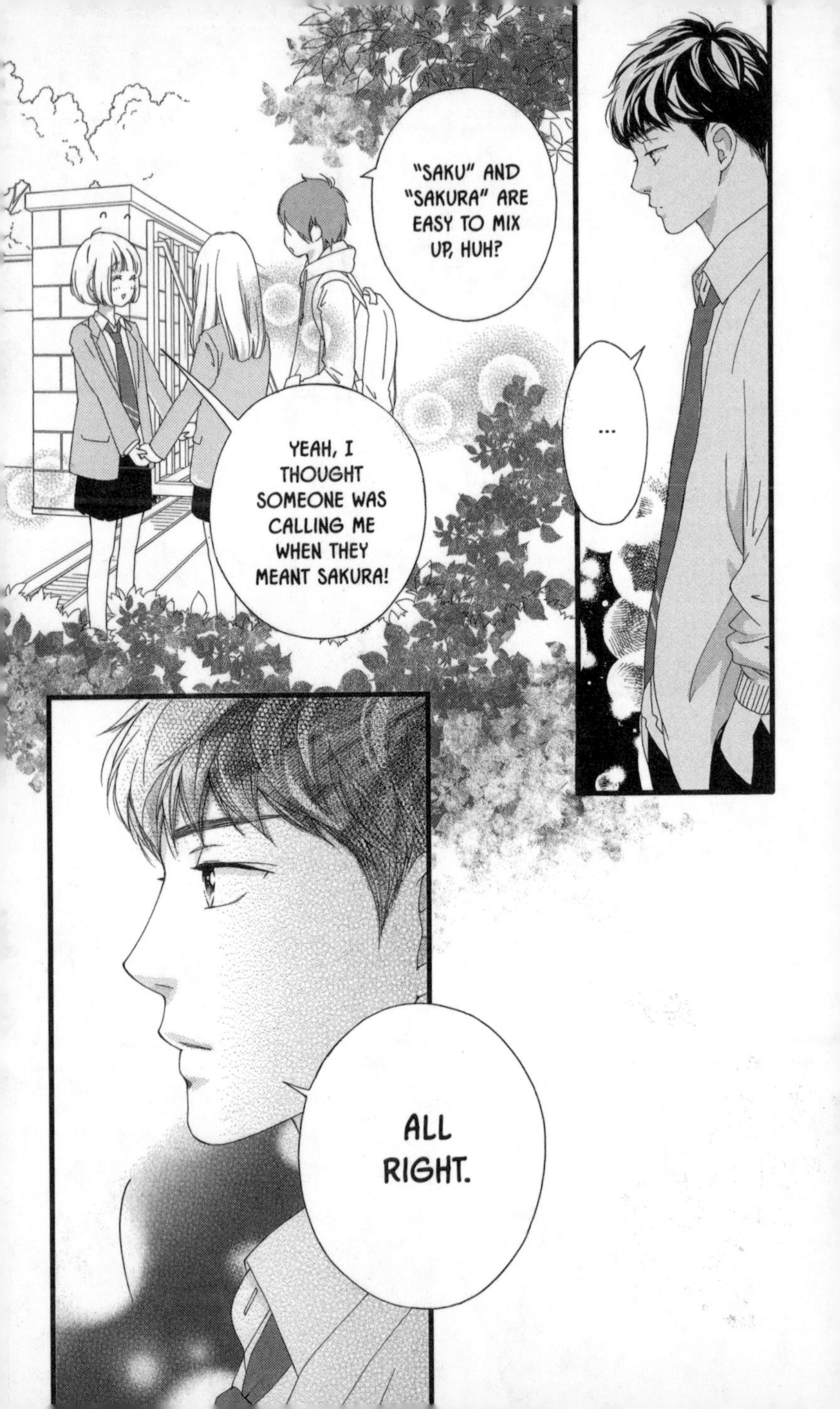
...
"SAKU" AND "SAKURA" ARE EASY TO MIX UP, HUH?
YEAH, I THOUGHT SOMEONE WAS CALLING ME WHEN THEY MEANT SAKURA!
ALL RIGHT.

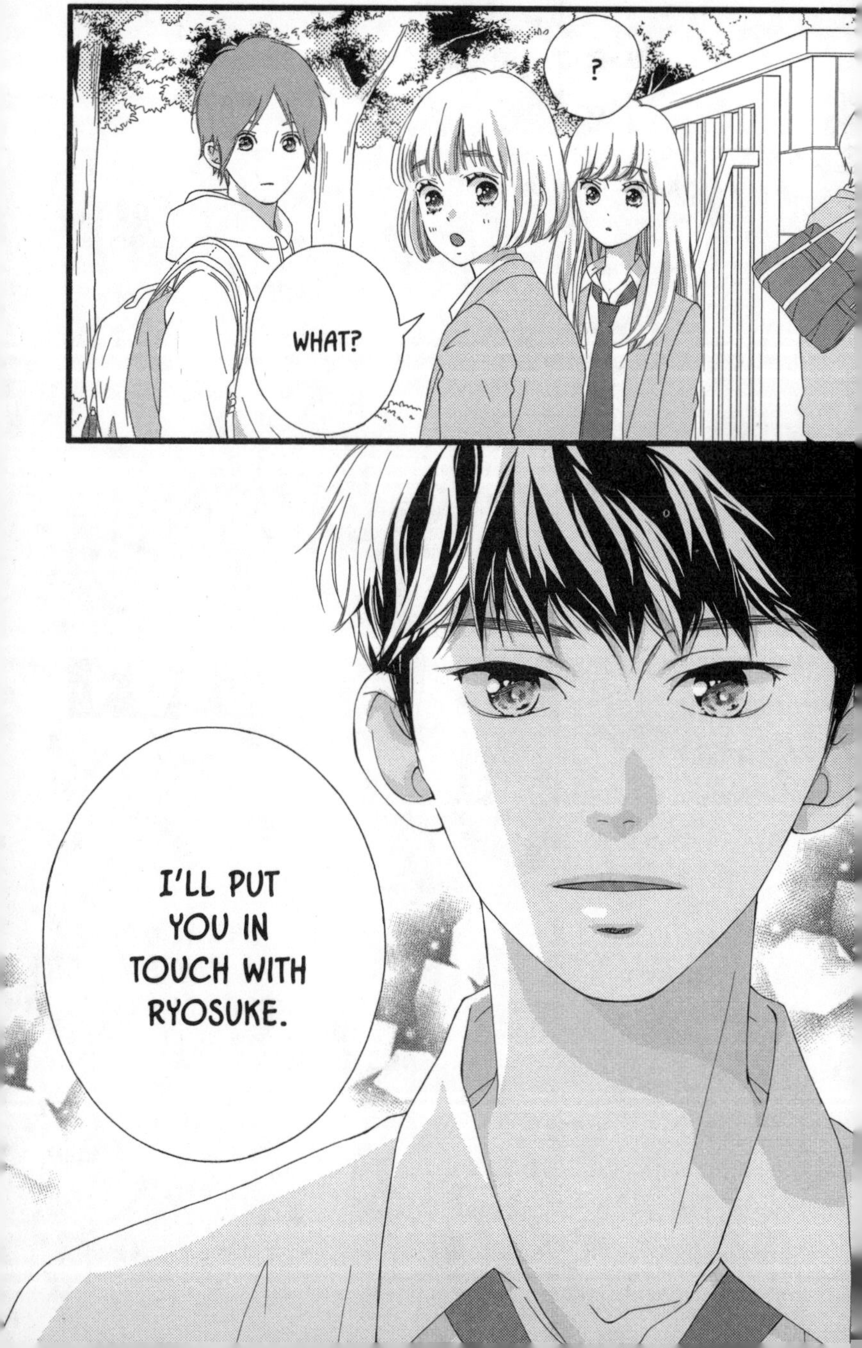
?
WHAT?
I'LL PUT YOU IN TOUCH WITH RYOSUKE.

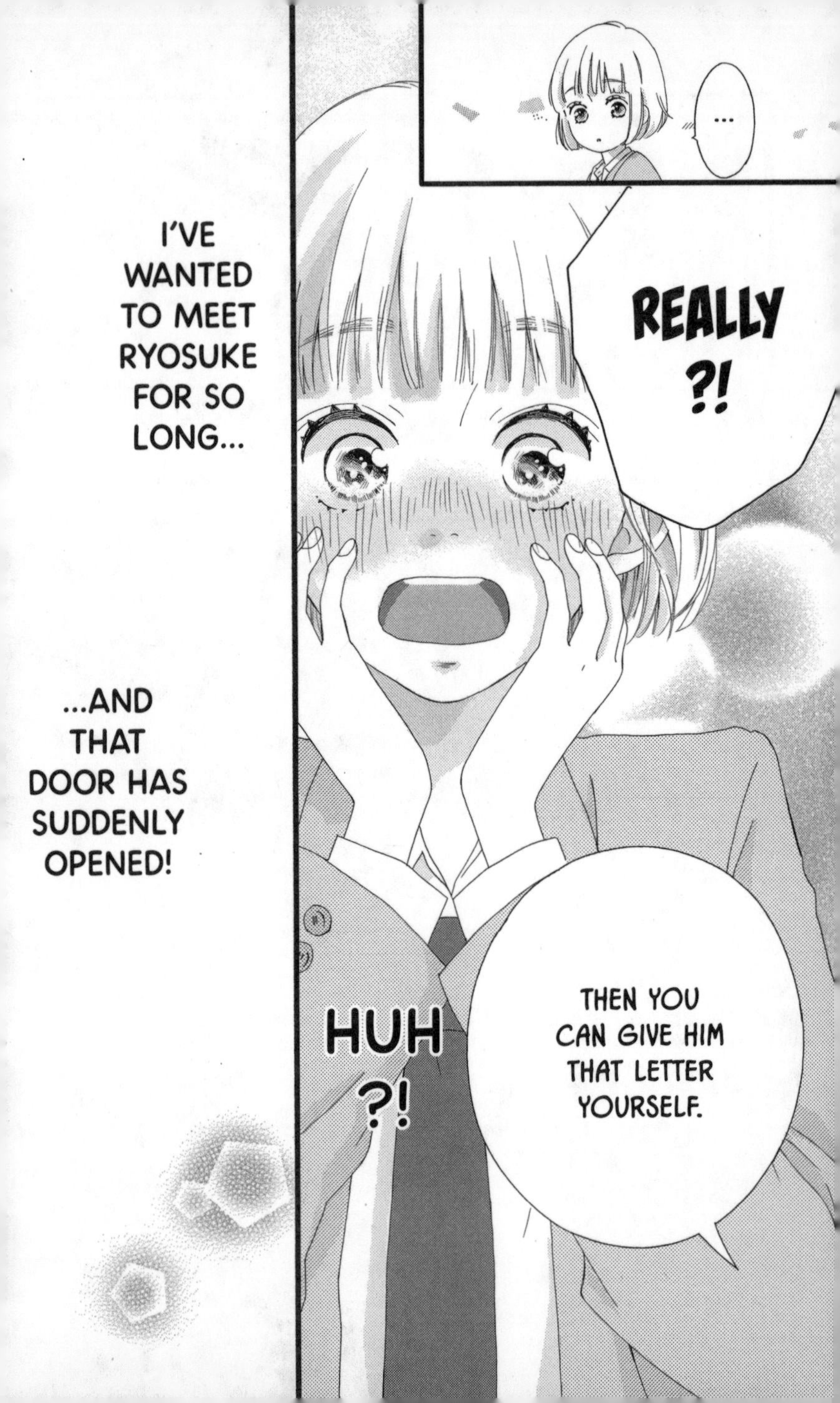
...
REALLY ?!
THEN YOU CAN GIVE HIM THAT LETTER YOURSELF.
HUH ?!
I'VE WANTED TO MEET RYOSUKE FOR SO LONG...
...AND THAT DOOR HAS SUDDENLY OPENED!

Bloom 2

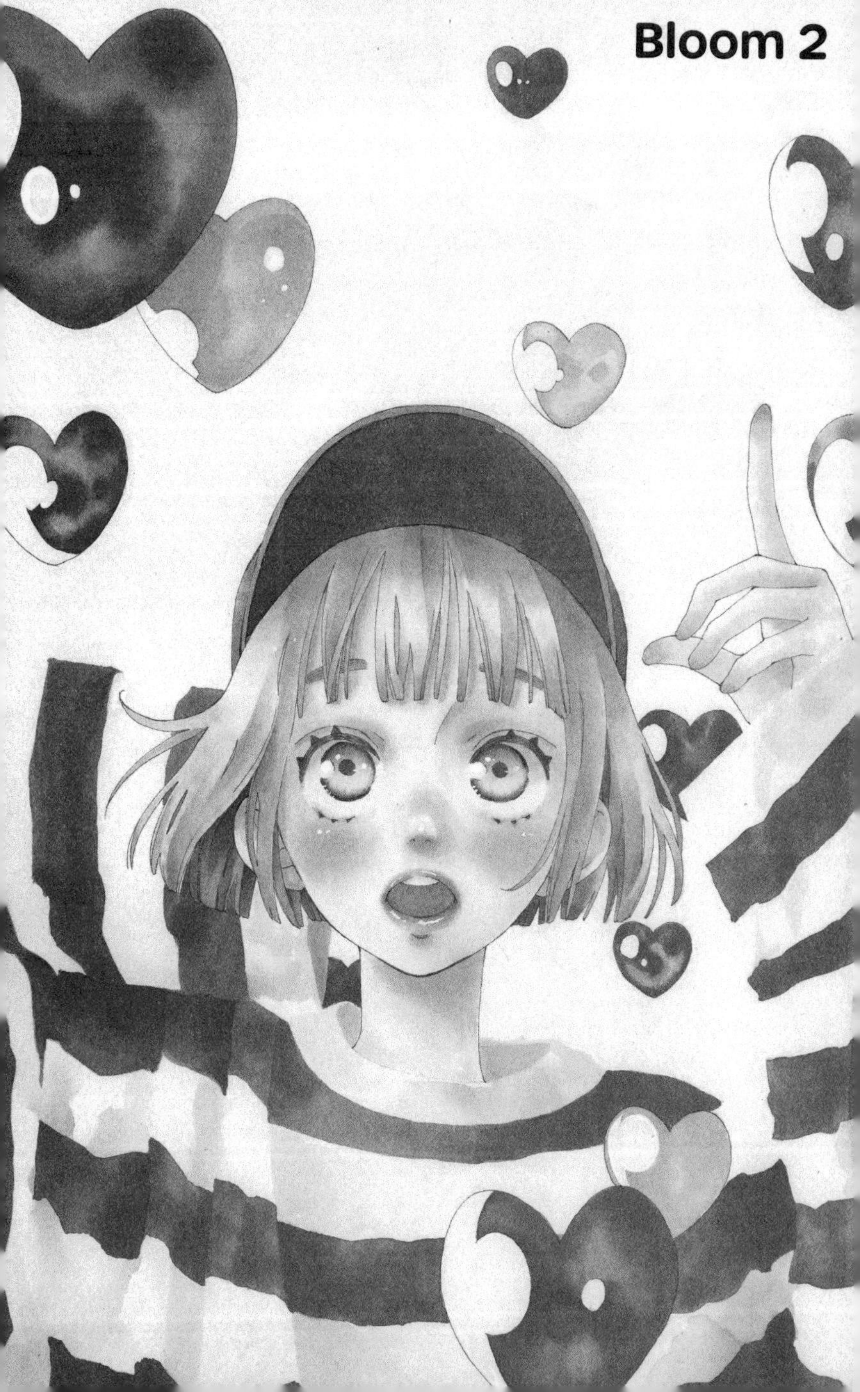

Sakura, Saku

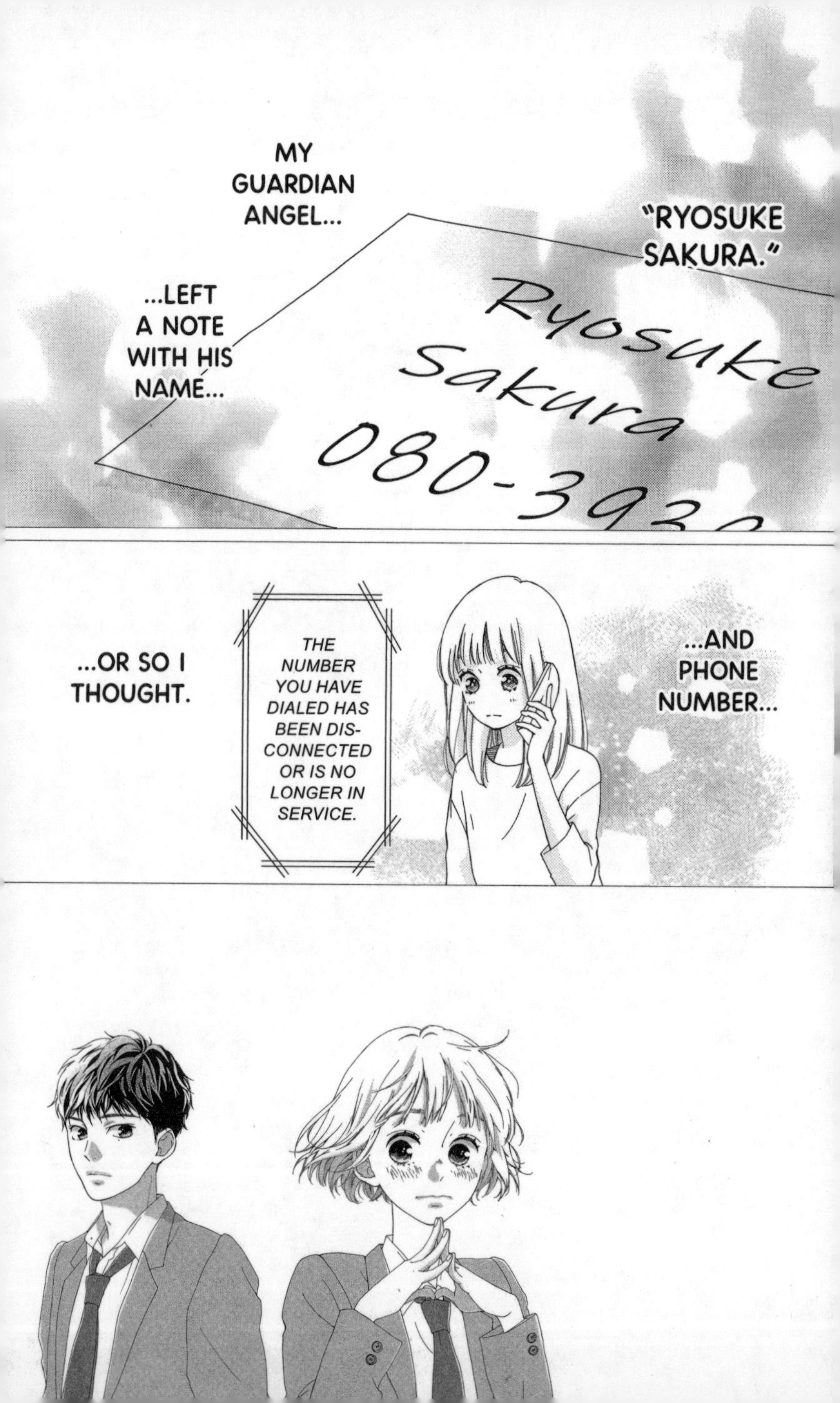
MY GUARDIAN ANGEL...
...LEFT A NOTE WITH HIS NAME...
"RYOSUKE SAKURA."
Ryosuke Sakura
080-393
...AND PHONE NUMBER...
THE NUMBER YOU HAVE DIALED HAS BEEN DIS-CONNECTED OR IS NO LONGER IN SERVICE.
...OR SO I THOUGHT.

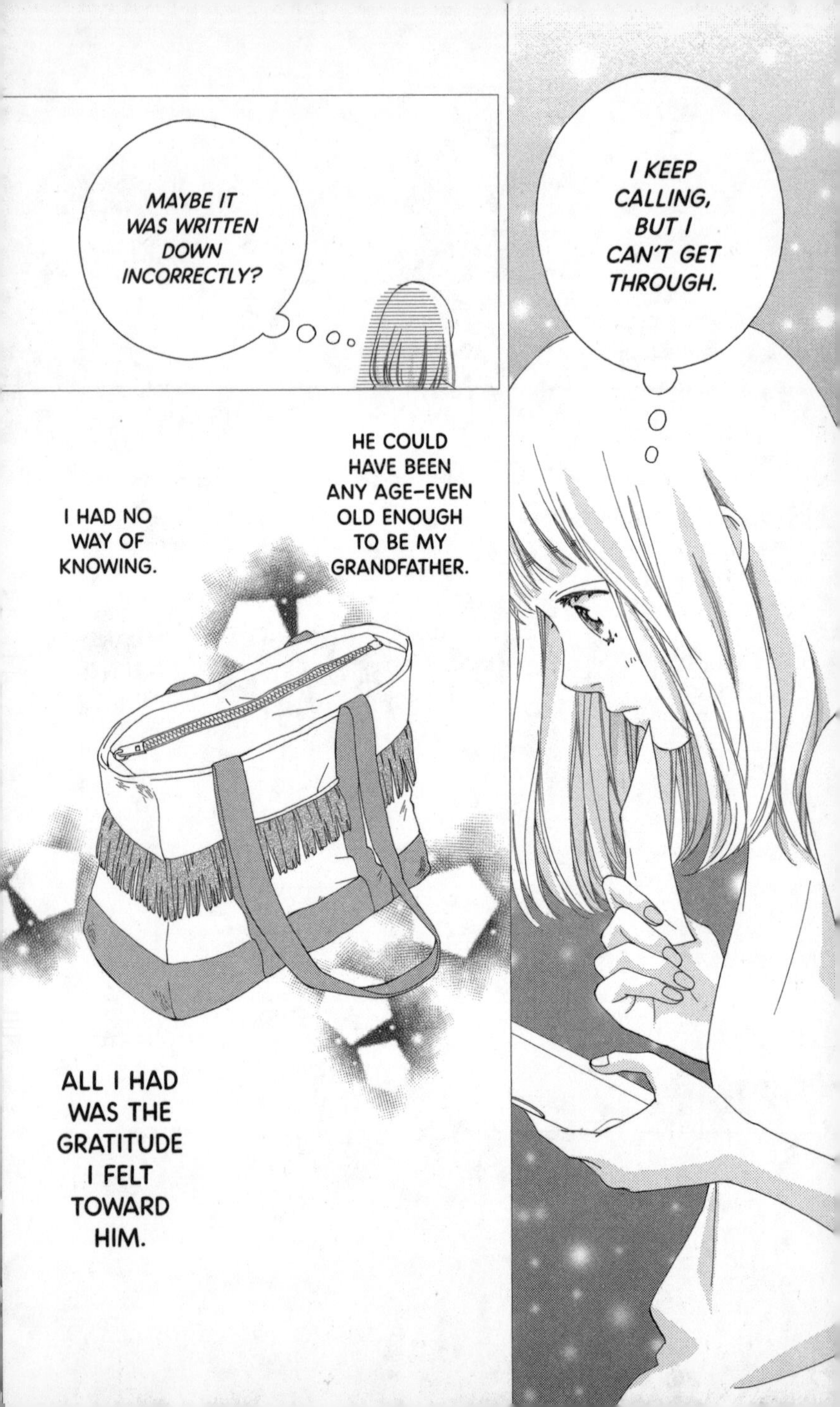
I KEEP CALLING, BUT I CAN'T GET THROUGH.
MAYBE IT WAS WRITTEN DOWN INCORRECTLY?
HE COULD HAVE BEEN ANY AGE—EVEN OLD ENOUGH TO BE MY GRANDFATHER.
I HAD NO WAY OF KNOWING.
ALL I HAD WAS THE GRATITUDE I FELT TOWARD HIM.

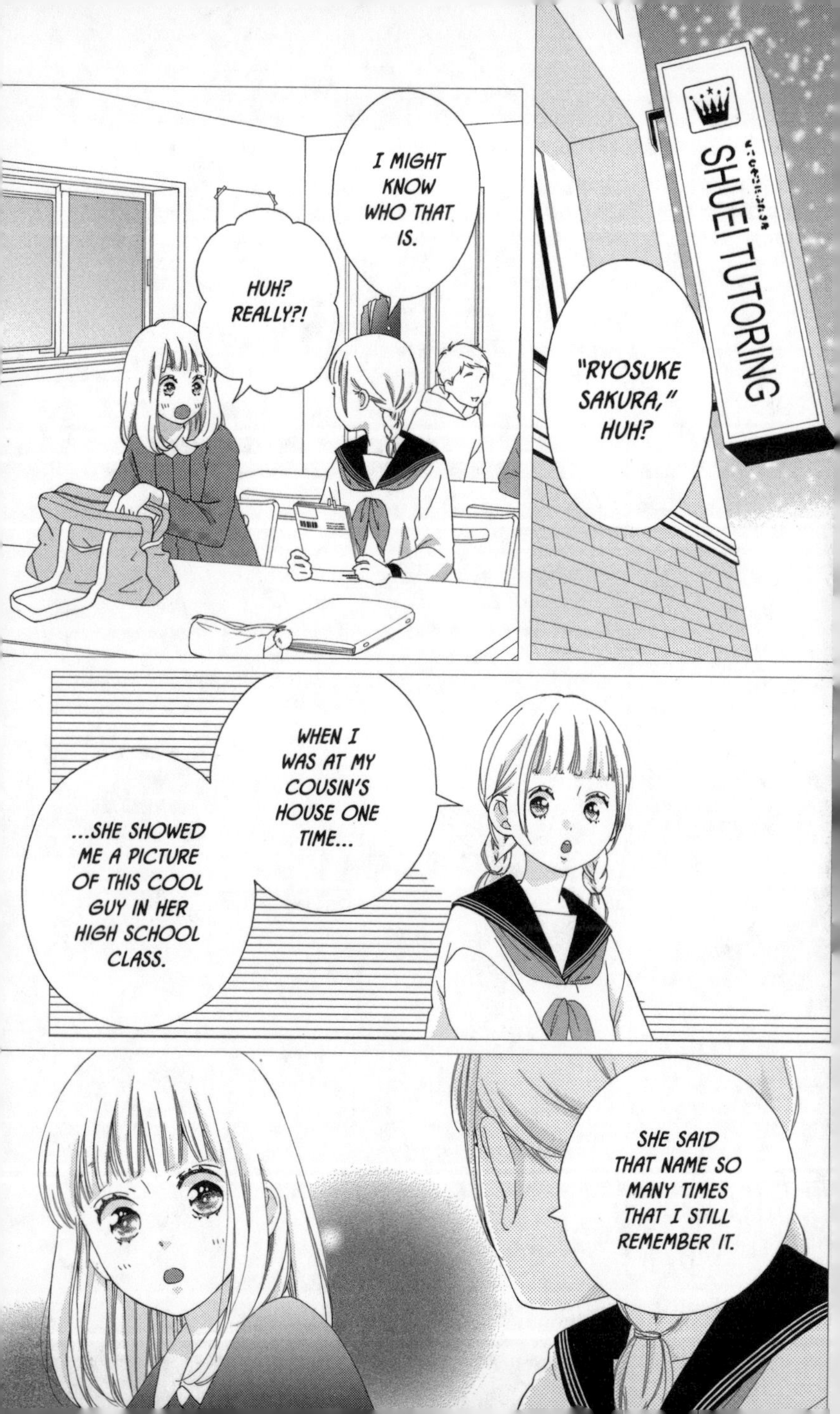
SHUEI TUTORING
"RYOSUKE SAKURA," HUH?
I MIGHT KNOW WHO THAT IS.
HUH? REALLY?!
WHEN I WAS AT MY COUSIN'S HOUSE ONE TIME...
...SHE SHOWED ME A PICTURE OF THIS COOL GUY IN HER HIGH SCHOOL CLASS.
SHE SAID THAT NAME SO MANY TIMES THAT I STILL REMEMBER IT.

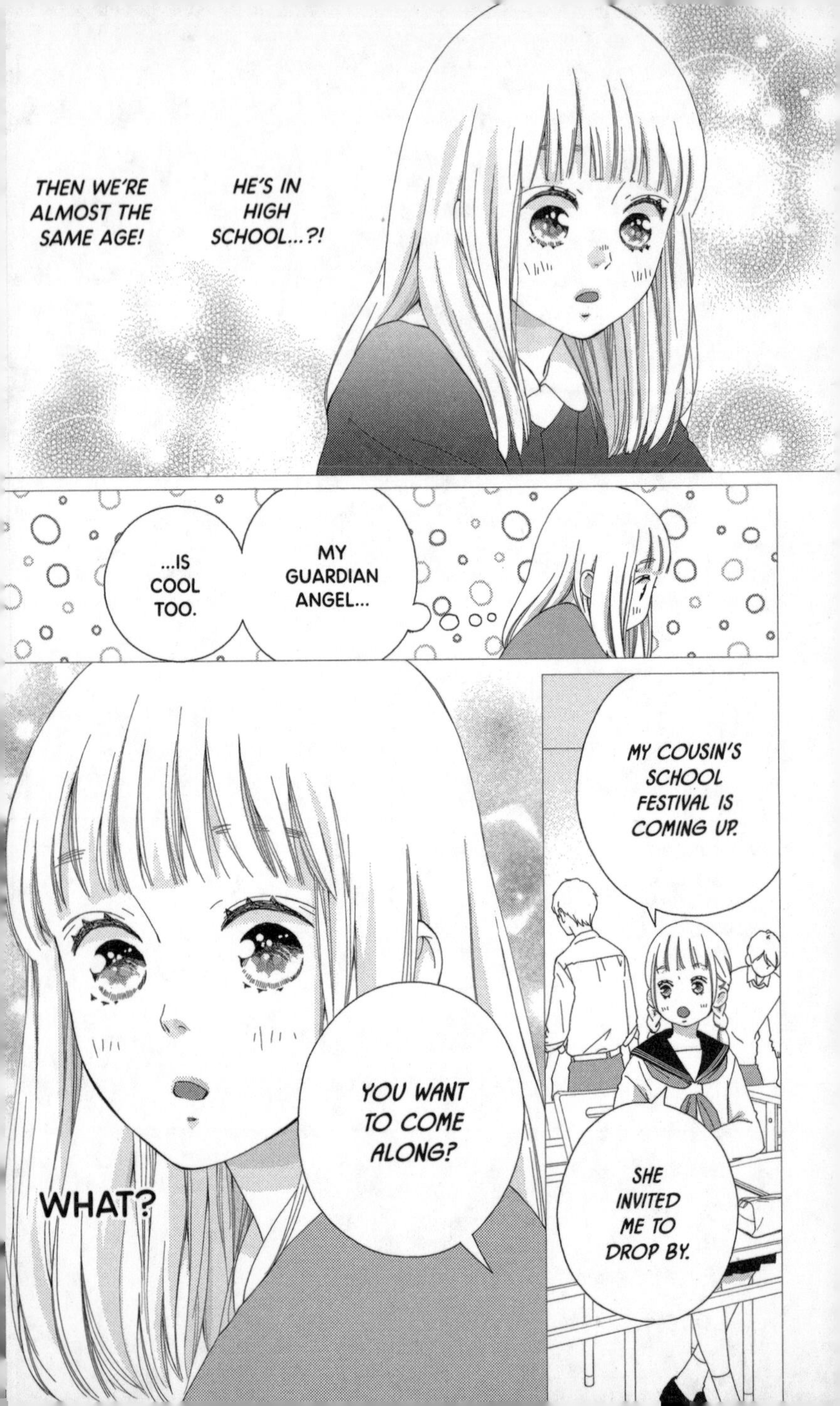
HE'S IN HIGH SCHOOL...?!
THEN WE'RE ALMOST THE SAME AGE!
MY GUARDIAN ANGEL...
...IS COOL TOO.
MY COUSIN'S SCHOOL FESTIVAL IS COMING UP.
SHE INVITED ME TO DROP BY.
YOU WANT TO COME ALONG?
WHAT?

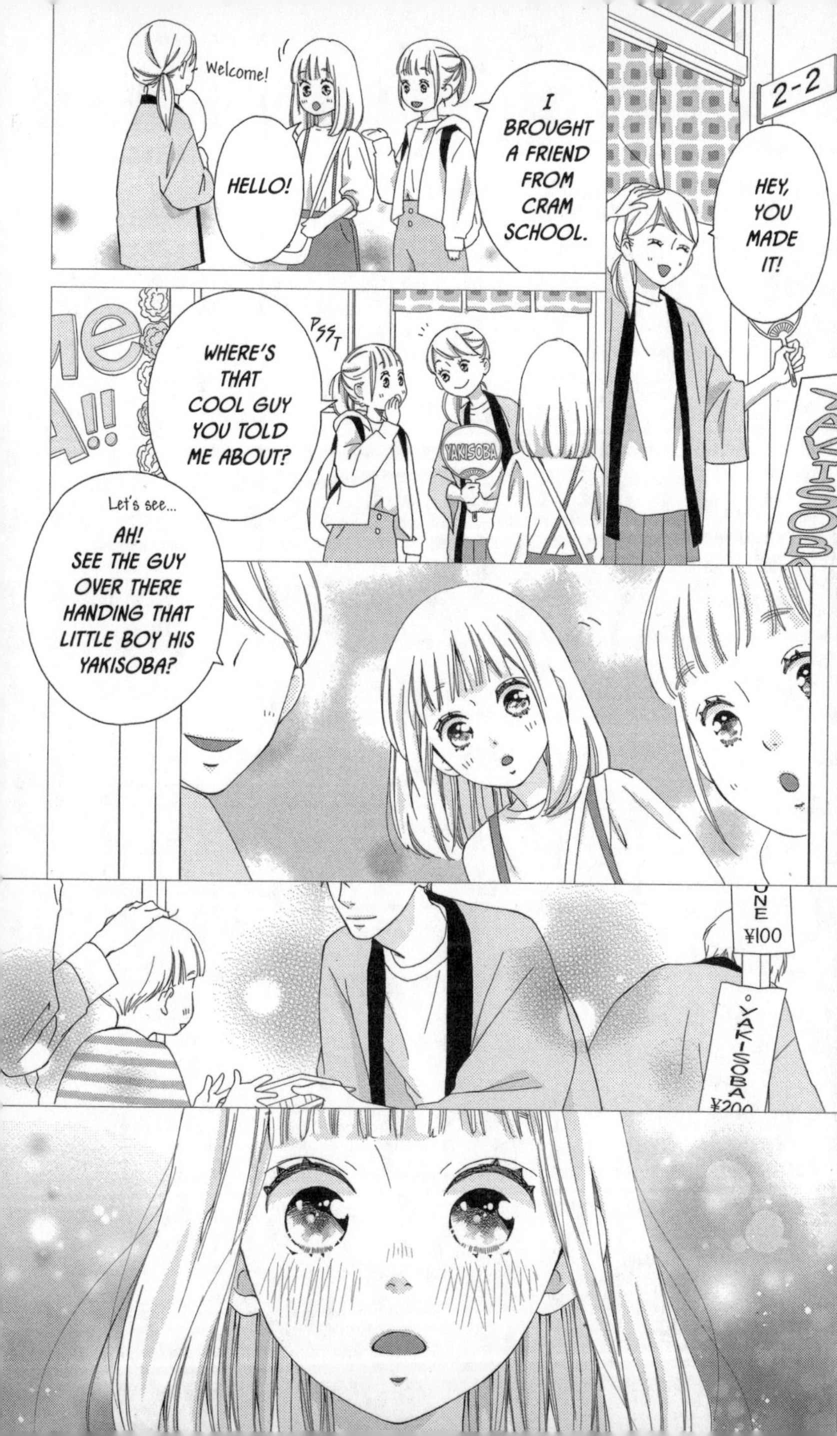
2-2
HEY, YOU MADE IT!
YAKISOBA
I BROUGHT A FRIEND FROM CRAM SCHOOL.
HELLO!
Welcome!
PSST
WHERE'S THAT COOL GUY YOU TOLD ME ABOUT?
YAKISOBA
Let's see... AH! SEE THE GUY OVER THERE HANDING THAT LITTLE BOY HIS YAKISOBA?
UNE ¥100
YAKISOBA ¥200

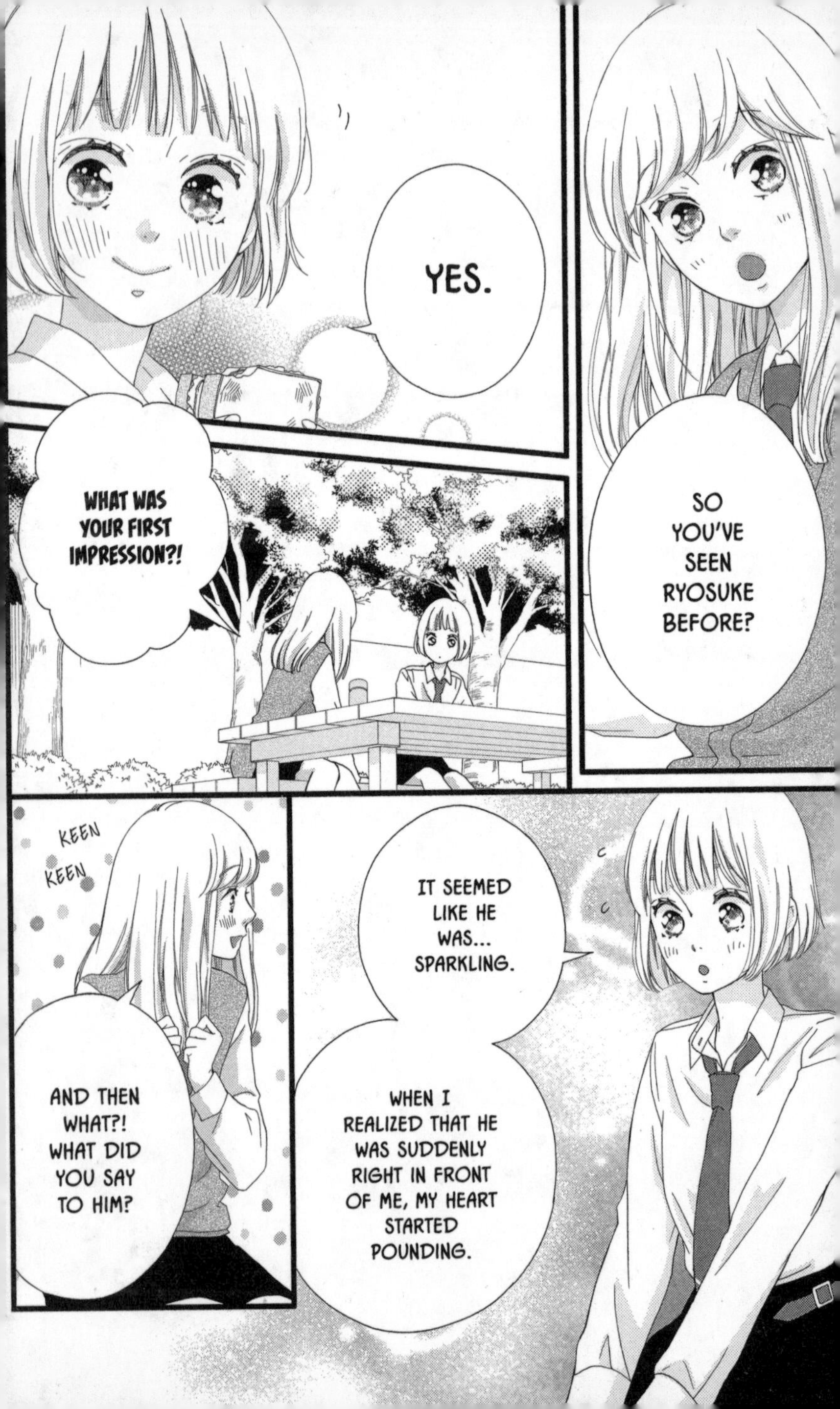
SO YOU'VE SEEN RYOSUKE BEFORE?
YES.
WHAT WAS YOUR FIRST IMPRESSION?!
IT SEEMED LIKE HE WAS... SPARKLING.
WHEN I REALIZED THAT HE WAS SUDDENLY RIGHT IN FRONT OF ME, MY HEART STARTED POUNDING.
KEEN
KEEN
AND THEN WHAT?! WHAT DID YOU SAY TO HIM?

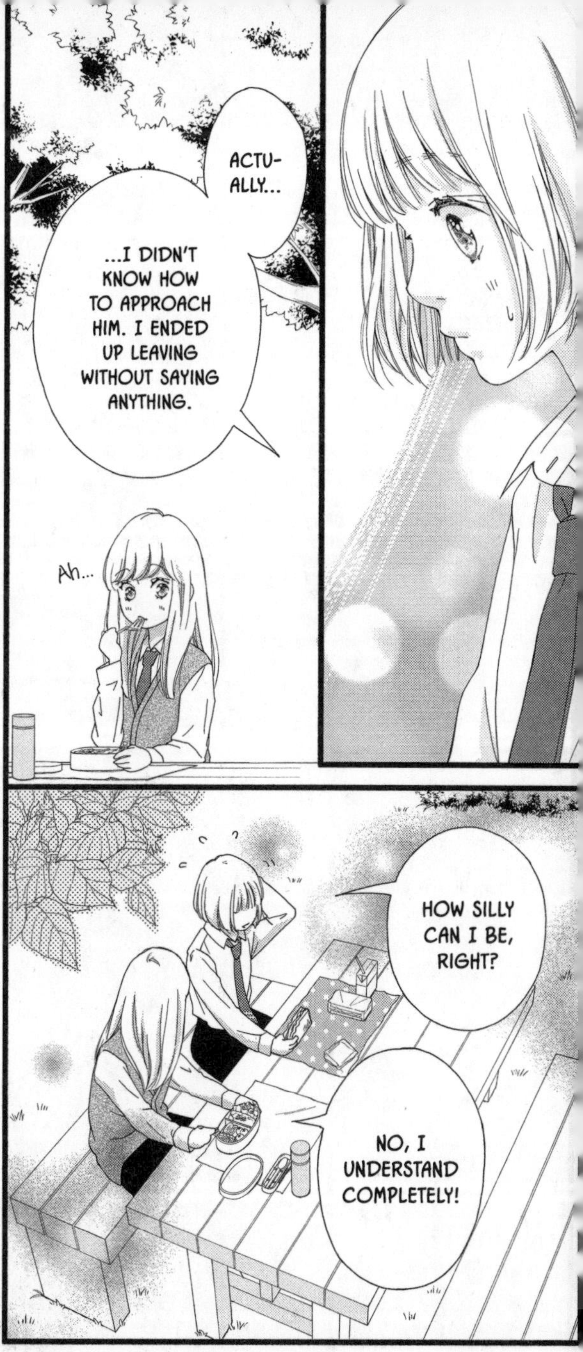
ACTU-ALLY...
...I DIDN'T KNOW HOW TO APPROACH HIM. I ENDED UP LEAVING WITHOUT SAYING ANYTHING.
Ah...
HOW SILLY CAN I BE, RIGHT?
NO, I UNDERSTAND COMPLETELY!

I don't normally have trouble falling asleep or waking up, but I definitely don't lead a regular lifestyle either. When my sleepiness level hits its max, I go to bed and drift off pretty easily. But I do have more trouble on some nights. When I'm worried about something, it stays in the back of my mind and keeps me awake. If I have important plans the next day, I'll go to bed early, but that makes it harder to fall asleep. At times like that, I watch the shapes and patterns that appear (or emerge) when I close my eyes. The point of this is to not have any opinions about what I'm seeing in my mind. I just watch the shapes constantly changing. This helps me get to sleep pretty quickly. Give it a try!

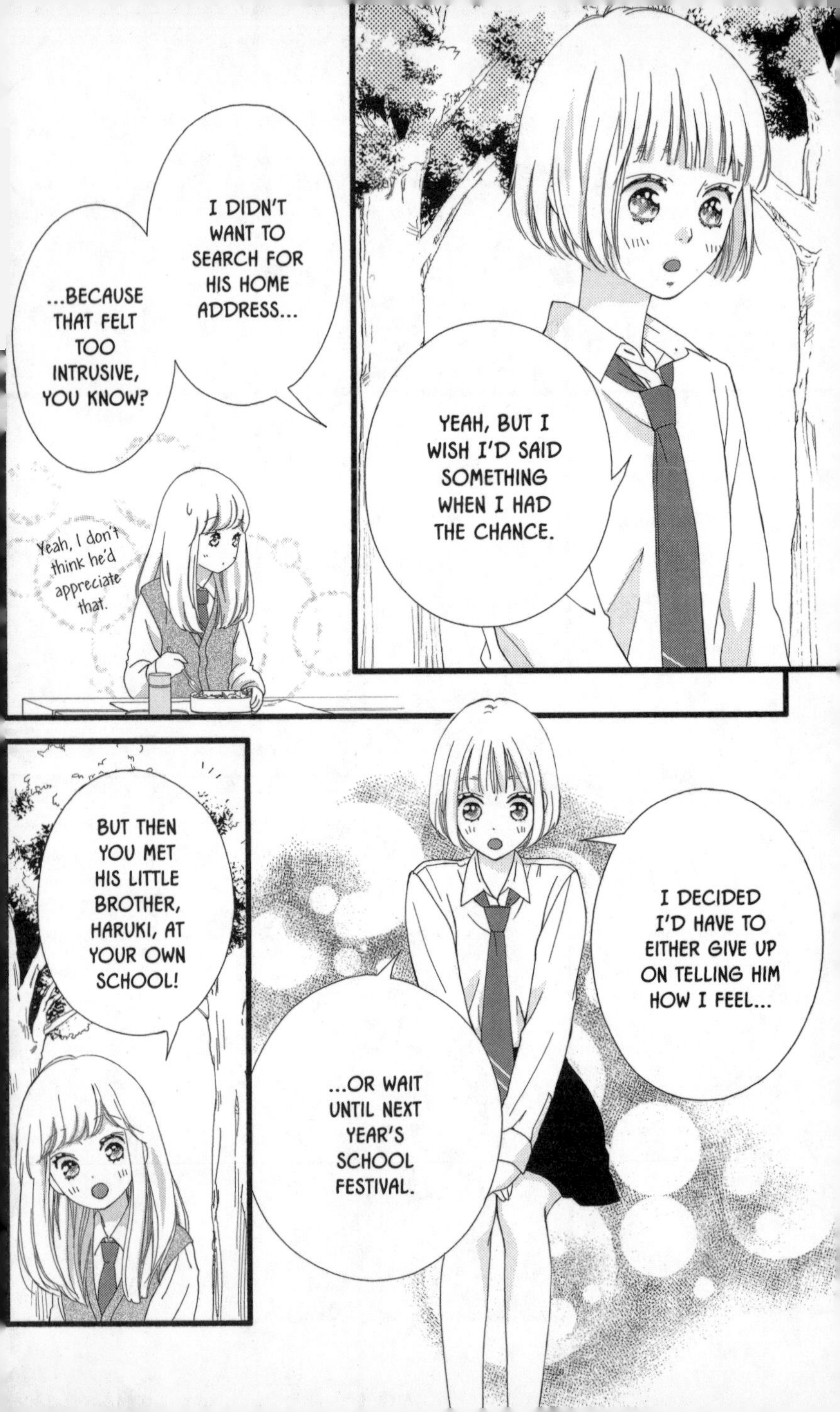
YEAH, BUT I WISH I'D SAID SOMETHING WHEN I HAD THE CHANCE.
I DIDN'T WANT TO SEARCH FOR HIS HOME ADDRESS...
...BECAUSE THAT FELT TOO INTRUSIVE, YOU KNOW?
Yeah, I don't think he'd appreciate that.
I DECIDED I'D HAVE TO EITHER GIVE UP ON TELLING HIM HOW I FEEL...
...OR WAIT UNTIL NEXT YEAR'S SCHOOL FESTIVAL.
BUT THEN YOU MET HIS LITTLE BROTHER, HARUKI, AT YOUR OWN SCHOOL!

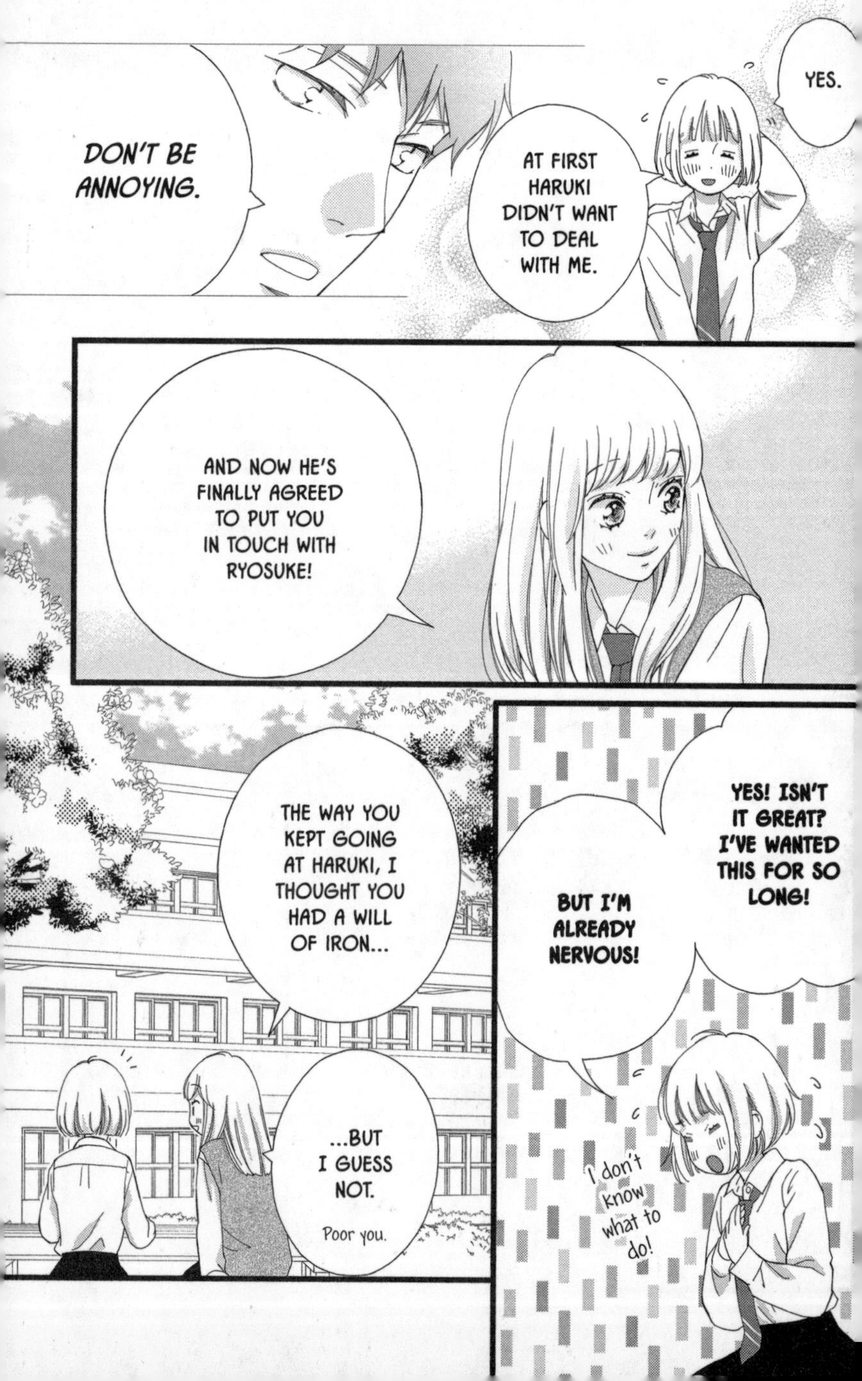
YES.
AT FIRST HARUKI DIDN'T WANT TO DEAL WITH ME.
DON'T BE ANNOYING.
AND NOW HE'S FINALLY AGREED TO PUT YOU IN TOUCH WITH RYOSUKE!
YES! ISN'T IT GREAT? I'VE WANTED THIS FOR SO LONG!
BUT I'M ALREADY NERVOUS!
I don't know what to do!
THE WAY YOU KEPT GOING AT HARUKI, I THOUGHT YOU HAD A WILL OF IRON...
...BUT I GUESS NOT.
Poor you.

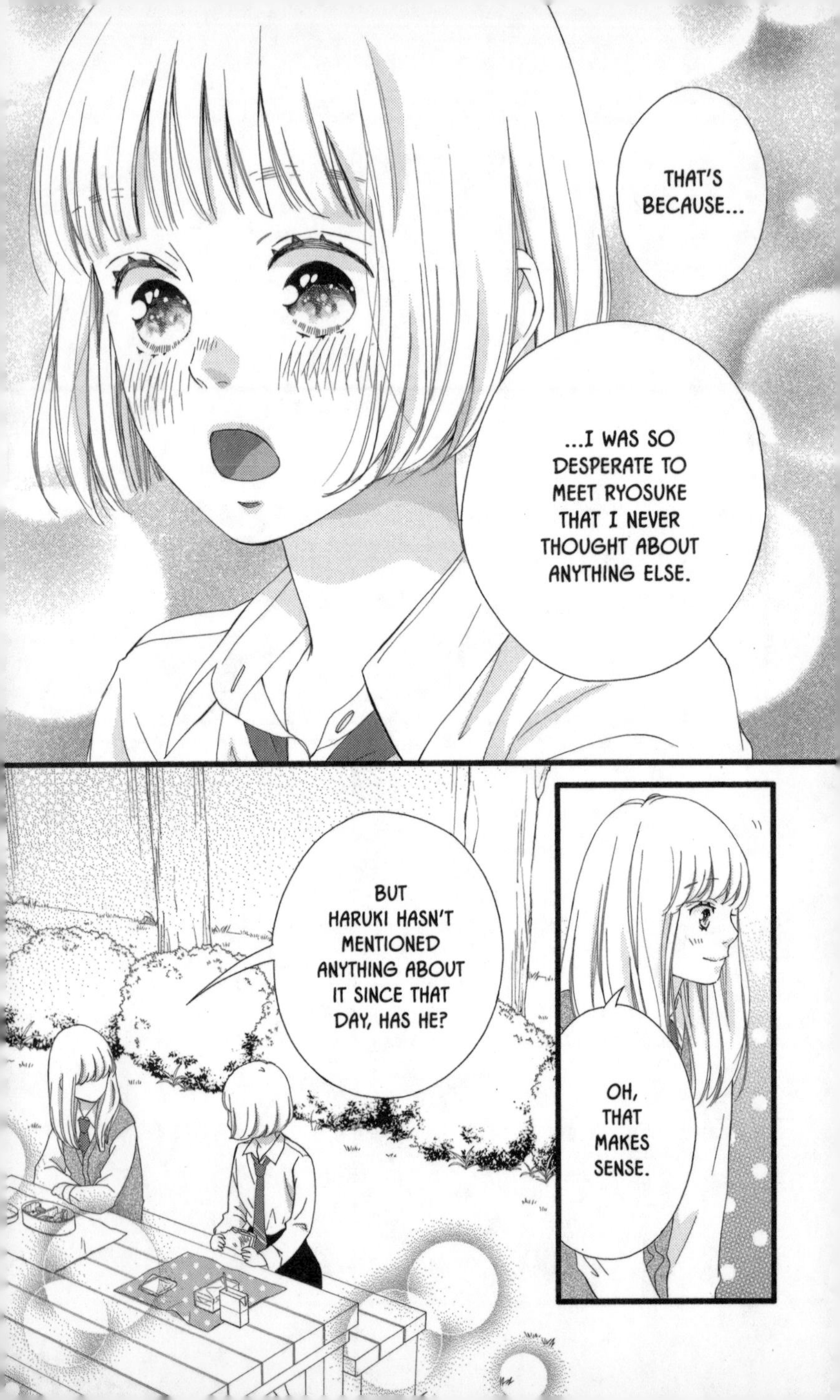
THAT'S BECAUSE...
...I WAS SO DESPERATE TO MEET RYOSUKE THAT I NEVER THOUGHT ABOUT ANYTHING ELSE.
OH, THAT MAKES SENSE.
BUT HARUKI HASN'T MENTIONED ANYTHING ABOUT IT SINCE THAT DAY, HAS HE?

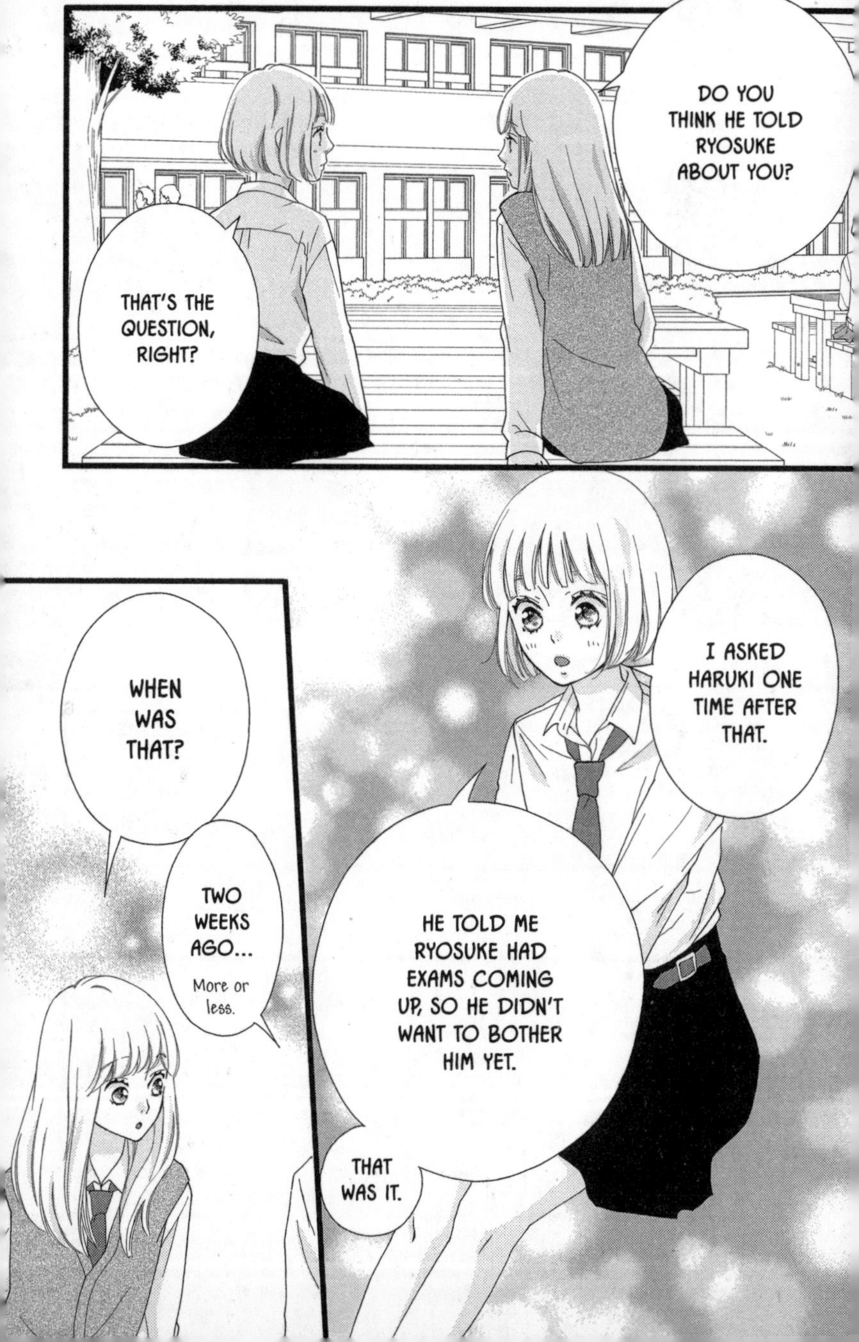
DO YOU THINK HE TOLD RYOSUKE ABOUT YOU?
THAT'S THE QUESTION, RIGHT?
I ASKED HARUKI ONE TIME AFTER THAT.
WHEN WAS THAT?
TWO WEEKS AGO...
More or less.
HE TOLD ME RYOSUKE HAD EXAMS COMING UP, SO HE DIDN'T WANT TO BOTHER HIM YET.
THAT WAS IT.

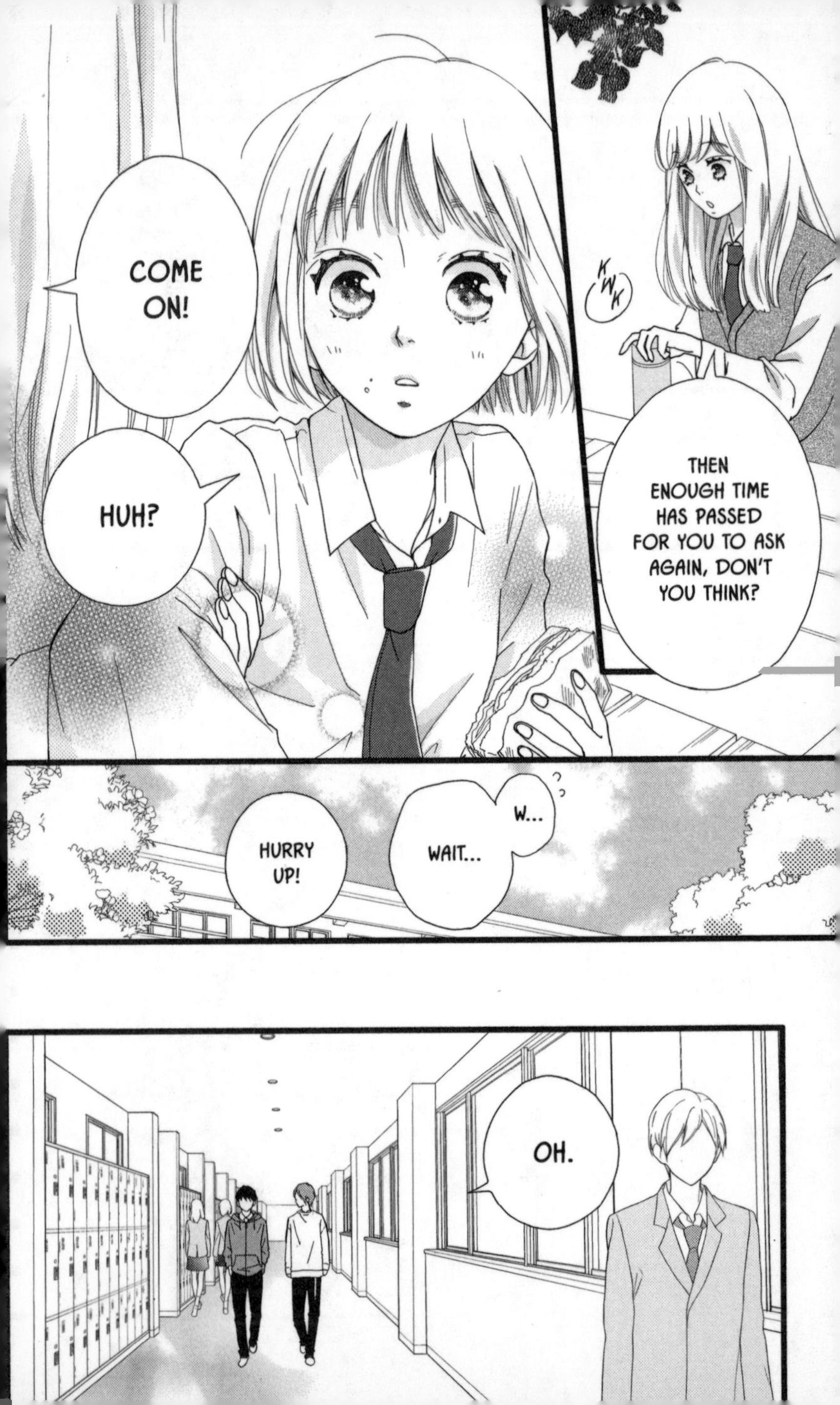
KWK
THEN ENOUGH TIME HAS PASSED FOR YOU TO ASK AGAIN, DON'T YOU THINK?
COME ON!
HUH?
W...
WAIT...
HURRY UP!
OH.

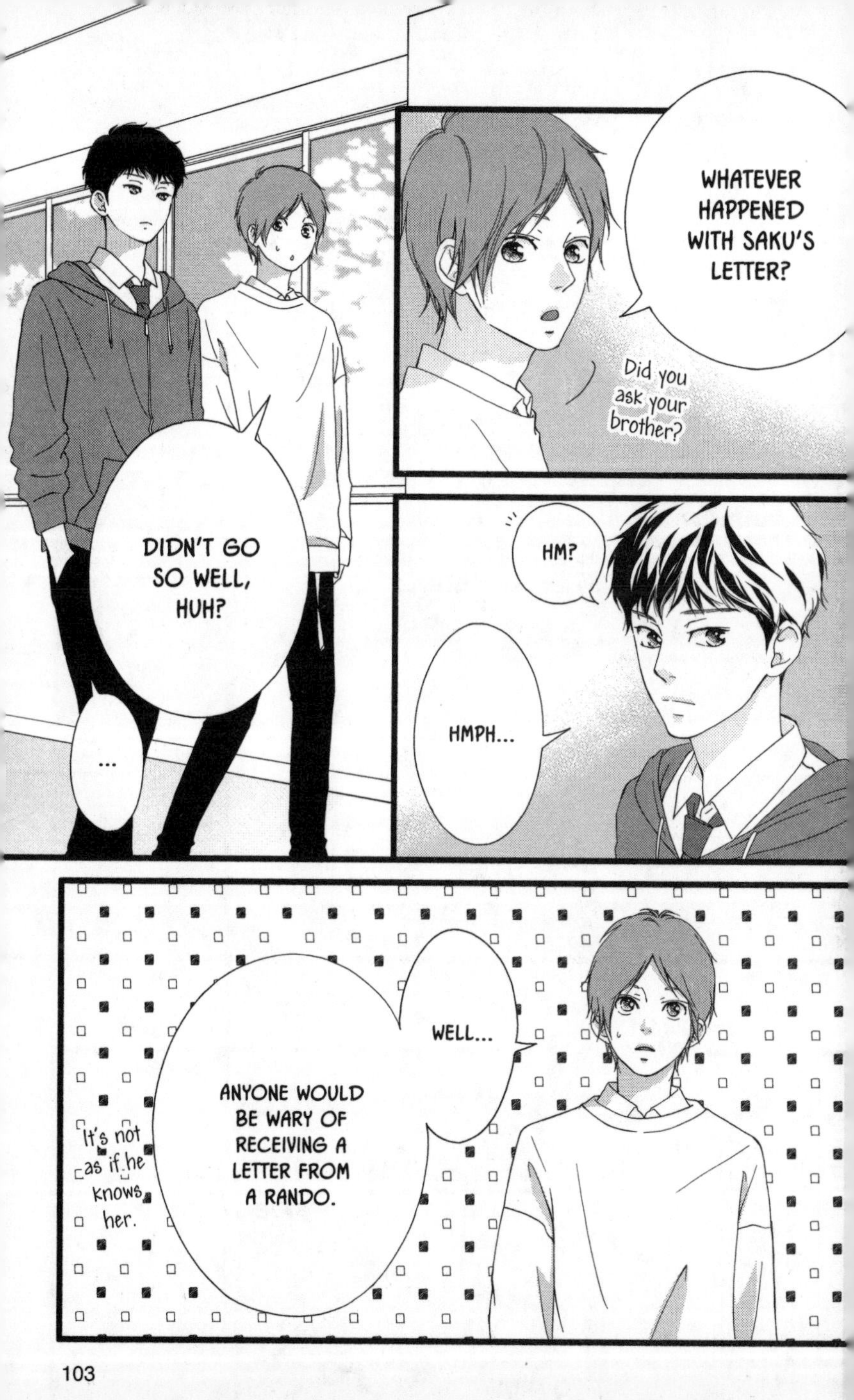
WHATEVER HAPPENED WITH SAKU'S LETTER?
Did you ask your brother?
HM?
HMPH...
DIDN'T GO SO WELL, HUH?
...
WELL...
ANYONE WOULD BE WARY OF RECEIVING A LETTER FROM A RANDO.
It's not as if he knows her.

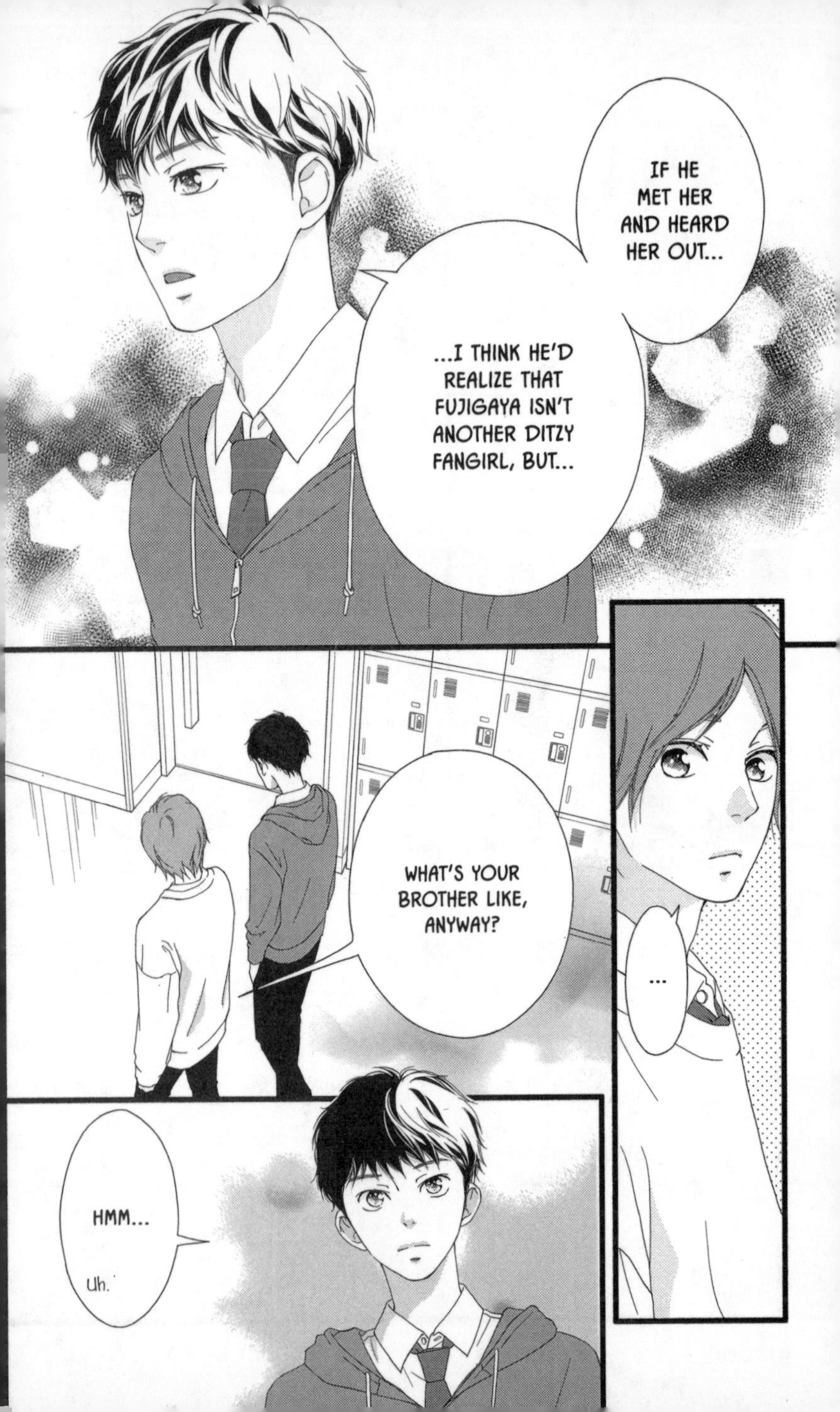
IF HE MET HER AND HEARD HER OUT...
...I THINK HE'D REALIZE THAT FUJIGAYA ISN'T ANOTHER DITZY FANGIRL, BUT...
...
WHAT'S YOUR BROTHER LIKE, ANYWAY?
HMM...
Uh.

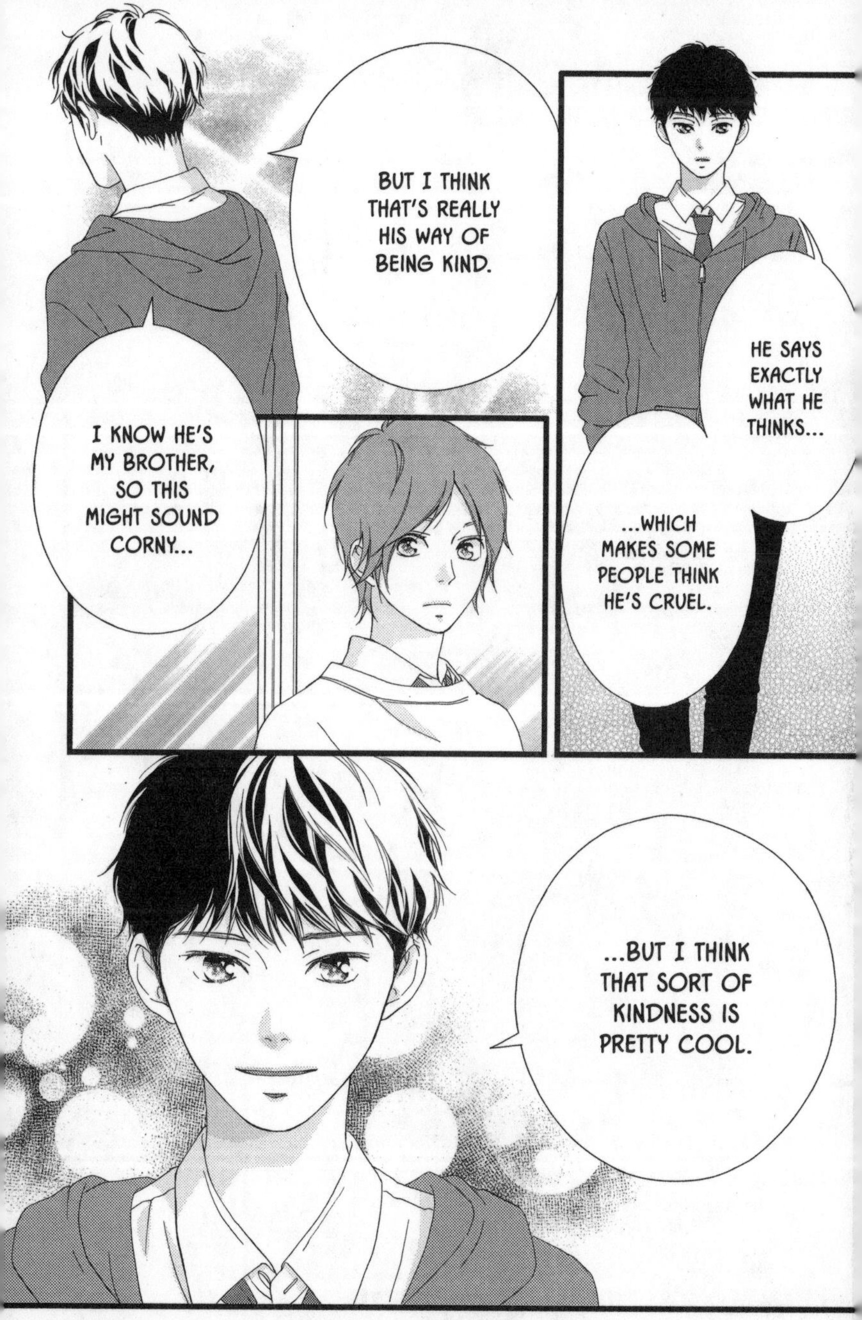
HE SAYS EXACTLY WHAT HE THINKS...
...WHICH MAKES SOME PEOPLE THINK HE'S CRUEL.
BUT I THINK THAT'S REALLY HIS WAY OF BEING KIND.
I KNOW HE'S MY BROTHER, SO THIS MIGHT SOUND CORNY...
...BUT I THINK THAT SORT OF KINDNESS IS PRETTY COOL.

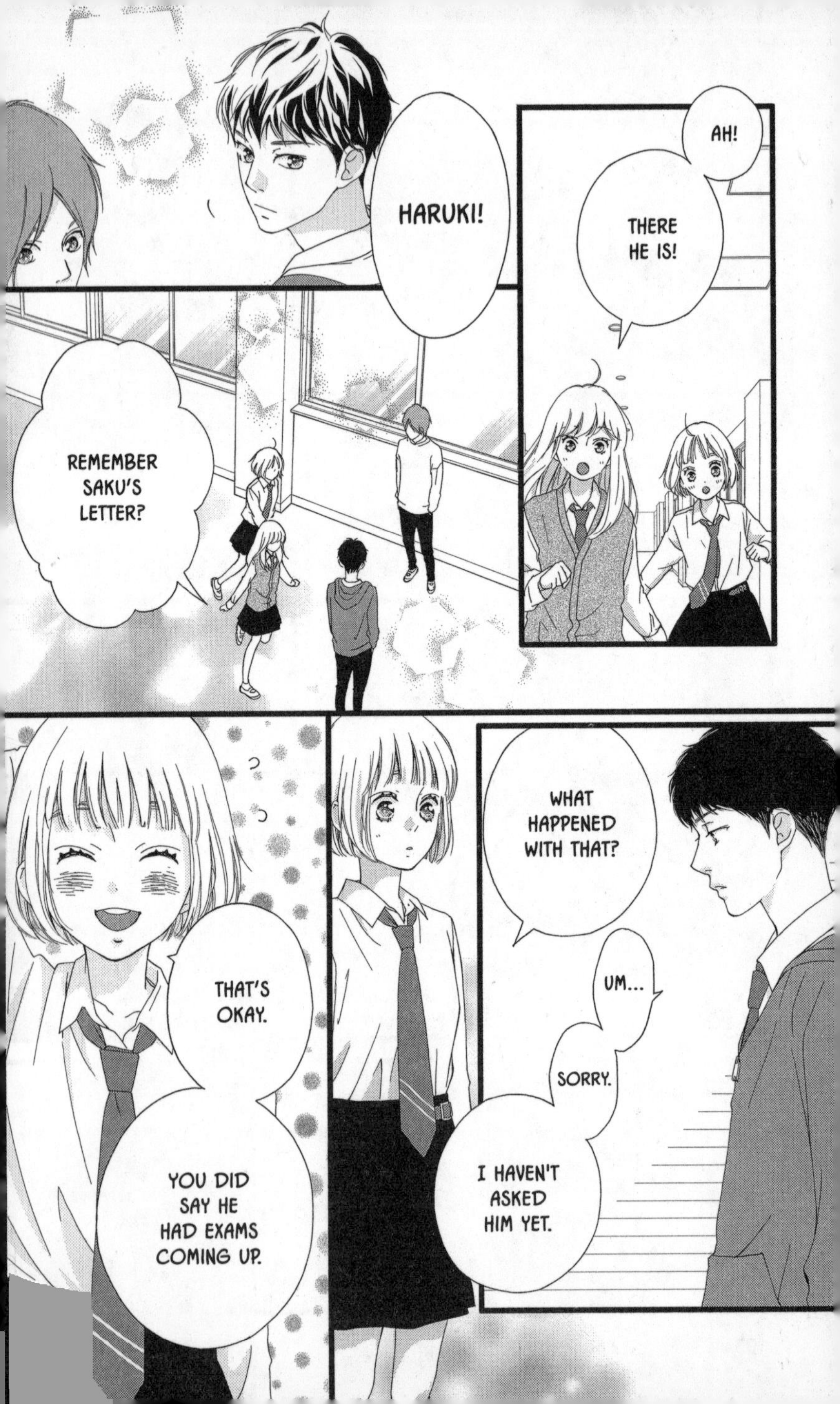
AH!
THERE HE IS!
HARUKI!
REMEMBER SAKU'S LETTER?
WHAT HAPPENED WITH THAT?
UM...
SORRY.
I HAVEN'T ASKED HIM YET.
THAT'S OKAY.
YOU DID SAY HE HAD EXAMS COMING UP.

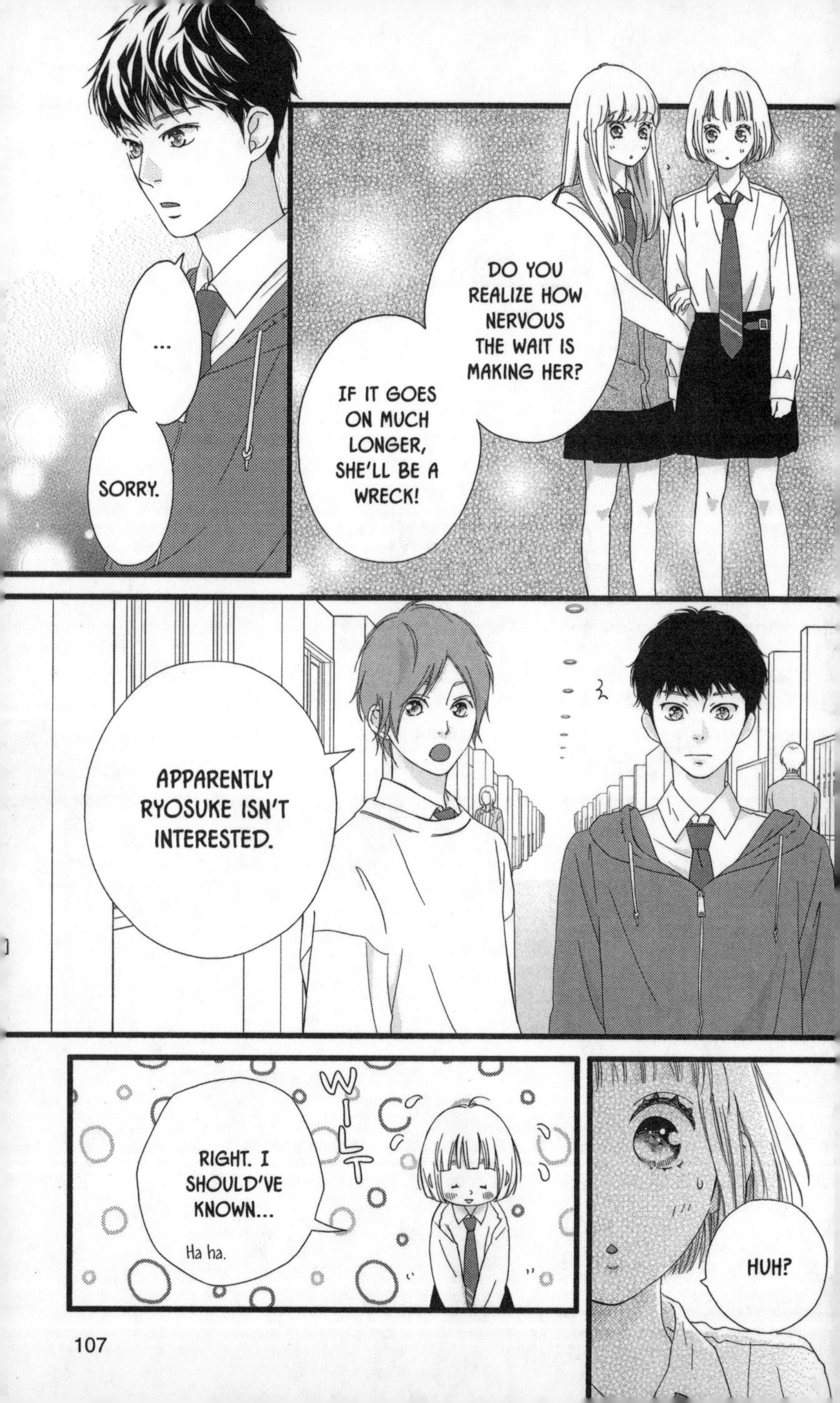
DO YOU REALIZE HOW NERVOUS THE WAIT IS MAKING HER?
IF IT GOES ON MUCH LONGER, SHE'LL BE A WRECK!
...
SORRY.
APPARENTLY RYOSUKE ISN'T INTERESTED.
HUH?
WILT
RIGHT. I SHOULD'VE KNOWN...
Ha ha.

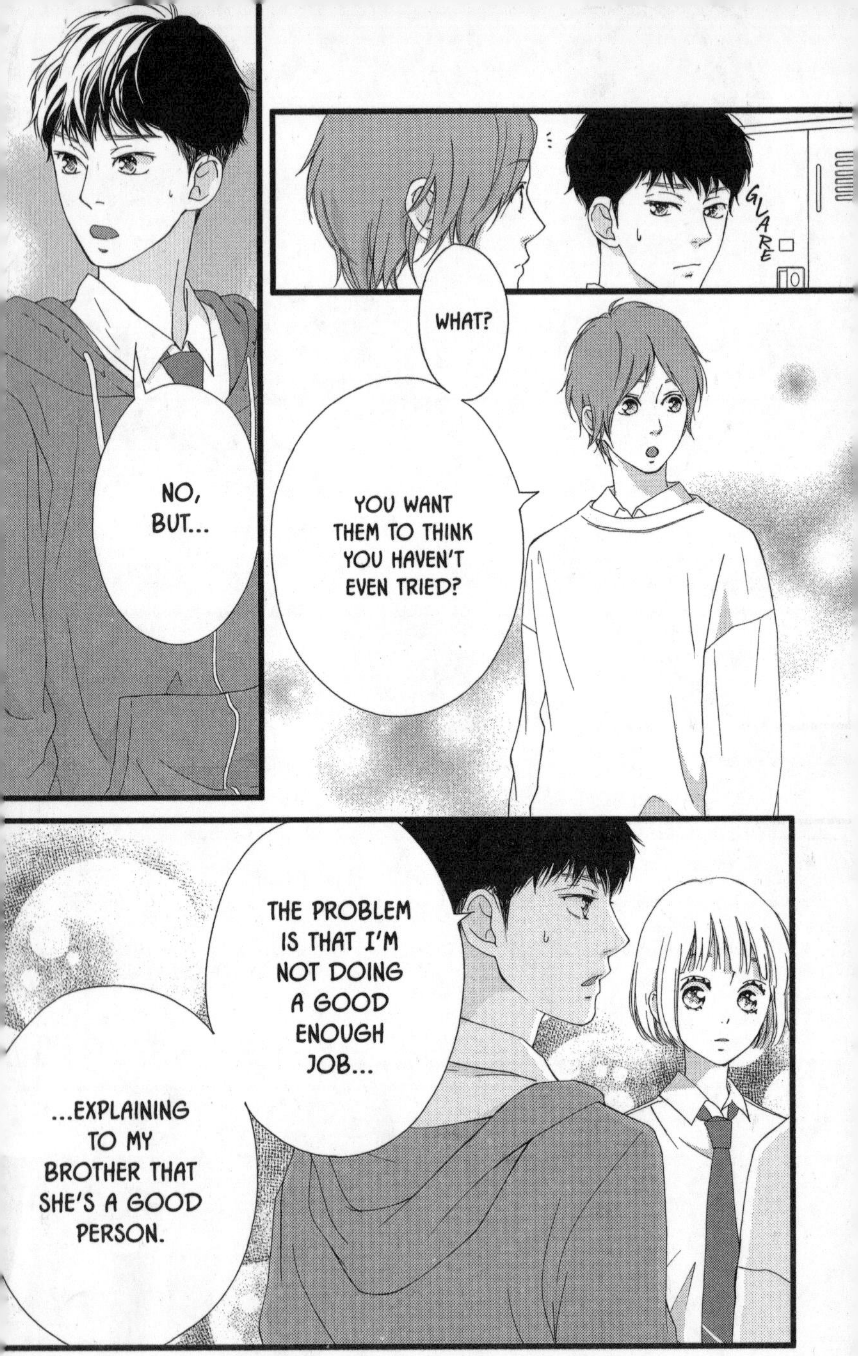
GLARE
WHAT?
YOU WANT THEM TO THINK YOU HAVEN'T EVEN TRIED?
NO, BUT...
THE PROBLEM IS THAT I'M NOT DOING A GOOD ENOUGH JOB...
...EXPLAINING TO MY BROTHER THAT SHE'S A GOOD PERSON.

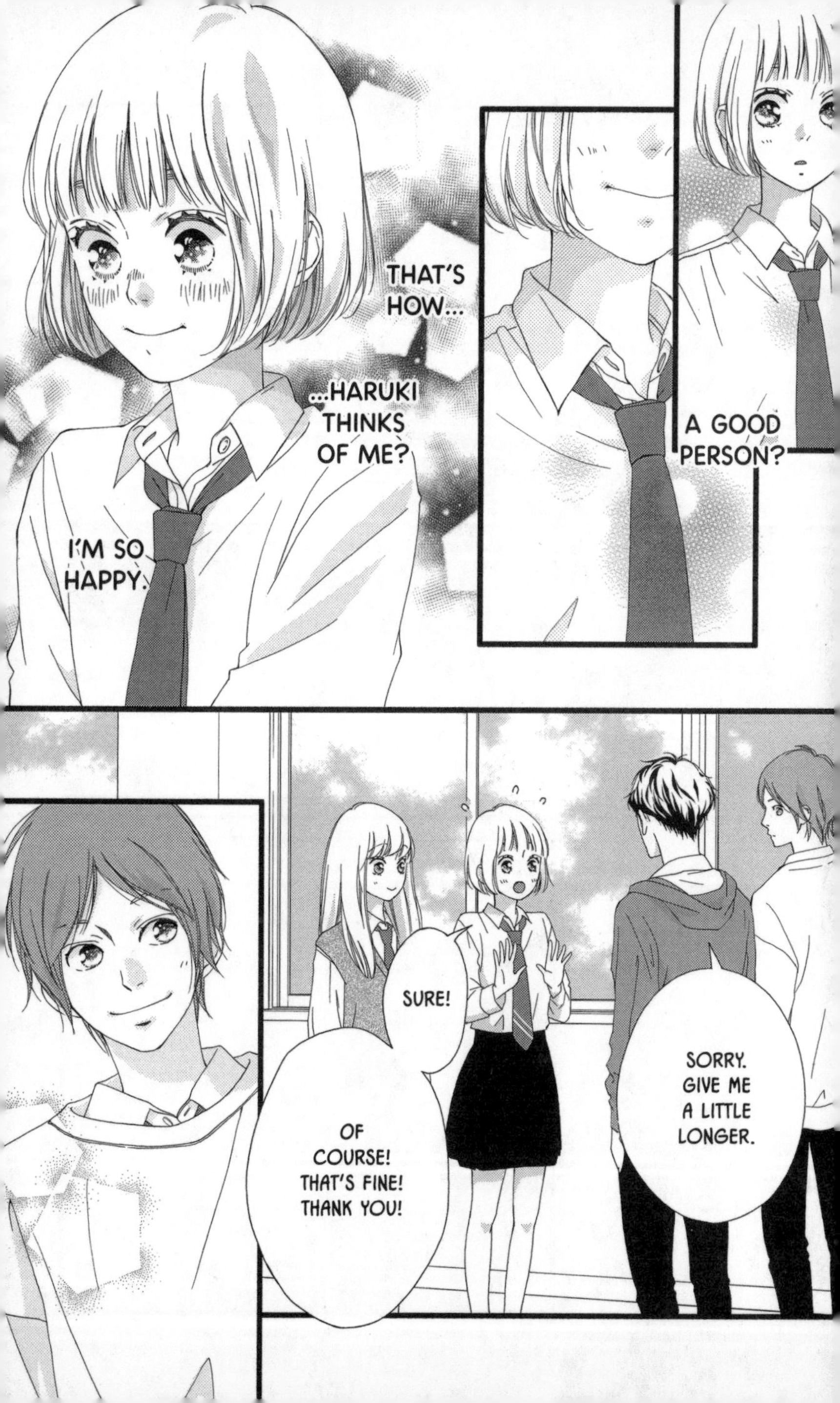
A GOOD PERSON?
THAT'S HOW...
...HARUKI THINKS OF ME?
I'M SO HAPPY.
SORRY. GIVE ME A LITTLE LONGER.
SURE!
OF COURSE! THAT'S FINE! THANK YOU!

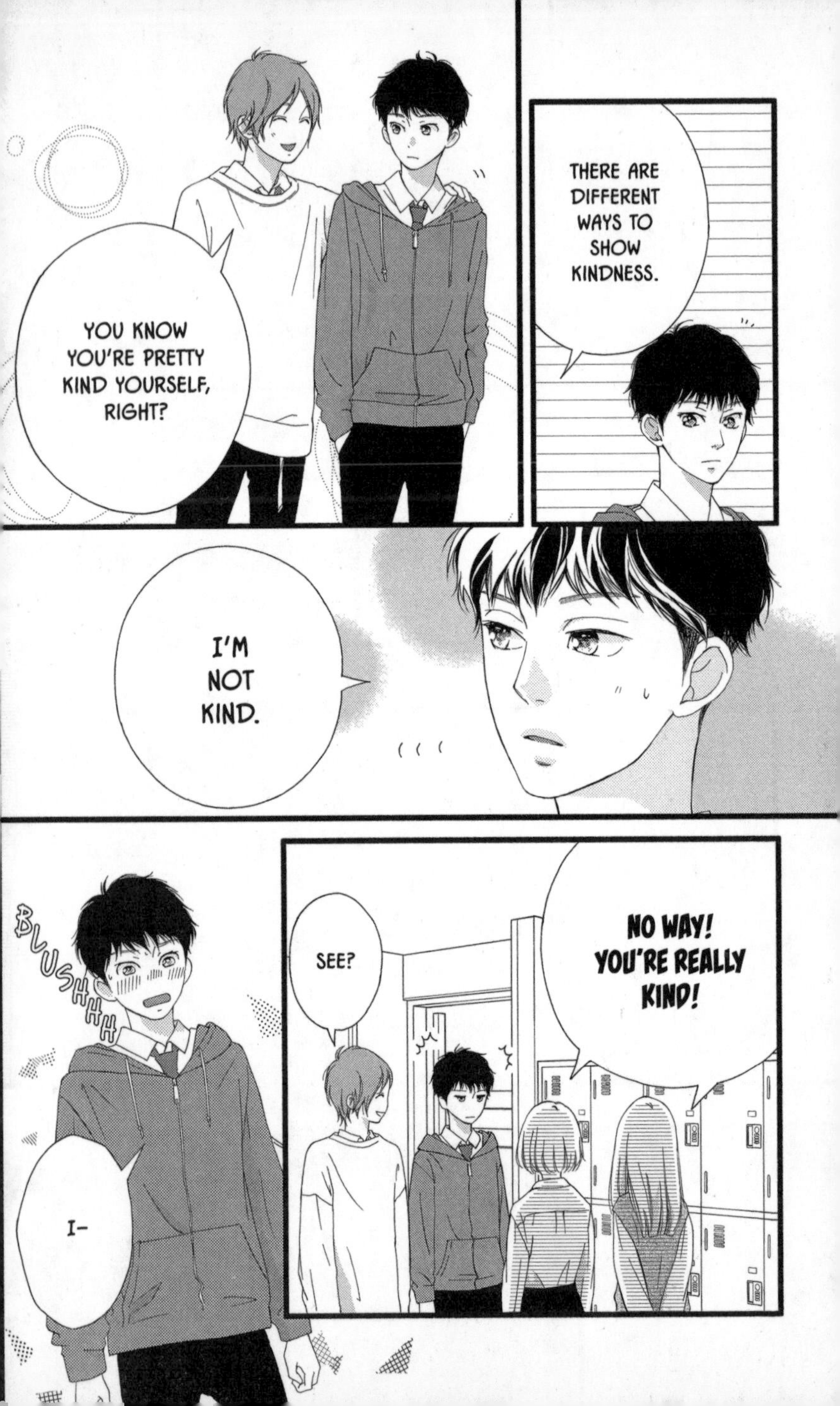
THERE ARE DIFFERENT WAYS TO SHOW KINDNESS.
YOU KNOW YOU'RE PRETTY KIND YOURSELF, RIGHT?
I'M NOT KIND.
NO WAY! YOU'RE REALLY KIND!
SEE?
BLUSHHH
I-

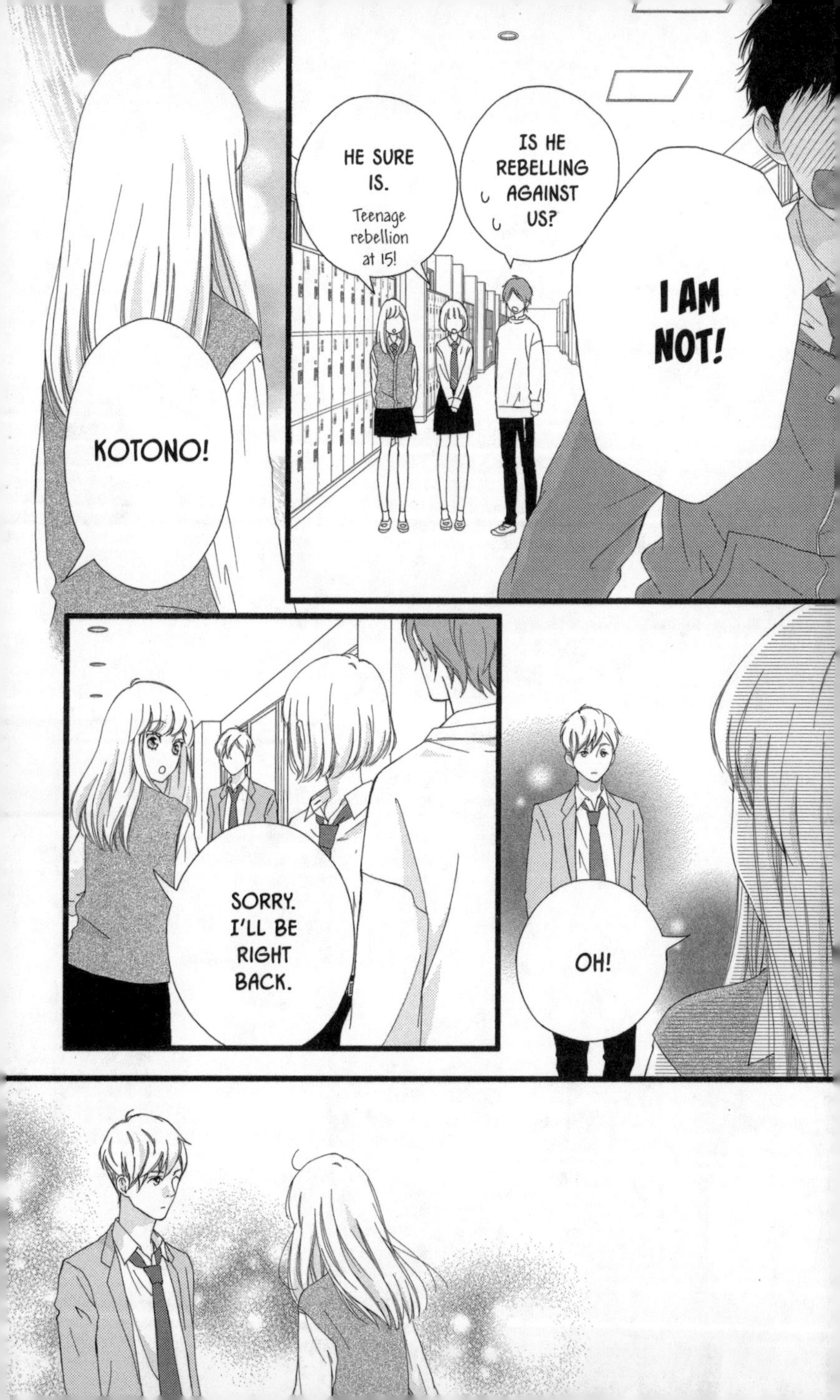
IS HE REBELLING AGAINST US?
HE SURE IS.
Teenage rebellion at 15!
I AM NOT!
KOTONO!
OH!
SORRY. I'LL BE RIGHT BACK.

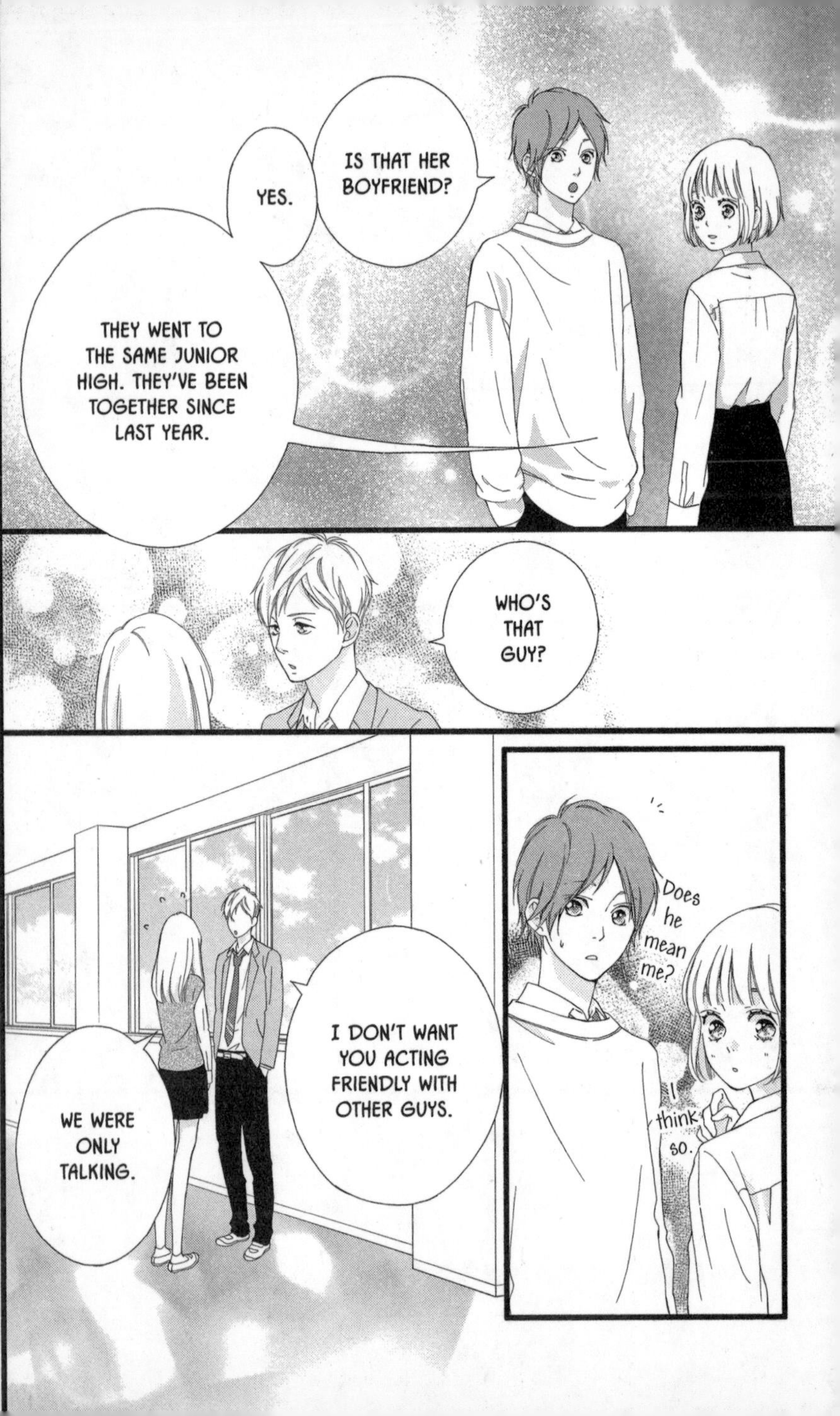
IS THAT HER BOYFRIEND?
YES.
THEY WENT TO THE SAME JUNIOR HIGH. THEY'VE BEEN TOGETHER SINCE LAST YEAR.
WHO'S THAT GUY?
Does he mean me?
I think so.
I DON'T WANT YOU ACTING FRIENDLY WITH OTHER GUYS.
WE WERE ONLY TALKING.

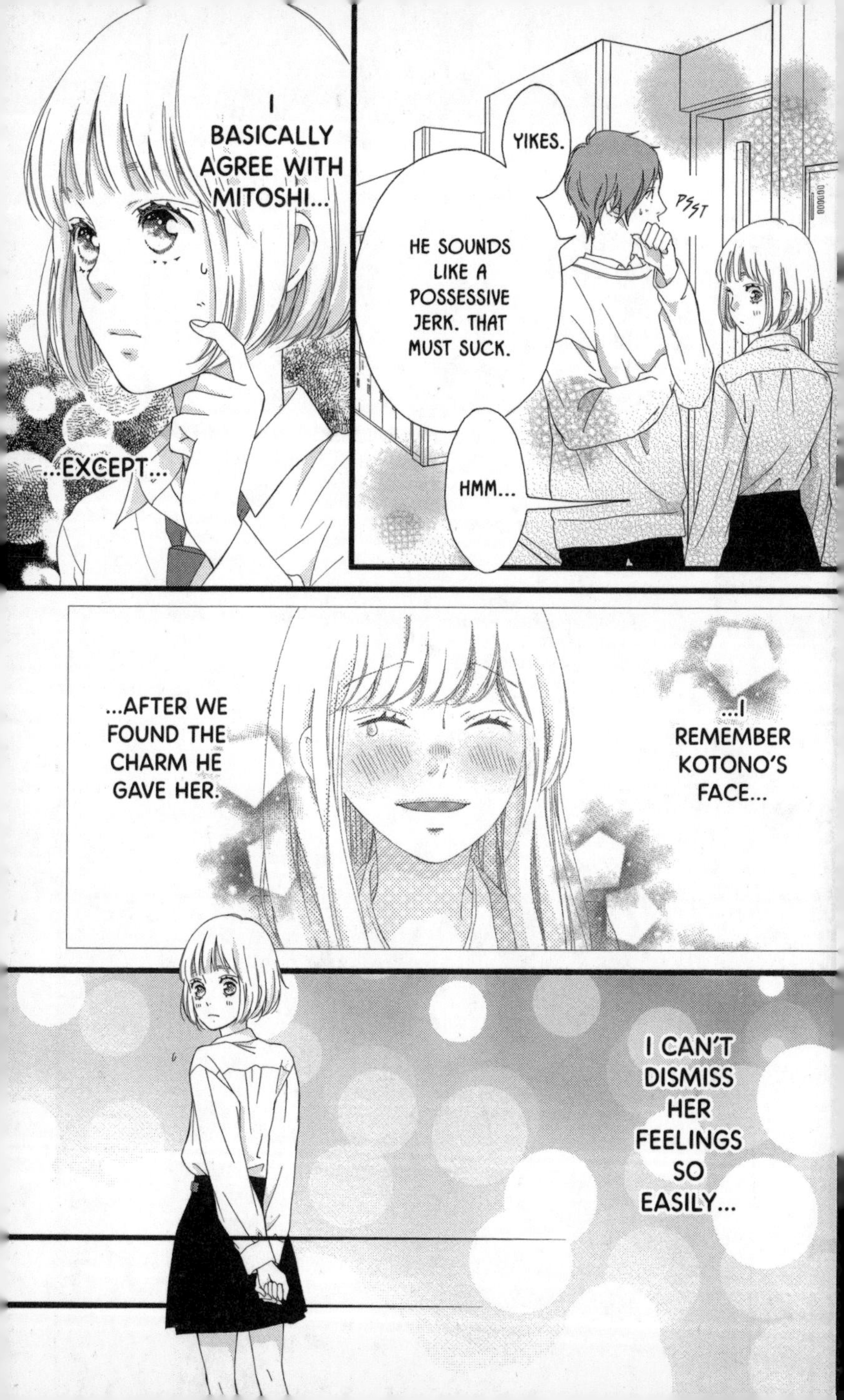
YIKES.
HE SOUNDS LIKE A POSSESSIVE JERK. THAT MUST SUCK.
PSST
HMM...
I BASICALLY AGREE WITH MITOSHI...
...EXCEPT...
...I REMEMBER KOTONO'S FACE...
...AFTER WE FOUND THE CHARM HE GAVE HER.
I CAN'T DISMISS HER FEELINGS SO EASILY...

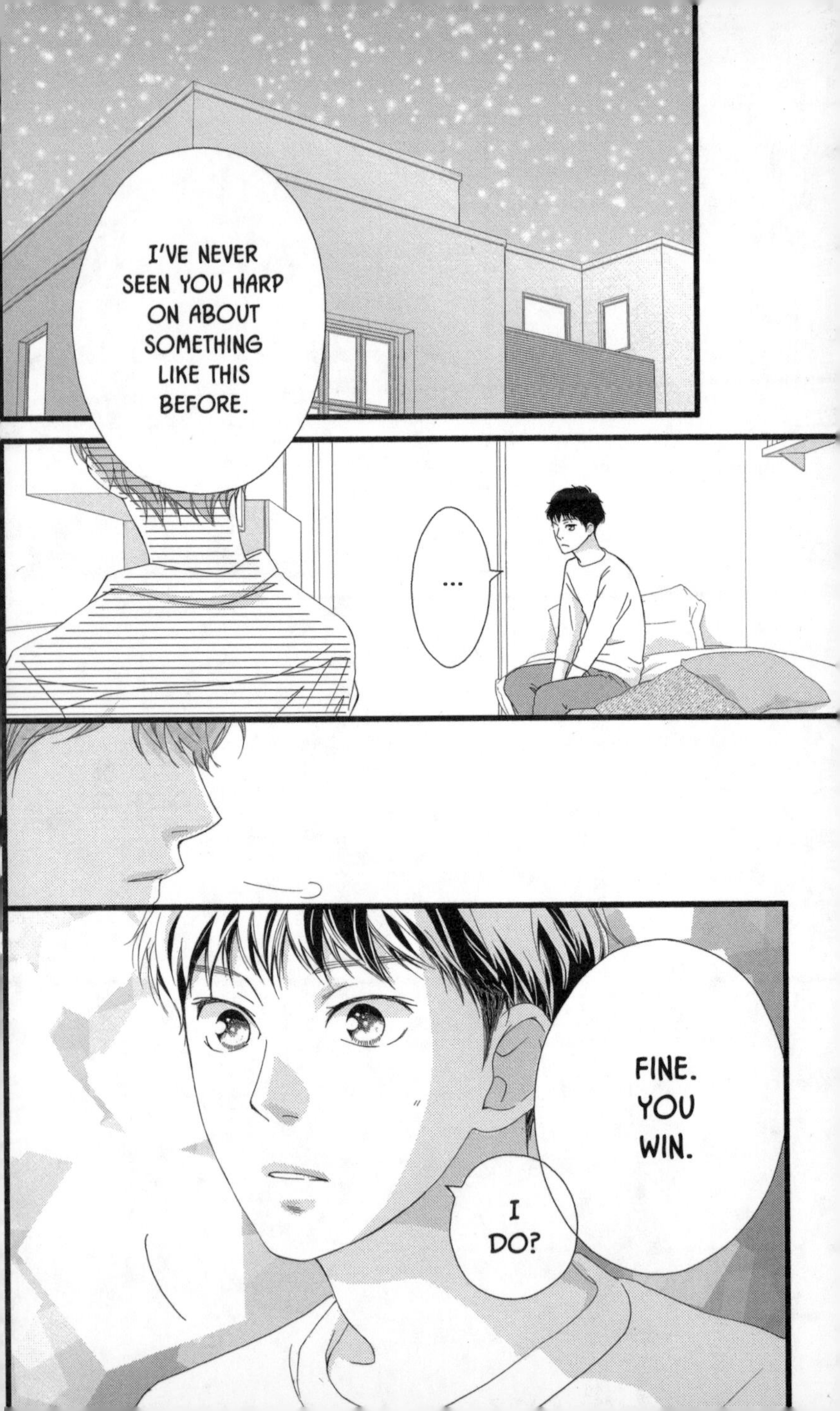
I'VE NEVER SEEN YOU HARP ON ABOUT SOMETHING LIKE THIS BEFORE.
...
FINE. YOU WIN.
I DO?

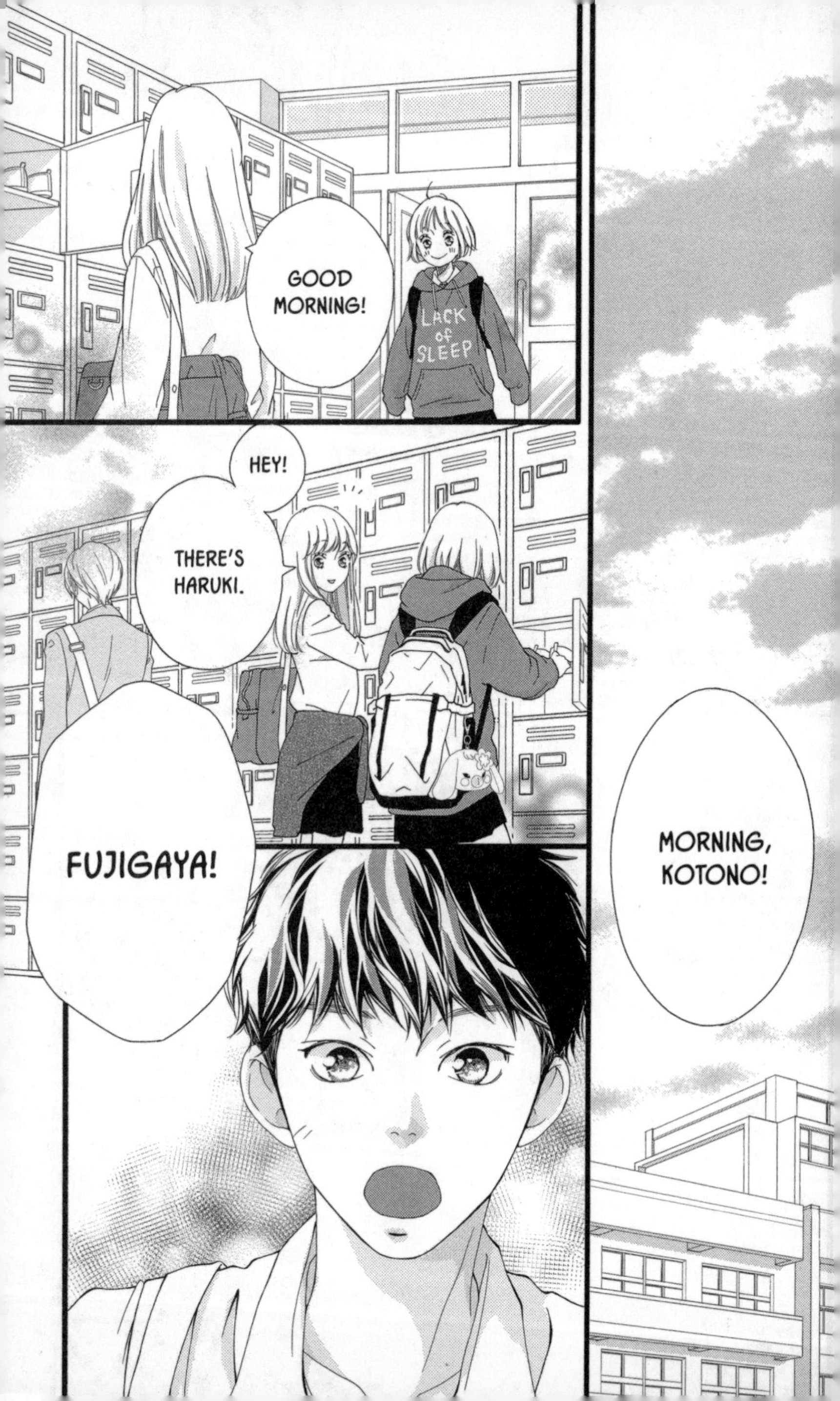
MORNING, KOTONO!
GOOD MORNING!
LACK of SLEEP
HEY!
THERE'S HARUKI.
FUJIGAYA!

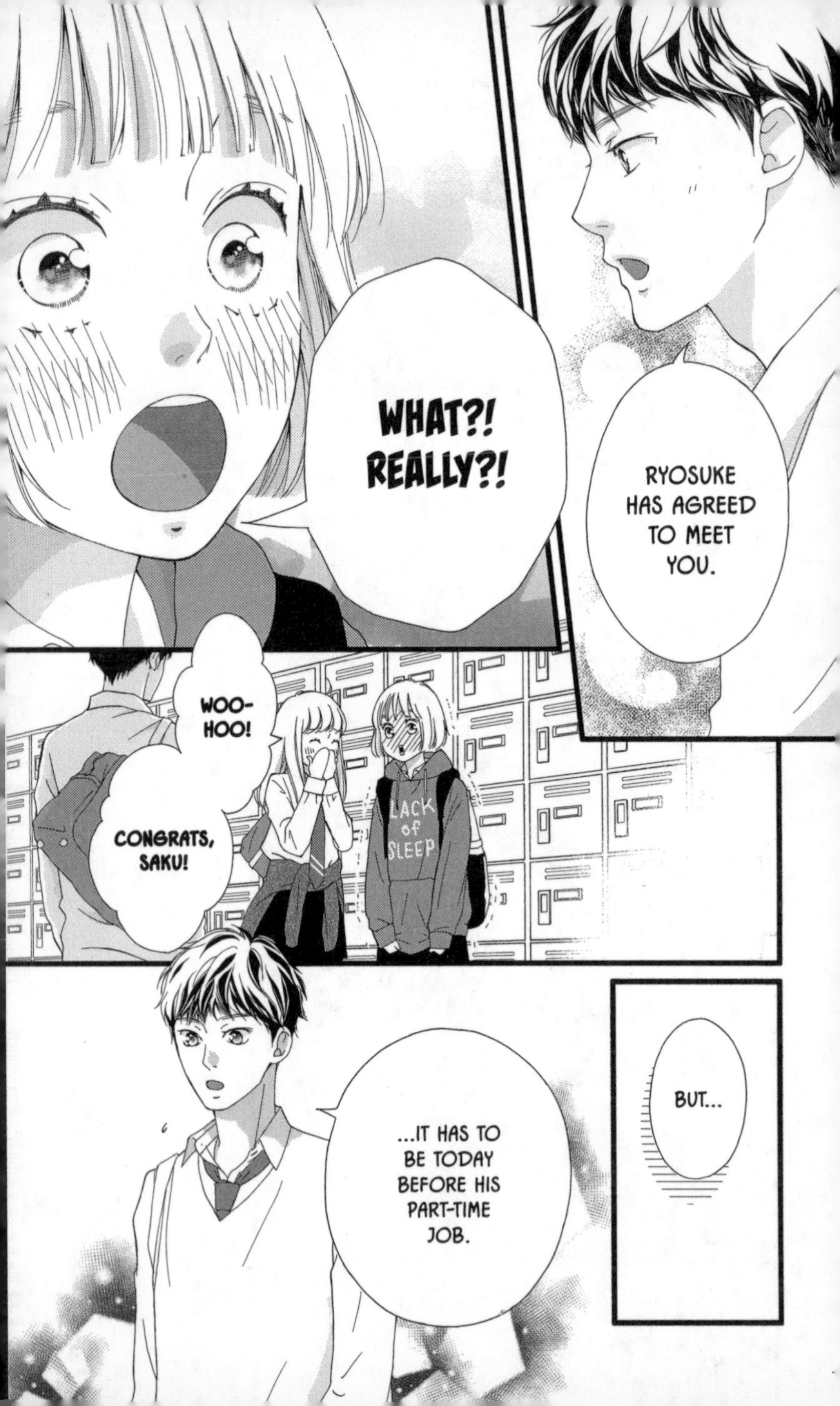
RYOSUKE HAS AGREED TO MEET YOU.
WHAT?! REALLY?!
WOO-HOO!
CONGRATS, SAKU!
BUT...
...IT HAS TO BE TODAY BEFORE HIS PART-TIME JOB.

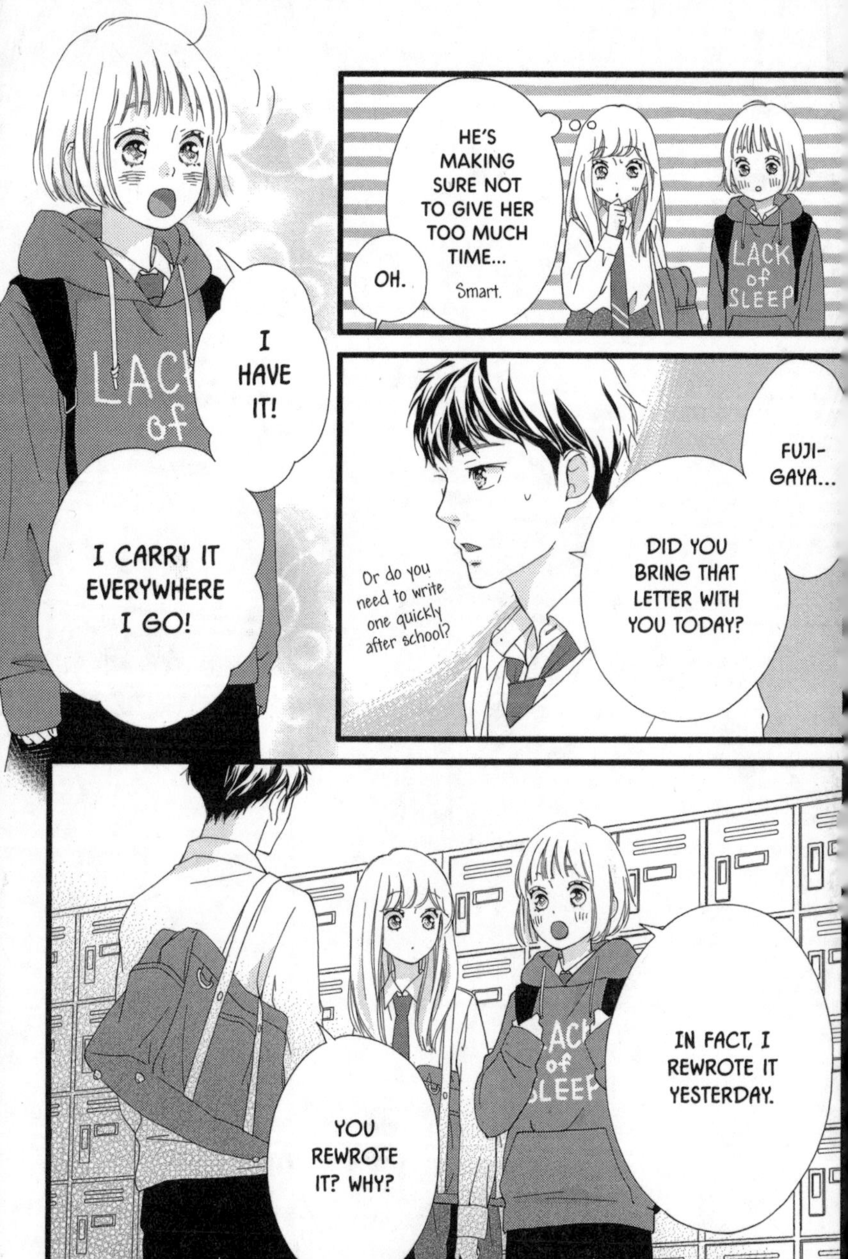
HE'S MAKING SURE NOT TO GIVE HER TOO MUCH TIME...
Smart.
OH.
FUJI-GAYA...
DID YOU BRING THAT LETTER WITH YOU TODAY?
Or do you need to write one quickly after school?
I HAVE IT!
I CARRY IT EVERYWHERE I GO!
IN FACT, I REWROTE IT YESTERDAY.
YOU REWROTE IT? WHY?

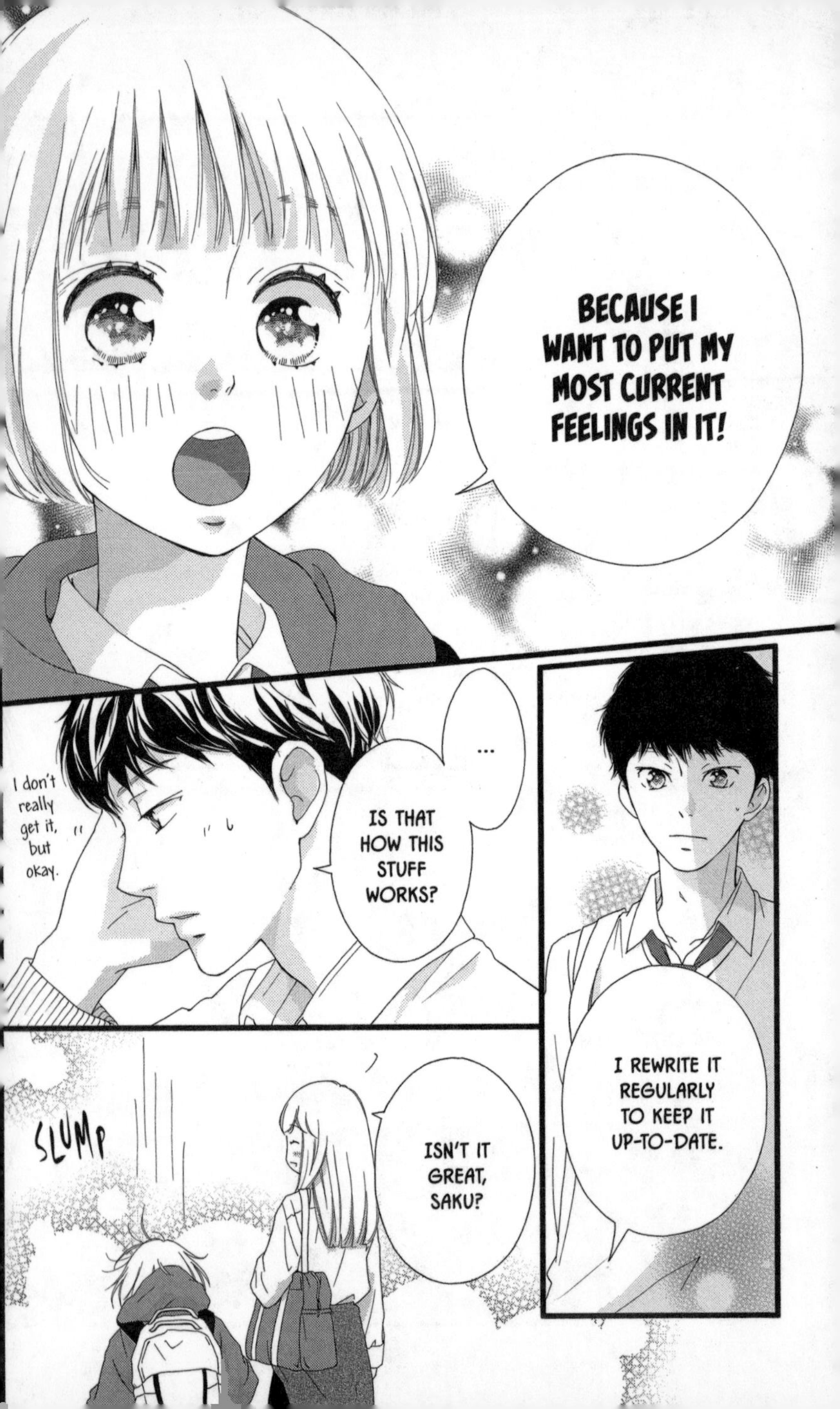
BECAUSE I WANT TO PUT MY MOST CURRENT FEELINGS IN IT!
I REWRITE IT REGULARLY TO KEEP IT UP-TO-DATE.
...
IS THAT HOW THIS STUFF WORKS?
I don't really get it, but okay.
ISN'T IT GREAT, SAKU?
SLUMP

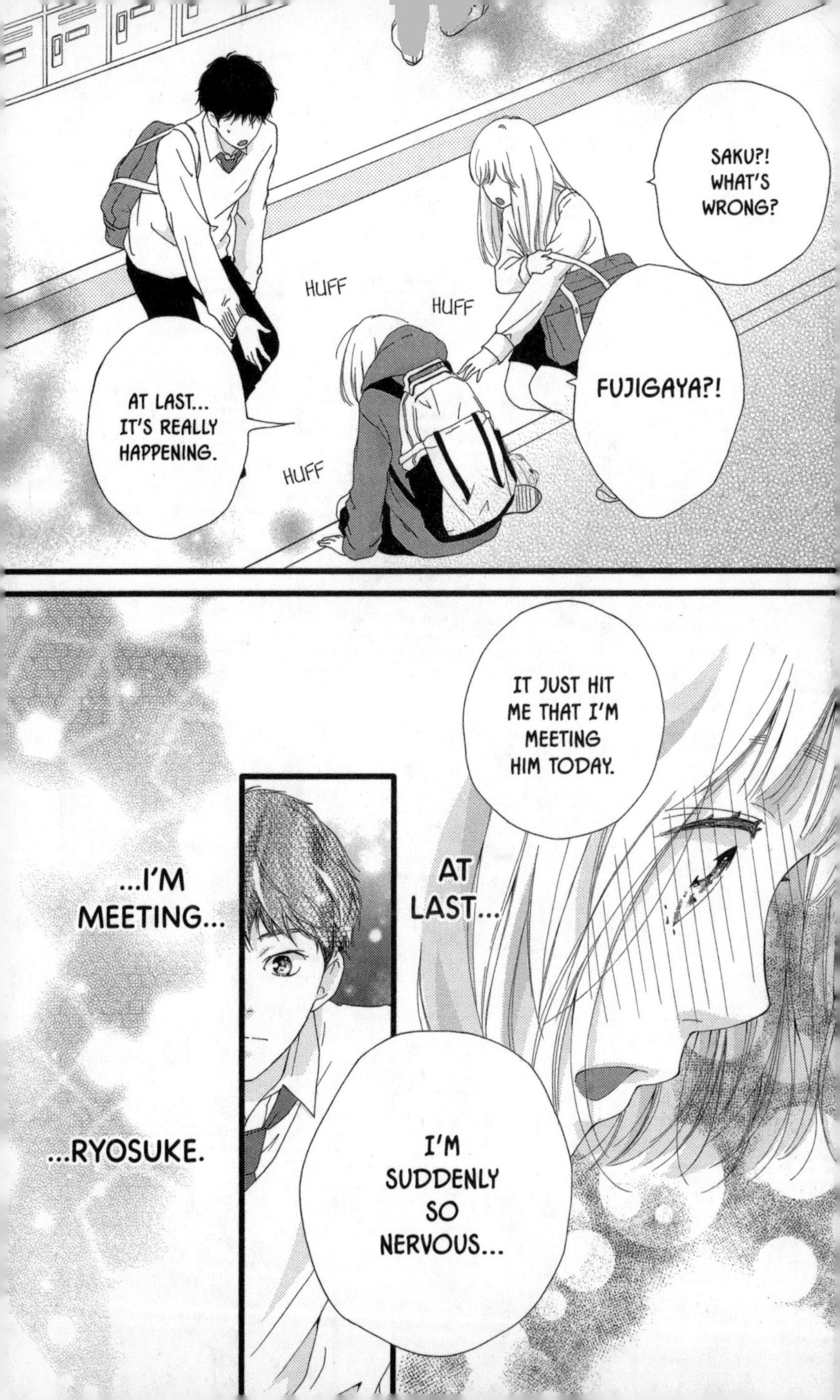
SAKU?! WHAT'S WRONG?
FUJIGAYA?!
HUFF
HUFF
HUFF
AT LAST... IT'S REALLY HAPPENING.
IT JUST HIT ME THAT I'M MEETING HIM TODAY.
I'M SUDDENLY SO NERVOUS...
AT LAST...
...I'M MEETING...
...RYOSUKE.

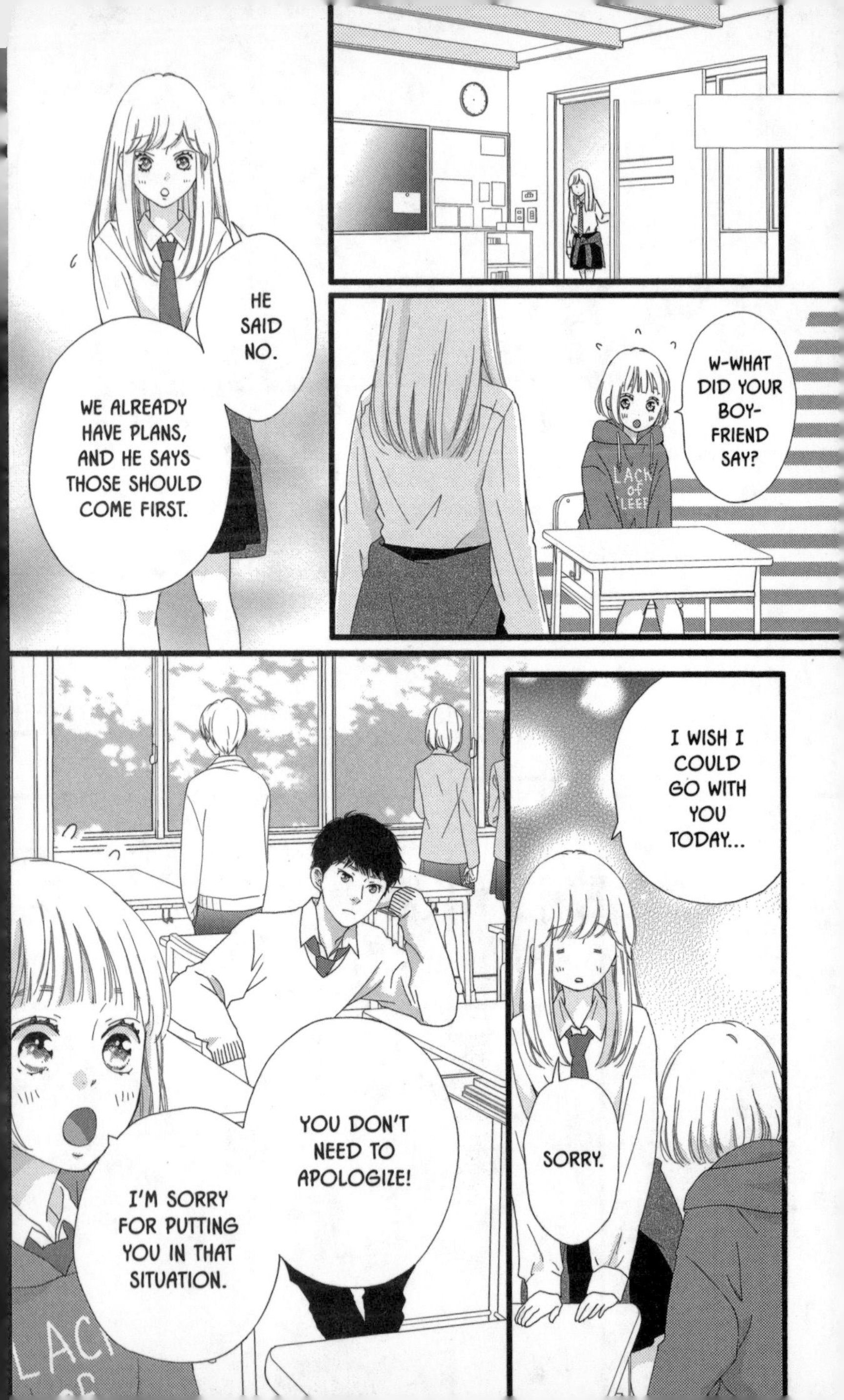
W-WHAT DID YOUR BOY-FRIEND SAY?
HE SAID NO.
WE ALREADY HAVE PLANS, AND HE SAYS THOSE SHOULD COME FIRST.
I WISH I COULD GO WITH YOU TODAY...
SORRY.
YOU DON'T NEED TO APOLOGIZE!
I'M SORRY FOR PUTTING YOU IN THAT SITUATION.

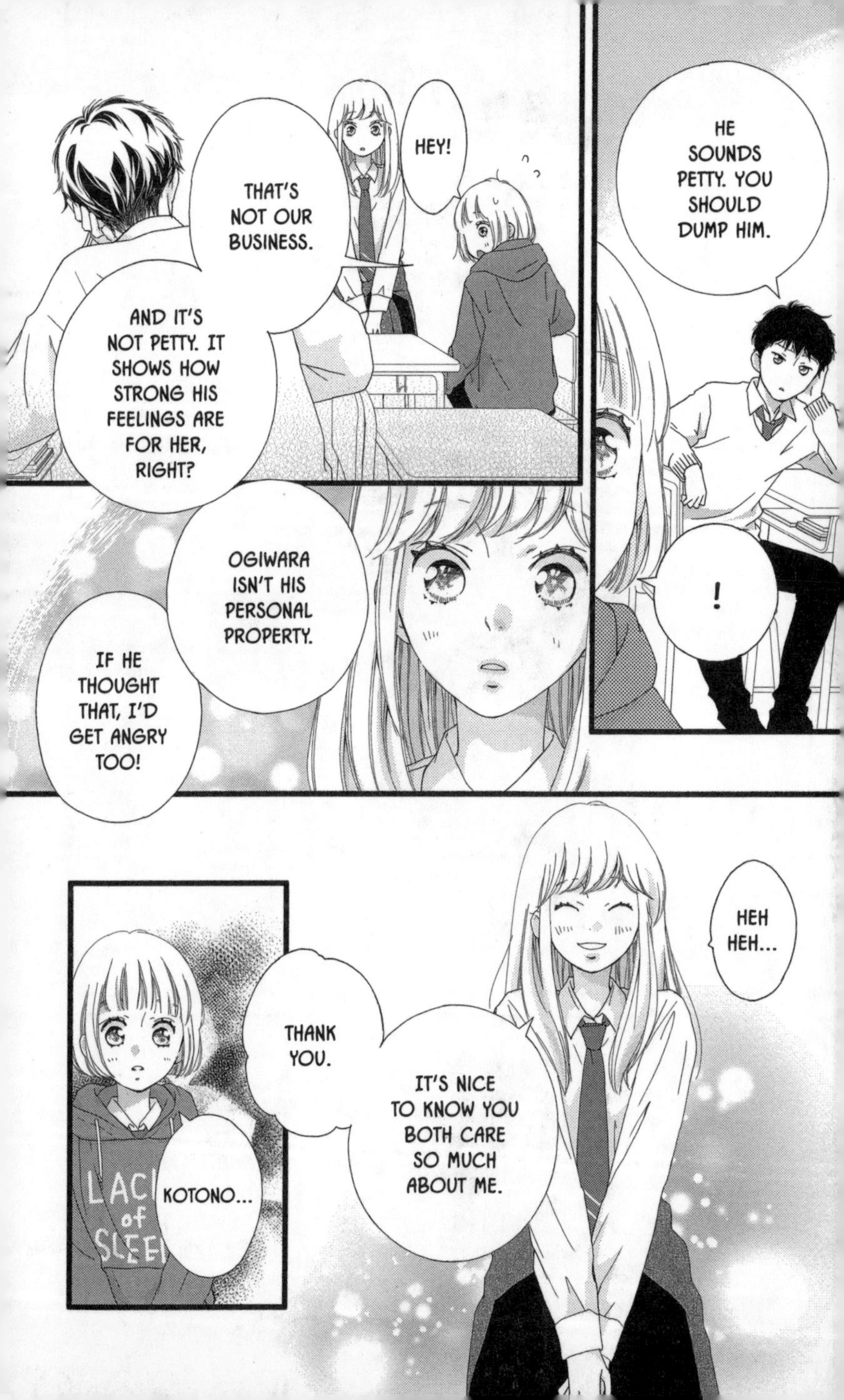
HE SOUNDS PETTY. YOU SHOULD DUMP HIM.
!
HEY!
THAT'S NOT OUR BUSINESS.
AND IT'S NOT PETTY. IT SHOWS HOW STRONG HIS FEELINGS ARE FOR HER, RIGHT?
OGIWARA ISN'T HIS PERSONAL PROPERTY.
IF HE THOUGHT THAT, I'D GET ANGRY TOO!
HEH HEH...
THANK YOU.
IT'S NICE TO KNOW YOU BOTH CARE SO MUCH ABOUT ME.
KOTONO...
LACK of SLEEP

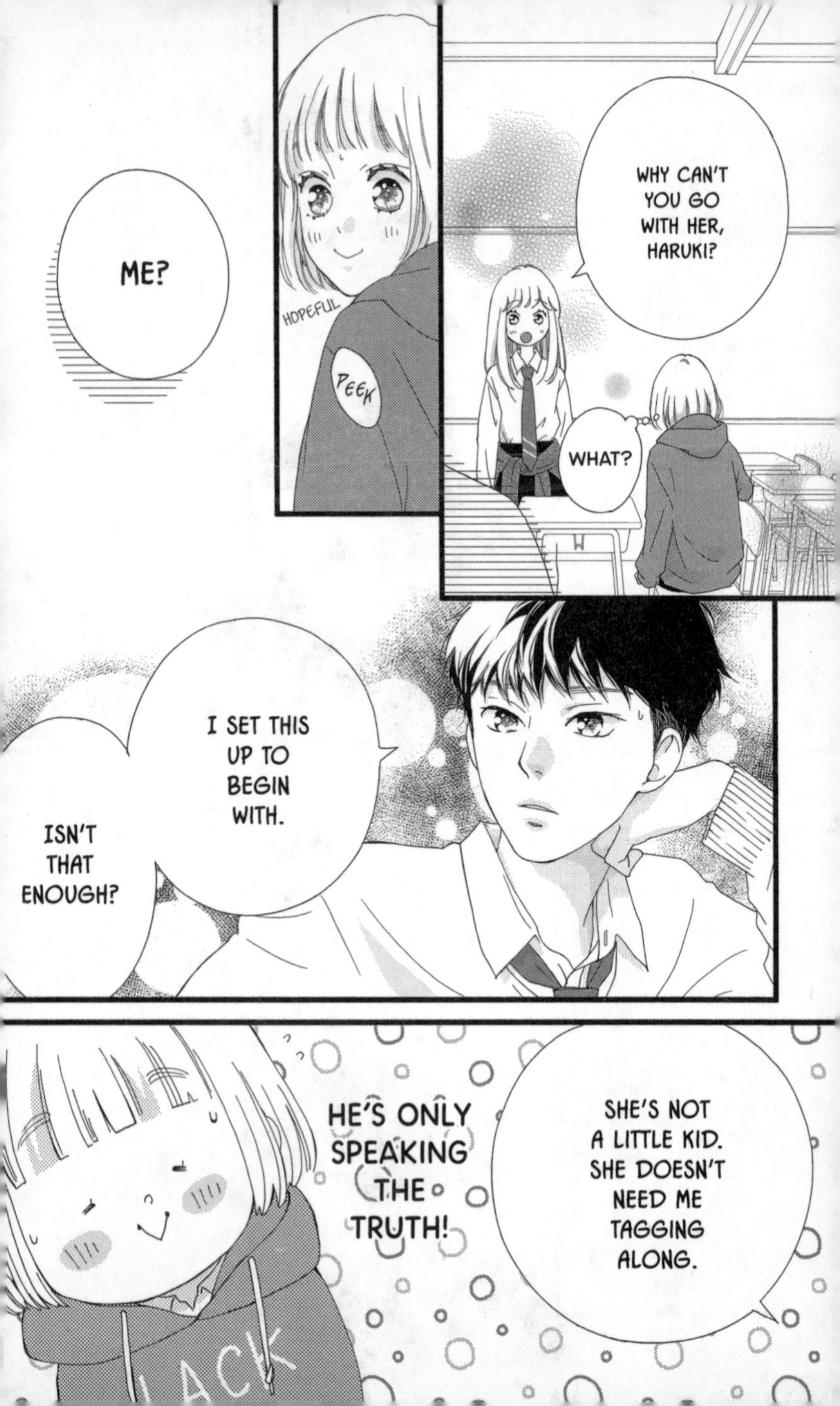
WHY CAN'T YOU GO WITH HER, HARUKI?
WHAT?
HOPEFUL
PEEK
ME?
I SET THIS UP TO BEGIN WITH.
ISN'T THAT ENOUGH?
SHE'S NOT A LITTLE KID. SHE DOESN'T NEED ME TAGGING ALONG.
HE'S ONLY SPEAKING THE TRUTH!

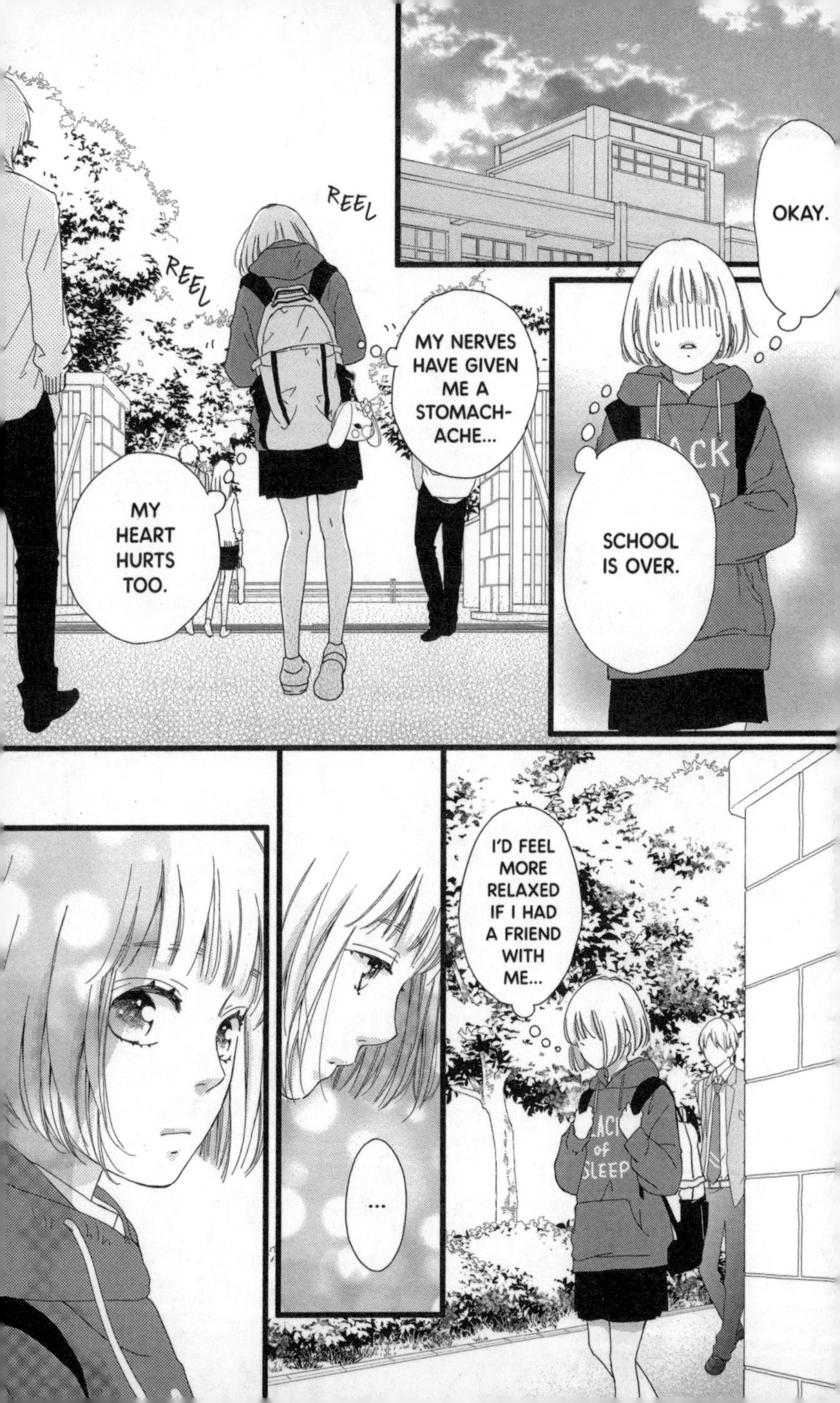
OKAY.
SCHOOL IS OVER.
REEL
REEL
MY NERVES HAVE GIVEN ME A STOMACH-ACHE...
MY HEART HURTS TOO.
I'D FEEL MORE RELAXED IF I HAD A FRIEND WITH ME...
...

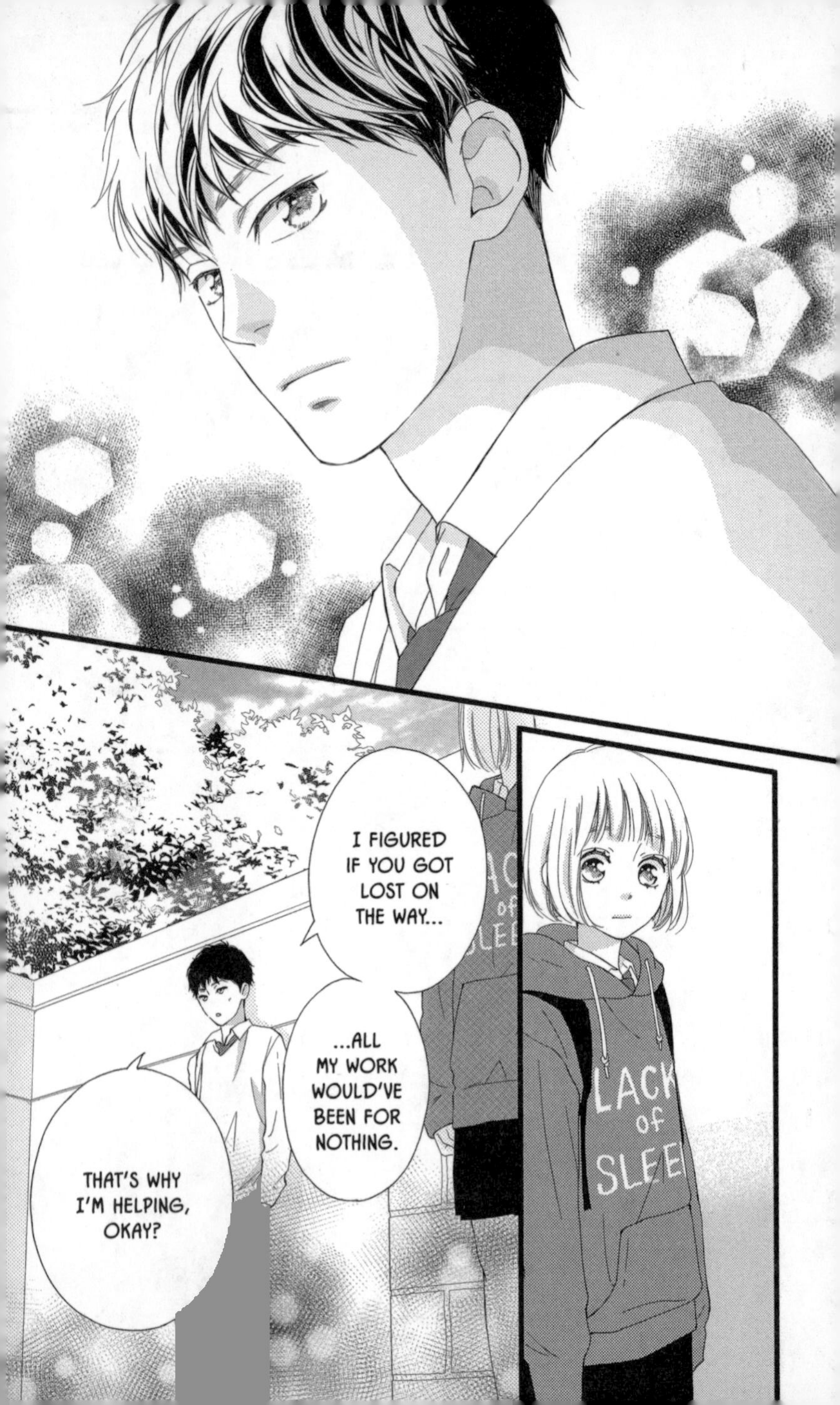
I FIGURED IF YOU GOT LOST ON THE WAY...
...ALL MY WORK WOULD'VE BEEN FOR NOTHING.
THAT'S WHY I'M HELPING, OKAY?
LACK of SLEEP

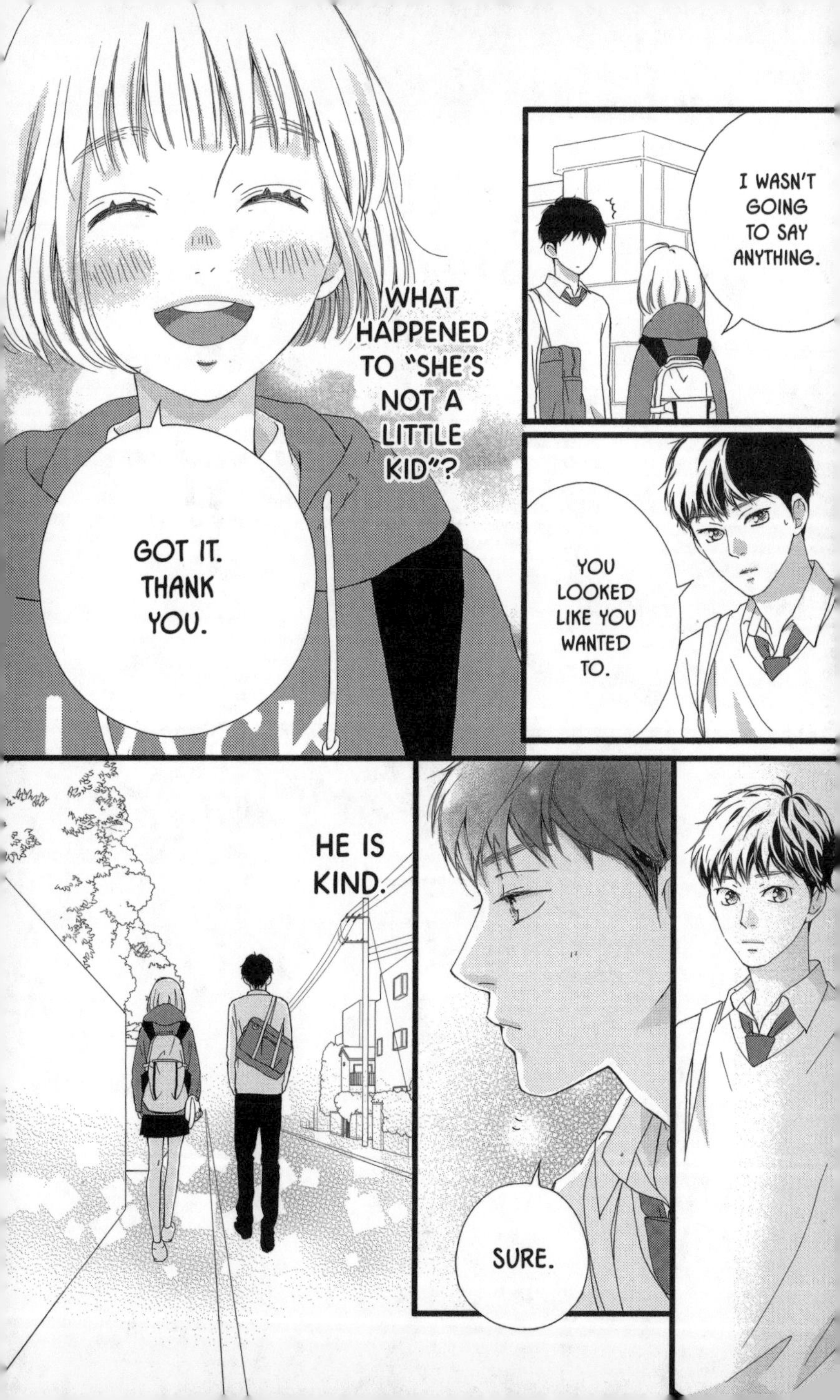
I WASN'T GOING TO SAY ANYTHING.
YOU LOOKED LIKE YOU WANTED TO.
WHAT HAPPENED TO "SHE'S NOT A LITTLE KID"?
GOT IT. THANK YOU.
SURE.
HE IS KIND.

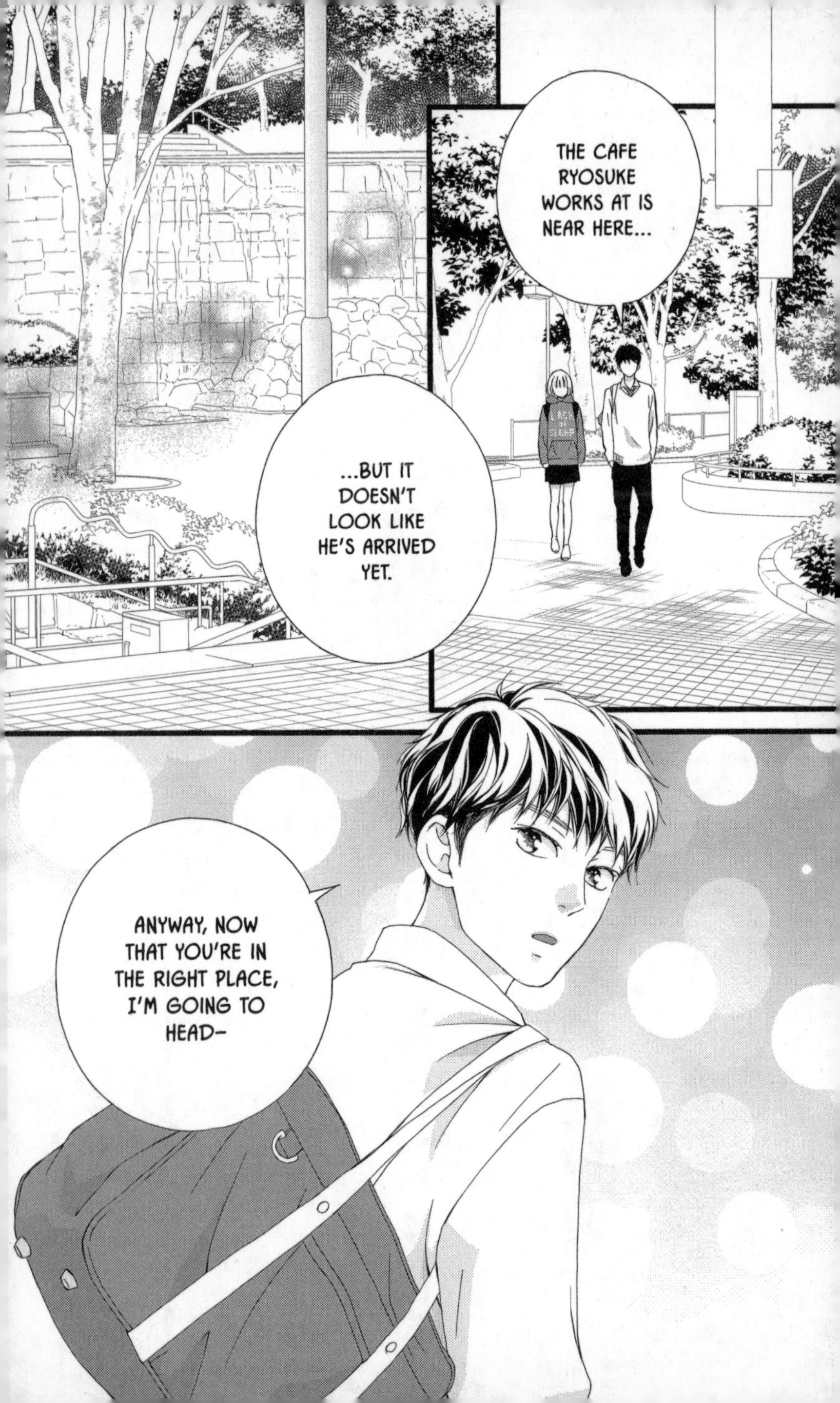
THE CAFE RYOSUKE WORKS AT IS NEAR HERE...
...BUT IT DOESN'T LOOK LIKE HE'S ARRIVED YET.
ANYWAY, NOW THAT YOU'RE IN THE RIGHT PLACE, I'M GOING TO HEAD-

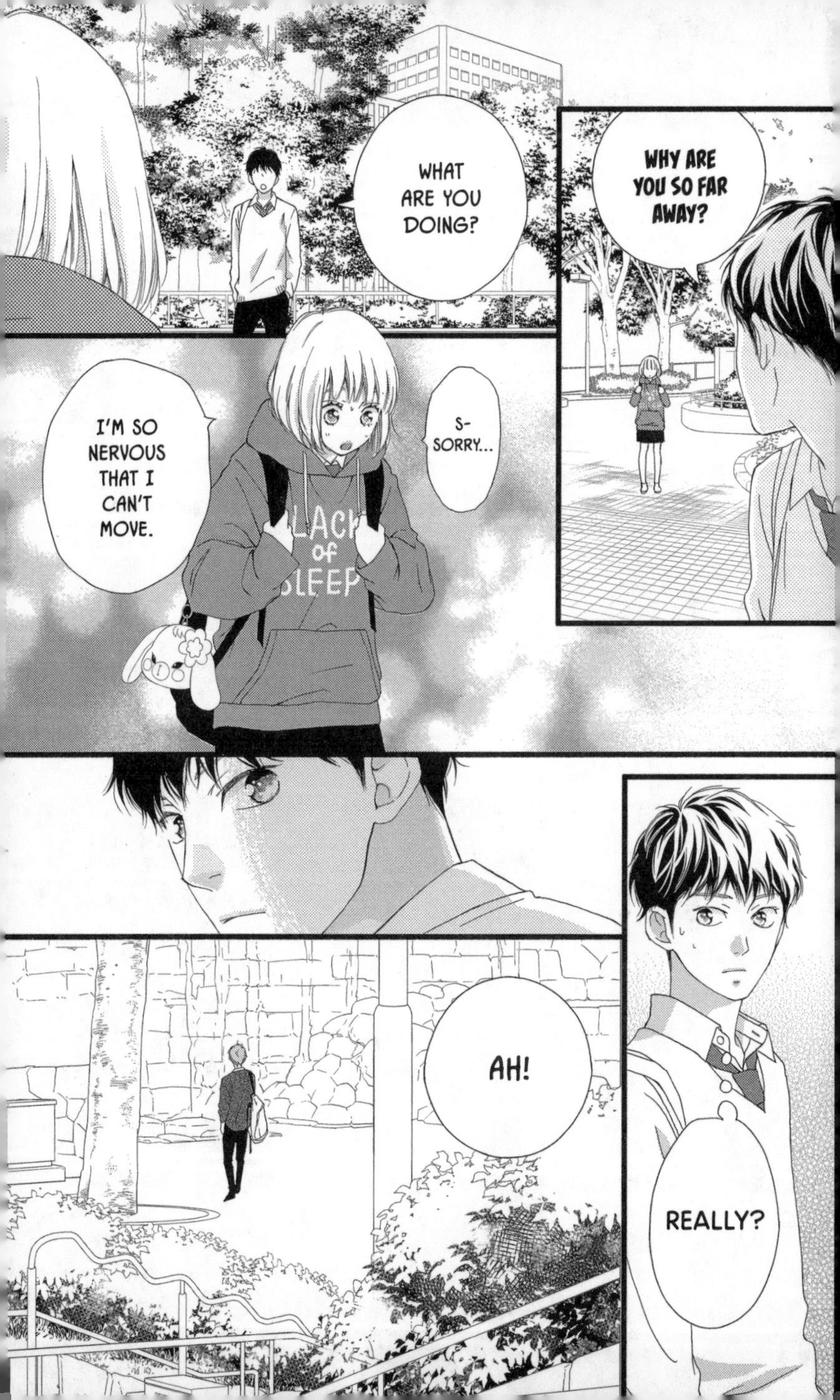
WHAT ARE YOU DOING?
WHY ARE YOU SO FAR AWAY?
S-SORRY...
I'M SO NERVOUS THAT I CAN'T MOVE.
LACK of SLEEP
AH!
REALLY?

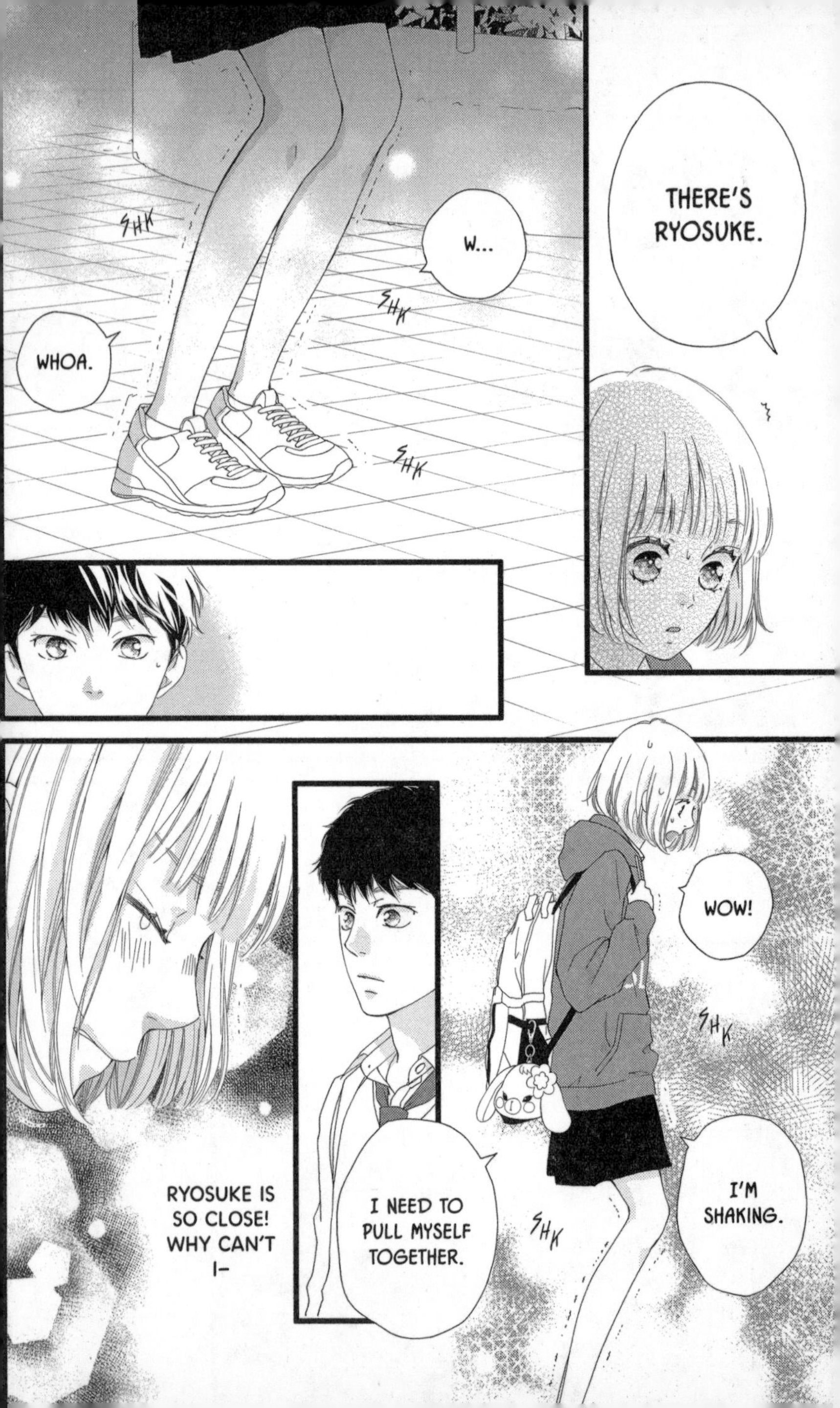
THERE'S RYOSUKE.
SHK
W...
SHK
SHK
WHOA.
WOW!
SHK
I'M SHAKING.
SHK
I NEED TO PULL MYSELF TOGETHER.
RYOSUKE IS SO CLOSE! WHY CAN'T I–

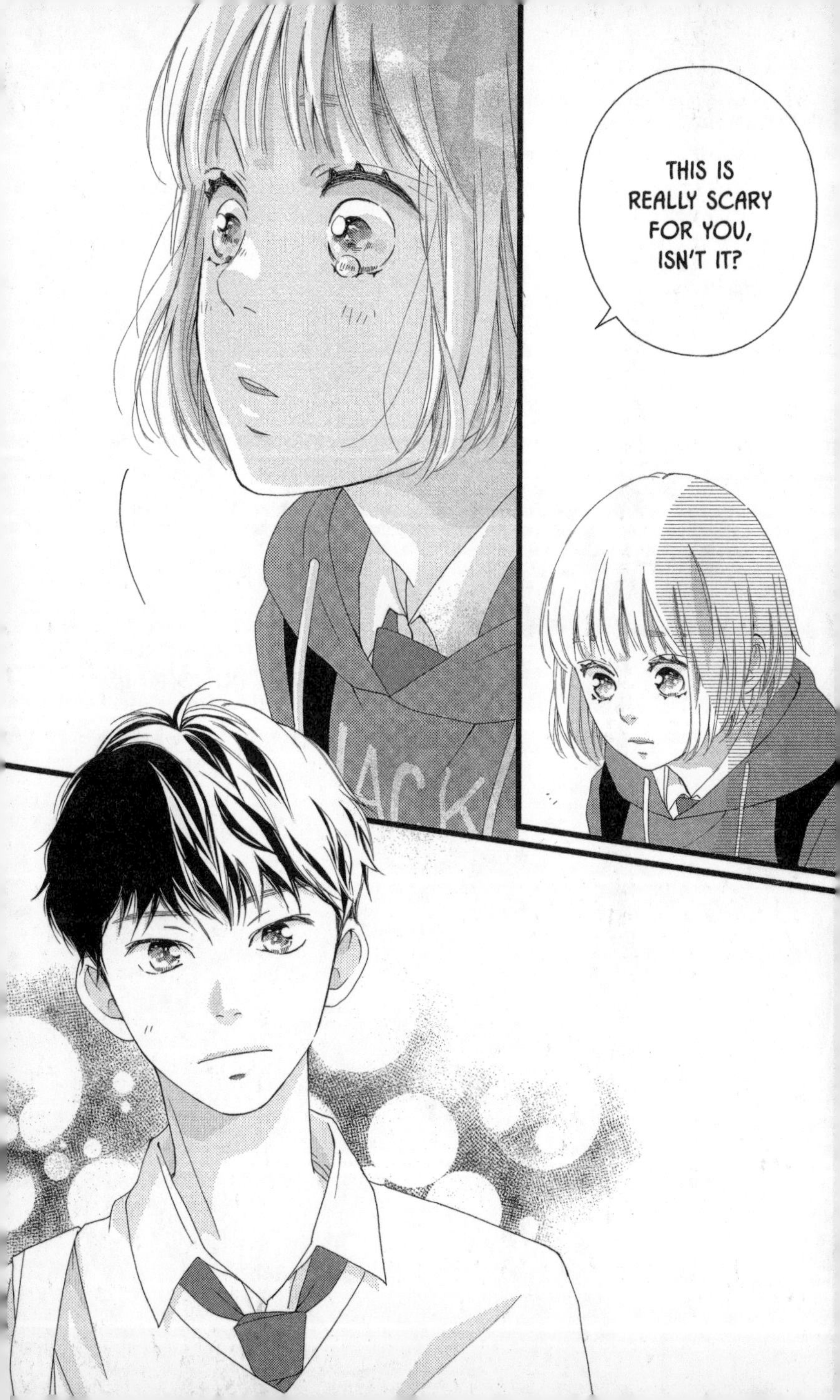
THIS IS REALLY SCARY FOR YOU, ISN'T IT?

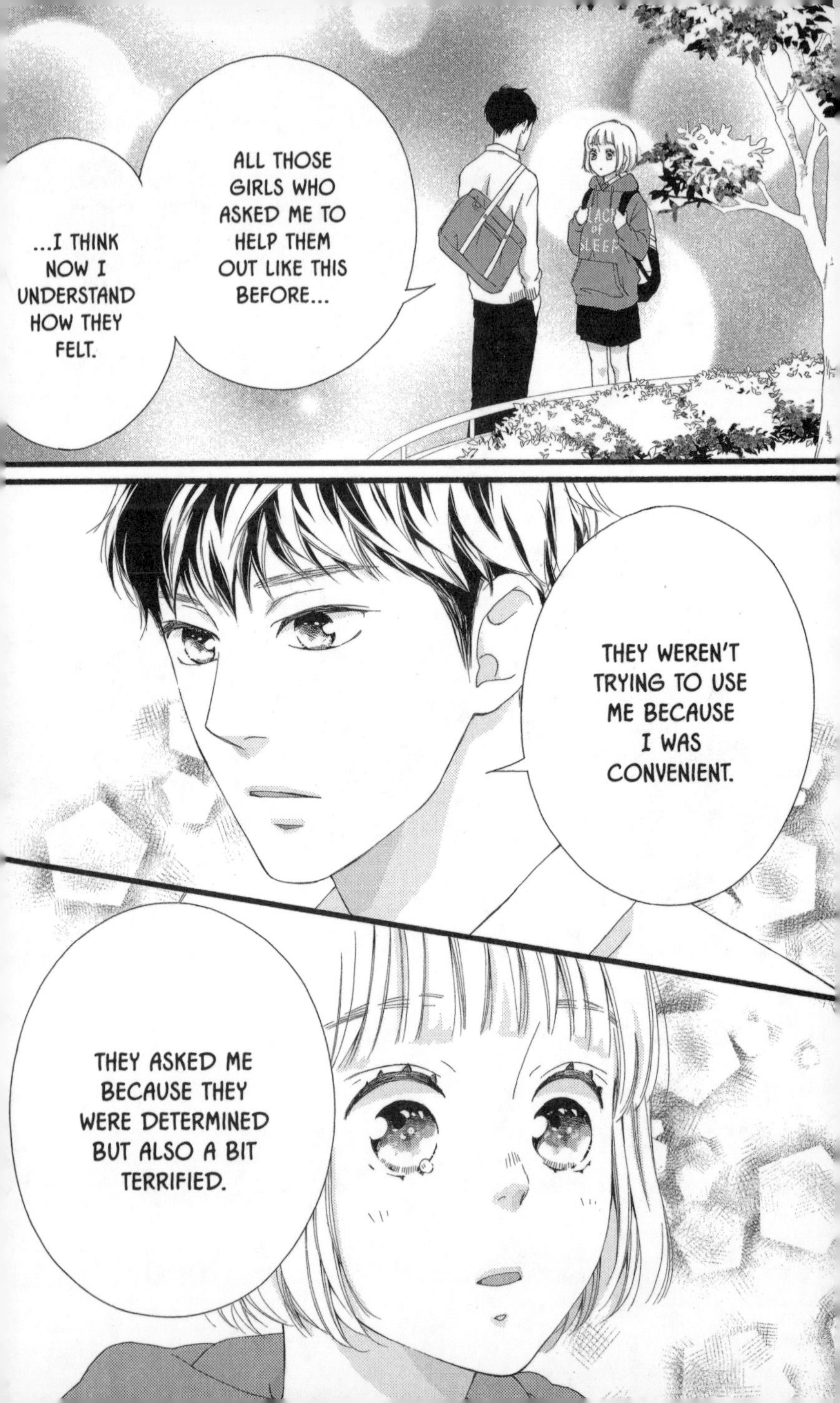
ALL THOSE GIRLS WHO ASKED ME TO HELP THEM OUT LIKE THIS BEFORE...
...I THINK NOW I UNDERSTAND HOW THEY FELT.
THEY WEREN'T TRYING TO USE ME BECAUSE I WAS CONVENIENT.
THEY ASKED ME BECAUSE THEY WERE DETERMINED BUT ALSO A BIT TERRIFIED.

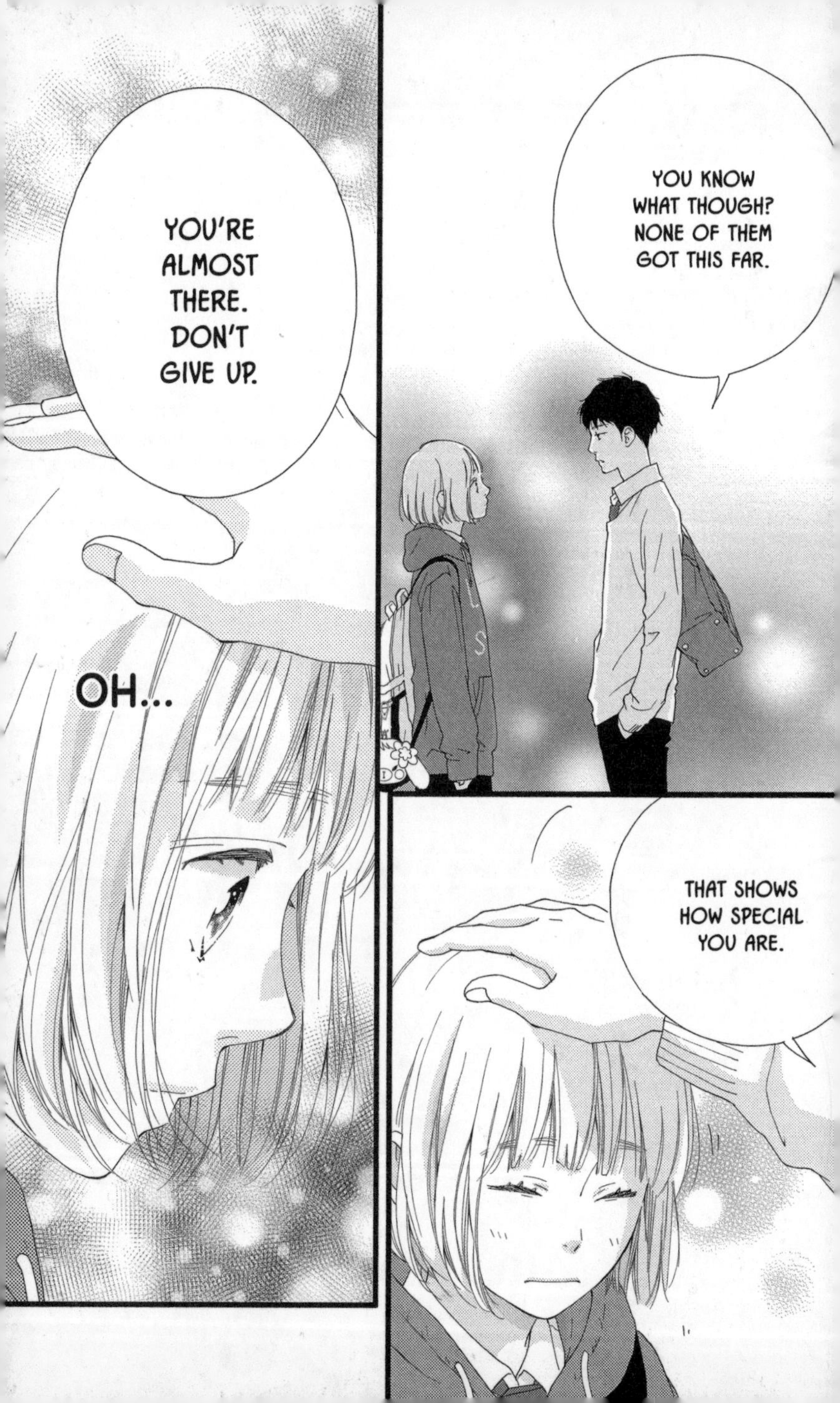
YOU KNOW WHAT THOUGH? NONE OF THEM GOT THIS FAR.
THAT SHOWS HOW SPECIAL YOU ARE.
YOU'RE ALMOST THERE. DON'T GIVE UP.
OH...

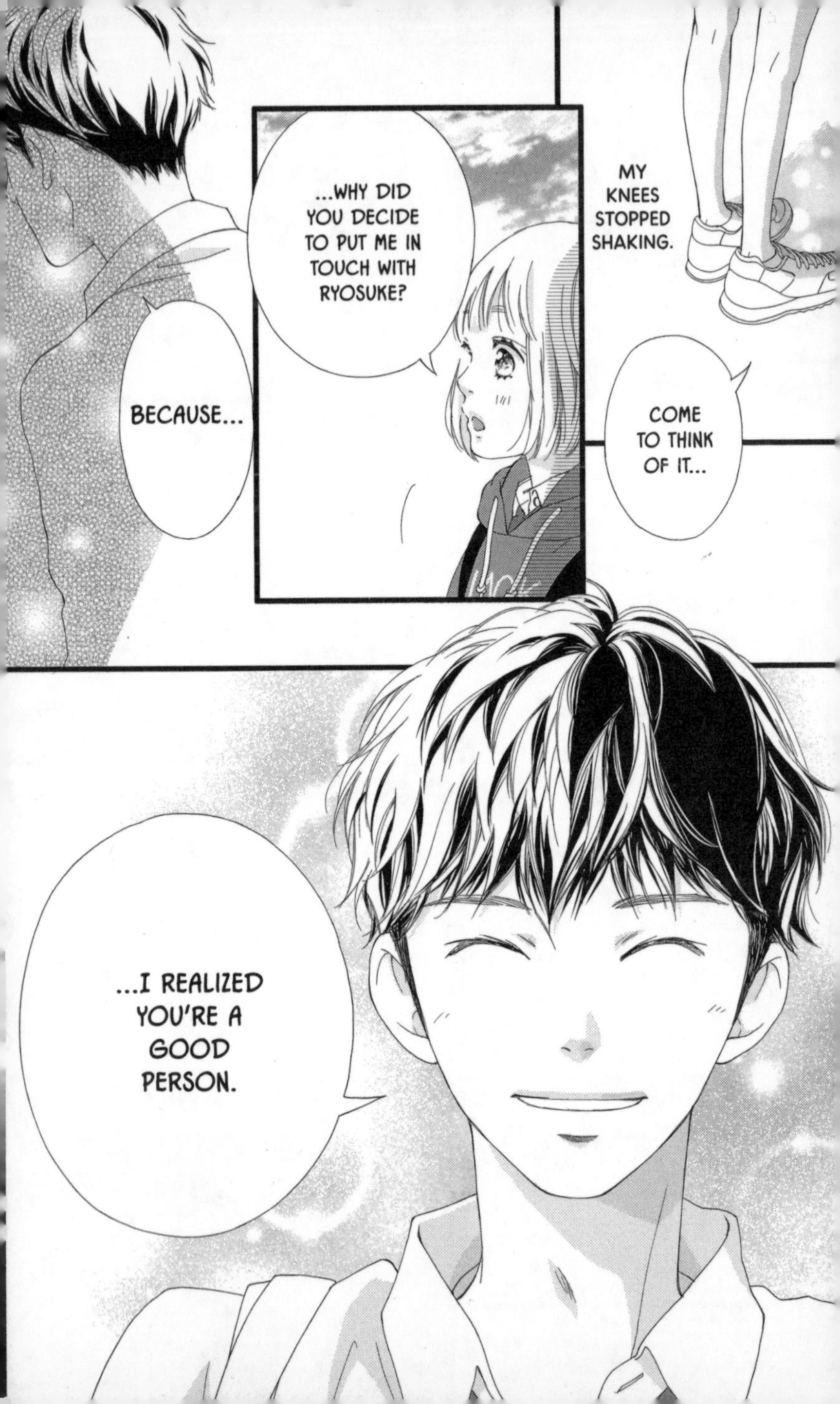

MY KNEES STOPPED SHAKING.
COME TO THINK OF IT...
...WHY DID YOU DECIDE TO PUT ME IN TOUCH WITH RYOSUKE?
BECAUSE...
...I REALIZED YOU'RE A GOOD PERSON.

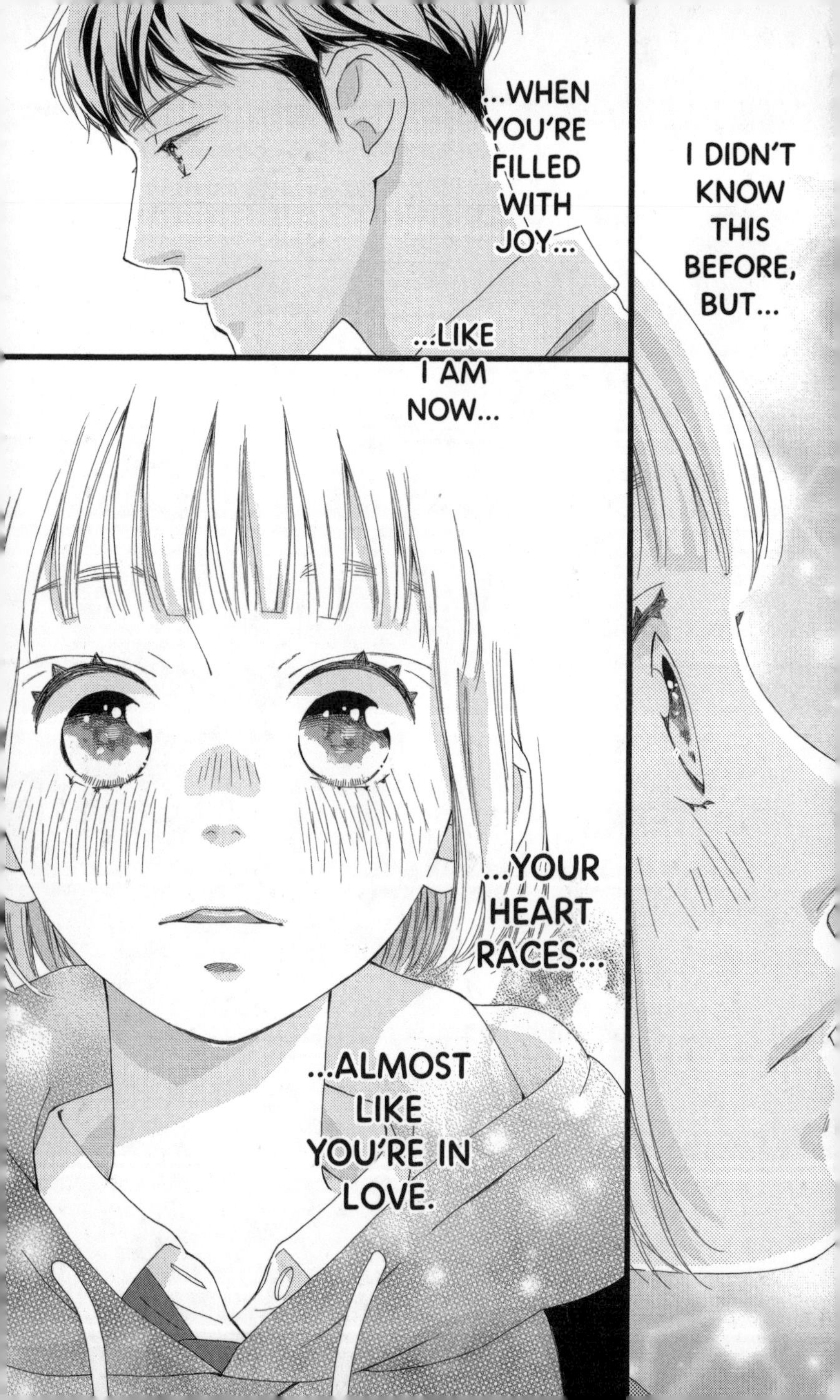
I DIDN'T KNOW THIS BEFORE, BUT...
...WHEN YOU'RE FILLED WITH JOY...
...LIKE I AM NOW...
...YOUR HEART RACES...
...ALMOST LIKE YOU'RE IN LOVE.

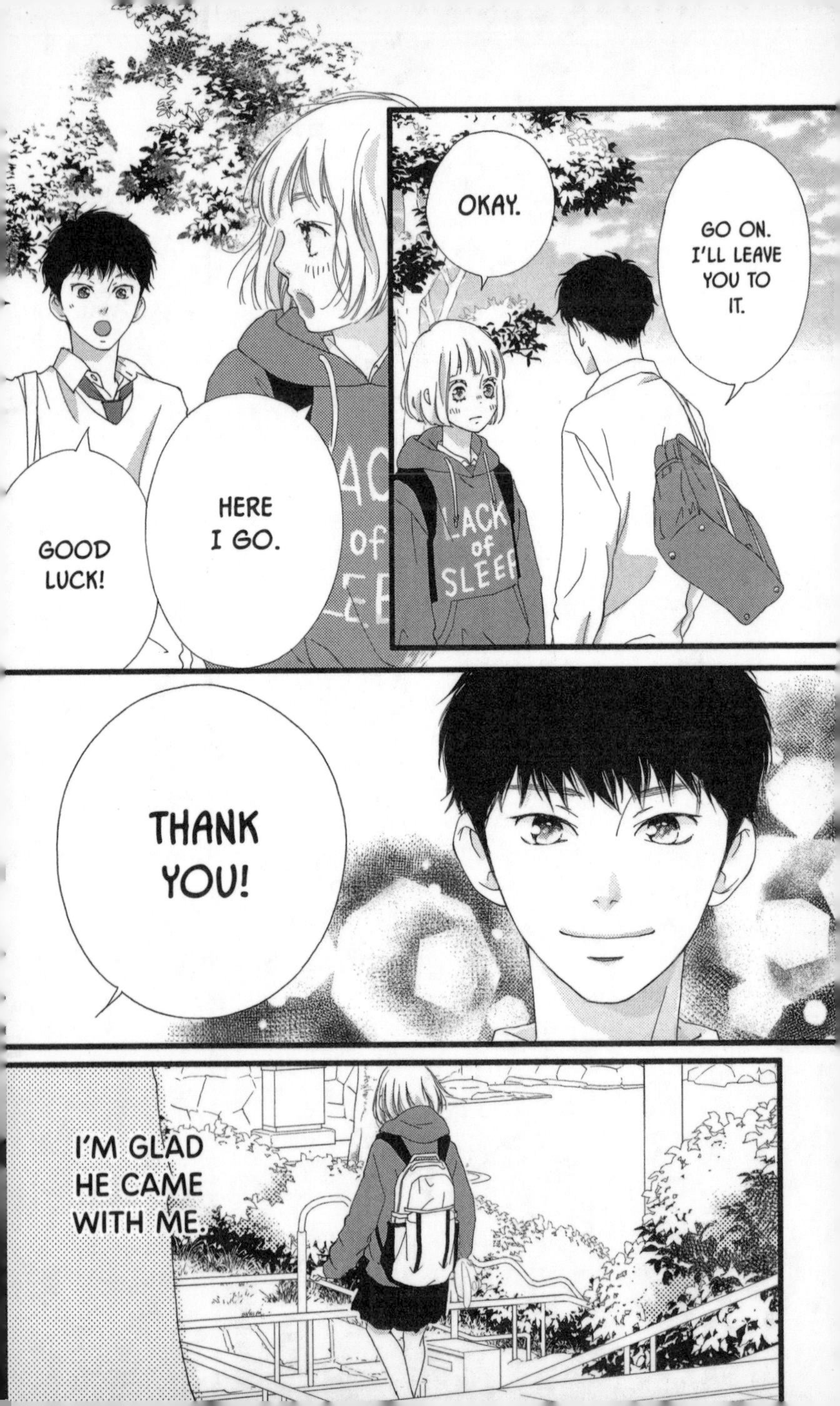
GO ON. I'LL LEAVE YOU TO IT.
OKAY.
HERE I GO.
GOOD LUCK!
THANK YOU!
I'M GLAD HE CAME WITH ME.

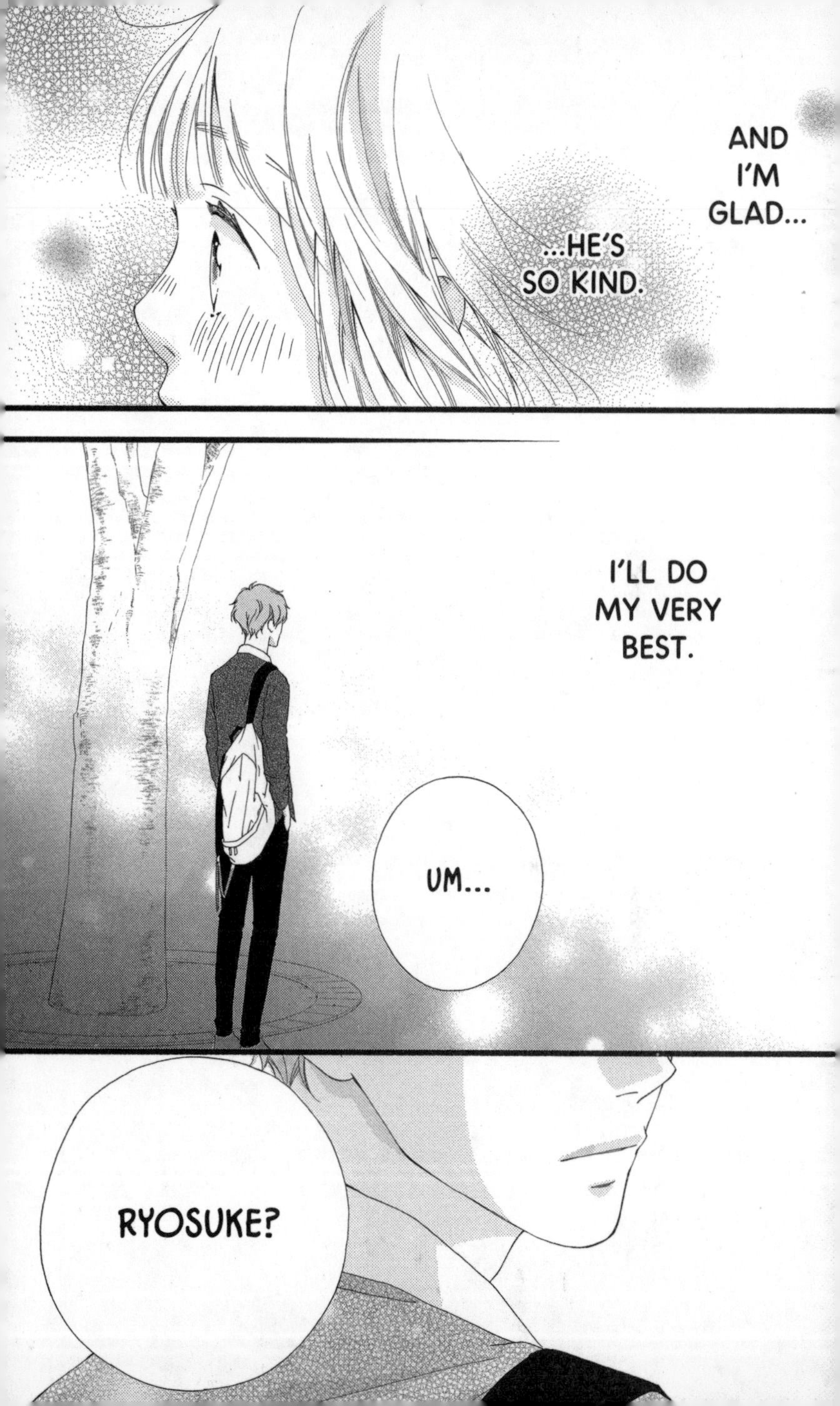
AND I'M GLAD...
...HE'S SO KIND.
I'LL DO MY VERY BEST.
UM...
RYOSUKE?

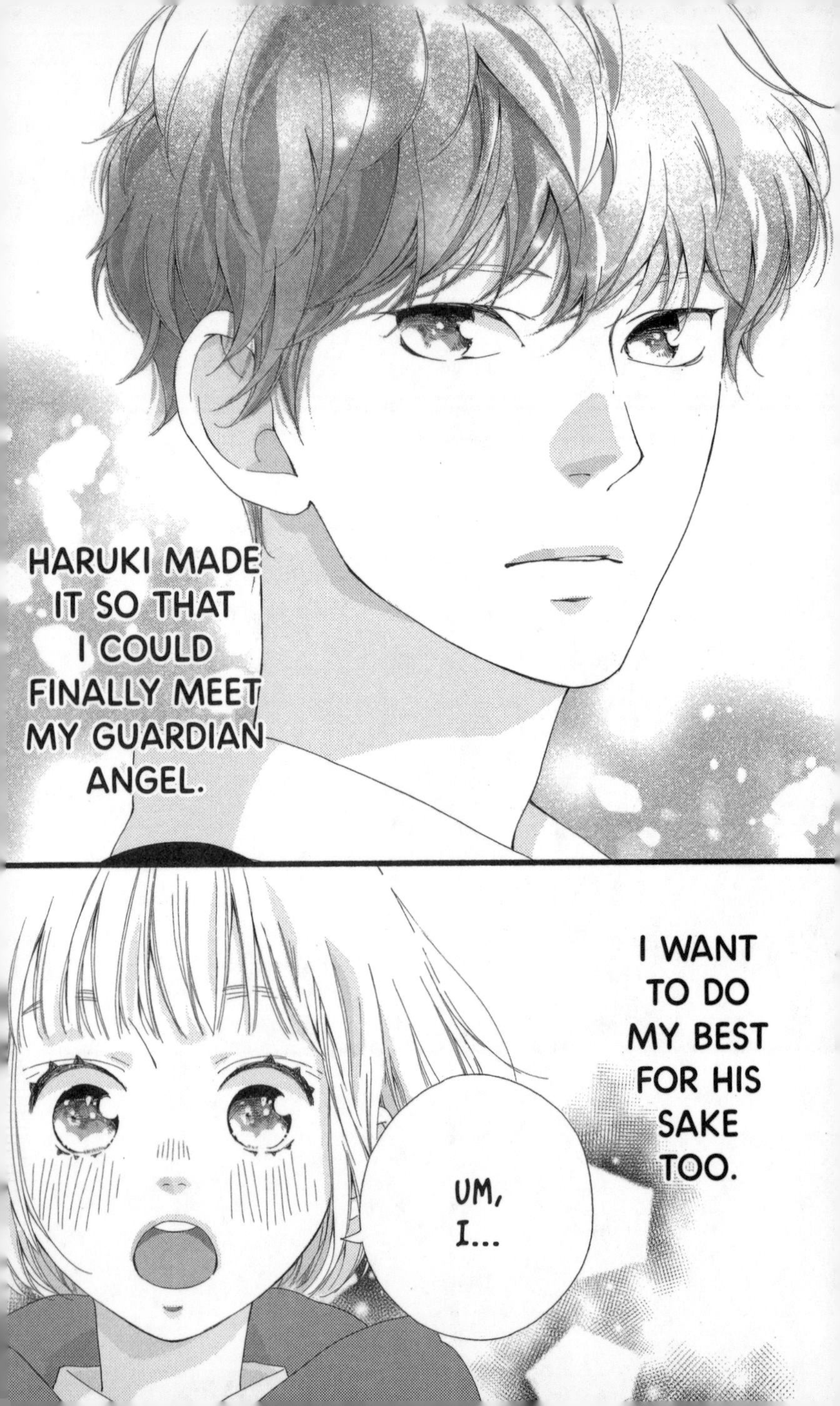
HARUKI MADE IT SO THAT I COULD FINALLY MEET MY GUARDIAN ANGEL.
I WANT TO DO MY BEST FOR HIS SAKE TOO.
UM, I...

Bloom 3

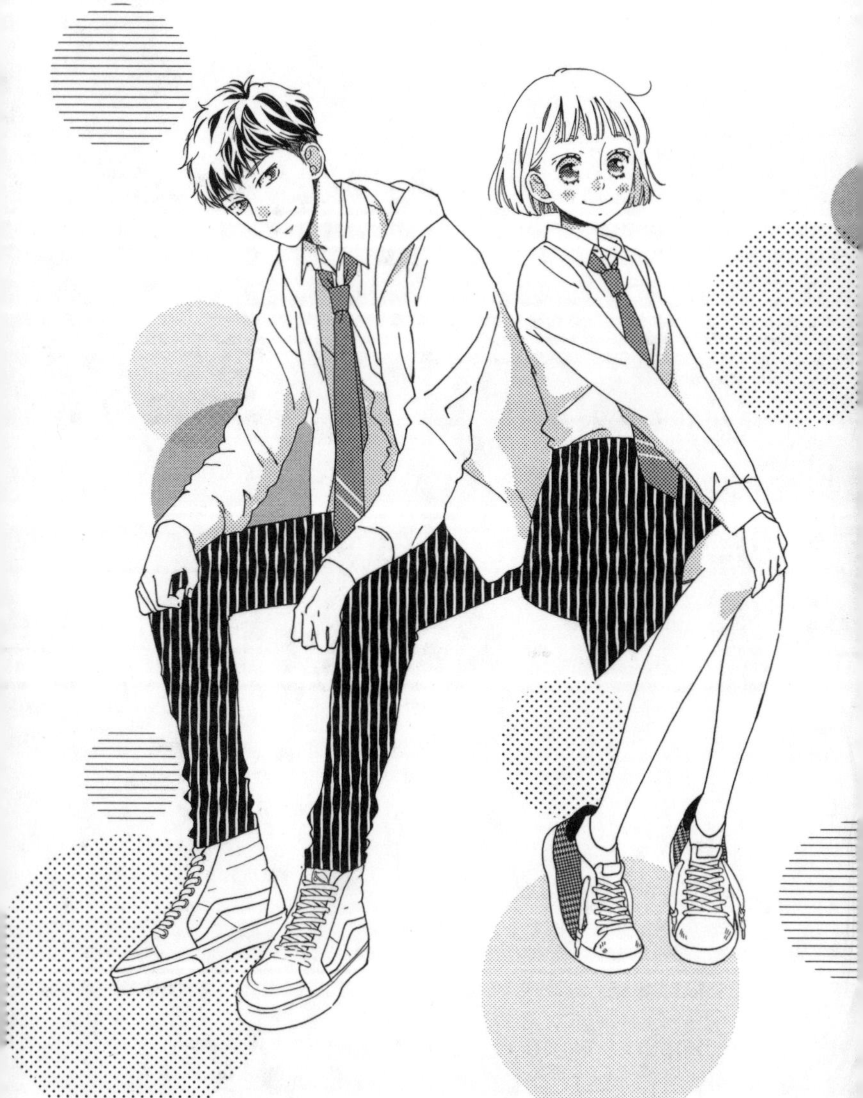

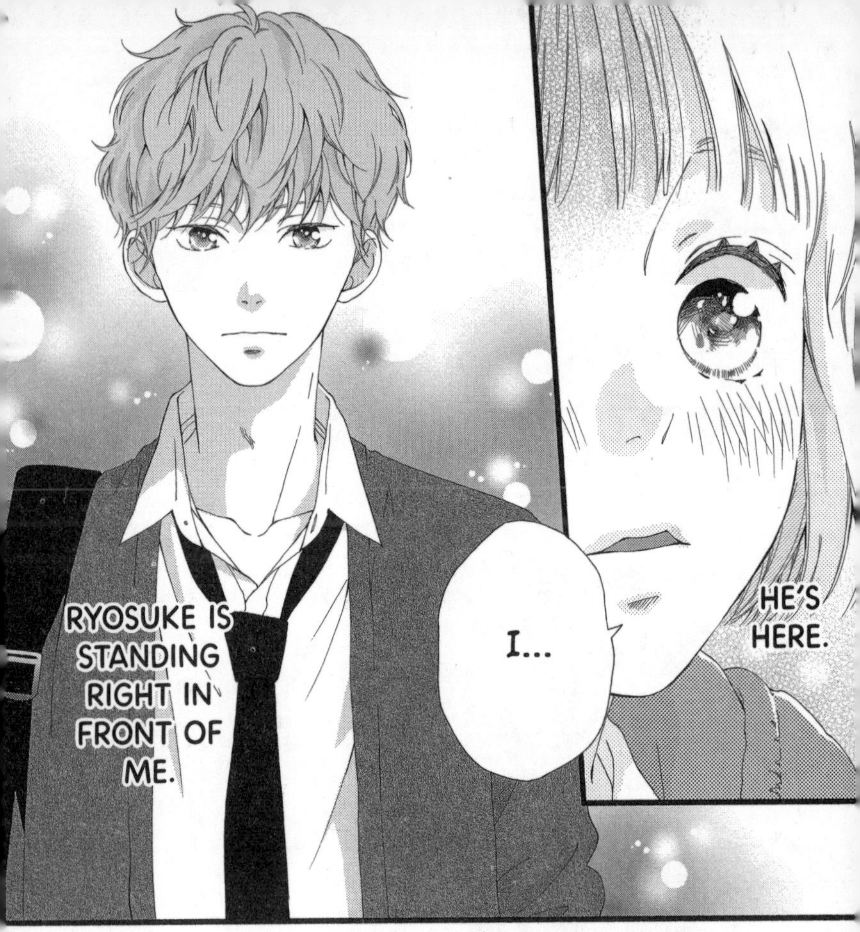
HE'S HERE.
I...
RYOSUKE IS STANDING RIGHT IN FRONT OF ME.
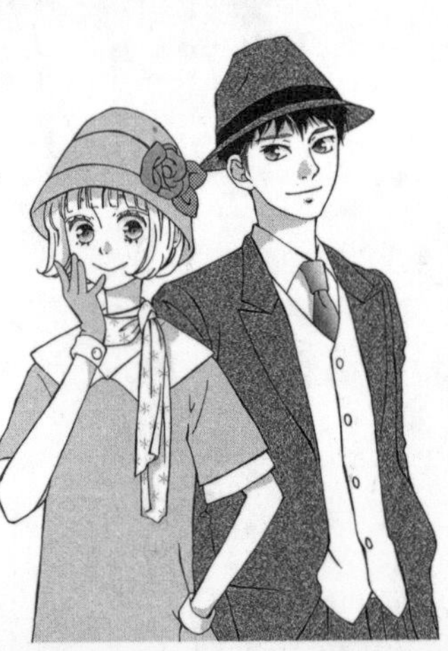

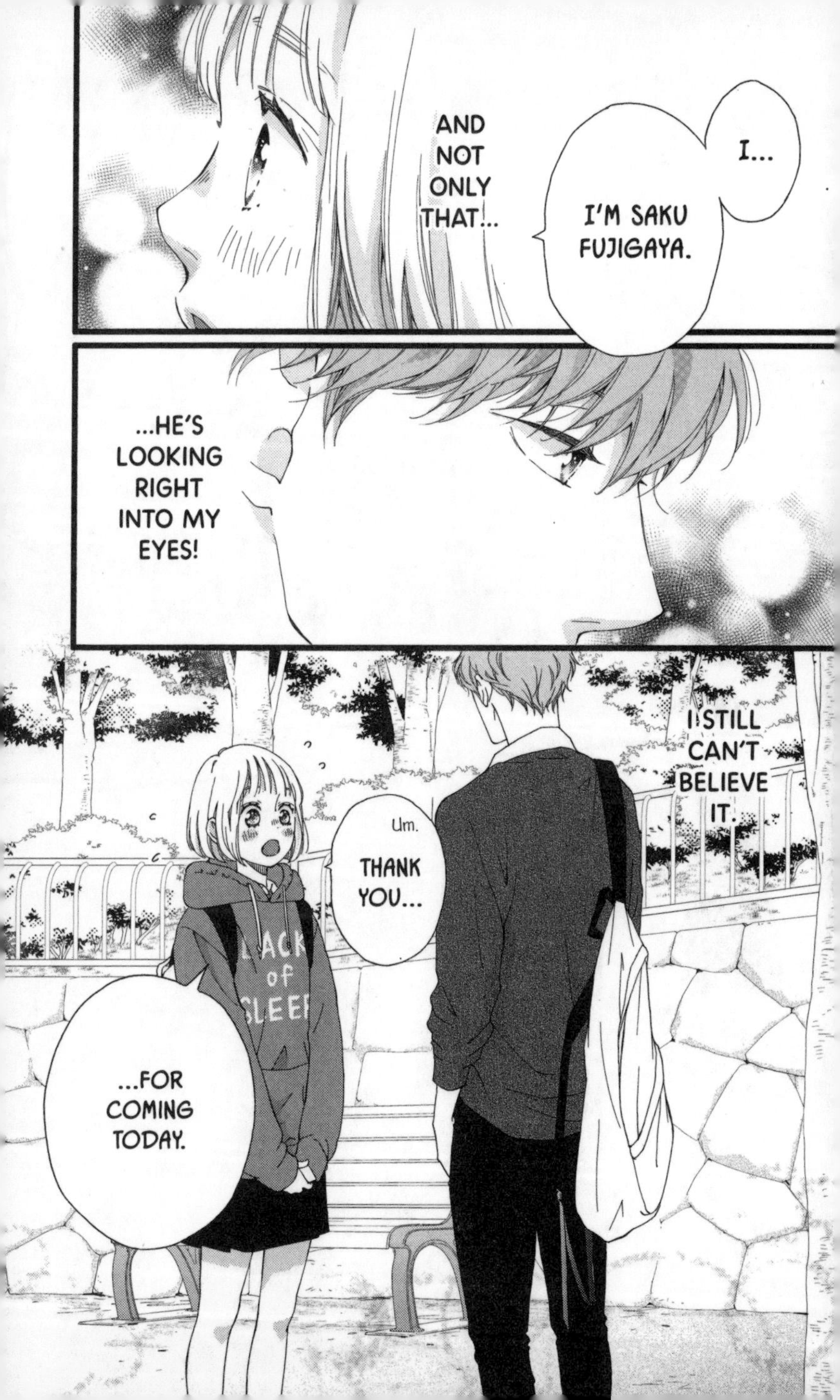
I...
I'M SAKU FUJIGAYA.
AND NOT ONLY THAT...
...HE'S LOOKING RIGHT INTO MY EYES!
I STILL CAN'T BELIEVE IT.
Um.
THANK YOU...
...FOR COMING TODAY.

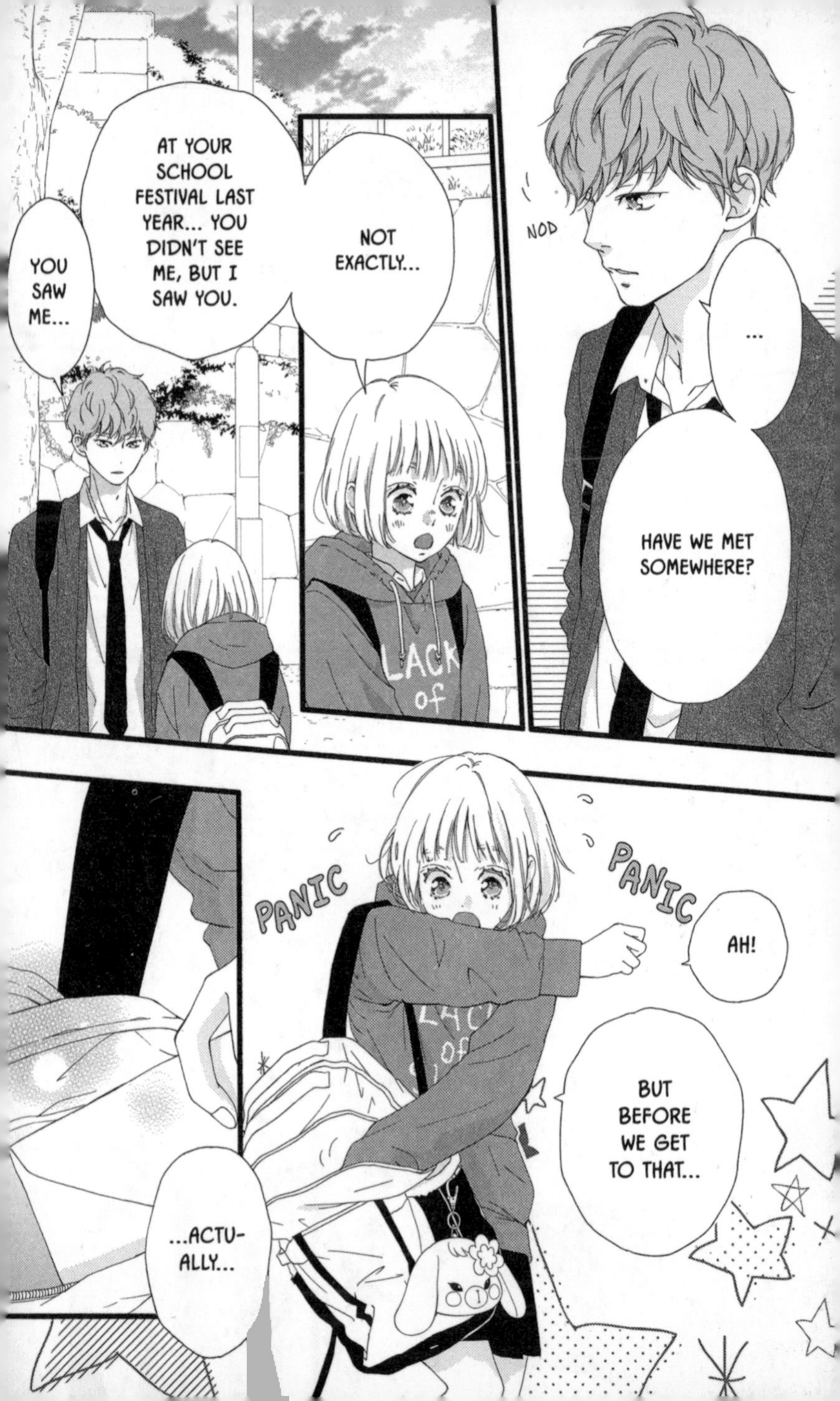
NOD
...
HAVE WE MET SOMEWHERE?
NOT EXACTLY...
AT YOUR SCHOOL FESTIVAL LAST YEAR... YOU DIDN'T SEE ME, BUT I SAW YOU.
YOU SAW ME...
AH!
PANIC
PANIC
BUT BEFORE WE GET TO THAT...
...ACTU-ALLY...

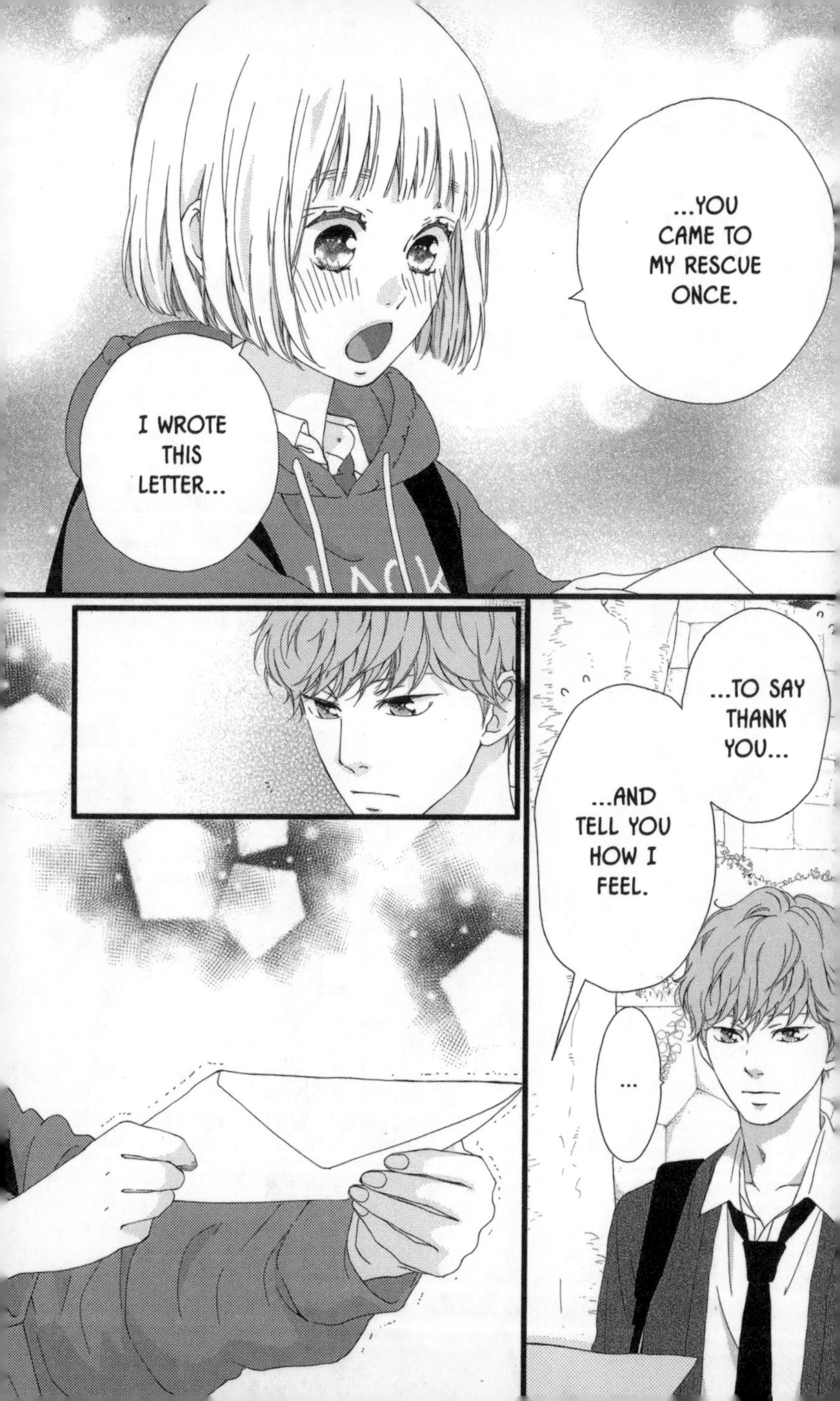
...YOU CAME TO MY RESCUE ONCE.
I WROTE THIS LETTER...
...TO SAY THANK YOU...
...AND TELL YOU HOW I FEEL.
...

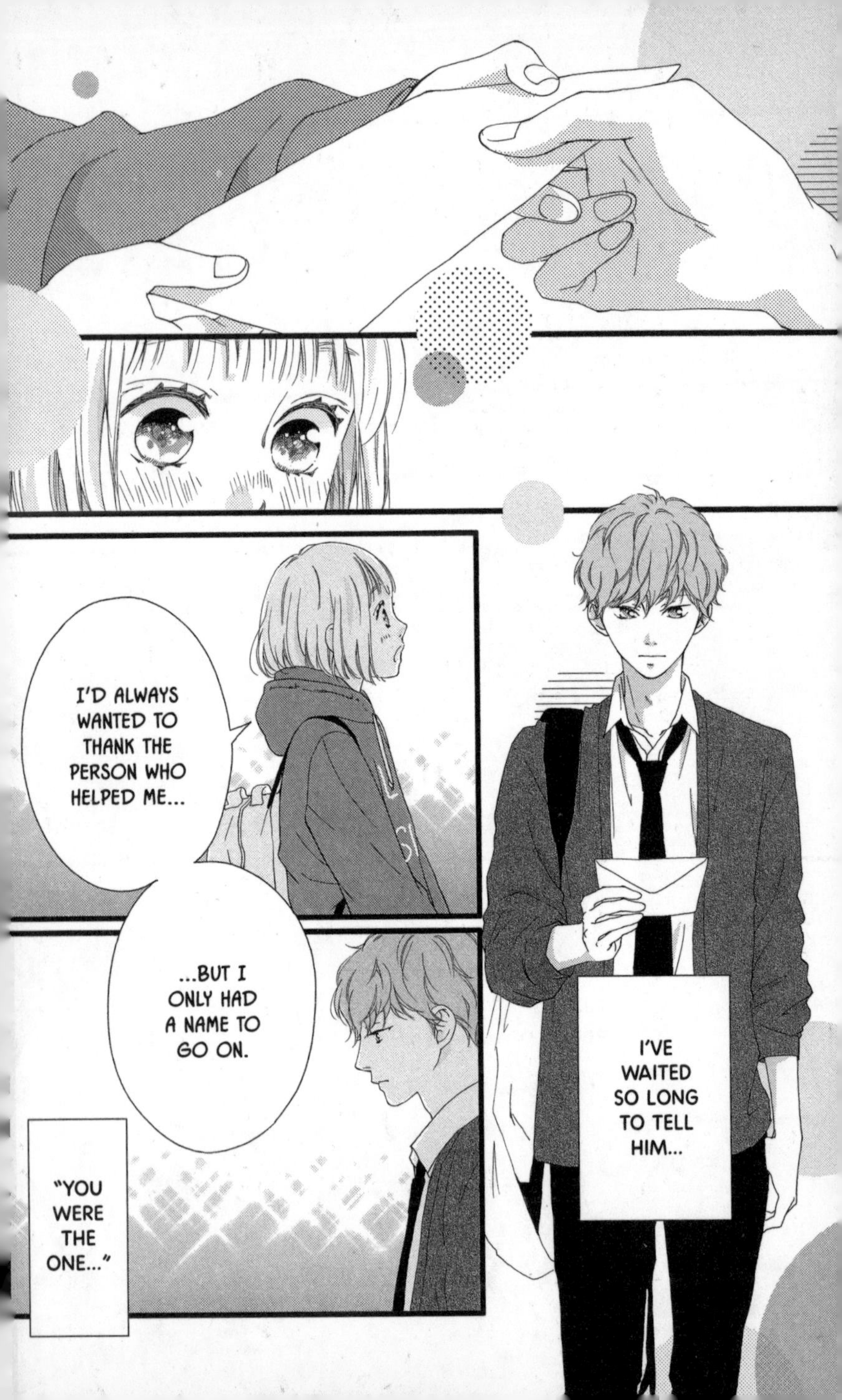
I'VE WAITED SO LONG TO TELL HIM...
I'D ALWAYS WANTED TO THANK THE PERSON WHO HELPED ME...
...BUT I ONLY HAD A NAME TO GO ON.
"YOU WERE THE ONE..."

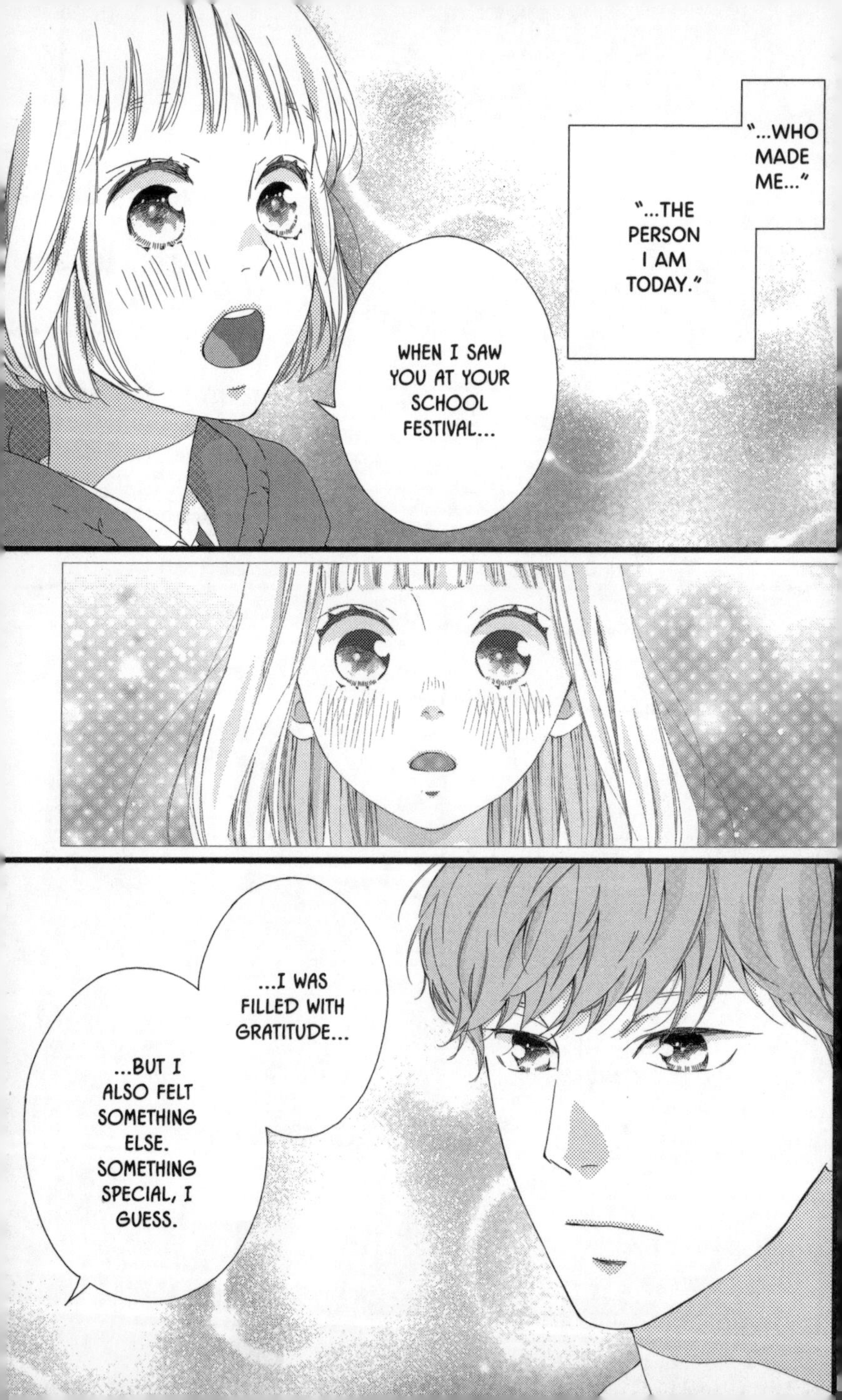
"...WHO MADE ME..."
"...THE PERSON I AM TODAY."
WHEN I SAW YOU AT YOUR SCHOOL FESTIVAL...
...I WAS FILLED WITH GRATITUDE...
...BUT I ALSO FELT SOMETHING ELSE. SOMETHING SPECIAL, I GUESS.

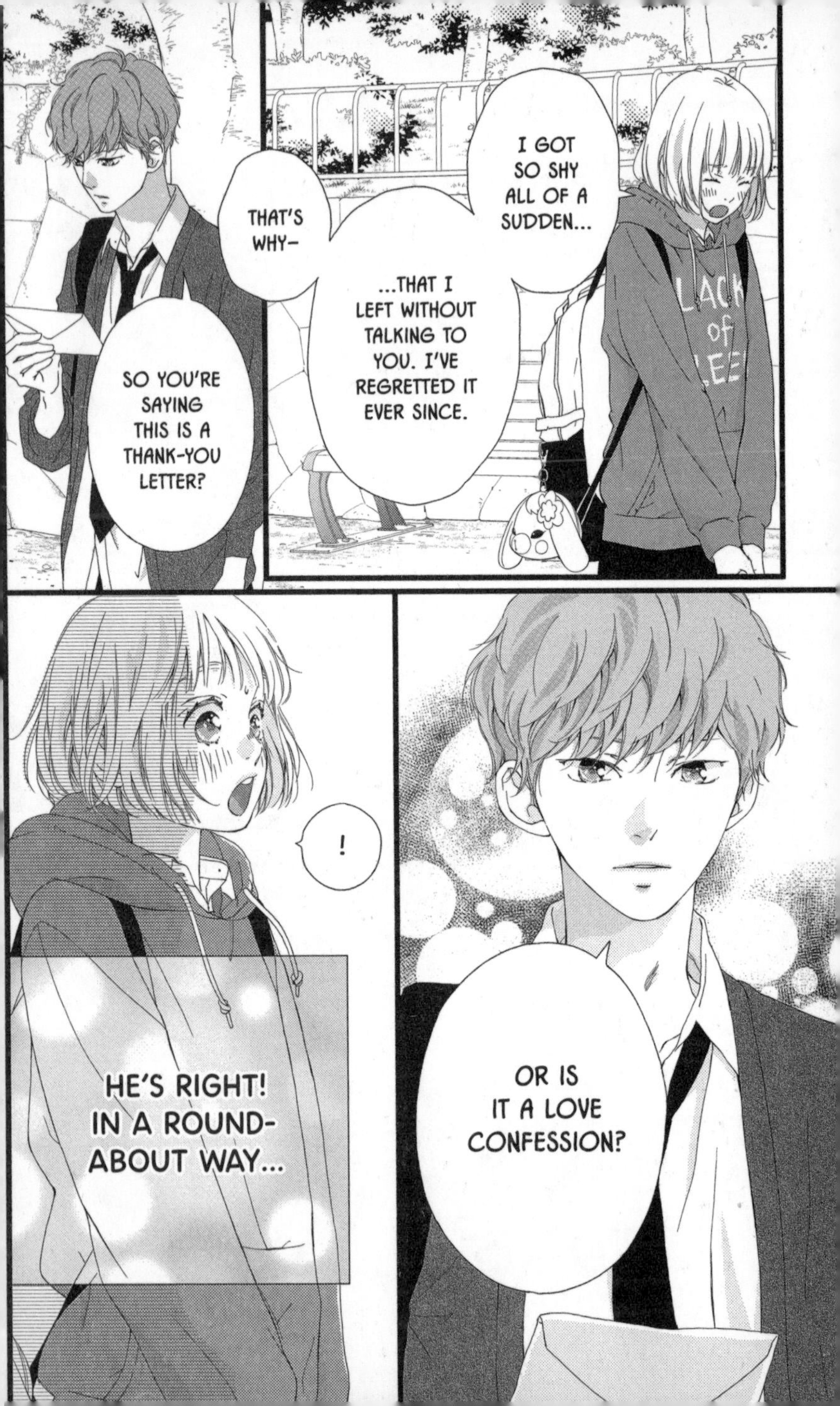
I GOT SO SHY ALL OF A SUDDEN...
THAT'S WHY—
...THAT I LEFT WITHOUT TALKING TO YOU. I'VE REGRETTED IT EVER SINCE.
SO YOU'RE SAYING THIS IS A THANK-YOU LETTER?
OR IS IT A LOVE CONFESSION?
!
HE'S RIGHT! IN A ROUND-ABOUT WAY...

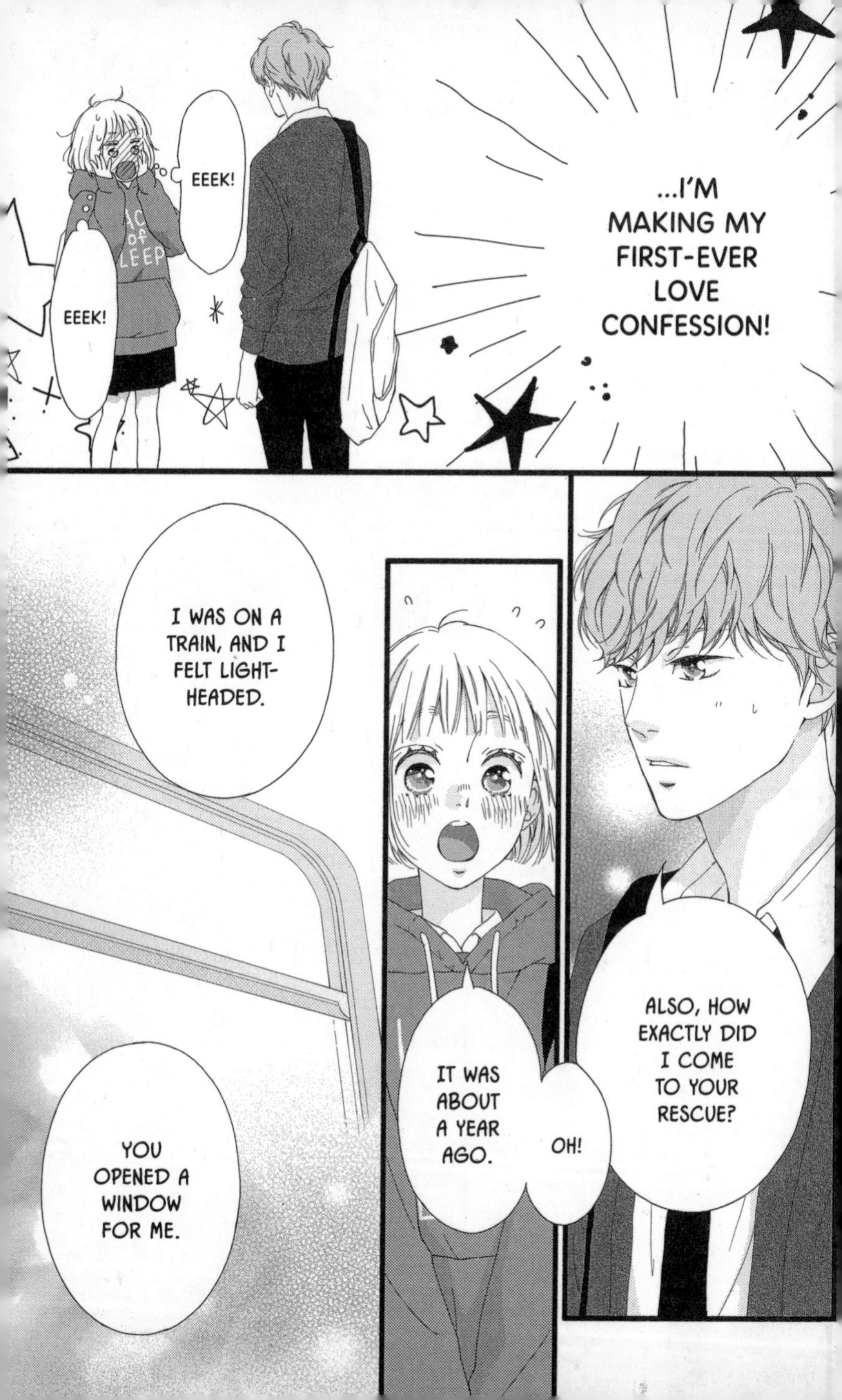
...I'M MAKING MY FIRST-EVER LOVE CONFESSION!
EEEK!
EEEK!
ALSO, HOW EXACTLY DID I COME TO YOUR RESCUE?
OH!
IT WAS ABOUT A YEAR AGO.
I WAS ON A TRAIN, AND I FELT LIGHT-HEADED.
YOU OPENED A WINDOW FOR ME.

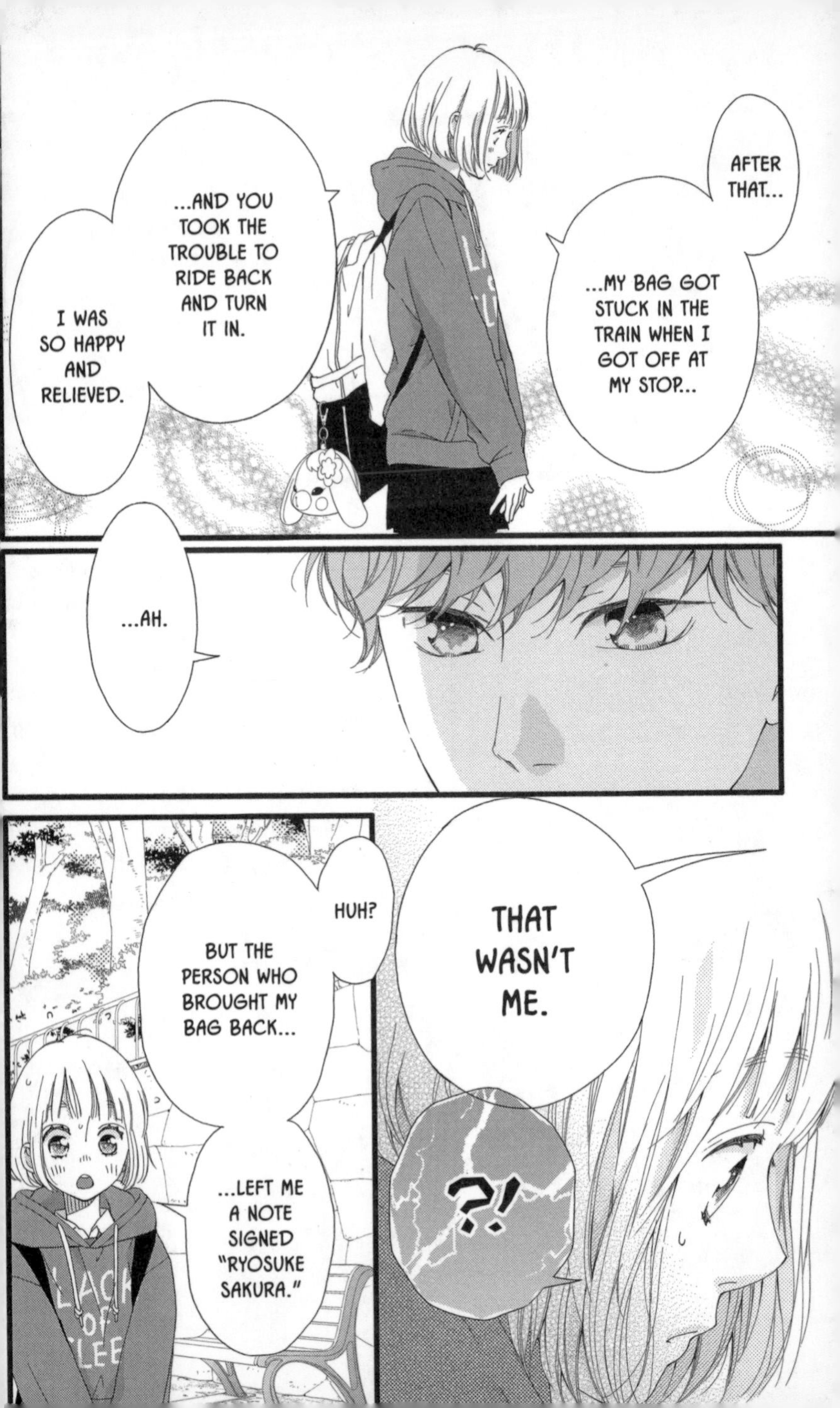
AFTER THAT...
...MY BAG GOT STUCK IN THE TRAIN WHEN I GOT OFF AT MY STOP...
...AND YOU TOOK THE TROUBLE TO RIDE BACK AND TURN IT IN.
I WAS SO HAPPY AND RELIEVED.
...AH.
THAT WASN'T ME.
?!
HUH?
BUT THE PERSON WHO BROUGHT MY BAG BACK...
...LEFT ME A NOTE SIGNED "RYOSUKE SAKURA."

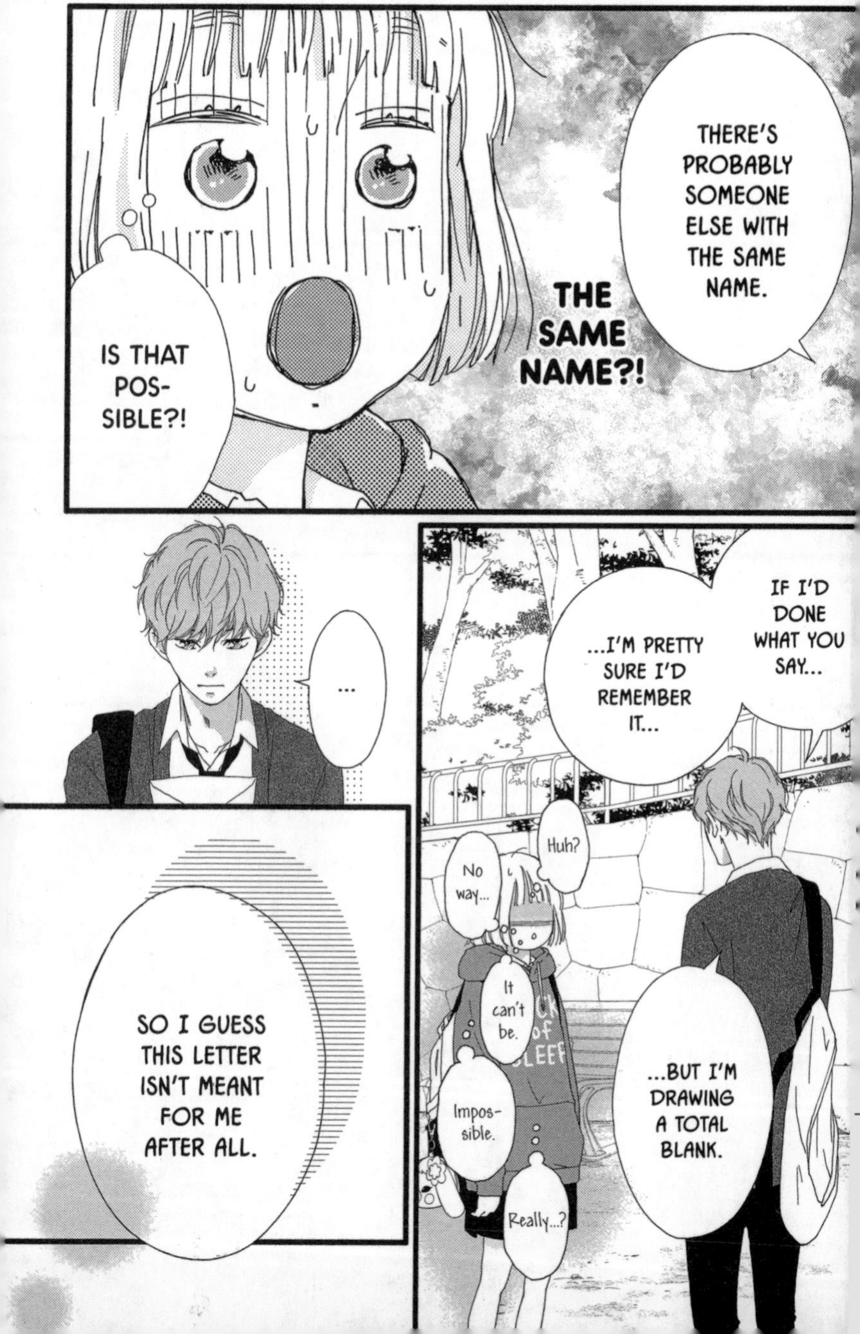
THERE'S PROBABLY SOMEONE ELSE WITH THE SAME NAME.
THE SAME NAME?!
IS THAT POS-SIBLE?!
IF I'D DONE WHAT YOU SAY...
...I'M PRETTY SURE I'D REMEMBER IT...
...BUT I'M DRAWING A TOTAL BLANK.
Huh?
No way...
It can't be.
Impos-sible.
Really...?
...
SO I GUESS THIS LETTER ISN'T MEANT FOR ME AFTER ALL.

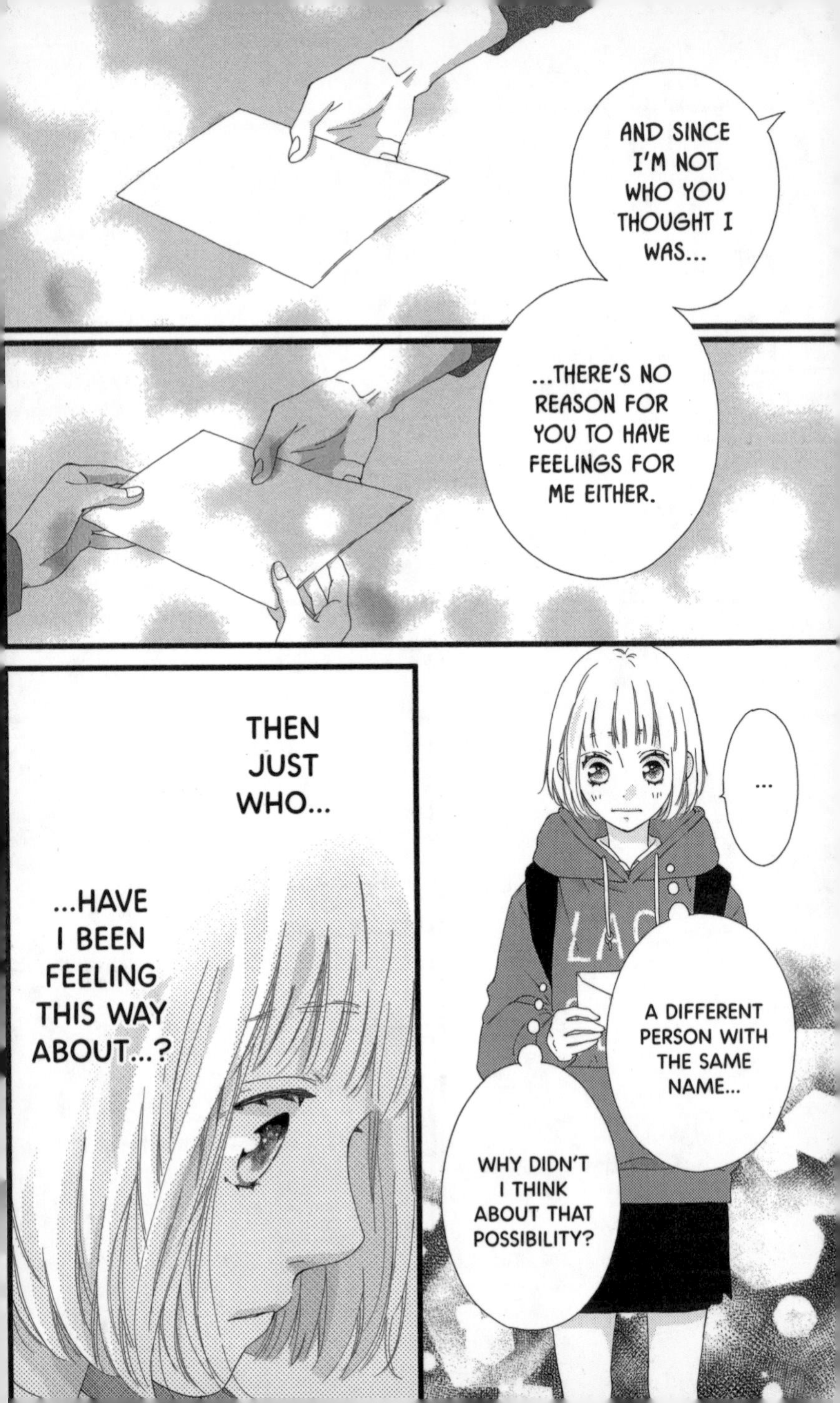
AND SINCE I'M NOT WHO YOU THOUGHT I WAS...
...THERE'S NO REASON FOR YOU TO HAVE FEELINGS FOR ME EITHER.
...
A DIFFERENT PERSON WITH THE SAME NAME...
WHY DIDN'T I THINK ABOUT THAT POSSIBILITY?
THEN JUST WHO...
...HAVE I BEEN FEELING THIS WAY ABOUT...?

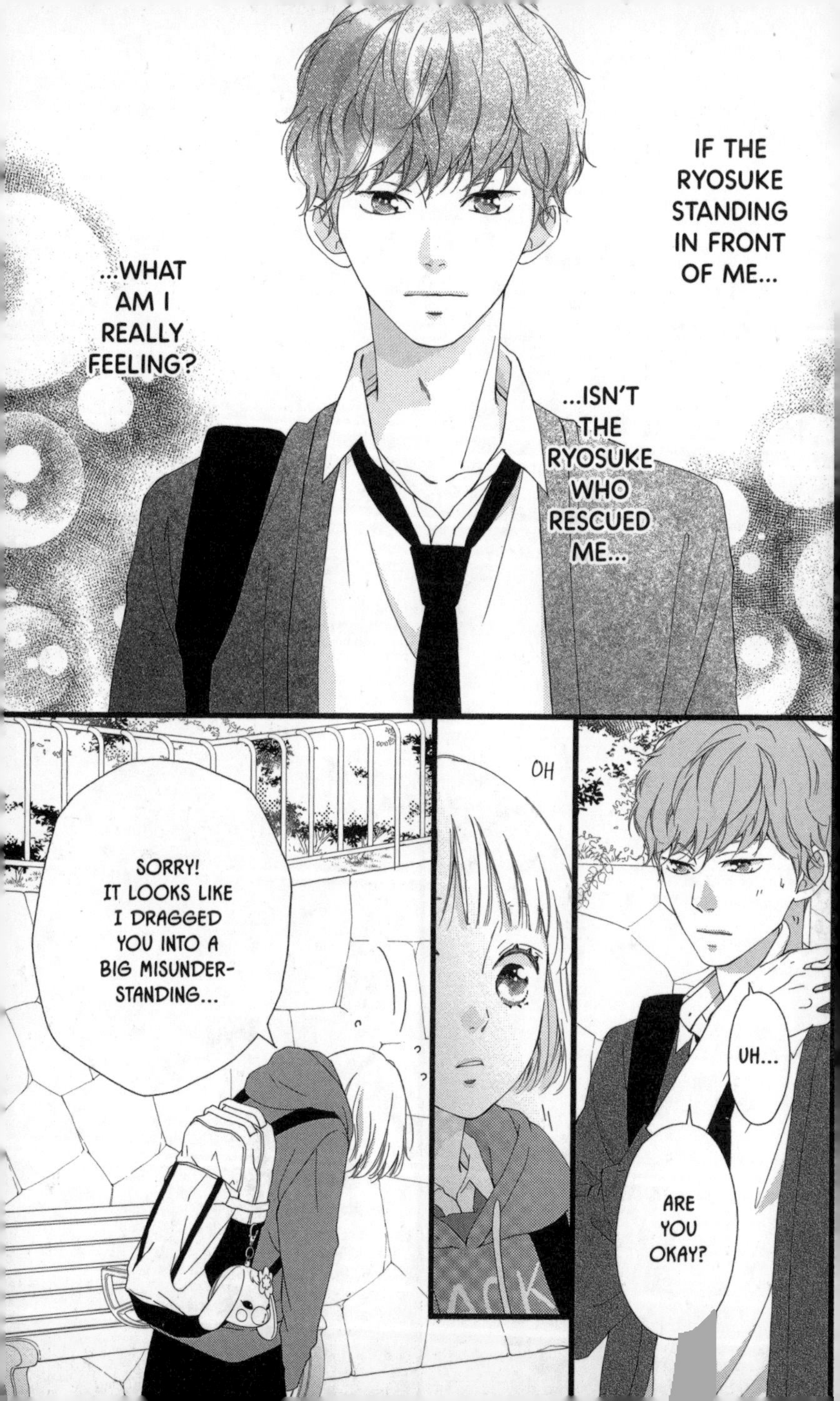
IF THE RYOSUKE STANDING IN FRONT OF ME...
...ISN'T THE RYOSUKE WHO RESCUED ME...
...WHAT AM I REALLY FEELING?
UH...
ARE YOU OKAY?
OH
SORRY! IT LOOKS LIKE I DRAGGED YOU INTO A BIG MISUNDER-STANDING...

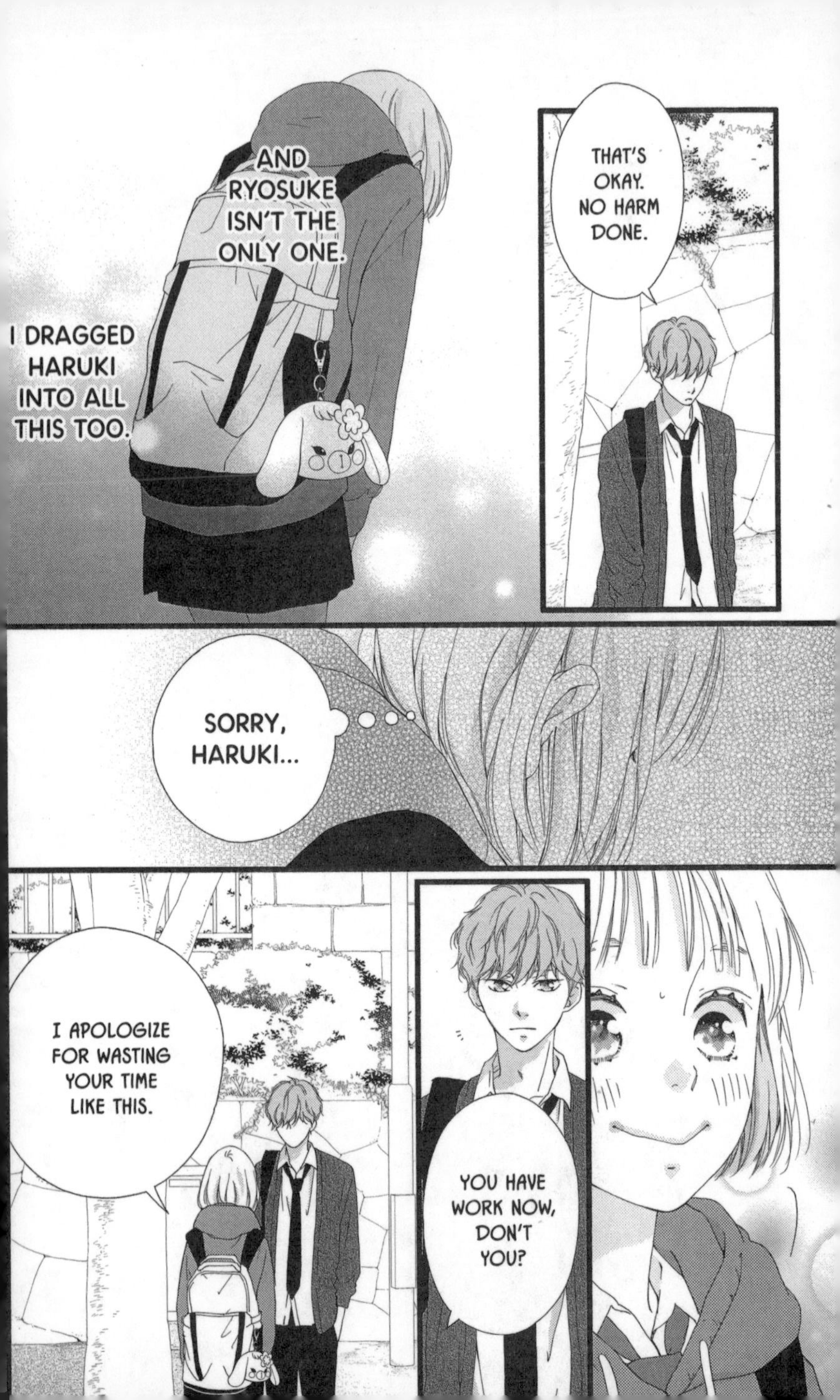
THAT'S OKAY. NO HARM DONE.
AND RYOSUKE ISN'T THE ONLY ONE.
I DRAGGED HARUKI INTO ALL THIS TOO.
SORRY, HARUKI...
YOU HAVE WORK NOW, DON'T YOU?
I APOLOGIZE FOR WASTING YOUR TIME LIKE THIS.

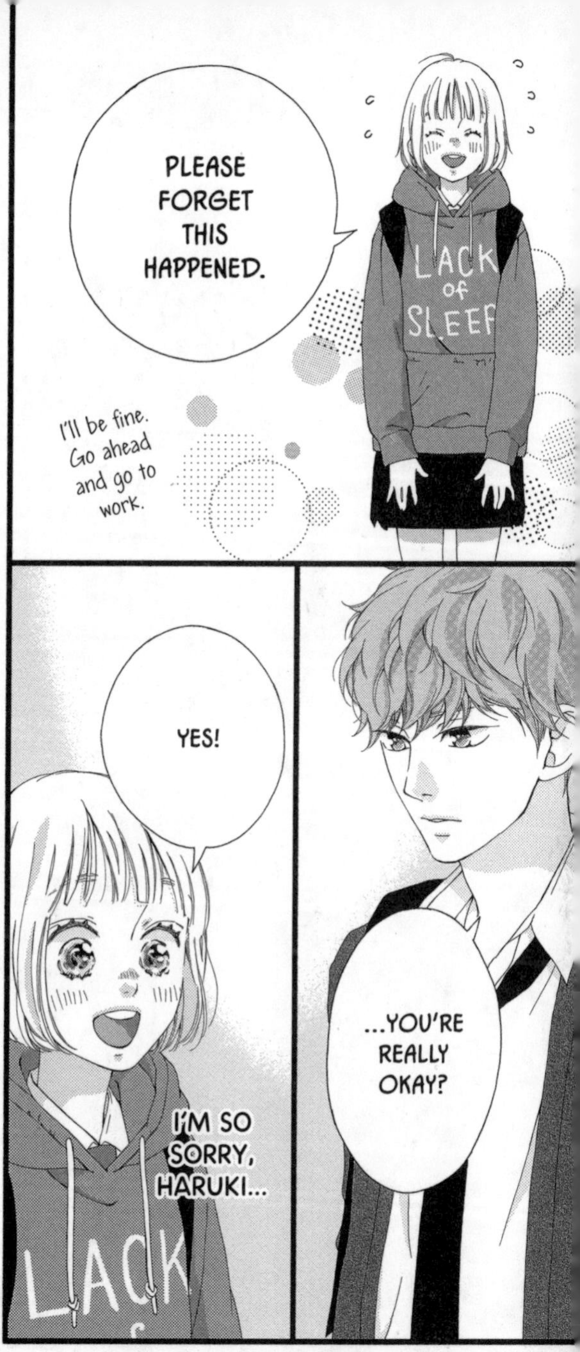
PLEASE FORGET THIS HAPPENED.
I'll be fine. Go ahead and go to work.
LACK of SLEEP
...YOU'RE REALLY OKAY?
YES!
I'M SO SORRY, HARUKI...
LACK

Some readers might know this already, but Haruki's brother, Ryosuke, appeared in my last series, *Love Me, Love Me Not*. I really liked him as a character and wanted to draw him a little more, so I brought him into this story too. If you want to know more about Ryosuke's past, please read *Love Me, Love Me Not*. Sorry this sounds like an advertisement. But while I'm in advertising mode, the rabbit rail pass case hanging from Saku's bag is real-life merch from *Ao Haru Ride*, the series I wrote before *Love Me, Love Me Not*. That's where the rabbit makes its first appearance, so please check out *Ao Haru Ride* as well!

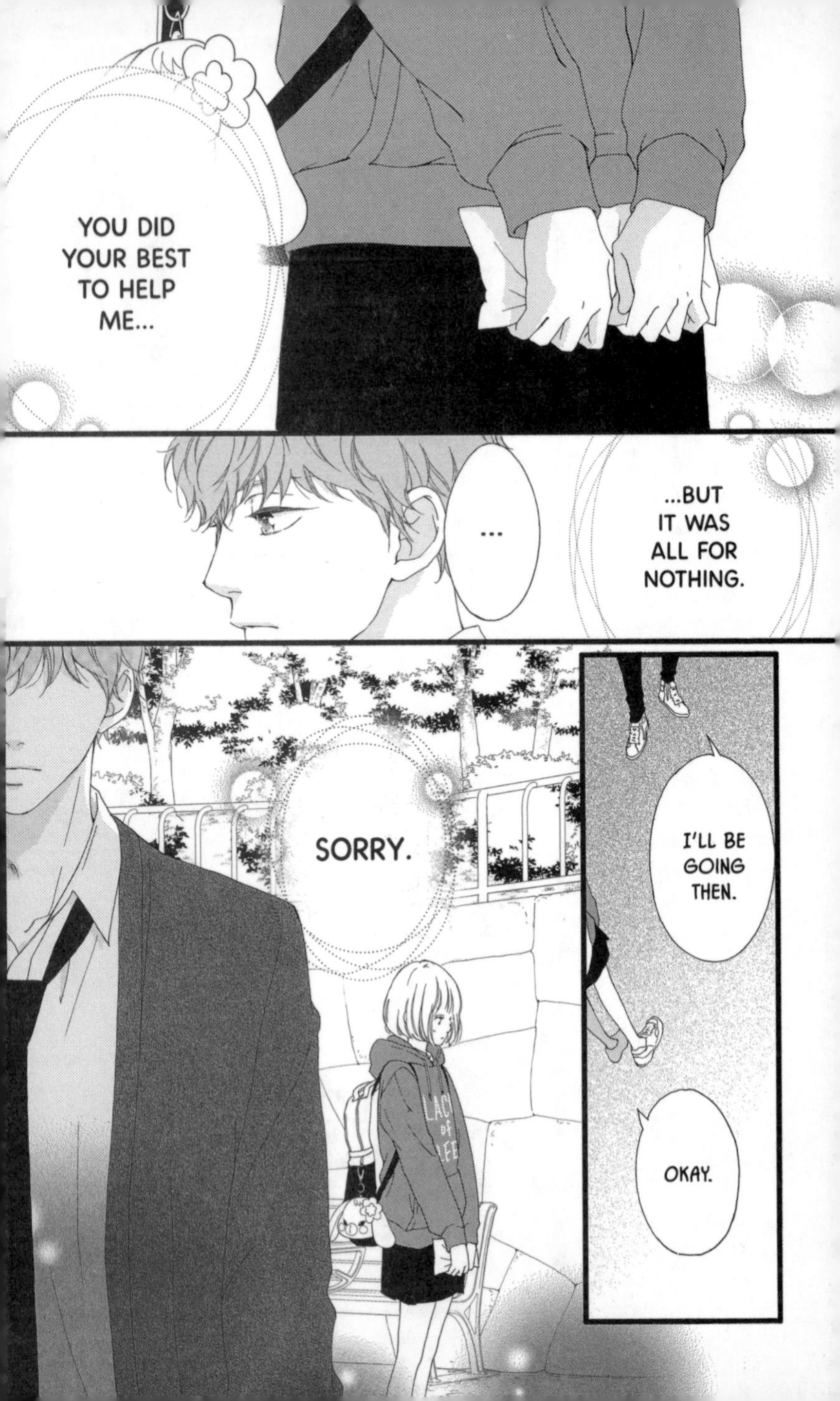
YOU DID YOUR BEST TO HELP ME...
...BUT IT WAS ALL FOR NOTHING.
...
I'LL BE GOING THEN.
OKAY.
SORRY.

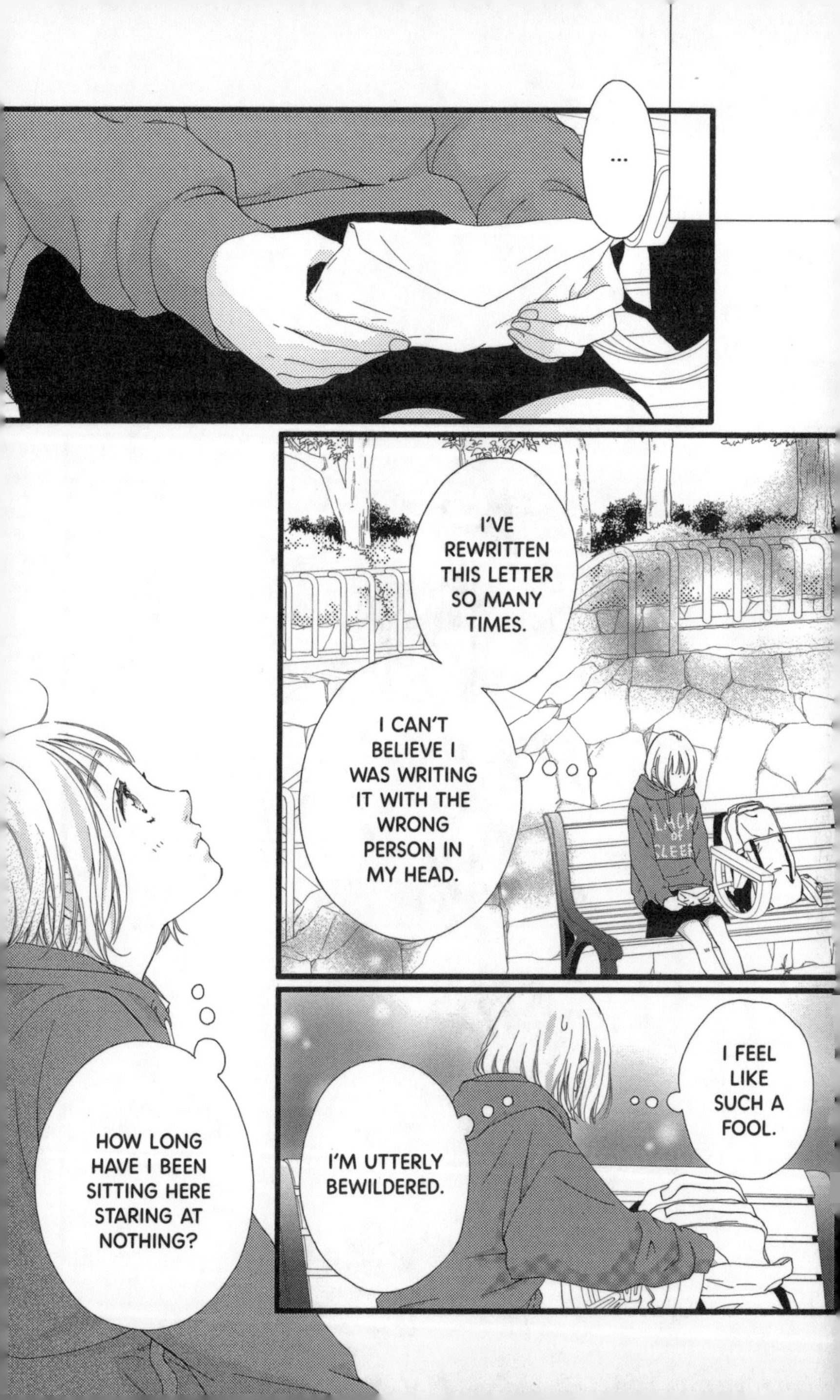
...
I'VE REWRITTEN THIS LETTER SO MANY TIMES.
I CAN'T BELIEVE I WAS WRITING IT WITH THE WRONG PERSON IN MY HEAD.
I FEEL LIKE SUCH A FOOL.
I'M UTTERLY BEWILDERED.
HOW LONG HAVE I BEEN SITTING HERE STARING AT NOTHING?

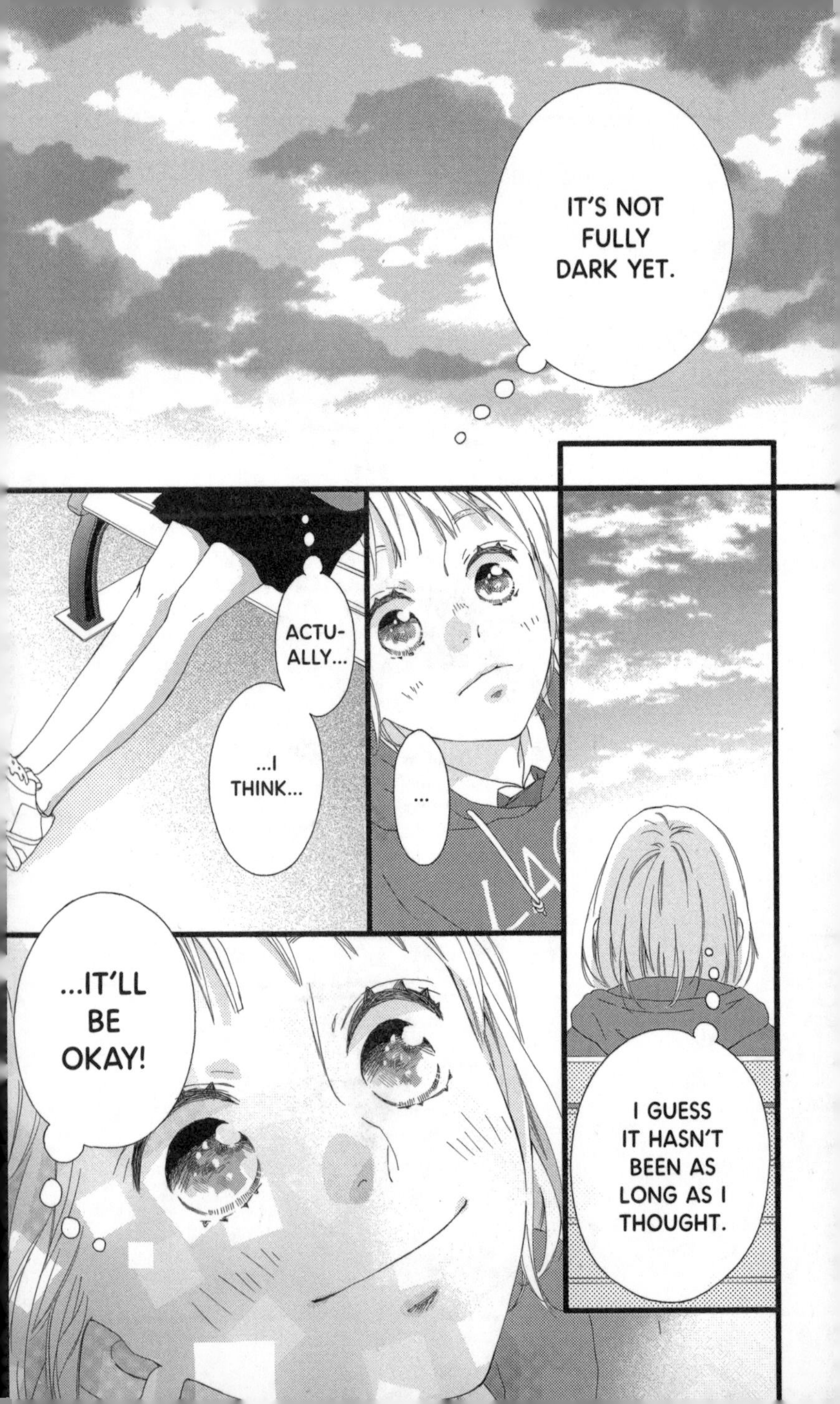
IT'S NOT FULLY DARK YET.
I GUESS IT HASN'T BEEN AS LONG AS I THOUGHT.
...
ACTU-ALLY...
...I THINK...
...IT'LL BE OKAY!

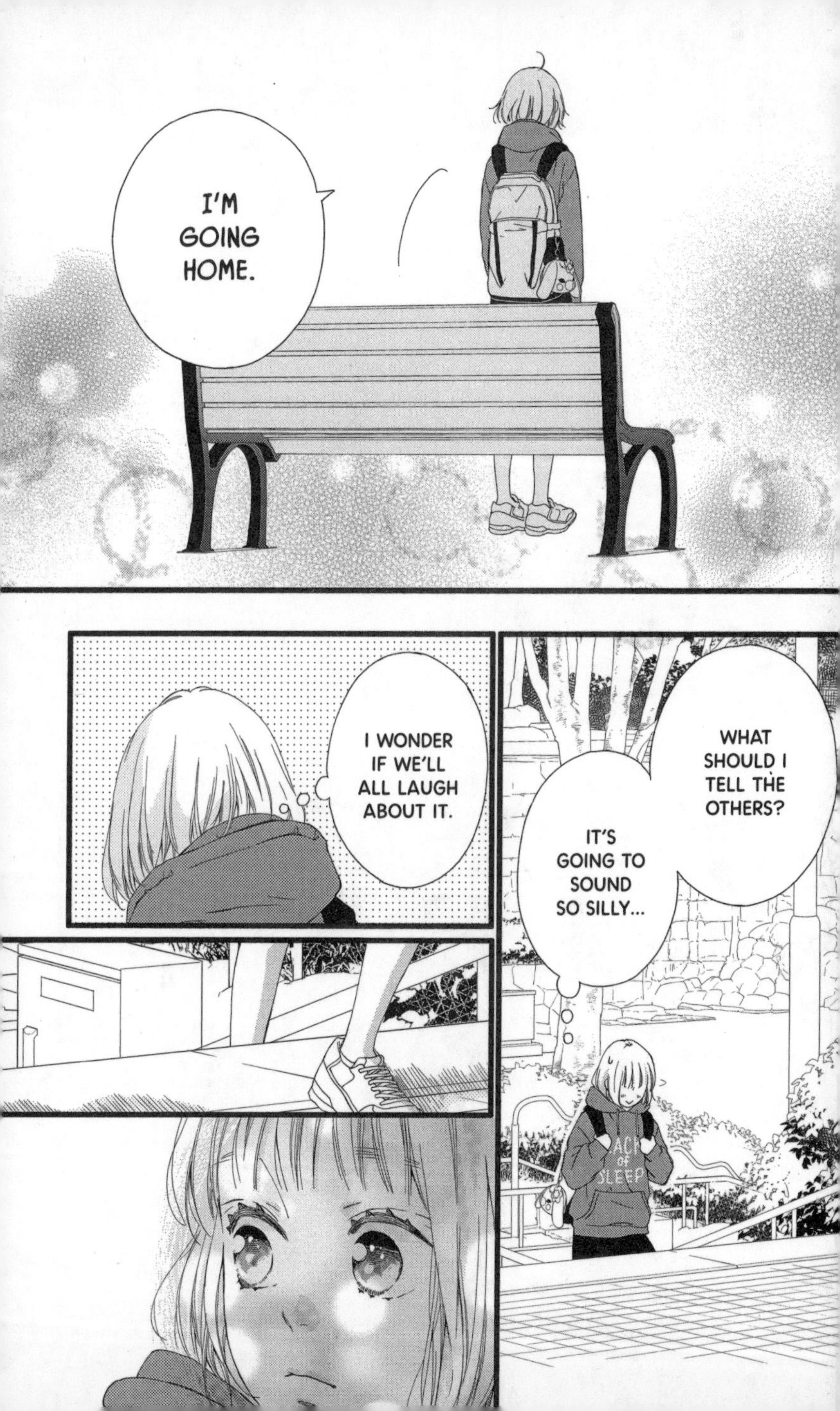
I'M GOING HOME.
WHAT SHOULD I TELL THE OTHERS?
IT'S GOING TO SOUND SO SILLY...
I WONDER IF WE'LL ALL LAUGH ABOUT IT.

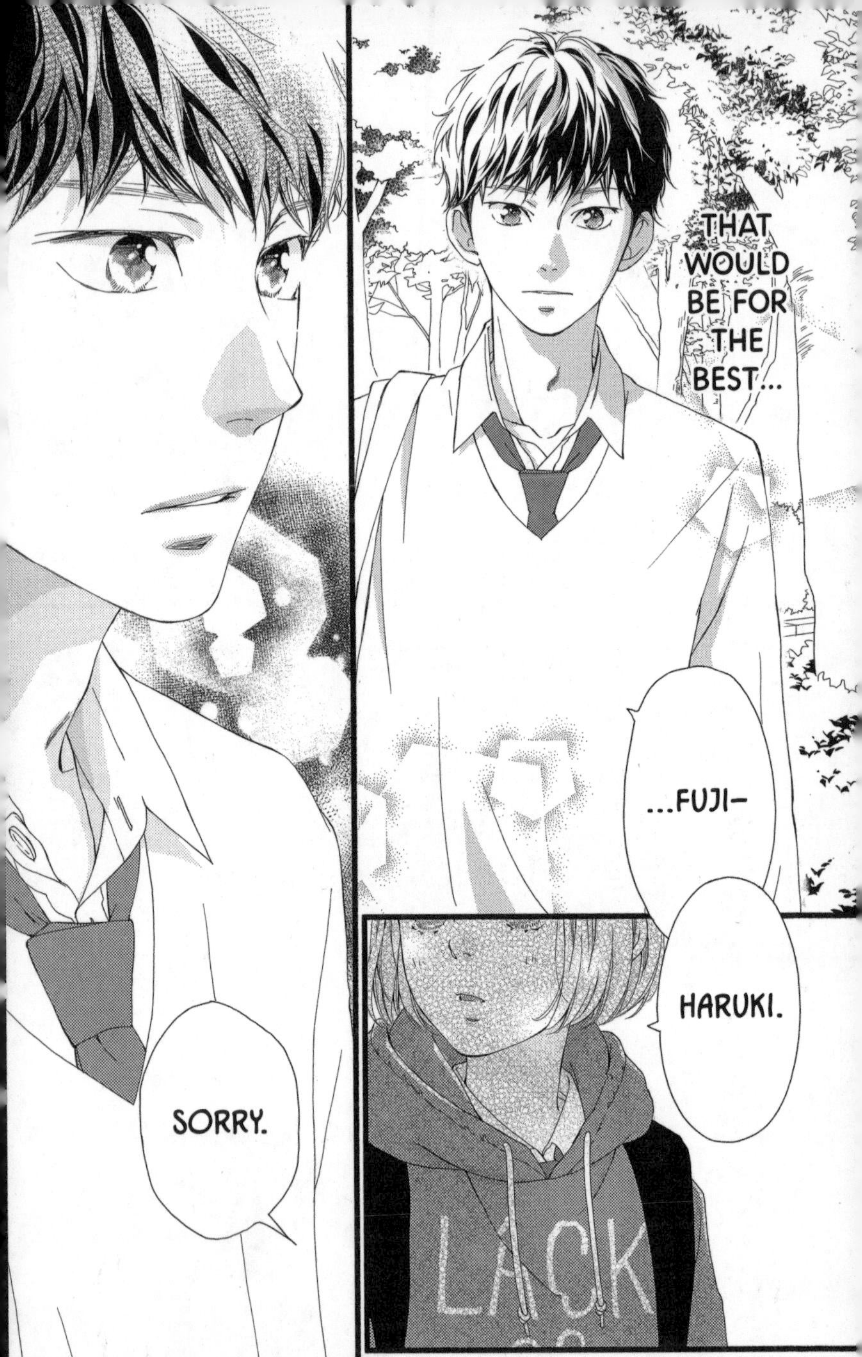
THAT WOULD BE FOR THE BEST...
...FUJI-
HARUKI.
SORRY.

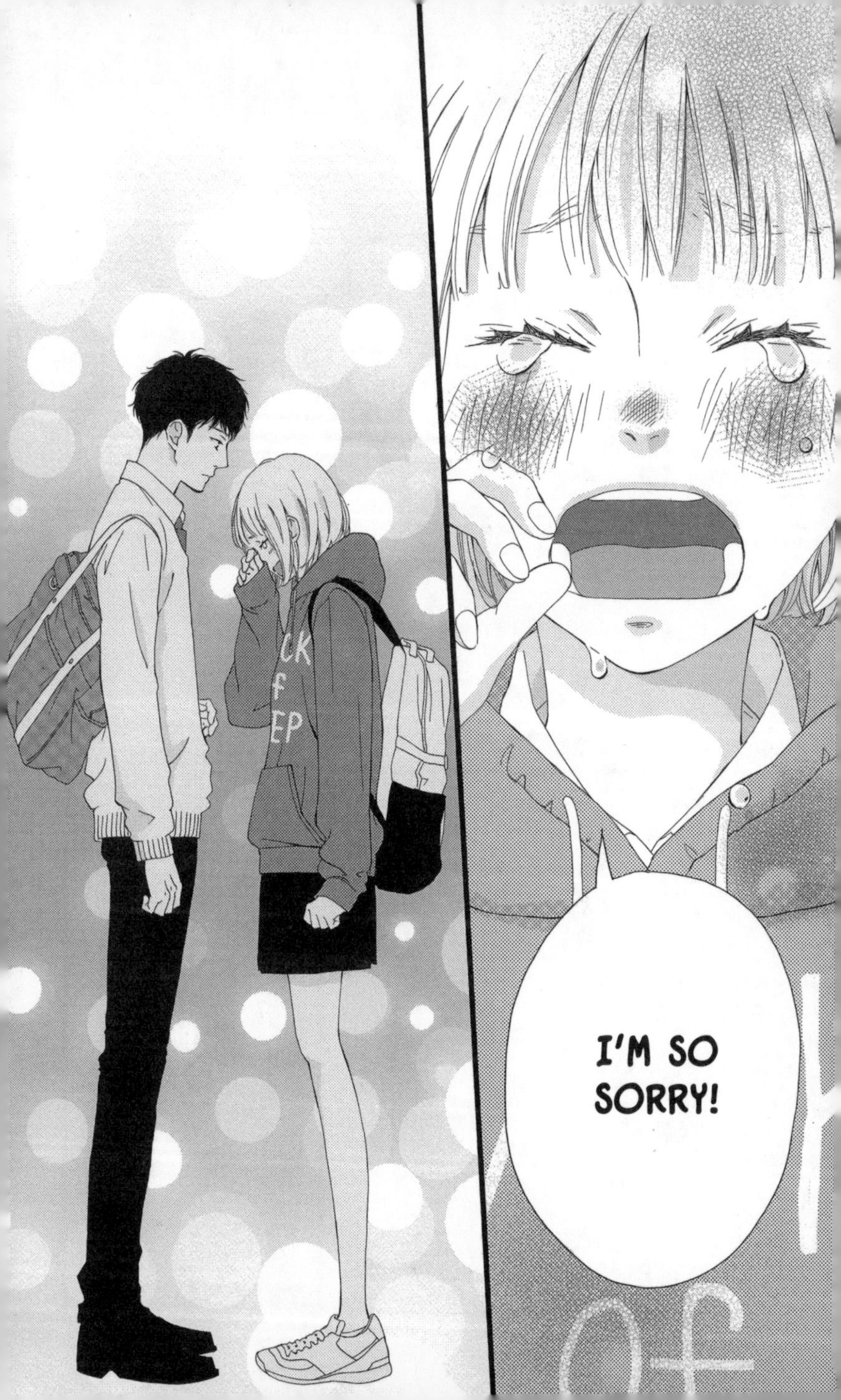
I'M SO SORRY!

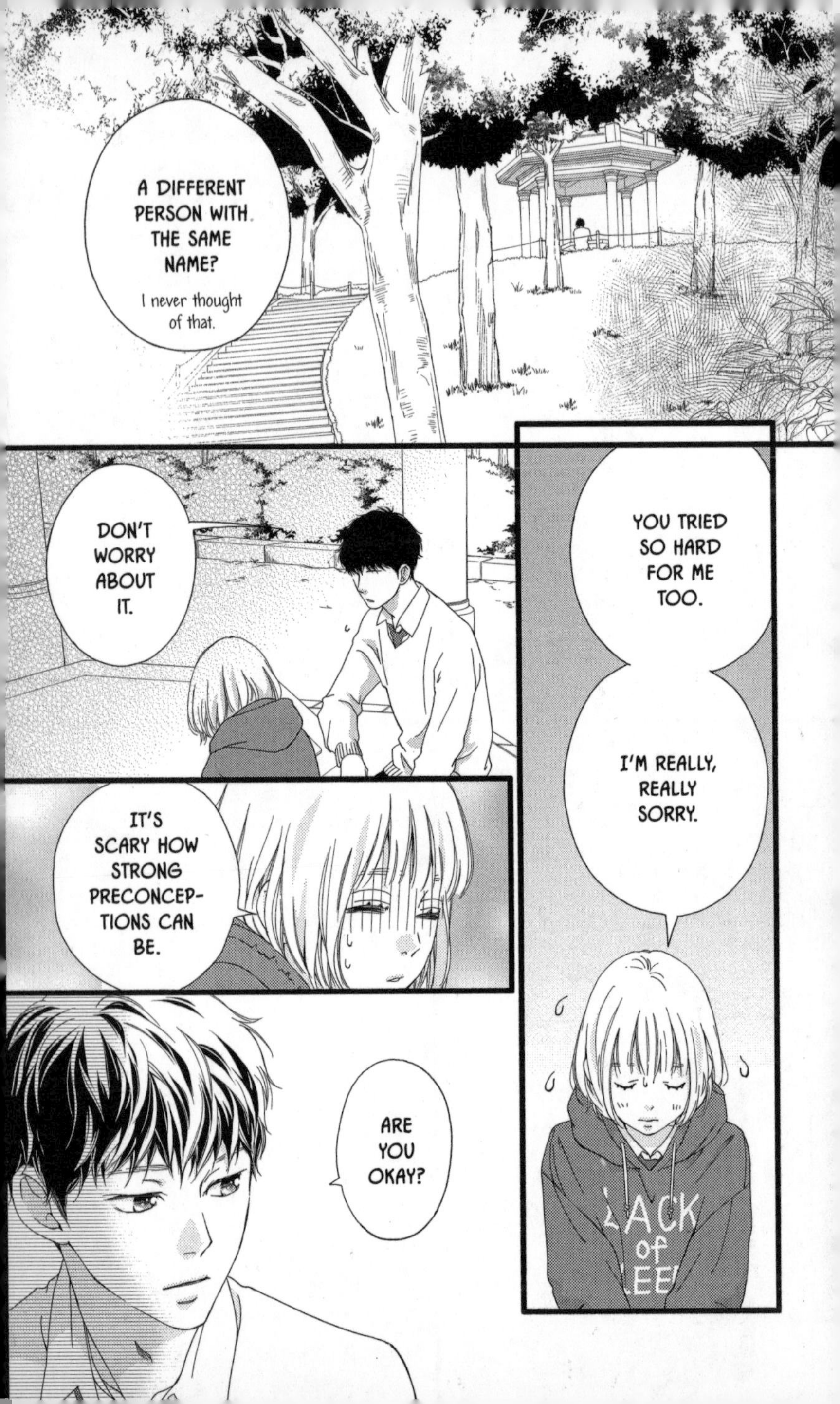
A DIFFERENT PERSON WITH THE SAME NAME?
I never thought of that.
YOU TRIED SO HARD FOR ME TOO.
I'M REALLY, REALLY SORRY.
DON'T WORRY ABOUT IT.
IT'S SCARY HOW STRONG PRECONCEP-TIONS CAN BE.
ARE YOU OKAY?

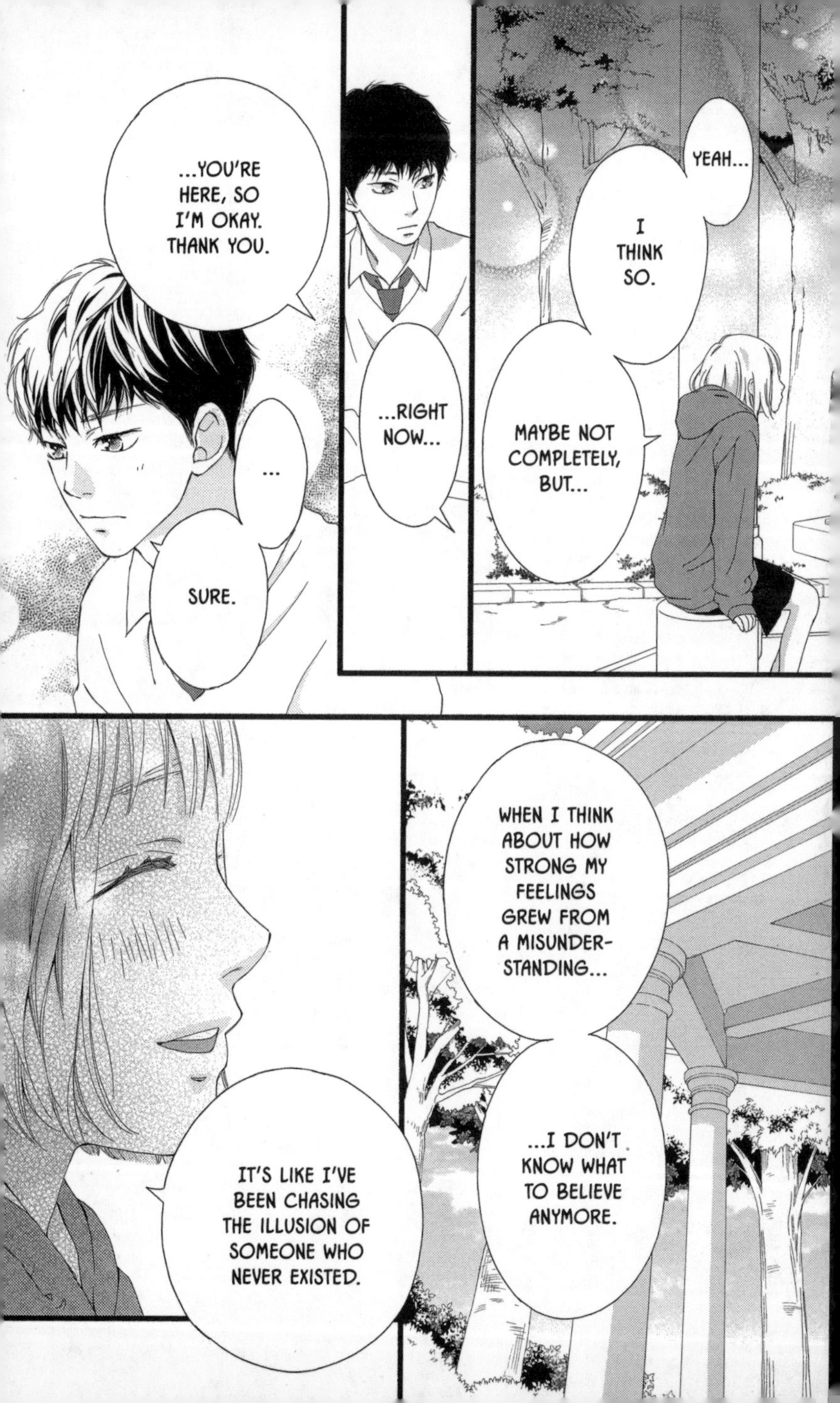
YEAH...
I THINK SO.
MAYBE NOT COMPLETELY, BUT...
...RIGHT NOW...
...YOU'RE HERE, SO I'M OKAY. THANK YOU.
...
SURE.
WHEN I THINK ABOUT HOW STRONG MY FEELINGS GREW FROM A MISUNDER-STANDING...
...I DON'T KNOW WHAT TO BELIEVE ANYMORE.
IT'S LIKE I'VE BEEN CHASING THE ILLUSION OF SOMEONE WHO NEVER EXISTED.

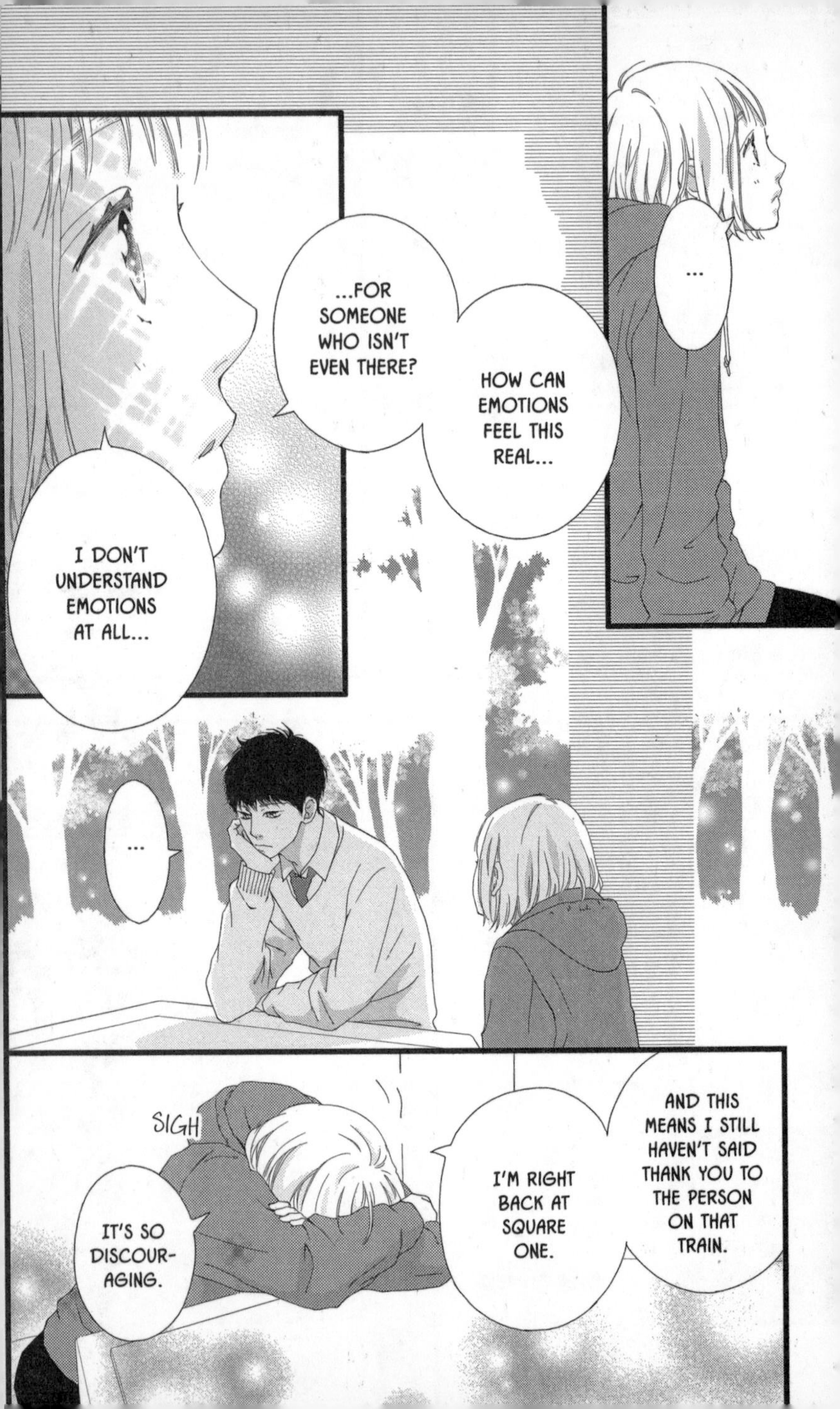
...
HOW CAN EMOTIONS FEEL THIS REAL...
...FOR SOMEONE WHO ISN'T EVEN THERE?
I DON'T UNDERSTAND EMOTIONS AT ALL...
...
AND THIS MEANS I STILL HAVEN'T SAID THANK YOU TO THE PERSON ON THAT TRAIN.
I'M RIGHT BACK AT SQUARE ONE.
SIGH
IT'S SO DISCOUR-AGING.

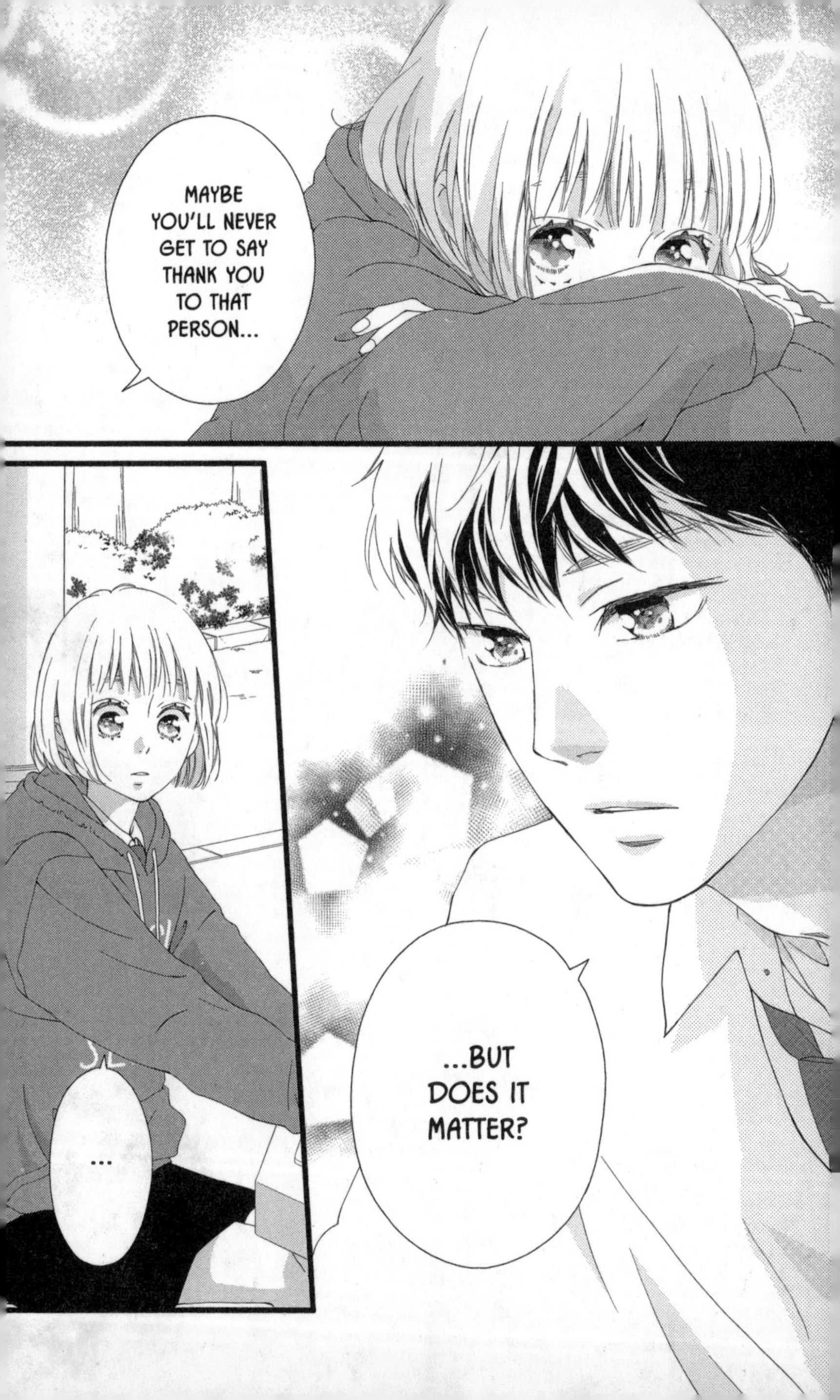
MAYBE YOU'LL NEVER GET TO SAY THANK YOU TO THAT PERSON...
...BUT DOES IT MATTER?
...

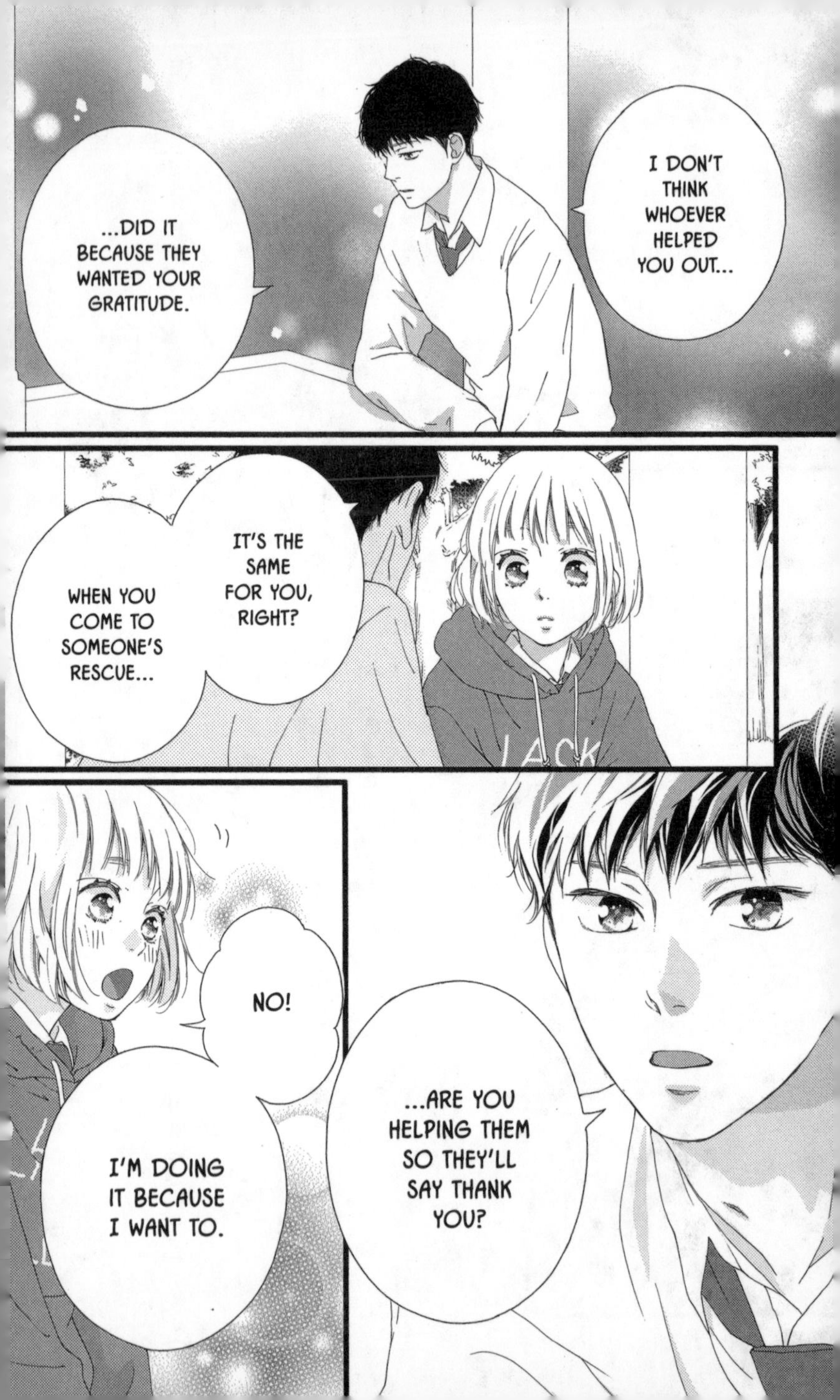
I DON'T THINK WHOEVER HELPED YOU OUT...
...DID IT BECAUSE THEY WANTED YOUR GRATITUDE.
IT'S THE SAME FOR YOU, RIGHT?
WHEN YOU COME TO SOMEONE'S RESCUE...
...ARE YOU HELPING THEM SO THEY'LL SAY THANK YOU?
NO!
I'M DOING IT BECAUSE I WANT TO.

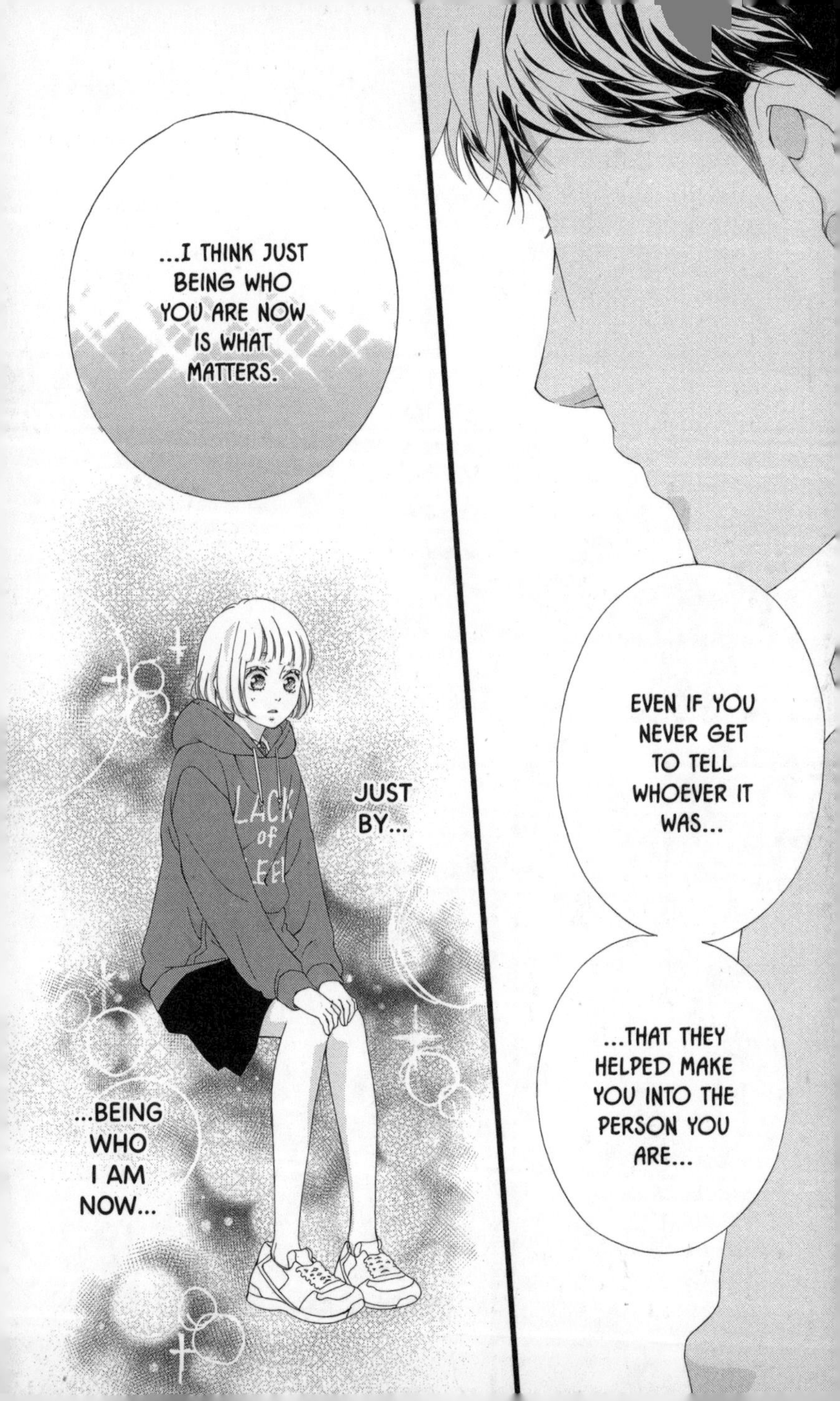
EVEN IF YOU NEVER GET TO TELL WHOEVER IT WAS...
...THAT THEY HELPED MAKE YOU INTO THE PERSON YOU ARE...
...I THINK JUST BEING WHO YOU ARE NOW IS WHAT MATTERS.
JUST BY...
...BEING WHO I AM NOW...

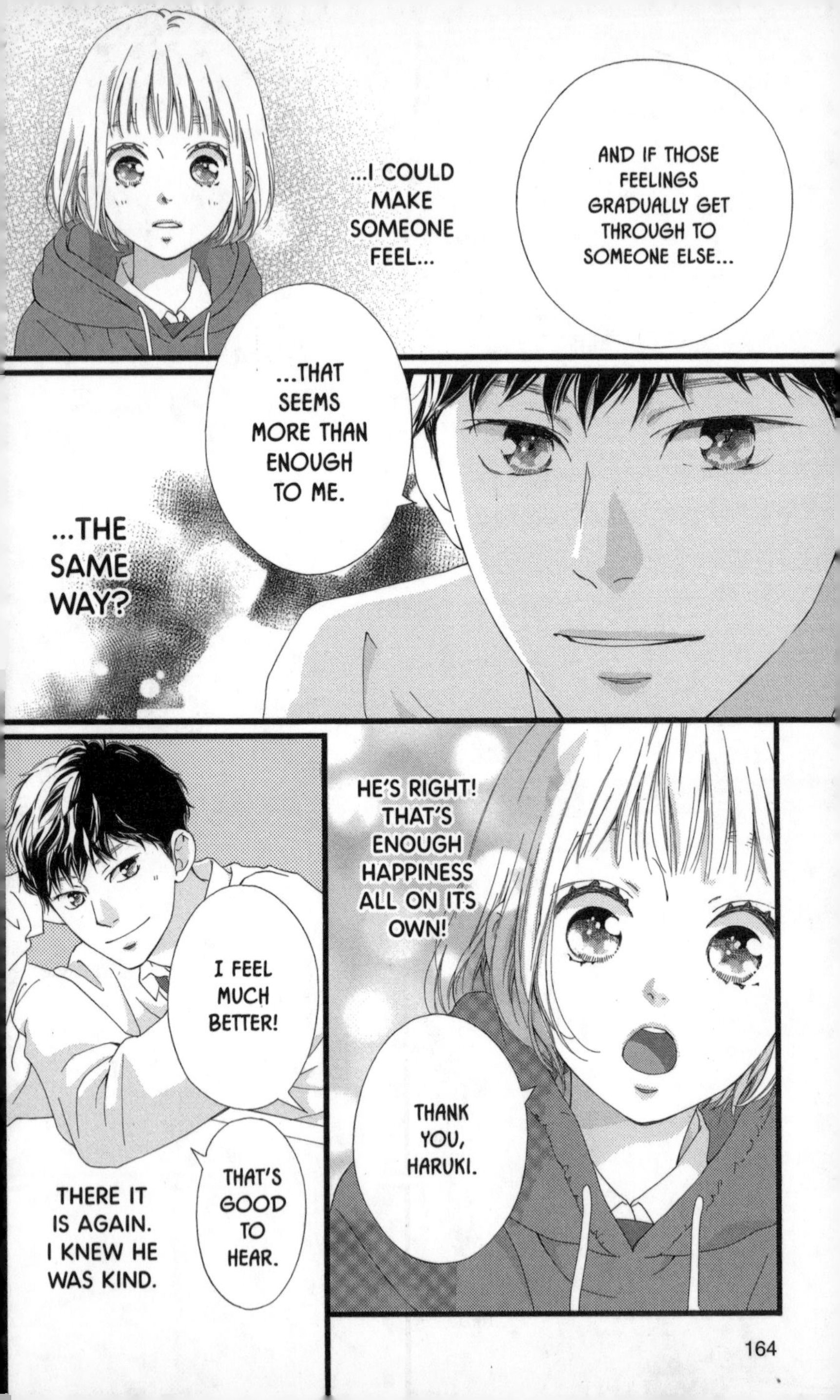

AND IF THOSE FEELINGS GRADUALLY GET THROUGH TO SOMEONE ELSE...
...I COULD MAKE SOMEONE FEEL...
...THE SAME WAY?
...THAT SEEMS MORE THAN ENOUGH TO ME.
HE'S RIGHT! THAT'S ENOUGH HAPPINESS ALL ON ITS OWN!
THANK YOU, HARUKI.
I FEEL MUCH BETTER!
THAT'S GOOD TO HEAR.
THERE IT IS AGAIN. I KNEW HE WAS KIND.

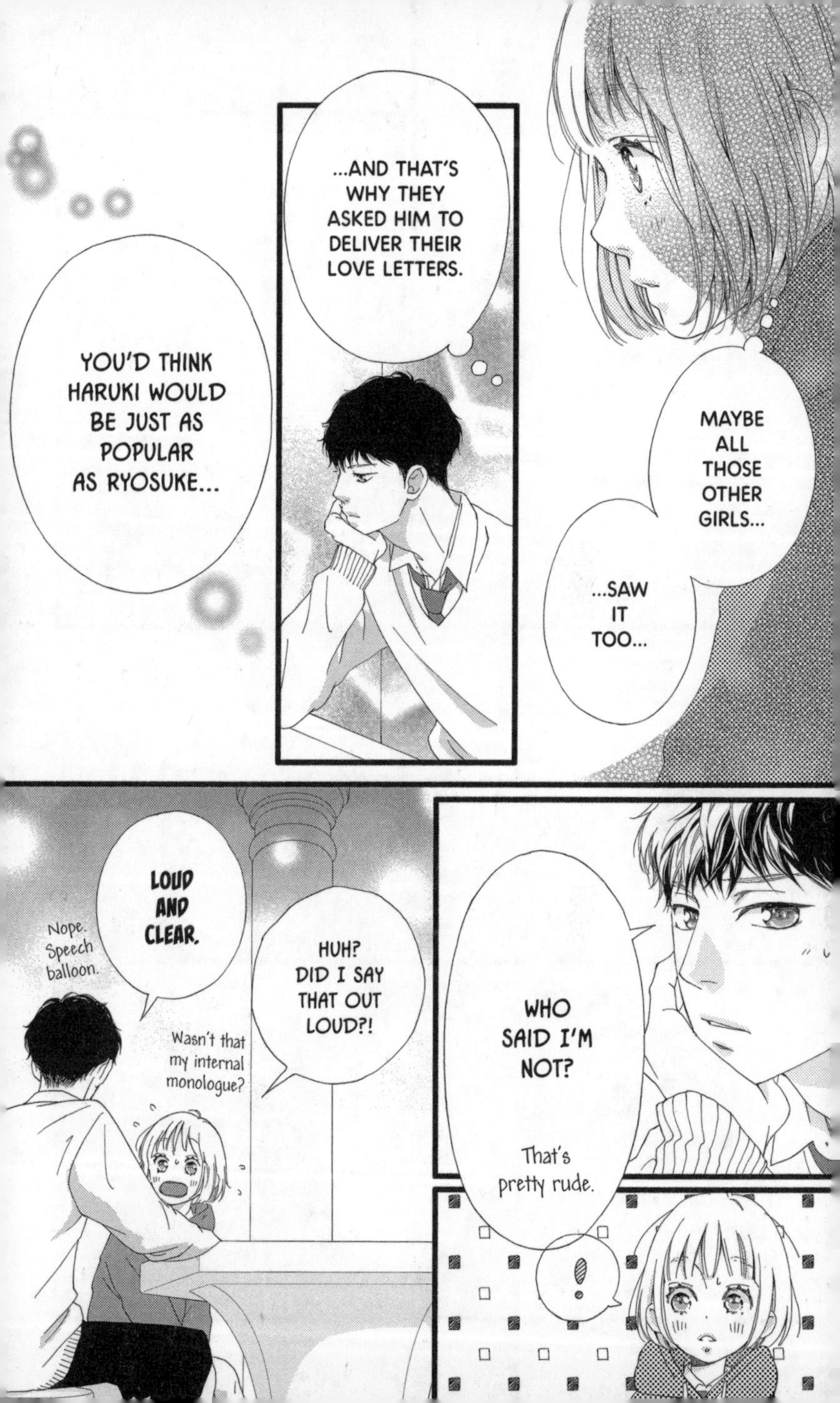
MAYBE ALL THOSE OTHER GIRLS...
...SAW IT TOO...
...AND THAT'S WHY THEY ASKED HIM TO DELIVER THEIR LOVE LETTERS.
YOU'D THINK HARUKI WOULD BE JUST AS POPULAR AS RYOSUKE...
WHO SAID I'M NOT?
That's pretty rude.
!
HUH? DID I SAY THAT OUT LOUD?!
Wasn't that my internal monologue?
LOUD AND CLEAR.
Nope. Speech balloon.

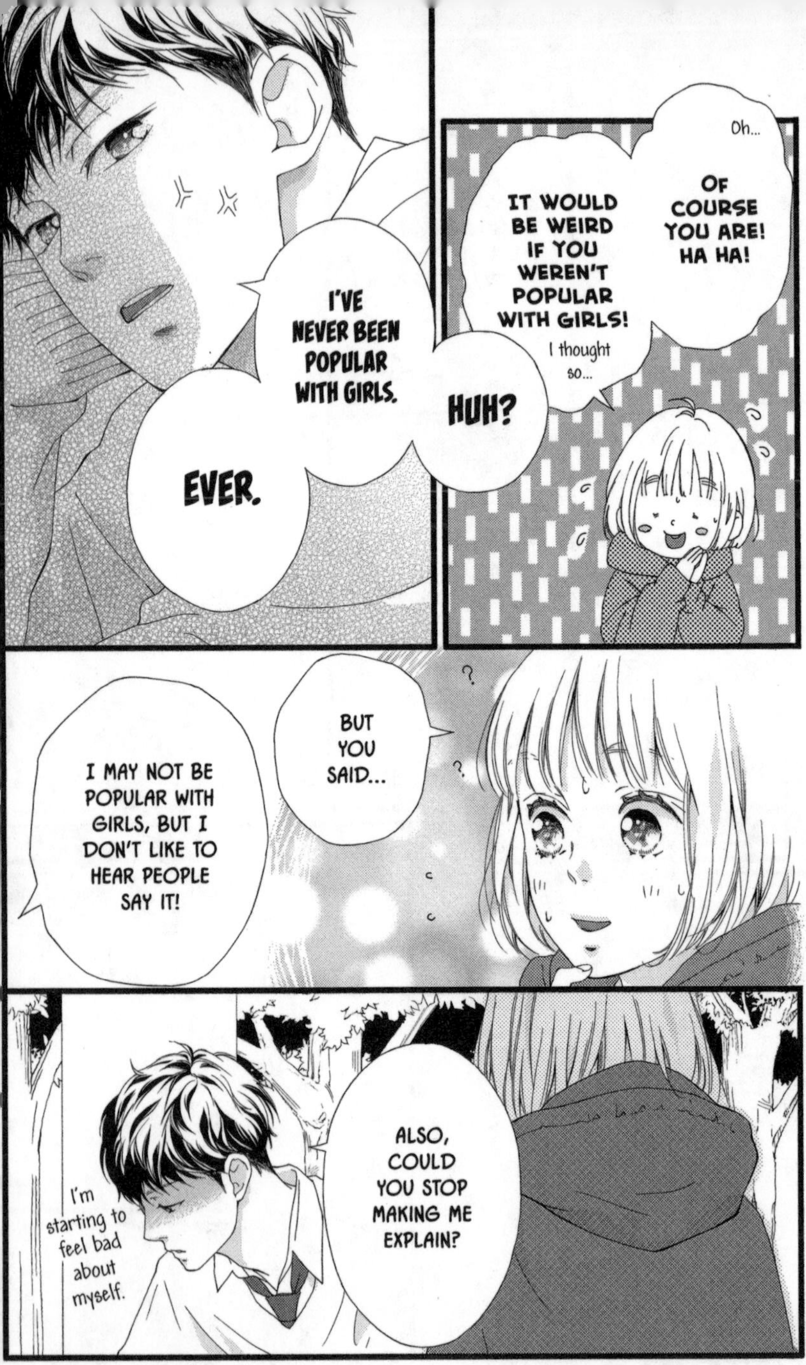

Oh...
OF COURSE YOU ARE! HA HA!
IT WOULD BE WEIRD IF YOU WEREN'T POPULAR WITH GIRLS!
I thought so...
I'VE NEVER BEEN POPULAR WITH GIRLS.
HUH?
EVER.
BUT YOU SAID...
I MAY NOT BE POPULAR WITH GIRLS, BUT I DON'T LIKE TO HEAR PEOPLE SAY IT!
ALSO, COULD YOU STOP MAKING ME EXPLAIN?
I'm starting to feel bad about myself.

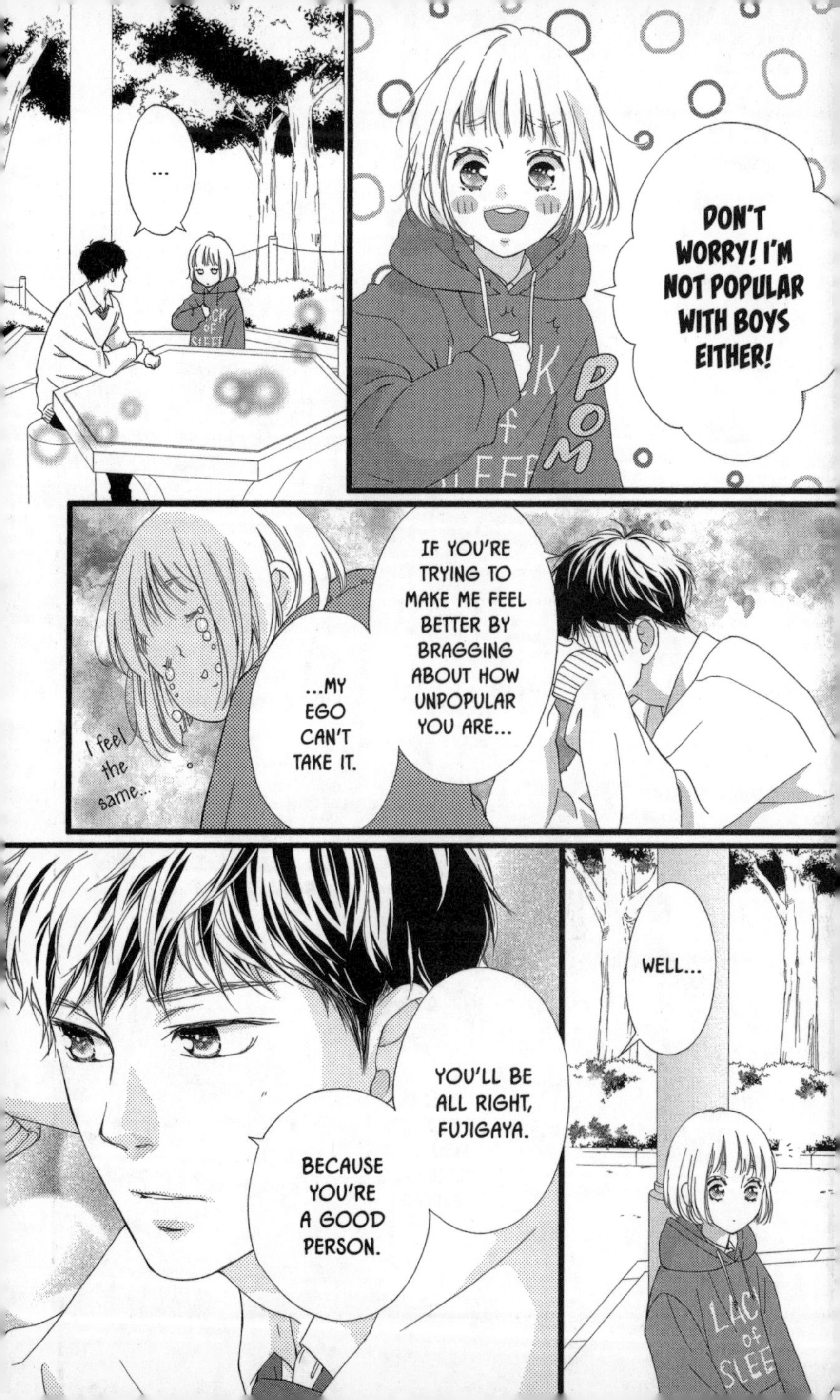
DON'T WORRY! I'M NOT POPULAR WITH BOYS EITHER!
POM
...
IF YOU'RE TRYING TO MAKE ME FEEL BETTER BY BRAGGING ABOUT HOW UNPOPULAR YOU ARE...
...MY EGO CAN'T TAKE IT.
I feel the same...
WELL...
YOU'LL BE ALL RIGHT, FUJIGAYA.
BECAUSE YOU'RE A GOOD PERSON.

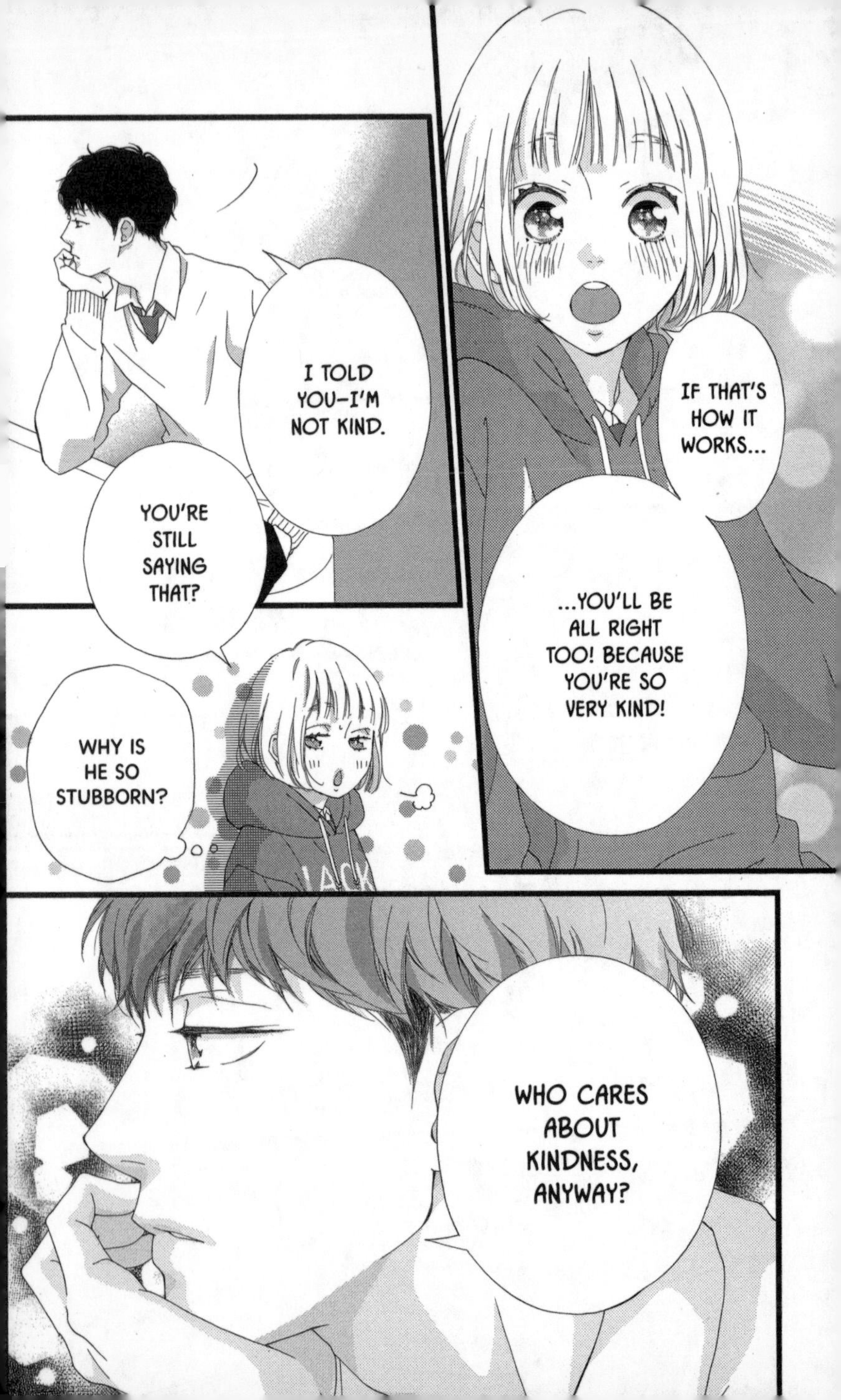
IF THAT'S HOW IT WORKS...
...YOU'LL BE ALL RIGHT TOO! BECAUSE YOU'RE SO VERY KIND!
I TOLD YOU—I'M NOT KIND.
YOU'RE STILL SAYING THAT?
WHY IS HE SO STUBBORN?
WHO CARES ABOUT KINDNESS, ANYWAY?

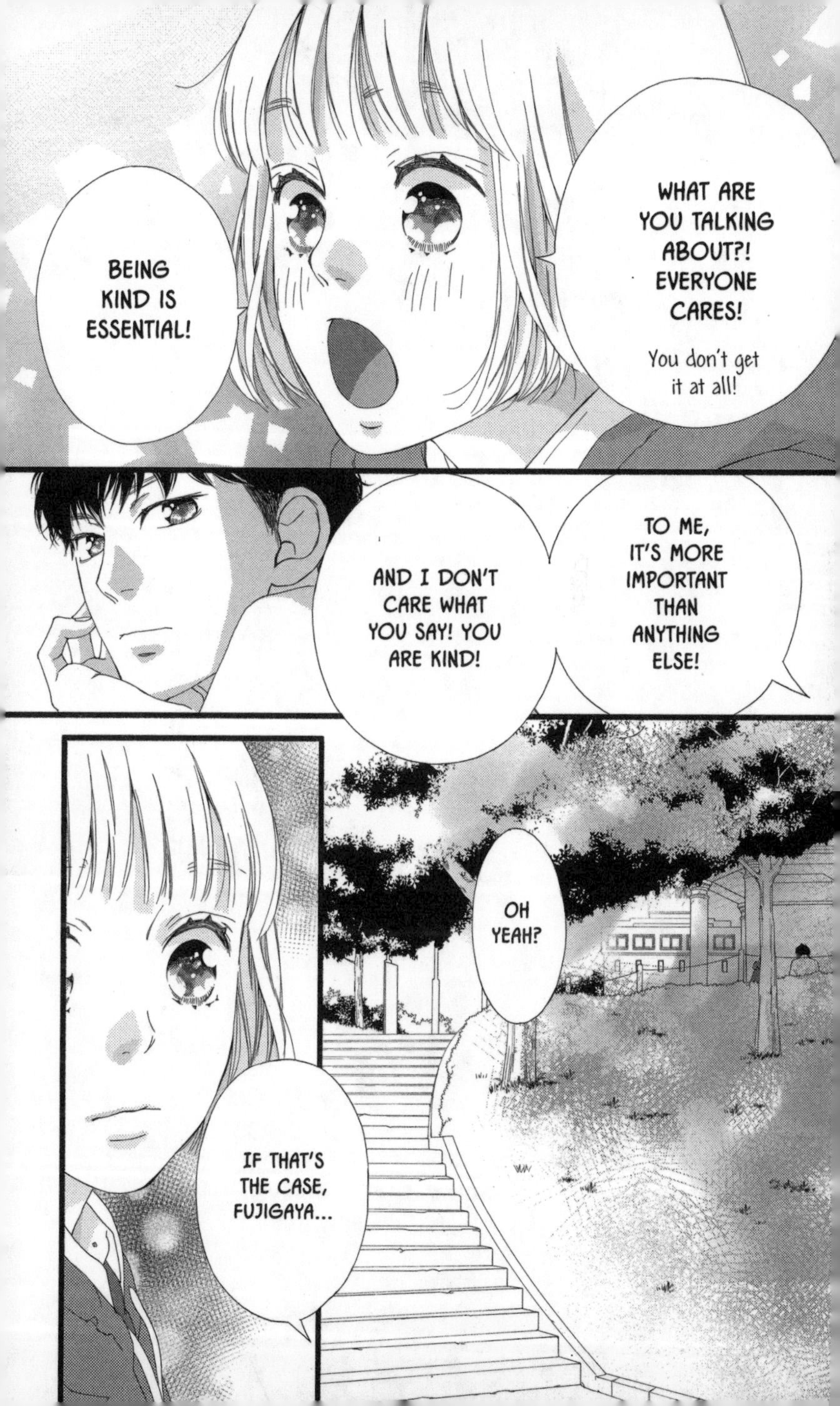
WHAT ARE YOU TALKING ABOUT?! EVERYONE CARES!
You don't get it at all!
BEING KIND IS ESSENTIAL!
TO ME, IT'S MORE IMPORTANT THAN ANYTHING ELSE!
AND I DON'T CARE WHAT YOU SAY! YOU ARE KIND!
OH YEAH?
IF THAT'S THE CASE, FUJIGAYA...

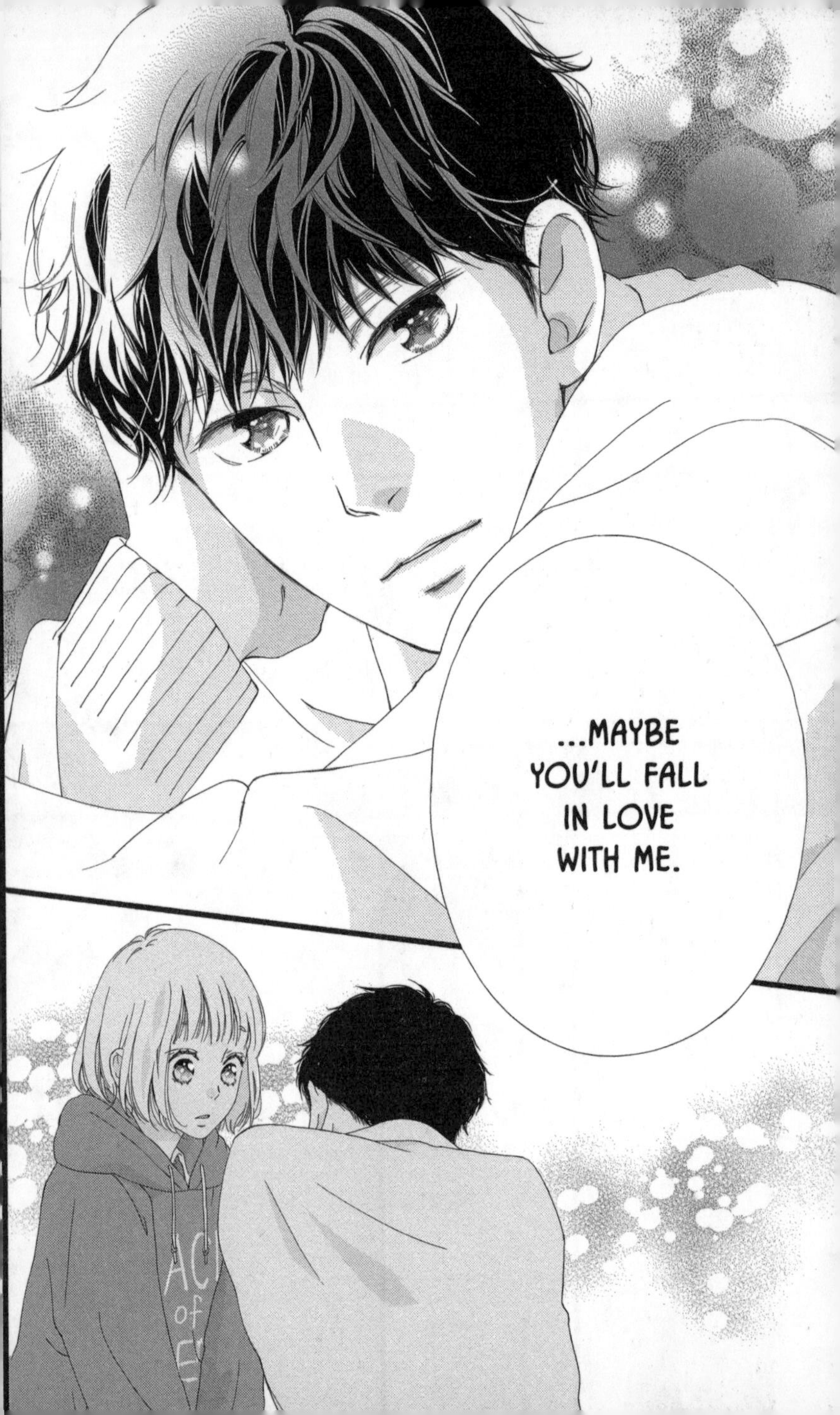
...MAYBE YOU'LL FALL IN LOVE WITH ME.

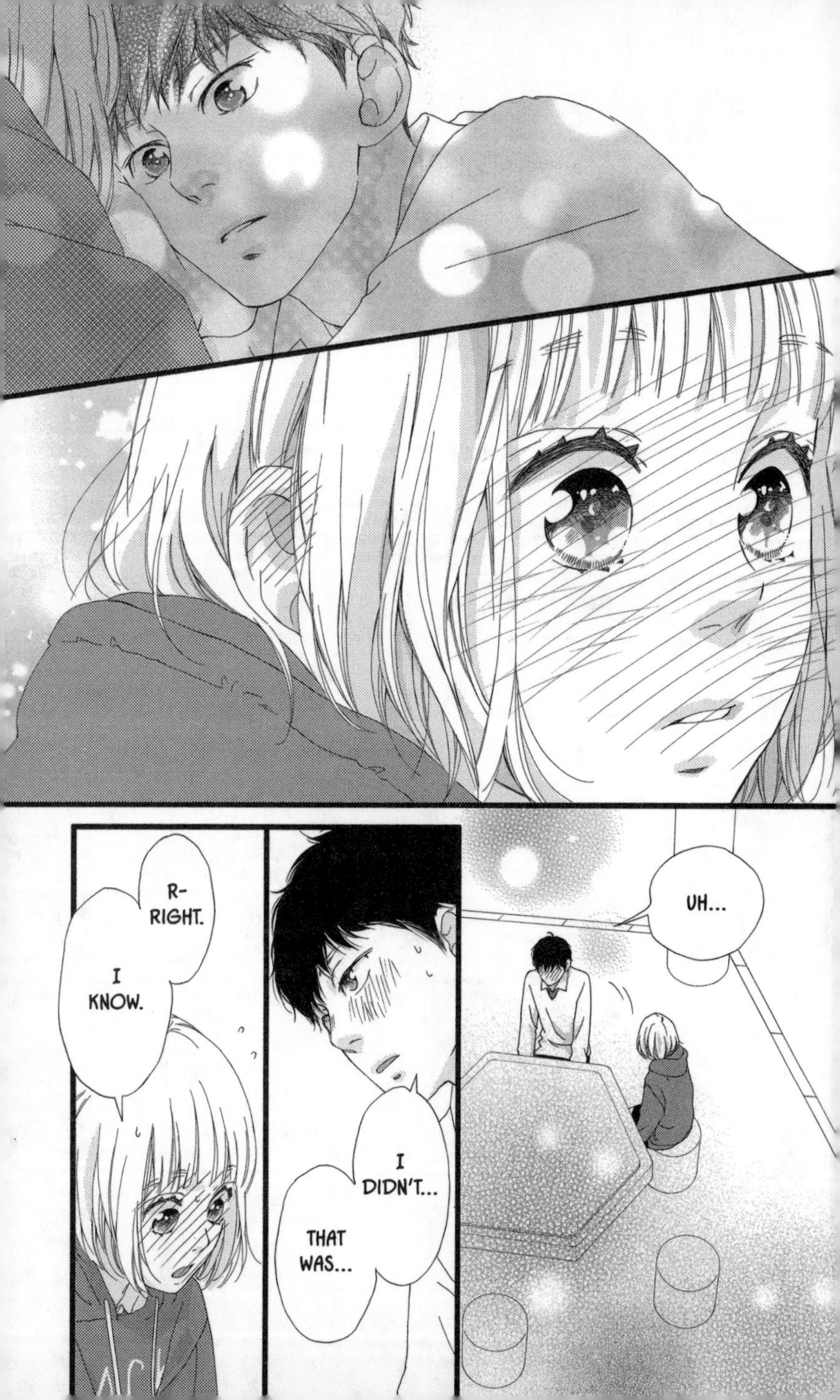
UH...
I DIDN'T...
THAT WAS...
R-RIGHT.
I KNOW.

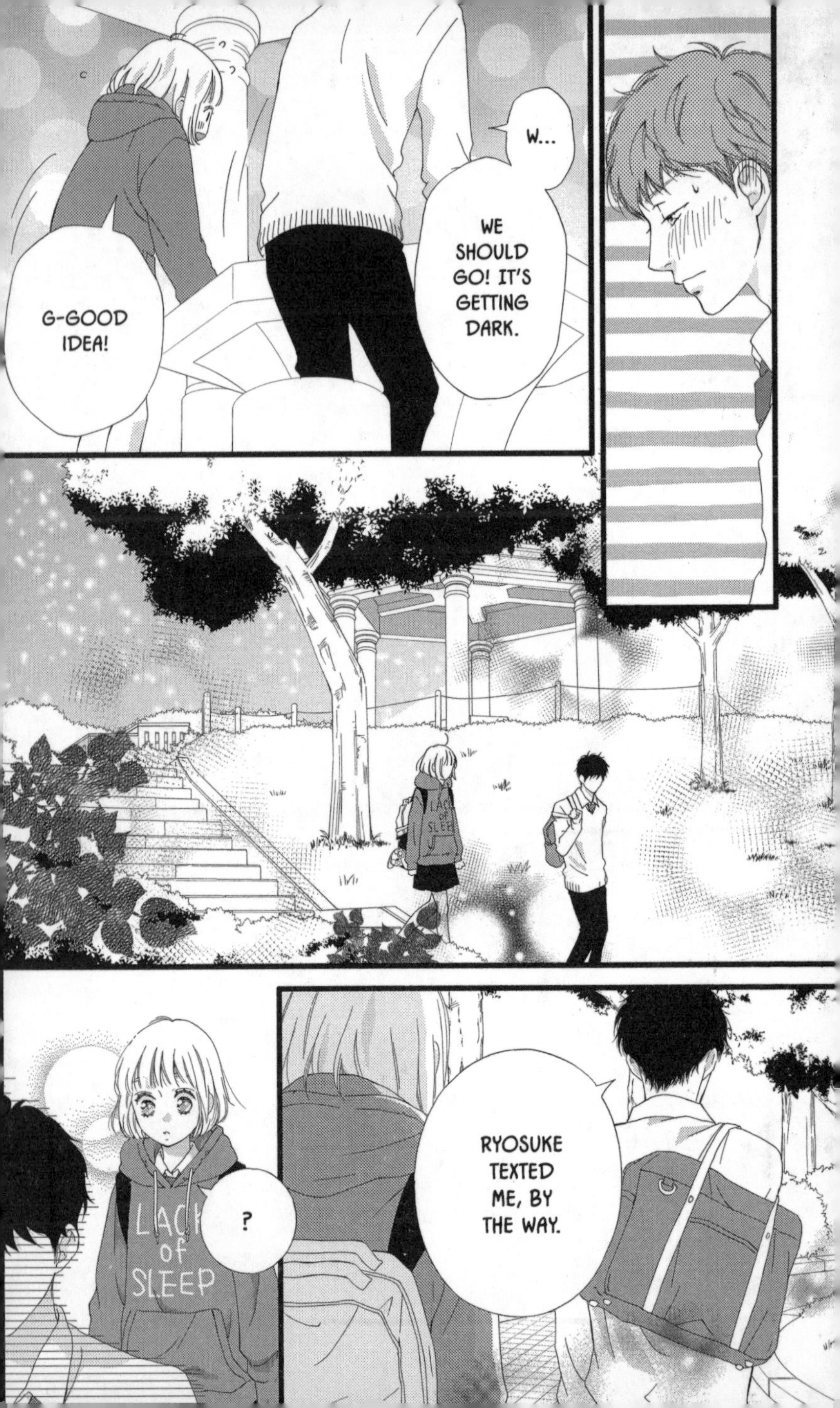
W...
WE SHOULD GO! IT'S GETTING DARK.
G-GOOD IDEA!
RYOSUKE TEXTED ME, BY THE WAY.
?

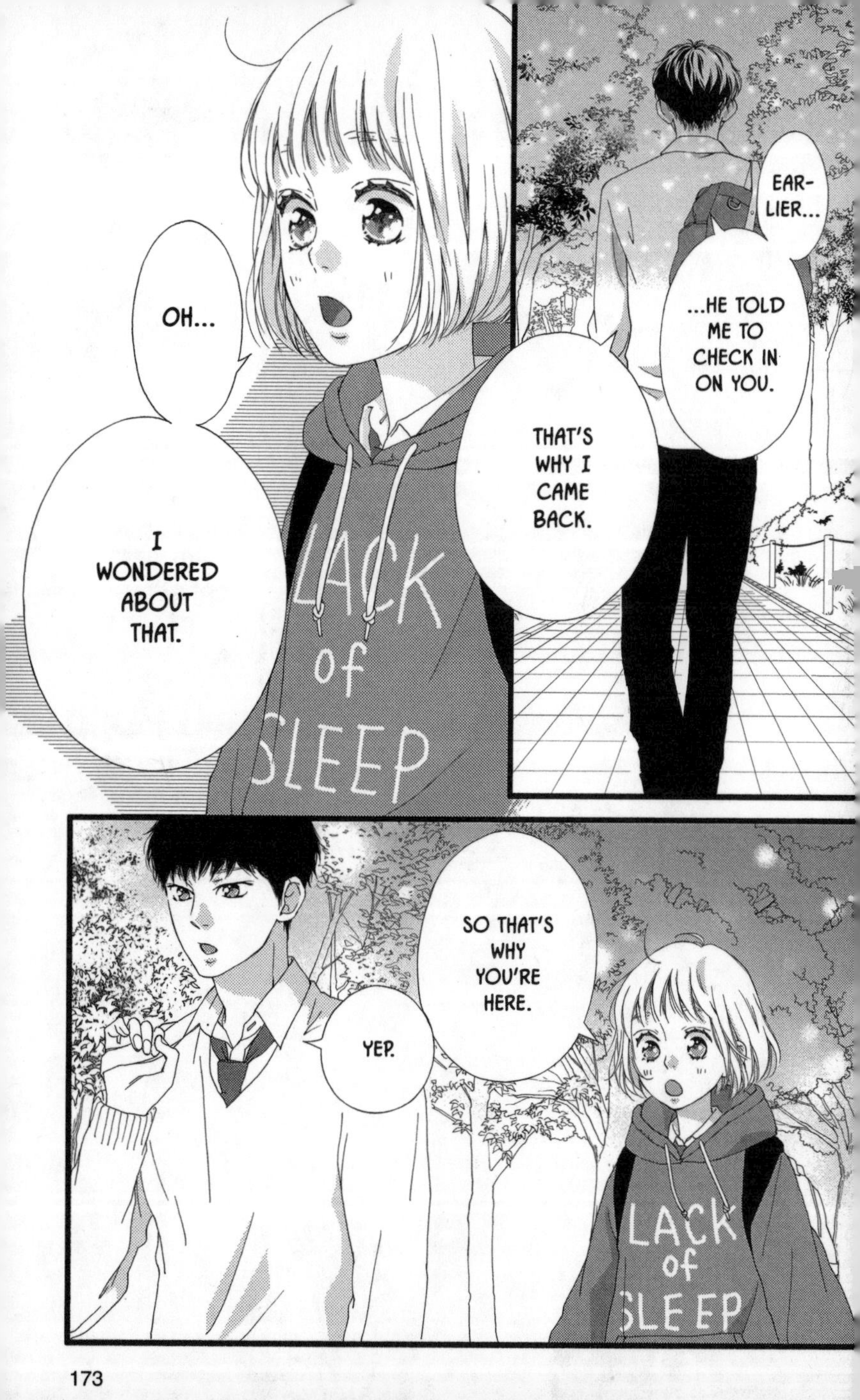
EAR-LIER...
...HE TOLD ME TO CHECK IN ON YOU.
THAT'S WHY I CAME BACK.
OH...
I WONDERED ABOUT THAT.
SO THAT'S WHY YOU'RE HERE.
YEP.

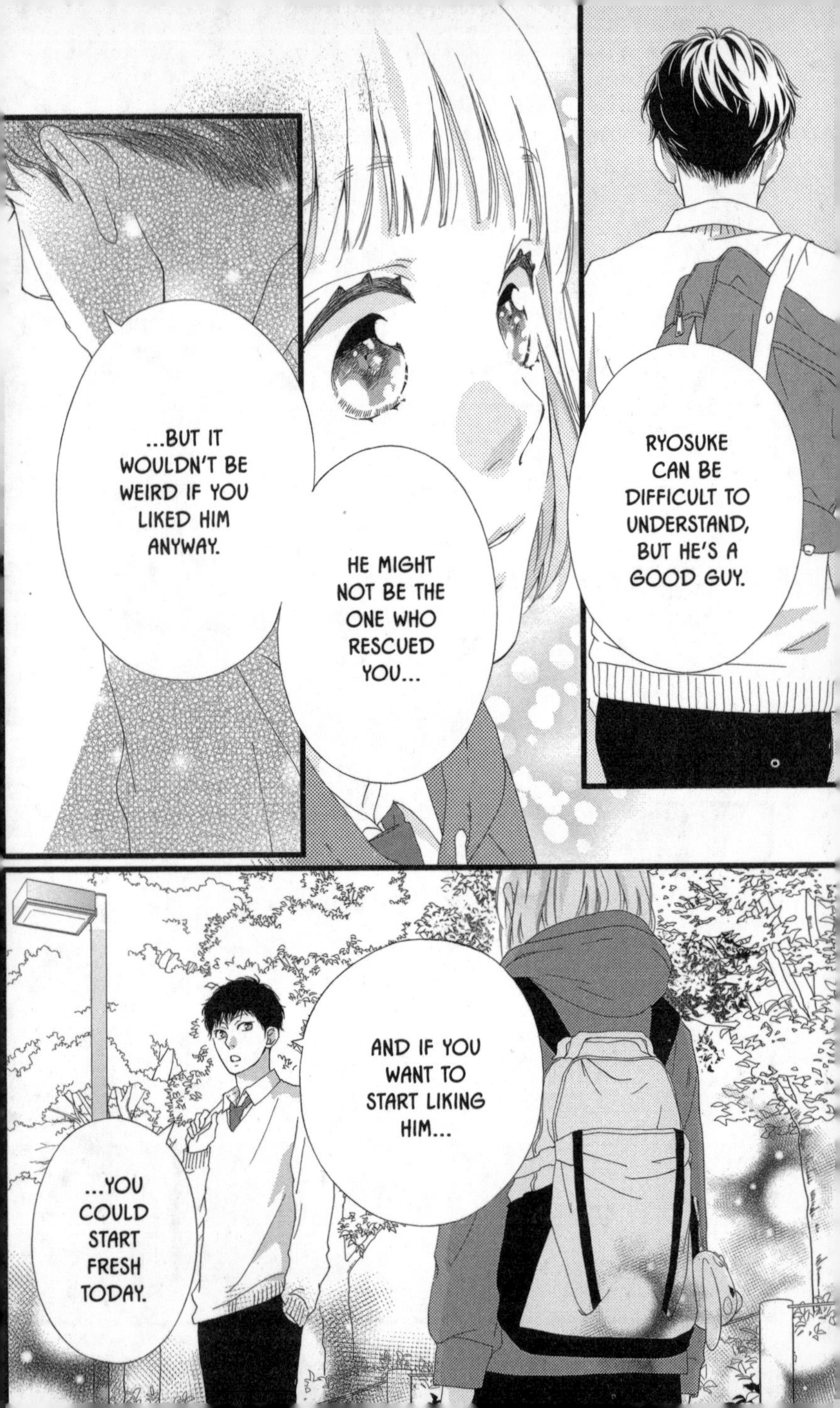
RYOSUKE CAN BE DIFFICULT TO UNDERSTAND, BUT HE'S A GOOD GUY.
HE MIGHT NOT BE THE ONE WHO RESCUED YOU...
...BUT IT WOULDN'T BE WEIRD IF YOU LIKED HIM ANYWAY.
AND IF YOU WANT TO START LIKING HIM...
...YOU COULD START FRESH TODAY.

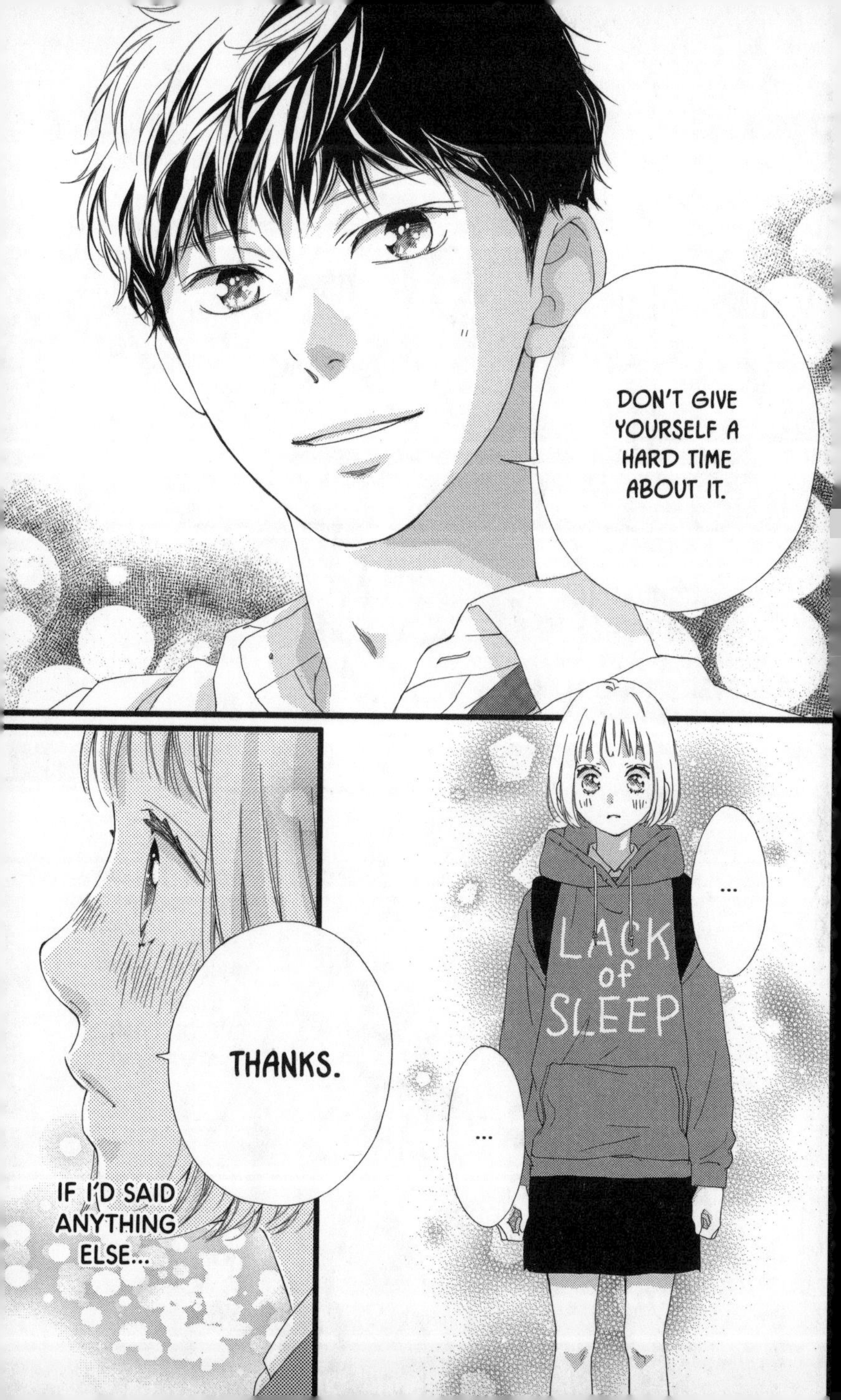
DON'T GIVE YOURSELF A HARD TIME ABOUT IT.
...
LACK of SLEEP
...
THANKS.
IF I'D SAID ANYTHING ELSE...

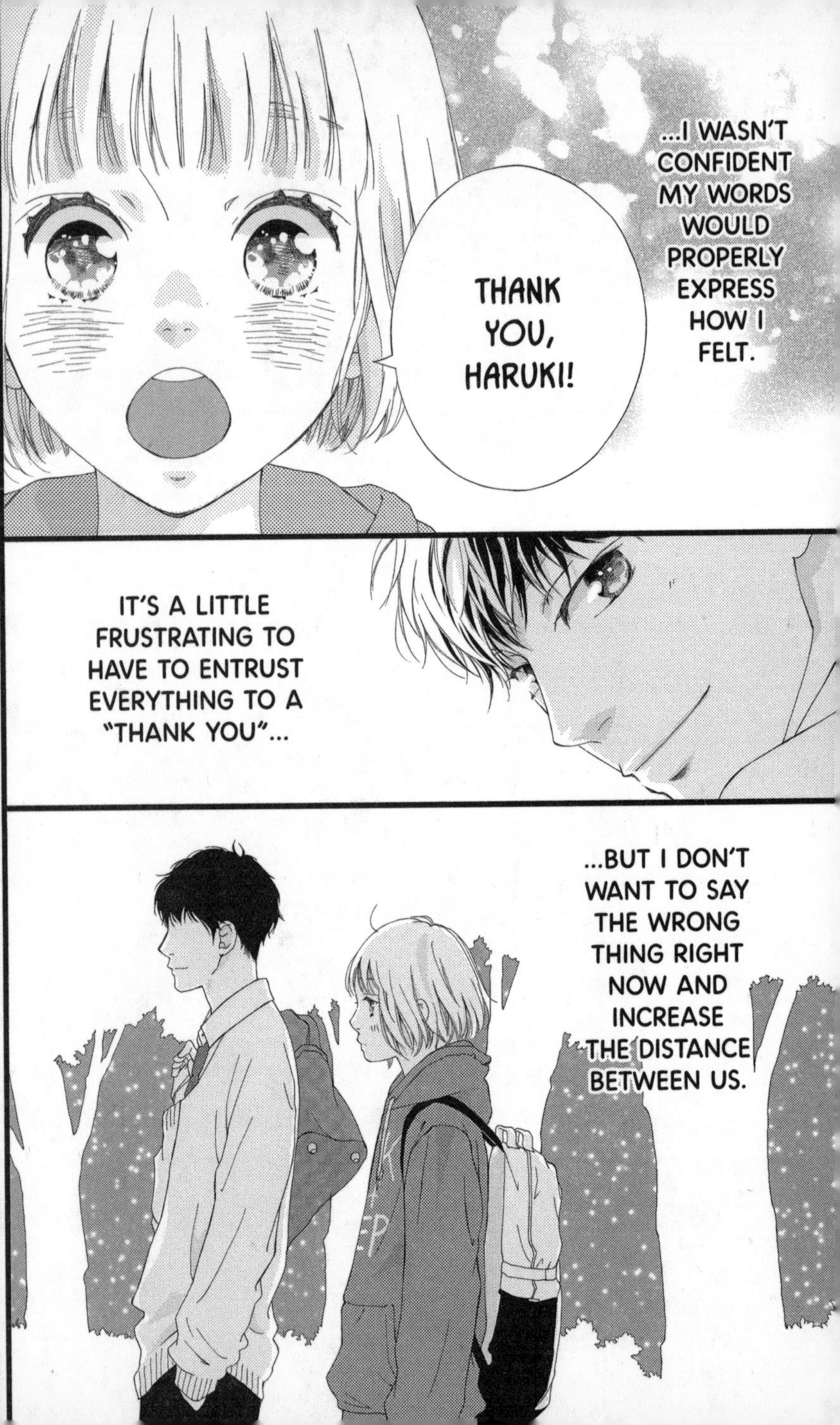
...I WASN'T CONFIDENT MY WORDS WOULD PROPERLY EXPRESS HOW I FELT.
THANK YOU, HARUKI!
IT'S A LITTLE FRUSTRATING TO HAVE TO ENTRUST EVERYTHING TO A "THANK YOU"...
...BUT I DON'T WANT TO SAY THE WRONG THING RIGHT NOW AND INCREASE THE DISTANCE BETWEEN US.

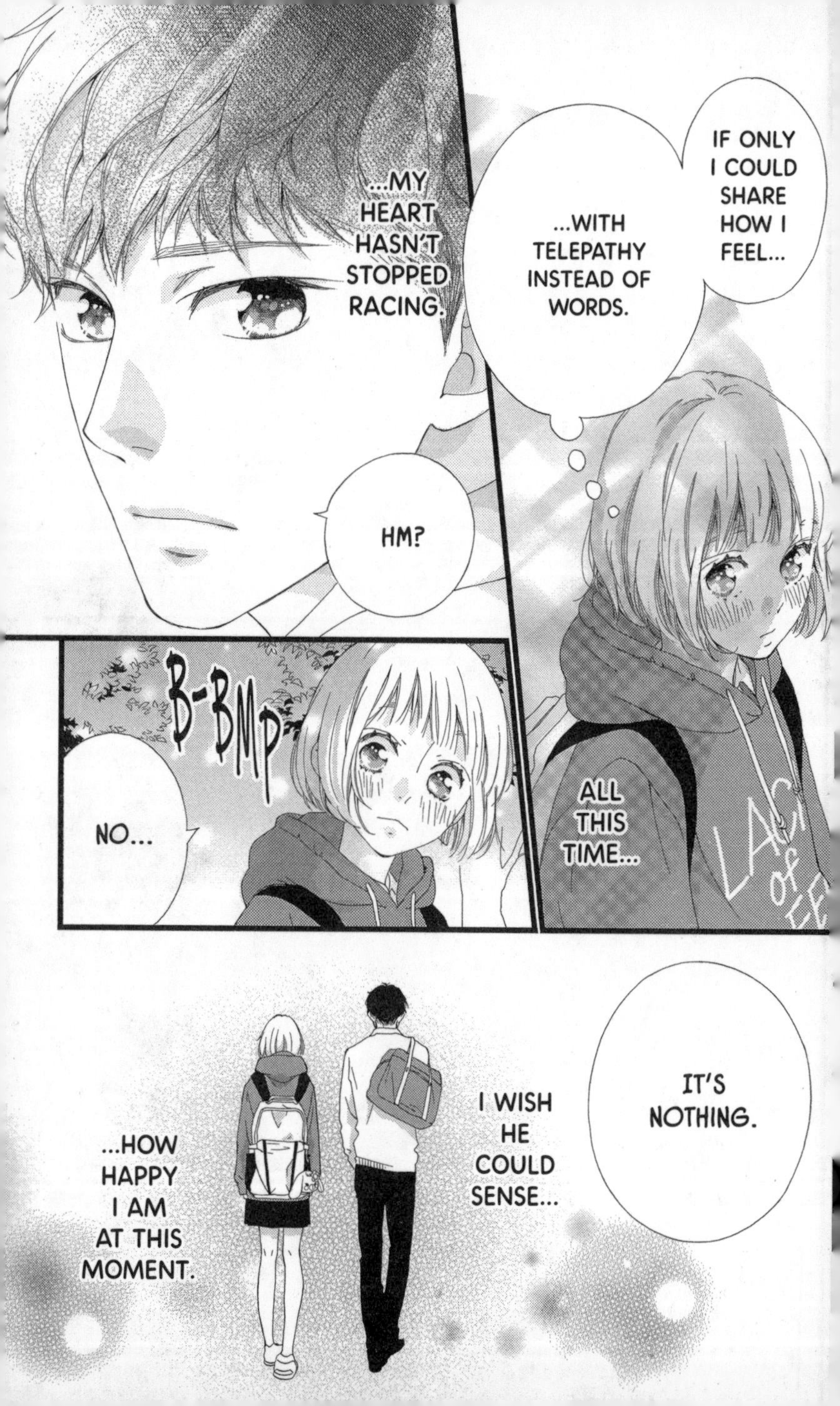
IF ONLY I COULD SHARE HOW I FEEL...
...WITH TELEPATHY INSTEAD OF WORDS.
ALL THIS TIME...
...MY HEART HASN'T STOPPED RACING.
HM?
B-BMP
NO...
IT'S NOTHING.
I WISH HE COULD SENSE...
...HOW HAPPY I AM AT THIS MOMENT.

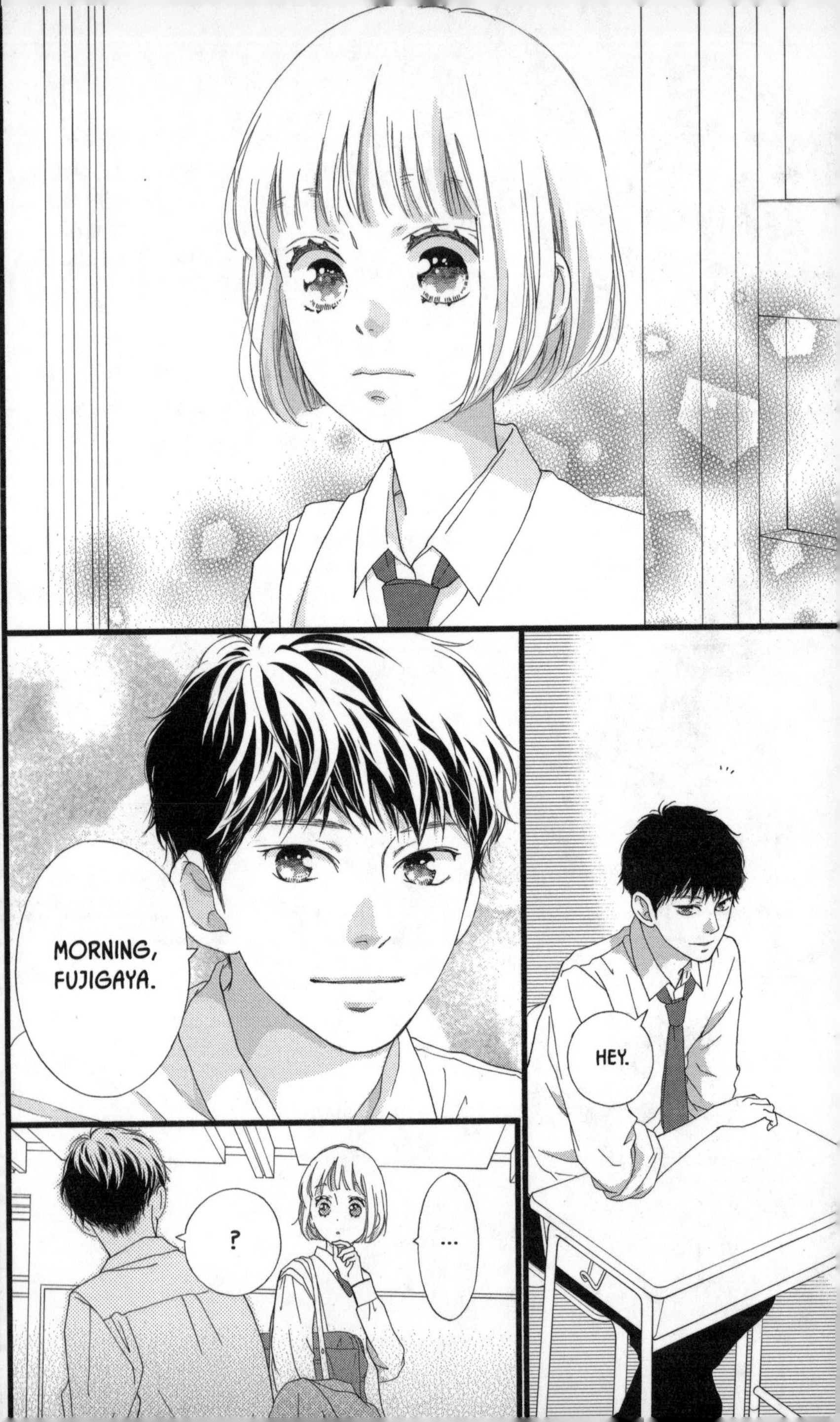
HEY.
MORNING, FUJIGAYA.
...
?

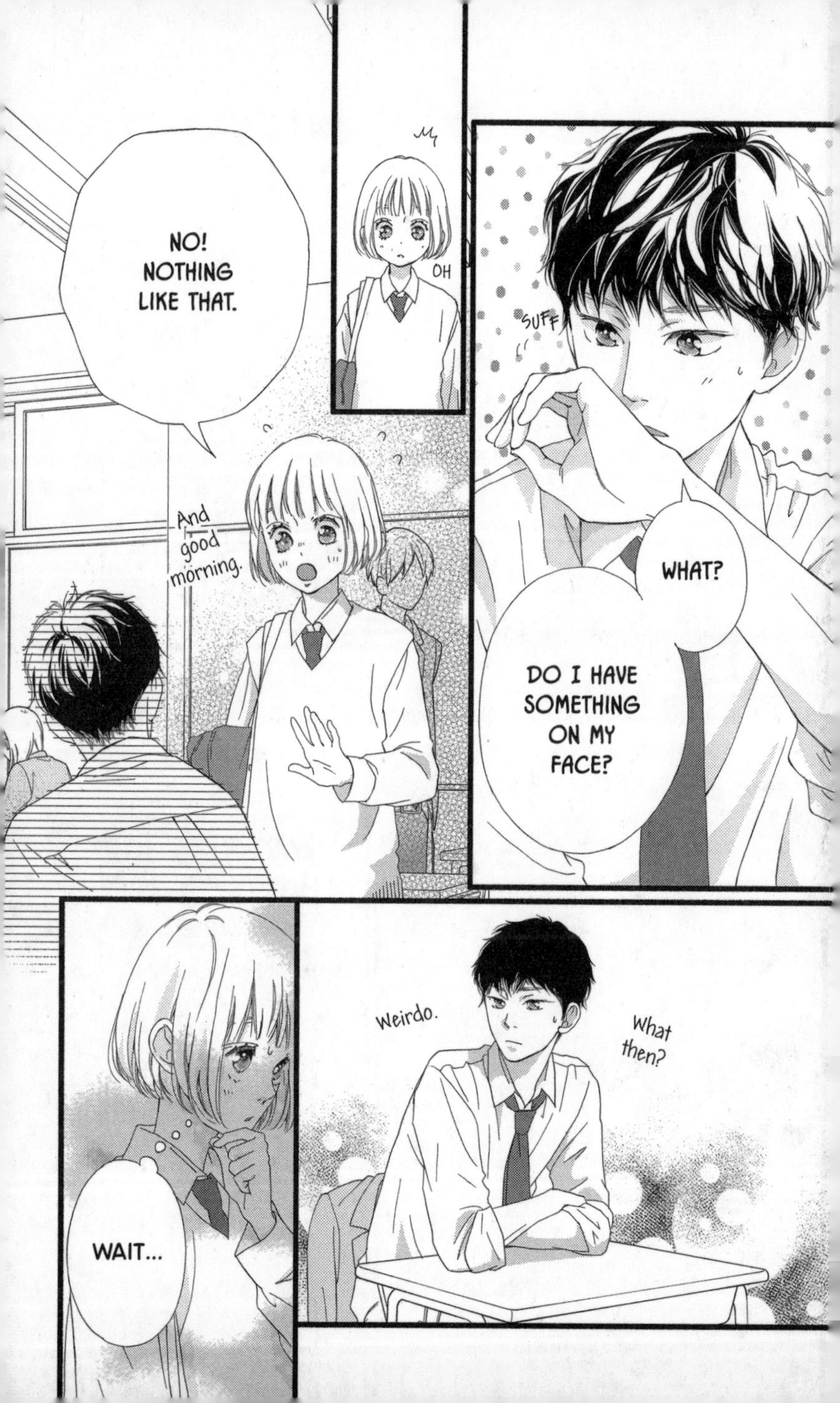
SUFF
WHAT?
DO I HAVE SOMETHING ON MY FACE?
OH
NO! NOTHING LIKE THAT.
And good morning.
What then?
Weirdo.
WAIT...

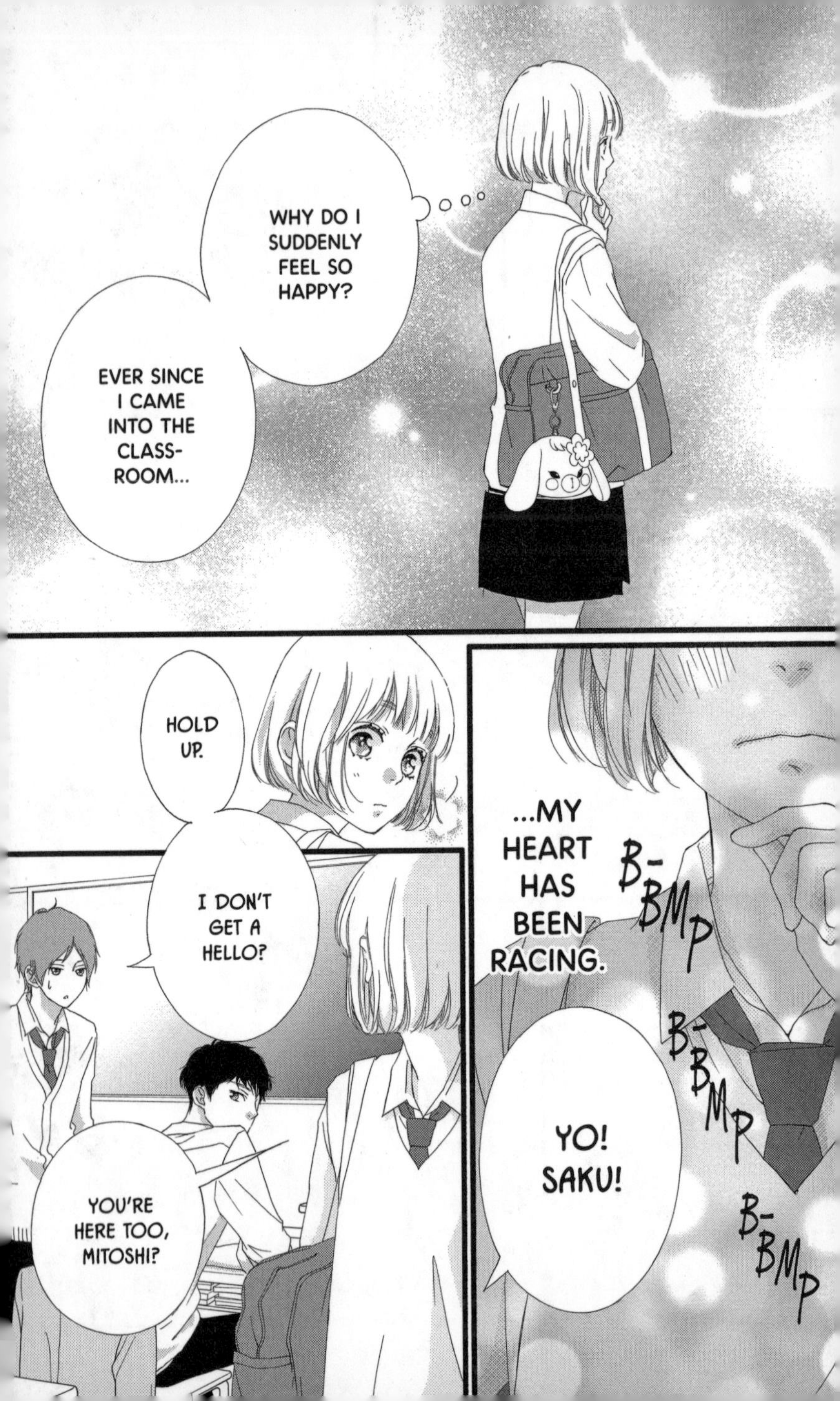
WHY DO I SUDDENLY FEEL SO HAPPY?
EVER SINCE I CAME INTO THE CLASS-ROOM...
...MY HEART HAS BEEN RACING.
B-BMP
B-BMP
YO! SAKU!
B-BMP
HOLD UP.
I DON'T GET A HELLO?
YOU'RE HERE TOO, MITOSHI?

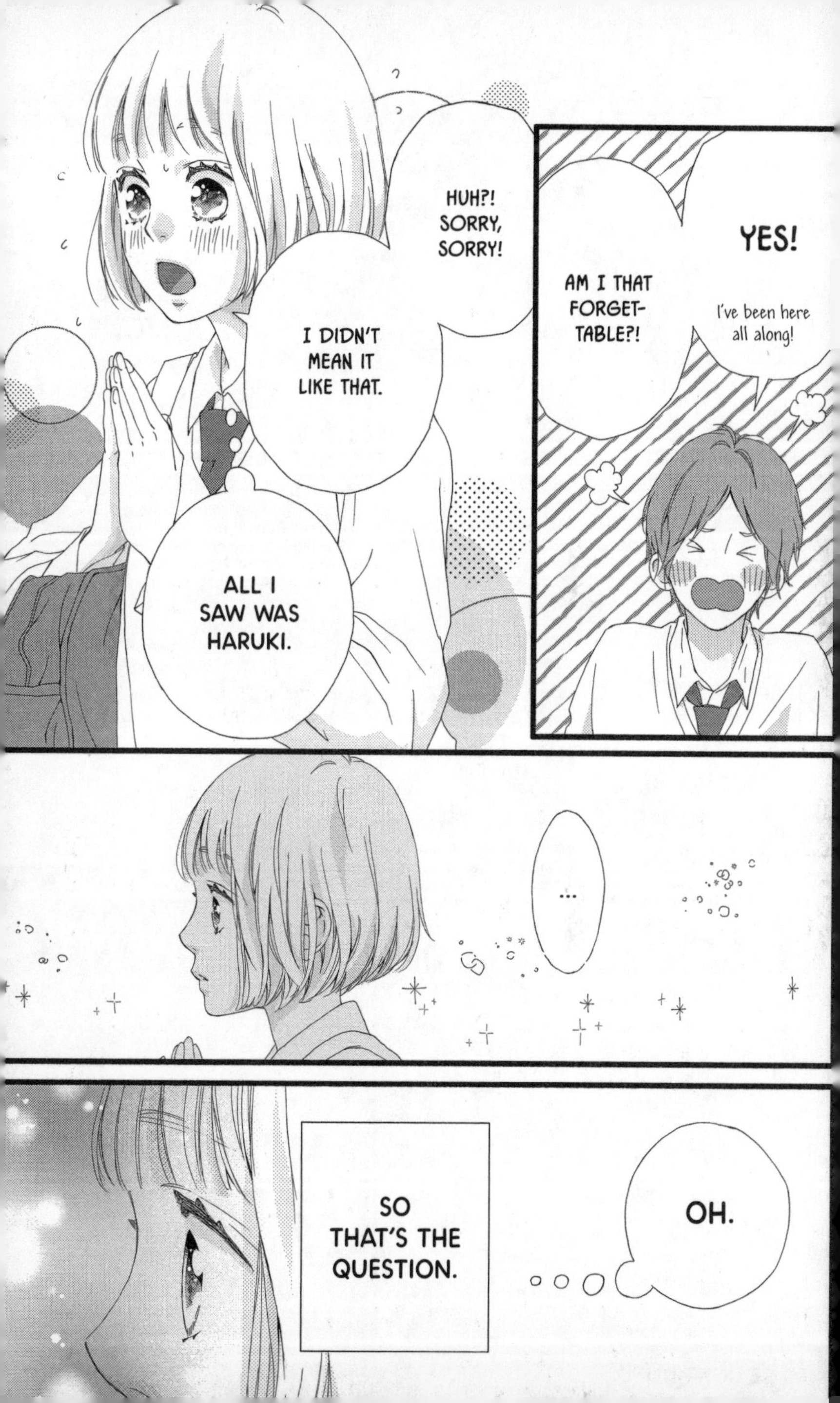
YES!
I've been here all along!
AM I THAT FORGET-TABLE?!
HUH?! SORRY, SORRY!
I DIDN'T MEAN IT LIKE THAT.
ALL I SAW WAS HARUKI.
...
OH.
SO THAT'S THE QUESTION.

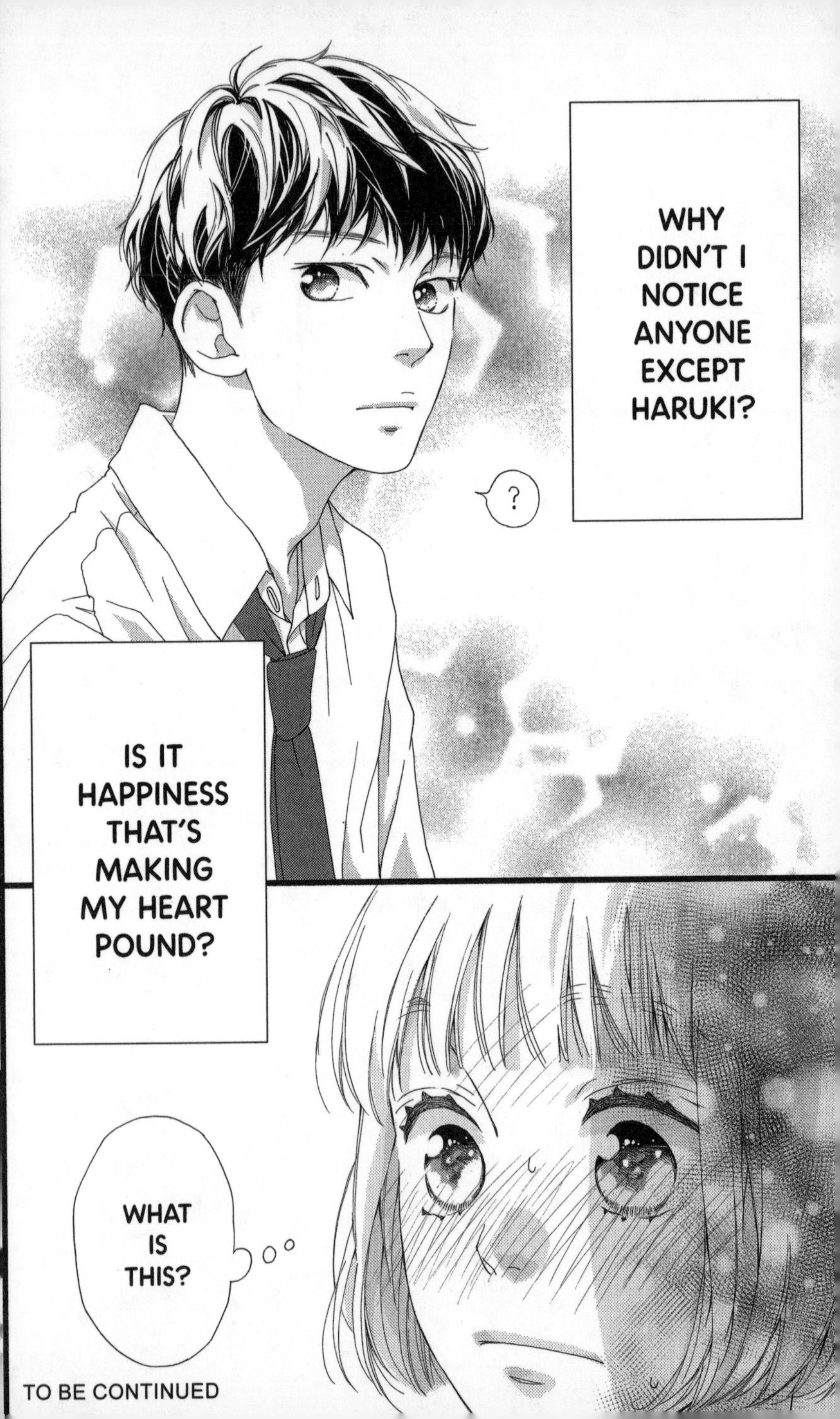
WHY DIDN'T I NOTICE ANYONE EXCEPT HARUKI?
?
IS IT HAPPINESS THAT'S MAKING MY HEART POUND?
WHAT IS THIS?
TO BE CONTINUED

AFTERWORD

Thank you for reading to the end of volume 1!

For this series I've gone digital. Well, sort of...
Everything up to inking is still analog like
before. So I still get tired of the huge pile of
eraser crumbs I end up with while working on the
manga pages. Also, going digital means so many
new things to remember, decisions to make, and
workflow changes to implement that I'll probably
be struggling with it for a while yet.

To my sensei for digital matters, all my assistants,
and my editor, thank you for tenaciously
supporting me as always. I'll try to adapt as soon
as I can. Let's hope things are going a little
smoother by the time the next book comes out...

And with that, see you all in the next volume!

Io Sakisaka

I'm delighted to be starting a new story. Even I'm looking forward to seeing how the lead characters develop. I'll do my best to deliver all kinds of emotions!

— IO SAKISAKA

Born on June 8, **Io Sakisaka** made her debut as a manga creator with *Sakura, Chiru*. *Strobe Edge* and *Ao Haru Ride* are published by VIZ Media's Shojo Beat imprint. *Ao Haru Ride* was adapted into an anime series in 2014, and *Love Me, Love Me Not* was made into an animated feature film. In her spare time, Sakisaka likes to paint things and sleep.

Sakura, Saku

SHOJO BEAT EDITION
Volume 1

Story & Art By
IO SAKISAKA

Translation & Adaptation
MAX GREENWAY

Touch-Up Art & Lettering
INORI FUKUDA TRANT

Design
ALICE LEWIS

Editor
NANCY THISTLETHWAITE

Published by VIZ Media, LLC
P.O. Box 77010
San Francisco, CA 94107

10 9 8 7 6 5 4 3 2 1
First printing, November 2023

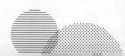

VIZ MEDIA
viz.com

Shojo Beat
shojobeat.com

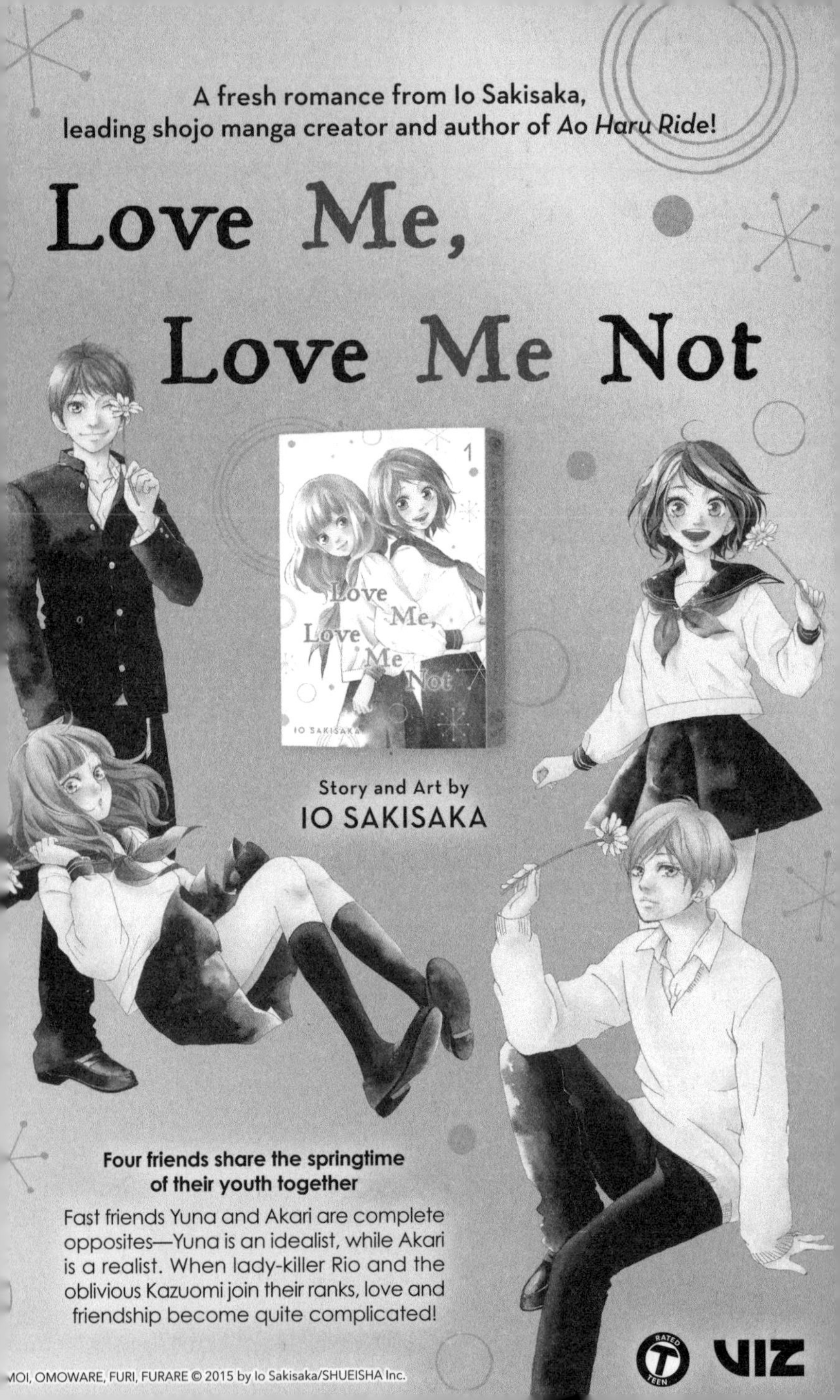
A fresh romance from Io Sakisaka,
leading shojo manga creator and author of *Ao Haru Ride*!
Love Me,
Love Me Not
Love Me, Love Me Not
1
IO SAKISAKA
Story and Art by
IO SAKISAKA
Four friends share the springtime of their youth together
Fast friends Yuna and Akari are complete opposites—Yuna is an idealist, while Akari is a realist. When lady-killer Rio and the oblivious Kazuomi join their ranks, love and friendship become quite complicated!
RATED T TEEN
VIZ
MOI, OMOWARE, FURI, FURARE © 2015 by Io Sakisaka/SHUEISHA Inc.

Ao Haru Ride

STORY AND ART BY
IO SAKISAKA

Futaba Yoshioka thought all boys were loud and obnoxious until she met Kou Tanaka in junior high. But as soon as she realized she really liked him, he had already moved away because of family issues. Now, in high school, Kou has reappeared, but is he still the same boy she fell in love with?

VIZ

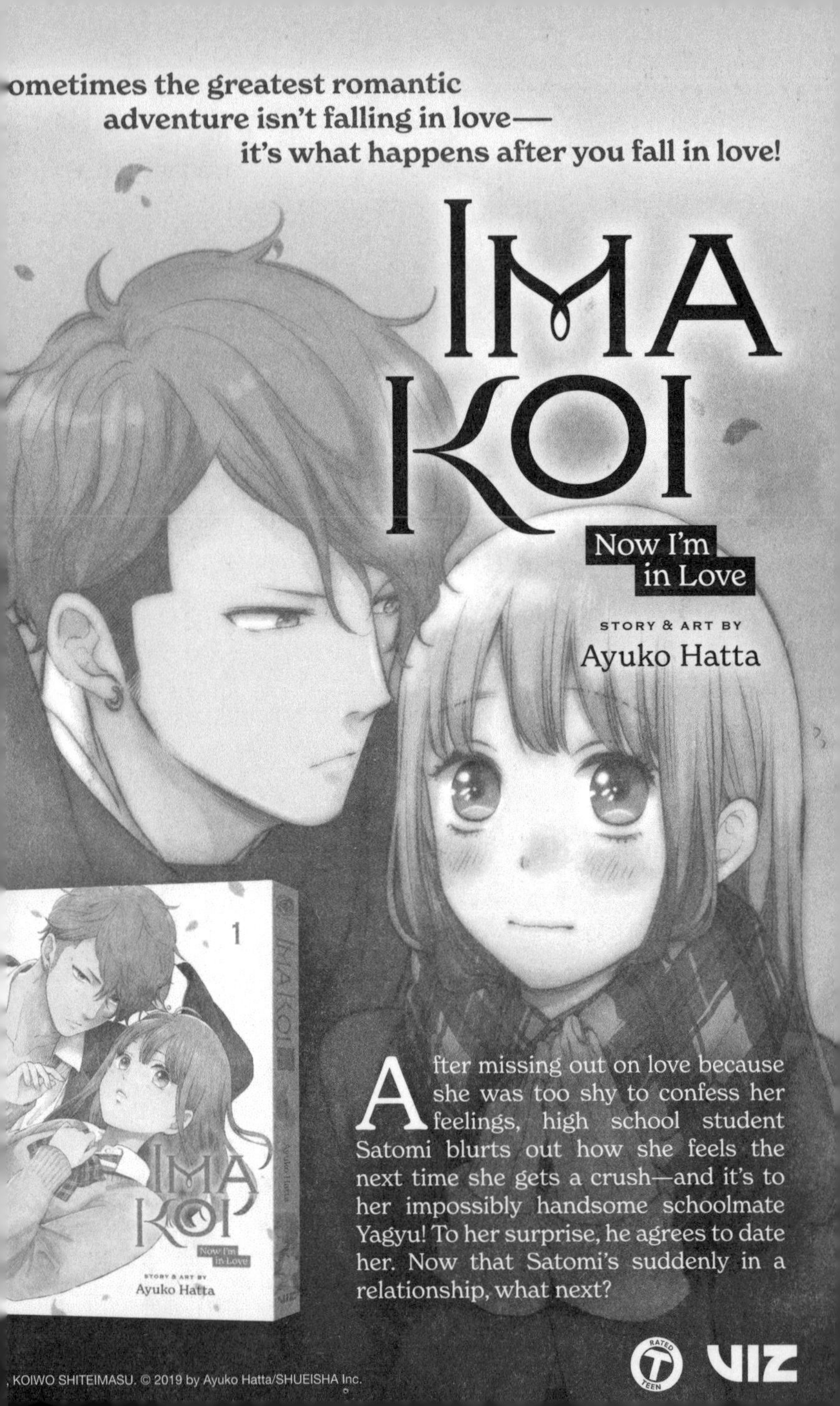

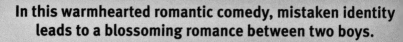

In this warmhearted romantic comedy, mistaken identity leads to a blossoming romance between two boys.

Art by **Aruko**
Story by **Wataru Hinekure**

Aoki has a crush on Hashimoto, the girl in the seat next to him in class. But he despairs when he borrows her eraser and sees she's written the name of another boy—Ida—on it. To make matters more confusing, Ida sees him holding that very eraser and thinks Aoki has a crush on him!

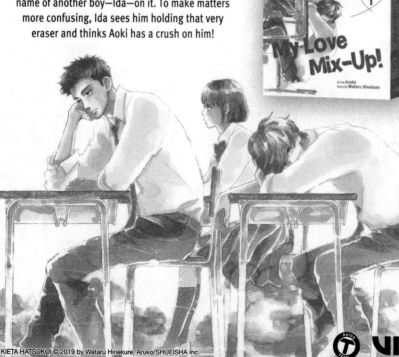

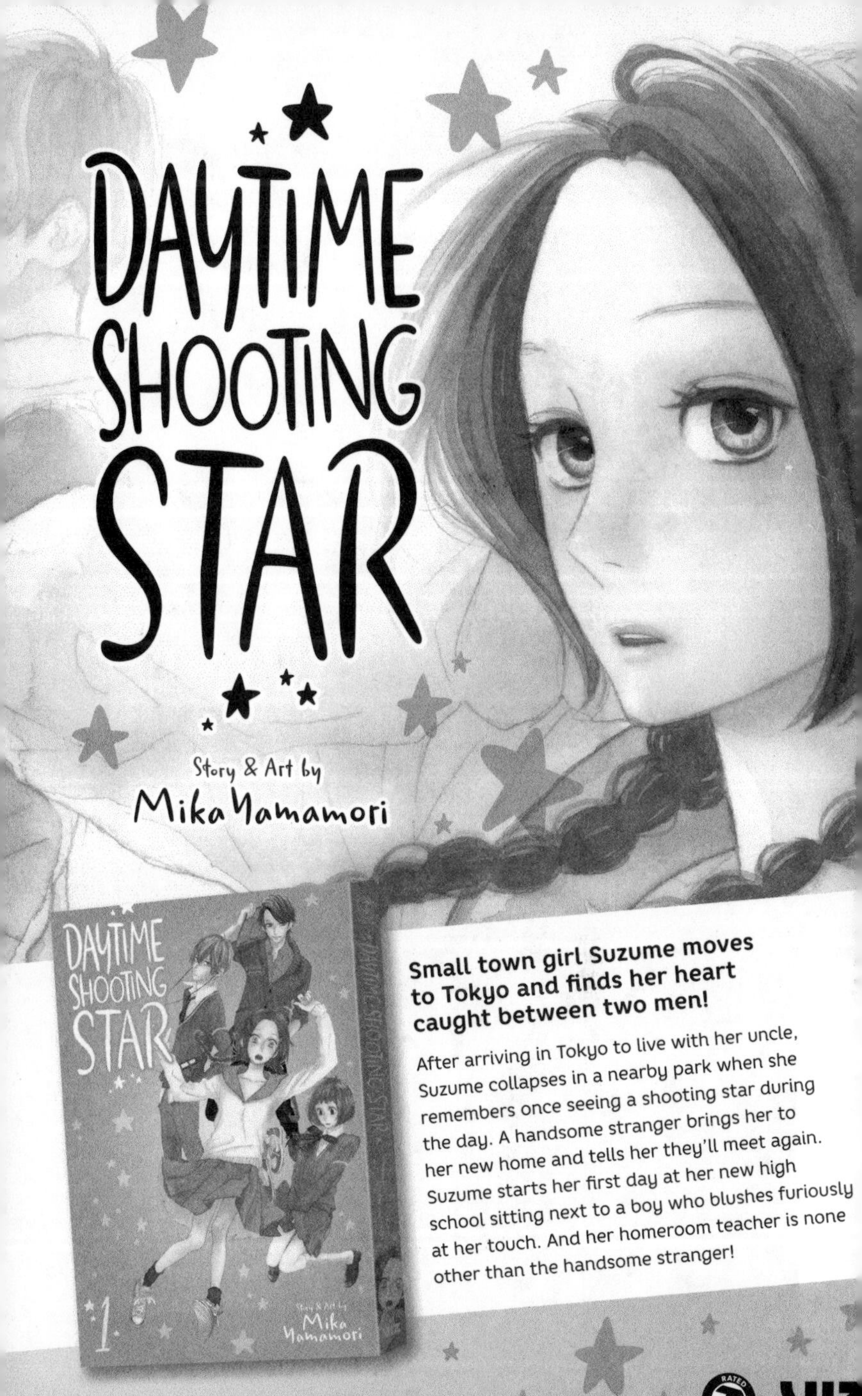
DAYTIME SHOOTING STAR
Story & Art by
Mika Yamamori
DAYTIME SHOOTING STAR
1
Story & Art by
Mika Yamamori
Small town girl Suzume moves to Tokyo and finds her heart caught between two men!
After arriving in Tokyo to live with her uncle, Suzume collapses in a nearby park when she remembers once seeing a shooting star during the day. A handsome stranger brings her to her new home and tells her they'll meet again. Suzume starts her first day at her new high school sitting next to a boy who blushes furiously at her touch. And her homeroom teacher is none other than the handsome stranger!
RATED T TEEN
VIZ

YOU'RE READING THE WRONG WAY!

Sakura, Saku reads from right to left, starting in the upper-right corner. Japanese is read from right to left, meaning that action, sound effects, and word-balloon order are completely reversed from English order. Check out the diagram shown here to get the hang of things, and then turn to the other side of the book to get started!

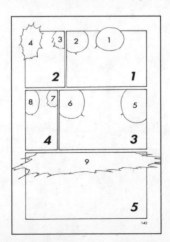